IN GOD'S NAME

The Vatican commented:
'Taking fantastic speculation to new levels of absurdity'
'Infamous rubbish'

The World's press disagreed:
'His book has two strengths. It brings up to date and tells well the story of how the Vatican has conducted its financial affairs. The portrayal of the hitherto little-known John Paul I is also excellently done . . . an engrossing and disturbing book. It reflects no credit on the Vatican that its spokesmen affect to view the charges with contempt and ignore the questions raised'
The Economist

'An important and at times frightening book. The consequences of its publication are incalculable'
Bolton Evening News

'Deft and accurate'
Morris West, Sydney Morning Herald

'You didn't know "the smiling Pope" was murdered after only a month in office? Read Yallop's . . . exhaustively researched, fascinating material and, if not convinced, you will certainly wonder . . . the case he makes is indeed impressive, shocking and frightening'
Variety

'Deeply disturbing . . . if only a small percentage of it is true then the Vatican and the world has much to fear, for God appears far from home'
Aberdeen Evening Express

'He has surely proved that there is a case to answer'
Irish Independent

'Compelling reading'
South Wales Argus

'An astounding book . . . a story of corruption, lies and disinformation'
The Daily Mail, Hull

'Was John Paul I murdered? He may have been. To the extent the Vatican does not address itself to a responsible discussion of the evidence Mr Yallop has gathered, the probability of murder goes up'
Father Andrew M. Greeley

'He weaves a skilful tale of intrigue . . . the story has all the elements of a first-rate thriller'
Calgary Herald

'The book is fascinating reading' *Derby Evening Telegraph*

'David Yallop's research is intensive, far-reaching and comprehensive . . . rich with plot arabesques and ingenious characters in a setting of international power and grandeur. However, this is no fiction; it is a documentary chronicle of greed, megalomania and the callous murder of the one geod man capable of halting it'
British Book News

'A ruthless investigation' *NZ Herald*

'This is one of the most disturbing books I have ever read and the Vatican will dismiss or ignore it at its peril, for those millions around the world who look to Rome in their faith must surely want answers'
Gloucester Citizen

'It all makes marvellous reading' *The Yorkshire Post*

'Impressively researched . . . readers will have to look far and wide for fiction as gripping and downright readable'
The Edmonton Journal

'I read this book with the absorbing interest aroused by an expert prosecutor at a sensational trial'
The Times

David Yallop's first book, *To Encourage the Others*, caused the British Government to reopen the Craig/Bentley murder case – a case which had been officially cleared for twenty years. The book, which provoked a major debate in the House of Lords, and the author's television drama-documentary, convinced many, ranging from the former Lord Chancellor, Lord Gardiner, Lords Arran and Goodman, to authors such as Arthur Koestler, that a miscarriage of justice had occurred.

Yallop's second book, *The Day the Laughter Stopped*, was widely acclaimed on both sides of the Atlantic as the definitive biography and posthumous rehabilitation of the silent film star Roscoe (Fatty) Arbuckle, which also solved a fifty-year-old murder mystery.

His third book, *Beyond Reasonable Doubt?* led directly to the freeing of a man serving a life sentence for double murder in New Zealand. Following publication of Yallop's book, Thomas was granted a Royal Pardon and, after a Royal Commission had deliberated, one million dollars compensation.

Yallop's fourth book, *Deliver Us From Evil* was stimulated by a desire to pull a man *into* prison, the Yorkshire Ripper, and his statements to Assistant Chief Constable George Oldfield in June 1980 proved uncannily accurate.

Thus, David Yallop has established a reputation as 'a seeker of justice'. He receives letters continuously from many parts of the world asking, demanding, pleading that he investigate this murder or that alleged miscarriage of justice. He received one particularly singular request, to investigate a very special death. The request came from within the Vatican, and the death was that of Pope John Paul I.

David Yallop then began the extensive research for *In God's Name*, which has been translated into nearly forty languages, sold more than 5 million copies worldwide, and won the Crime Writers' Gold Dagger Award for the best non-fiction book of the year in 1984.

In God's Name

David Yallop

CARROLL & GRAF PUBLISHERS
NEW YORK

Carroll & Graf Publishers
An imprint of Avalon Publishing Group, Inc.
245 W. 17th Street, 11th Floor
New York NY 10011-5300
www.carrollandgraf.com

AVALON

First published in the UK by Jonathan Cape Ltd, 1984

This paperback edition published in the UK by Robinson,
an imprint of Constable & Robinson Ltd, 2007

First Carroll & Graf edition, 2007

ISBN-13: 978-0-78671-984-6
ISBN-10: 0-7867-1984-2

Printed and bound in the EU

Contents

✥

Illustrations

❧❧

PLATES

PICTURE CREDITS

The author and publishers wish to thank the following for permission to reproduce black and white photographs: Agenzia Ansa, 1, 2, 3, 4, 6, 24, 26, 29, 33, 35, 47, 51, 52, 54, 60; Associated Press, 7, 10, 15, 21, 25, 31, 32, 34, 36, 39, 40, 43, 45, 48; 49, 50, 57, 58, 61, 63, 64; Camera Press (photo by Michelle Noon), 62; *Chicago Sunday Times*, 11; Dufoto, 5, 8, 9, 14, 16, 19, 20, 22, 23, 46, 53, 55, 65; Bruno Ferrario, 12, 13, 17, 18, 37; Fotoattualita, 28; Foto Felici, 42; Liverani Foto Notizie d'Attualita per *La Stampa* (photo by Gianni di Mango), 56; *L'Osservatore Romano* Citta del Vaticano Servizio Fotografico (photos by Art uro Man), 27, 30, 38, 44; Private Collections, 59; Philip Willan, 41.

Introduction to this Edition

❧❧

This book was first published in June 1984 and appeared simultaneously in many countries. To date it has been translated into thirty languages and the various editions have sold over six million copies. I have received many thousands of letters from readers; just seven letters were critical, the remainder were kind enough to praise the book and, more importantly, record the writers' belief that Albino Luciani was in their view murdered and that the case has been powerfully proved.

Vatican response was swift. Within days of publication *and before any of these spokesmen had read the book* the reaction that I had predicted in the first edition was there for all to hear.'Taking fantastic speculation to new levels of absurdity.' An Article of the Apostolic Constitution specifically ruled out post mortems on Popes.' As this book demonstrates, that particular Vatican lie had served them well in 1978.

The lies about the life and death of 'The Smiling Pope' began on the day his body was discovered. They have continued down the years to the present day. In June 1985 when the British paperback edition was first published I decided to make the Vatican's task childishly simple:

'If the Vatican can prove me wrong on just two simple questions of fact – if they can prove that my account of who found the dead body of Albino Luciani is incorrect and can prove that my account of the papers he was holding in his hands is incorrect, then I will donate every penny of my royalties from the sales of this book to cancer research.' The Vatican account of who found the body was their first lie. The papers that Albino Luciani was clutching were the smoking gun.

In the light of the Vatican's initial statements that this book was 'Infamous rubbish' and 'Absurd fantasies' the Vatican should have been able to demonstrate how incorrect my evidence and conclusions were within hours of reading my offer. That challenge was the subject of worldwide media comment.

Nearly twenty-two years later I am still waiting for the Vatican to respond. In the light of subsequent revelations the continuing failure within the Vatican City State to take up that challenge was a wise decision.

Nothing has come to light from any quarter since 1984 to cause me to alter the conclusions I had arrived during the research and writing of this book. Indeed the additional evidence that has come to hand which is examined in a postscript to this edition further confirms those original conclusions.

David A. Yallop
January 27th 2007

Preface

꿈

This book, the product of nearly three years' intensive research, would not exist without the active help and co-operation of many people and many organizations. Very many of these only agreed to help on the strict understanding that they remained publicly unidentified. As with previous books I have written under similar conditions I respect their wishes. On this occasion there is an even greater need to protect their identity. As will become clear to the reader, murder is a frequent accompaniment to the events recorded here. A considerable number of those murders remain officially unsolved. No one should doubt that the individuals responsible for those deaths have the capacity to murder again. To reveal the names of men and women who provided me with crucial help and who are now at risk would be an act of criminal irresponsibility. To them I owe a particular debt. Their reasons for divulging a wide range of information were many and varied but again and again I heard the remark, 'The truth must be told. If you are prepared to tell it, then so be it.' I am deeply grateful to all of them and to the following, who with the greatest respect I classify as the tip of the iceberg:

Professor Amedeo Alexandre, Professor Leonardo Ancona, William Aronwald, Linda Attwell, Josephine Ayres, Alan Bailey, Dr Shamus Banim, Dr Derek Barrowcliff, Pia Basso, Father Aldo Belli, Cardinal Giovanni Benelli, Marco Borsa, Vittore Branca, David Buckley, Father Roberto Busa, Dr Renato Buzzonetti, Roberto Calvi, Emilio Cavaterra, Cardinal Mario Ciappi, Brother Clemente, Joseph Coffey, Annaloa Copps, Rupert Cornwall, Monsignor Ausilio Da Rif, Dr Guiseppe Da Ros, Maurizio De Luca, Danielle Doglio, Monsignor Mafeo Ducoli,

Father François Evain, Cardinal Pericle Felici, Father Mario Ferrarese, Professor Luigi Fontana, Mario di Francesco, Dr Carlo Frizziero, Professor Piero Fucci, Father Giovanni Gennari, Monsignor Mario Ghizzo, Father Carlo Gonzalez, Father Andrew Greeley, Diane Hall, Doctor John Henry, Father Thomas Hunt, William Jackson, John J. Kenney, Peter Lemos, Dr David Levison, Father Diego Lorenzi, Edoardo Luciani, William Lynch, Ann McDiarmid, Father John Magee, Sandro Magister, Alexander Manson, Professor Vincenzo Masini, Father Francis Murphy, Monsignor Giulio Nicolini, Anna Nogara, Father Gerry O'Collins, Father Romeo Panciroli, Father Gianni Pastro, Lena Petri, Nina Petri, Professor Pier Luigi Prati, Professor Giovanni Rama, Roberto Rosone, Professor Fausto Rovelli, Professor Vincenzo Rulli, Ann Ellen Rutherford, Monsignor Tiziano Scalzotto, Monsignor Mario Senigaglia, Arnaldo Signoracci, Ernesto Signoracci, Father Bartolomeo Sorges, Lorana Sullivan, Father Francesco Taffarel, Sister Vincenza, Professor Thomas Whitehead, Phillip Willan. I am also grateful to the following organizations: the Augustinian Residence, Rome, Banco San Marco, the Bank of England, the Bank of International Settlements, Basle, the Bank of Italy, Catholic Central Library, Catholic Truth Society, City of London Police, the Department of Trade, Statistics and Market Intelligence Library, the English College, Rome, the Federal Bureau of Investigation, the Gregorian University, Rome, New Cross Hospital Poisons Unit, Opus Dei, the Pharmaceutical Society of Great Britain, the Tribunal of the Ward of Luxembourg, US Department of State, US District Court Southern District of New York, Vatican Press Office, and Vatican Radio.

Among those I cannot thank publicly are the people resident within Vatican City who contacted me and initiated my investigation of the events surrounding the death of Pope John Paul I, Albino Luciani. The fact that men and women living within the heart of the Roman Catholic Church cannot speak openly and be identified is an eloquent comment on the state of affairs within the Vatican.

Doubtless this book will be attacked by some and dismissed by others. It will be seen by some as an assault on the Roman Catholic faith in particular and on Christianity in general. It is neither of these. To a degree it is an indictment of specifically named men who were born Roman Catholics but who have never become Christians.

As such this book is not an attack on 'The Faith' of the Church's devout millions who follow it. What they hold sacred is too important to be left in the hands of men who have conspired to drag the message of Christ into the muddy market place – a conspiracy that has met with frightening success.

As already indicated I am met with an insurmountable difficulty when faced with the task of naming specific sources within the text. Who exactly told me what or provided the documentary information must remain secret. I can assure the reader that all the information, all the details, all the facts, have been checked and double checked to the extent multiple sources were available. I take the responsibility for putting the evidence together and for the conclusions reached.

I am sure that the fact that I recount conversations between men dead before my investigation began will be cause for comment. How for example could I know what passed between Pope John Paul I and Cardinal Jean Villot on the day they discussed the issue of birth control? Within the Vatican there is no such thing as a private audience that remains completely private. Quite simply both men subsequently talked to others of what had transpired. These secondary sources, sometimes with deeply differing personal opinions on the issue discussed by the Pope and his Secretary of State, provided the words attributed. Therefore while the dialogue within this book is reconstructed, it is not fabricated.

Prologue

꩜

The spiritual leader of nearly one-fifth of the world's population wields immense power: but any uninformed observer of Albino Luciani at the beginning of his reign as Pope John Paul I would have found it difficult to believe that this man truly embodied such power. The diffidence and humility emanating from this small, quiet, 65-year-old Italian had led many to conclude that this Papacy would not be particularly noteworthy. The well-informed, however, knew differently: Albino Luciani had embarked on a revolution.

On September 28th, 1978 he had been Pope for thirty-three days. In little more than a month he had initiated various courses of action which, if completed, would have a direct and dynamic effect upon us all. The majority in this world would applaud his decisions, a minority would be appalled. The man who had quickly been labelled 'The Smiling Pope' intended to remove the smiles from a number of faces on the following day.

That evening Luciani sat down to dinner in the third-floor dining-room of the Apostolic Palace within Vatican City. With him were his two secretaries, Father Diego Lorenzi, who had worked closely with him in Venice for over two years when, as a Cardinal, Luciani had been Patriarch there, and Father John Magee, newly acquired since the Papal election. As the nuns who worked in the Papal Apartments hovered anxiously, Albino Luciani ate a frugal meal of clear soup, veal, fresh beans and a little salad. He sipped occasionally from a glass of water and considered the events of the day and the decisions he had made. He had not wanted the job. He had not sought or canvassed for the Papacy. Now as Head of State the awesome responsibilities were his.

While Sisters Vincenza, Assunta, Clorinda and Gabrietta quietly served the three men as they watched on television the events which preoccupied Italy that evening, other men in other places were being caused deep anxiety by the activities of Albino Luciani.

One floor below the Papal Apartments the lights were still on in the Vatican Bank. Its head, Bishop Paul Marcinkus, had other more pressing problems on his mind than his evening meal. Chicago-born Marcinkus had learned about survival on the back-streets of Cicero, Illinois. During his meteoric rise to the position of 'God's Banker' he had survived many moments of crisis. Now he was confronted with the most serious he had ever faced. In the past thirty-three days his colleagues in the Bank had noticed a remarkable change in the man who controlled the Vatican's millions. The 6ft 3in, 16-stone extrovert had become moody and introspective. He was visibly losing weight and his face had acquired a grey pallor. Vatican City in many respects is a village and secrets are hard to keep in a village. Word had reached Marcinkus that the new Pope had quietly begun his own personal investigation of the Vatican Bank and specifically into the methods Marcinkus was using to run that Bank. Countless times since the arrival of the new Pope, Marcinkus had regretted that business in 1972 concerning the Banca Cattolica del Veneto.

Vatican Secretary of State Cardinal Jean Villot was another who was still at his desk on that September evening. He studied the list of appointments, resignations to be asked for, and transfers which the Pope had handed to him one hour previously. He had advised, argued, remonstrated but to no avail. Luciani had been adamant.

It was by any standards a dramatic reshuffle. It would set the Church in new directions; directions which Villot, and the others on the list who were about to be replaced, considered highly dangerous. When these changes were announced there would be millions of words written and uttered by the world's media, analyzing, dissecting, prophesying, explaining. The real explanation, however, would not be discussed, would not be given a public airing – there was one common denominator, one fact that linked each of the men about to be replaced. Villot was aware of it. More important, so was the Pope. It had been one of the factors that had caused him to act: to strip these men of real power and put them into relatively harmless positions. It was Freemasonry.

The evidence the Pope had acquired indicated that within the Vatican City State there were over 100 Masons, ranging from

Cardinals to priests. This despite the fact that Canon Law stated that to be a Freemason ensured automatic excommunication. Luciani was further preoccupied with an illegal masonic lodge which had penetrated far beyond Italy in its search for wealth and power. It called itself P2. The fact that it had penetrated the Vatican walls and formed masonic links with priests, bishops and even Cardinals made P2 anathema to Albino Luciani.

Villot had already become deeply concerned about the new Papacy before this latest bombshell. He was one of the very few who was aware of the dialogue taking place between the Pope and the State Department in Washington. He knew that on October 23rd the Vatican would be receiving a Congressional delegation, and that on October 24th the delegation would be having a private audience with the Pope. The subject: birth control.

Villot had looked carefully at the Vatican dossier on Albino Luciani. He had also read the secret memorandum that Luciani, then Bishop of Vittorio Veneto, had sent to Paul VI before the Papal announcement of the encyclical *Humanae Vitae*, an encyclical which prohibited Catholics using any artificial form of birth control. His own discussions with Luciani had left him in no doubt where the new Pope stood on this issue. Equally, in Villot's mind, there was no doubt what Paul's successor was now planning to do. There was to be a dramatic change of position. Some would agree with Villot's view that it was a betrayal of Paul VI. Many would acclaim it as the Church's greatest contribution to the twentieth century.

In Buenos Aires, another banker, Roberto Calvi, had Pope John Paul I on his mind as September 1978 drew to a close. In the preceding weeks he had discussed the problems posed by the new Pope with his protectors, Licio Gelli and Umberto Ortolani, two men who could list among their many assets their complete control of Calvi, chairman of Banco Ambrosiano. Calvi had been beset with problems even before the Papal election that placed Albino Luciani upon St Peter's chair. The Bank of Italy had been secretly investigating Calvi's Milan bank since April. It was an investigation prompted by a mysterious poster campaign against Calvi which had erupted in late 1977: posters which gave details of some of Calvi's criminal activities and hinted at a world-wide range of criminal acts.

Calvi was aware of exactly what progress the Bank of Italy was making with its investigation. His close friendship with Licio Gelli ensured a day-by-day account of it. He was equally aware of the Papal investigation into the Vatican Bank. Like Marcinkus he knew it was only a matter of time before the two independent investigations realized that to probe one of these financial empires was to probe both. He was doing everything within his considerable power to thwart the Bank of Italy and protect his financial empire, from which he was in the process of stealing over one billion dollars.

Careful analysis of Roberto Calvi's position in September 1978 makes it abundantly clear that if Pope Paul was succeeded by an honest man then Calvi faced total ruin, the collapse of his bank and certain imprisonment. There is no doubt whatever that Albino Luciani was just such a man.

In New York, Sicilian banker Michele Sindona had also been anxiously monitoring Pope John Paul's activities. For over three years Sindona had been fighting the Italian Government's attempts to have him extradited. They wanted him brought to Milan to face charges involving fraudulent diversion of 225 million dollars. Earlier that year, in May, it appeared that Sindona had finally lost the long battle. A Federal Judge had ruled that the extradition request should be granted.

Sindona remained on a 3 million dollar bail while his lawyers prepared to play one last card. They demanded that the United States Government prove that there was well-founded evidence to justify extradition. Sindona asserted that the charges brought against him by the Italian Government were the work of Communist and other left-wing politicians. His lawyers also asserted that the Milan prosecutor had concealed evidence that would clear Sindona and that if their client was returned to Italy he would almost certainly be assassinated. The hearing was scheduled for November.

That summer, in New York, others were equally active on behalf of Michele Sindona. One Mafia member, Luigi Ronsisvalle, a professional killer; was threatening the life of witness Nicola Biase, who had earlier given evidence against Sindona in the extradition proceedings. The Mafia also had a contract out on the life of assistant United States attorney John Kenney, who was Chief Prosecutor in the extradition proceedings. The fee being offered for the murder of the Government attorney was 100,000 dollars.

If Pope John Paul I continued to dig into the affairs of the Vatican Bank then no amount of Mafia contracts would help Sindona in his fight against being returned to Italy. The web of corruption at the Vatican Bank, which included the laundering of Mafia money through that Bank, went back beyond Calvi: back to Michele Sindona.

In Chicago another Prince of the Catholic Church worried and fretted about events in the Vatican City: Cardinal John Cody, head of the richest archdiocese in the world. Cody ruled over two-and-a-half million Catholics and nearly 3,000 priests, over 450 parishes and an annual income that he refused to reveal in its entirety to anyone. It was in fact in excess of 250 million dollars. Fiscal secrecy was only one of the problems that whirled around Cody. By 1978 he had ruled Chicago for thirteen years. In those years the demands for his replacement had reached extraordinary proportions. Priests, nuns, lay workers, people from many secular professions had petitioned Rome in their thousands for the removal of a man they regarded as a despot.

Pope Paul had agonized for years about removing Cody. He had on at least one occasion actually steeled himself and made the decision, only to revoke the order at the last moment. The complex, tortured personality of Paul was only part of the reason for the vacillation. Paul knew that other secret allegations had been made against Cody, with a substantial amount of evidence which indicated the urgent need to replace the Cardinal of Chicago.

During late September, Cody received a phone call from Rome. The Vatican City village had leaked another piece of information – information well paid for over the years by Cardinal Cody. The caller told the Cardinal that where Pope Paul had agonized his successor John Paul had acted. The Pope had decided that Cardinal John Cody was to be replaced.

Over at least three of these men lurked the shadow of another, Licio Gelli. Men called him 'Il Burattinaio' – the Puppet Master. The puppets were many and were placed in numerous countries. He controlled P2 and through it he controlled Italy. In Buenos Aires, the city where he discussed the problem of the new Pope with Calvi, the Puppet Master had organized the triumphant return to power of General Peron – a fact that Peron subsequently acknowledged by kneeling at Gelli's feet. If Marcinkus, Sindona or Calvi were threatened by the various courses of action planned by Albino Luciani, it was in Licio Gelli's direct interests that the threat should be removed.

It was abundantly clear that on September 28th, 1978, these six men, Marcinkus, Villot, Calvi, Sindona, Cody and Gelli had much to fear if the Papacy of John Paul I continued. It is equally clear that all of them stood to gain in a variety of ways if Pope John Paul I should suddenly die.

He did.

Sometime during the late evening of September 28th, 1978 and the early morning of September 29th, 1978, thirty-three days after his election, Albino Luciani died.

Time of death: unknown. Cause of death: unknown.

I am convinced that the full facts and the complete circumstances which are merely outlined in the preceding pages hold the key to the truth of the death of Albino Luciani. I am equally convinced that one of these six men had, by the early evening of September 28th, 1978, already initiated a course of action to resolve the problems that Albino Luciani's Papacy was posing. One of these men was at the very heart of a conspiracy that applied a uniquely Italian solution.

Albino Luciani had been elected Pope on August 26th, 1978. Shortly after that Conclave, the English Cardinal Basil Hume said: 'The decision was unexpected. But once it had happened, it seemed totally and entirely right. The feeling he was just what we want was so general that he was unmistakably God's candidate.'

Thirty-three days later 'God's candidate' died.

What follows is the product of three years' continuous and intensive investigation into that death. I have evolved a number of rules for an investigation of this nature. Rule One: begin at the beginning. Ascertain the nature and personality of the dead subject. What manner of man was Albino Luciani?

The Road to Rome

❧❧

The Luciani family lived in the small mountain village of Canale d'Agordo,* nearly 1,000 metres above sea level and approximately 120 kilometres north of Venice.

At the time of Albino's birth on October 17th, 1912, his parents Giovanni and Bortola were already caring for two daughters from the father's first marriage. As a young widower with two girls and lacking a regular job Giovanni would not have been every young woman's dream come true. Bortola had been contemplating the life of a convent nun. Now she was mother to three children. The birth had been long and arduous and Bortola, displaying an over-anxiety that would become a feature of the boy's early life, feared that the child was about to die. He was promptly baptized, with the name Albino, in memory of a close friend of his father who had been killed in a blast furnace accident while working alongside Giovanni in Germany. The boy came into a world that within two years would be at war, after the Archduke Francis Ferdinand and his wife had been assassinated.

The first fourteen years of this century are considered by many Europeans to have been a golden age. Countless writers have described the stability, the general feeling of well-being, the widespread increase in mass culture, the satisfying spiritual life, the broadening of horizons and the reduction of social inequalities. They extol the freedom of thought and the quality of life as if it were an

*At the time of Albino Luciani's birth the village was called Forno di Canale. It was changed to Canale d'Agordo in 1964 at the instigation of Luciani's brother, Edoardo. The village thus reverted to its original name.

Edwardian Garden of Eden. Doubtless all this existed, but so did appalling poverty, mass unemployment, social inequality, hunger, illness and early death. Much of the world was divided by these two realities. Italy was no exception.

Naples was besieged by thousands of people who wanted to emigrate to the USA, or England, or anywhere. Already the United States had written some small print under the heroic declaration, 'Give me your tired, your poor. Your huddled masses yearning to breathe free.' The 'wretched refuse' now discovered that disease, insufficient funds, contract labour, criminality, and physical deformity were a few of the grounds for rejection from admission to the United States.

In Rome, within sight of St Peter's, thousands lived on a permanent basis in huts of straw and brushwood. In the summer many moved to the caves in the surrounding hills. Some did dawn to dusk work in vineyards at fourpence a day. On farms others worked the same hours and received no money at all. Payment was usually in rotten maize, one of the reasons that so many agricultural labourers suffered from a skin disease called pellagra. Standing waist deep in the rice fields of Pavia ensured that many contracted malaria from the frequent mosquito bites. Illiteracy was over 50 per cent. While Pope after Pope yearned for the return of the Papal States, these conditions were the reality of life for many who lived in this united Italy.

The village of Canale was dominated by children, women and old men. The majority of men of working age were forced to seek work further afield. Giovanni Luciani would travel to Switzerland, Austria, Germany and France, leaving in the spring and returning in the autumn.

The Luciani home, partly converted from an old barn, had one source of heating, an old wood-burning stove which heated the room where Albino was born. There was no garden – such items are considered luxuries by the mountain people. The scenery more than compensated: pine forests and, soaring directly above the village, the stark snow-capped mountains; the river Bioi cascaded down close to the village square.

Albino Luciani's parents were an odd mix. The deeply religious Bortola spent as much time in the church as she did in her small home, worrying over her increasingly large family. She was the kind of mother who at the slightest cough would over-anxiously rush any of her children to the nearby medical officers stationed on the border. Devout, with aspirations to martyrdom, she was prone to tell the children frequently of the many sacrifices she was obliged to make on their behalf. The father,

Giovanni, wandered a Europe at war seeking work that ranged from bricklaying and engineering to being an electrician and mechanic. As a committed Socialist he was regarded by devout Catholics as a priest-eating, crucifix-burning devil. The combination produced inevitable frictions. The memory of his mother's reaction when she saw her husband's name on posters which were plastered all over the village announcing that he was standing in a local election as a Socialist stayed with the young Albino for the rest of his life.

Albino was followed by another son, Edoardo, then a girl, Antonia. Bortola added to their small income by writing letters for the illiterate and working as a scullery maid.

The family diet consisted of polenta (corn meal), barley, macaroni and any vegetables that came to hand. On special occasions there might be a dessert of carfoni, pastry full of ground poppy seeds. Meat was a rarity. In Canale if a man was wealthy enough to afford the luxury of killing a pig it would be salted and last his family for a year.

Albino's vocation for the priesthood came early and was actively encouraged by his mother and the local parish priest, Father Filippo Carli. Yet if any single person deserves credit for ensuring that Albino Luciani took his first steps towards priesthood it is the irreligious Socialist, Giovanni. If Albino was to attend the minor seminary at nearby Feltre it was going to cost the Luciani family a considerable sum. Mother and son discussed this shortly before the boy's eleventh birthday. Eventually Bortola told her son to sit down and write to his father, then working in France. Albino was later to say it was one of the most important letters of his life.

His father received the letter and thought the problem over for a while before replying. Then he gave his permission and accepted the added burden with the words, 'Well, we must make this sacrifice'.

So, in 1923, the eleven-year-old Luciani went off to the seminary – to the internal war that was raging within the Roman Catholic Church. This was a Church where books such as Antonio Rosmini's *The Five Wounds of the Church* were banned. Rosmini, an Italian theologian and priest, had written in 1848 that the Church faced a crisis of five evils: social remoteness of the clergy from the people; the low standard of education of the priests; disunity and acrimony among the bishops; the dependence of lay appointments on secular authorities; and Church ownership of property and enslavement to wealth. Rosmini had hoped for liberalizing reform. What he got, largely as a result of Jesuit intrigue, was the condemnation of his book and the withdrawal of the cardinal's hat which Pius IX had offered him.

Only fifty-eight years before Luciani's birth the Vatican had proclaimed the *Syllabus of Errors* and an accompanying encyclical, *Quanta Cura*. In these the Papacy denounced unrestricted liberty of speech and the freedom of press comment. The concept of equal status for all religions was totally rejected. The Pope responsible for these measures was Pius IX. He also made it clear that he disliked intensely the concept of democratic government and that his preference was for absolute monarchies. He further denounced 'the proponents of freedom of conscience and freedom of religion' as well as 'all of those who assert that the Church may not use force'.

In 1870, this same pope, having summoned a Vatican Council, indicated to the assembled bishops that the main item on the agenda was Papal infallibility. *His* infallibility. After much intensive lobbying and some very unChristian-like pressure the Pope suffered a major moral defeat when, out of over 1,000 members entitled to take part in the Council, only 451 bishops voted for the concept. By an agreed strategy all but two of the dissenters left Rome before the final vote was taken. At the last meeting of the Council on July 18th, 1870, it was decided by 535 votes to 2 that the Pope was infallible when defining a doctrine concerning faith or morals.

Until they were liberated by Italian troops in 1870 the Jews in Rome had been locked in a ghetto by the Pope who became infallible. He was equally intolerant of Protestants and recommended the introduction of prison sentences for non-Catholics who were preaching in Tuscany. At the time of writing considerable efforts are being made to have Pius IX canonized and made a saint.

After Pius IX came Leo XIII, considered by many historians to have been an enlightened and humane man. He was followed by Pius X, thought by many of the same historians to have been a total disaster. He reigned until 1914 and the damage he did was still very evident when Albino Luciani entered the Feltre seminary.

The Index of books which no Roman Catholic was allowed to read grew ever longer. Publishers, editors, and authors were excommunicated. When critical books were published anonymously, the authors, whoever they were, were excommunicated. The Pope coined a word to encapsulate all that he was attempting to destroy: 'modernism'. Any who questioned the current teachings of the Church were anathema. With the Pope's blessing and financial help an Italian prelate, Umberto Benigni, created a spy system. The purpose was to hunt and destroy all modernists. Thus in the twentieth century the Inquisition was re-born.

With the diminution of his worldly powers through the loss of the

Papal States the self-proclaimed 'prisoner in the Vatican' was not in a position to order any burnings at the stake, but a nudge here, a wink there, anonymous and unsupported allegations about a colleague or possible rival were enough to destroy many careers within the Church. The mother was eating her own children. The majority of those whom Pius and the men around him destroyed were loyal and faithful members of the Roman Catholic Church.

Seminaries were closed. Those that were allowed to remain open to teach the next generation of priests were carefully monitored. In one encyclical the Pope declared that everyone who preached or taught in an official capacity had to take a special oath abjuring all errors of modernism. He further declared a general prohibition against the reading of newspapers by all seminarians and theological students, specifically adding that his rule also applied to the very best journals.

Every year Father Benigni, the man in charge of the spy ring that eventually reached through every single diocese in Italy and right across Europe, received a subsidy of 1,000 lire ($5,000 is an approximate modern equivalent) directly from the Pope. This secret organization of spies was not disbanded until 1921. Father Benigni then became an informant and spy for Mussolini.

Pius X died on August 20th, 1914. He was canonized in 1954.

So at Feltre Luciani found it was a crime to read a newspaper or periodical. He was in an austere world where the teachers were as vulnerable as the pupils. A word or comment that did not meet with the entire approval of a colleague might result in a teaching priest losing the right to teach, because of Father Benigni's spy ring. Although officially disbanded in 1921, two years before Luciani entered Feltre, its influence was still prevalent throughout his entire period of training for the priesthood. Critical questioning of what was being taught would have been anathema. The system was designed to give answers, not to encourage questions. The teachers who had been marked and scarred by the purge in turn would mark and scar the next generation.

Albino Luciani's generation of priests had to cope with the full force of the *Syllabus of Errors* and anti-modernism mentality. Luciani himself might easily have become, under such dominant influences, yet another priest with a closed mind. A variety of factors saved him from that fate. Not the least was a simple but great gift, a thirst for knowledge.

Despite his mother's exaggeration about his early health there was one considerable bonus in her over-protectiveness. By refusing to let the boy enjoy the rough and tumble of his friends and by replacing the ball with a book she opened the entire world to her son. He began to read voraciously at an early age the complete works of Dickens and Jules Verne. Mark Twain, for example, he read at the age of seven, unusual in a country where still nearly half the adults could not read at all at that time.

At Feltre he absorbed every book they had. More significantly he remembered virtually everything he read. He was endowed with an astonishing memory. Consequently, though provocative questions might be frowned upon, Luciani would from time to time have the temerity to ask them. His teachers considered him diligent but 'too lively'.

In the summers the young seminarian would return home and, dressed in his long black cassock, work in the fields. When not helping with the harvest he could be found 're-organizing' Father Filippo's library. The school terms would be enlivened from time to time by a visit from his father. The first act performed by Giovanni upon returning home in the autumn was always a visit to the seminary. He would then spend the winter campaigning on behalf of the Socialists.

From Feltre, Luciani graduated to the major seminary at Belluno. One of his contemporaries recalled for me the regime at Belluno:

> We were woken up at 5.30 a.m. No heating, indeed the water would often be solid ice. I used to lose my vocation every morning for five minutes. We had thirty minutes to get washed and make our beds.
>
> I met Luciani there in September 1929. He was then sixteen. He was always amiable, quiet, serene – unless you stated something that was inaccurate – then he was like a spring. I learned that in front of him one had to speak carefully. Any muddled thinking and you were in danger with him.

Among the books Luciani read were a number of works by Antonio Rosmini. Conspicuous by its absence from the seminary library was *The Five Wounds of the Church*. In 1930 it still remained on the Index of Forbidden Books. Aware by now of the furore that the book had caused, Luciani quietly acquired his own copy. It was to have a deep and lasting influence upon his life.

To Luciani's teachers the *Syllabus of Errors* proclaimed in 1864 by Pius IX was to be considered in the 1930s as the ultimate truth. The toleration of a non-Catholic opinion in any country where Catholics were in a majority was inconceivable. Mussolini's version of Fascism was not the only one being taught in Italy in the years immediately preceding the Second World War. Error had no rights. The exception apparently was if it was the teacher who was in error, then its rights were absolute.

Luciani's vision, far from being expanded by his teachers, began, in certain respects, to shrink. Fortunately he was subjected to influences other than his teachers. Another former class-mate at Belluno recalled:

> He read Goldoni's dramas. He read French novelists of the nineteenth century. He bought a collection of the writings of the seventeenth century French Jesuit, Pierre Couwase and read them from cover to cover.

So strongly did the writings of Couwase influence him that Luciani began to think seriously of becoming a Jesuit. He watched as first one, then a second, of his close friends went to the Rector, Bishop Giosué Cattarossi, and asked for permission to join the Jesuit order. In both instances the permission was granted. Luciani went and asked for permission. The Bishop considered the request then responded, 'No, three is one too many. You had better stay here.'

At the age of twenty-three he was ordained priest, on July 7th, 1935 in San Pietro, Belluno. The following day he celebrated his first mass in his home town. His delight at being appointed curate in Forno di Canale was total. The fact that this is the humblest clerical position within the Church was of no consequence to him. In the congregation of friends, relations, local priests and immediate family was a very proud Giovanni Luciani, who now had a permanent job relatively close to home as a glass-blower on the island of Murano near Venice.

In 1937 Luciani was appointed Vice-Rector at his old seminary in Belluno. If the content of his teaching at this time differed little from that of his own tutors, his manner certainly did. He lifted what was often dull and tedious theology to something fresh and memorable. After four years he felt the need to expand. He wanted to gain a doctorate in theology. This would mean moving to Rome and studying at the Gregorian University. His superiors in Belluno wanted him to continue teaching there while he studied for his doctorate. Luciani was agreeable but the Gregorian University insisted on at least one year's obligatory attendance in Rome.

After the intervention of Angelo Santin, the director at Belluno, and Father Felice Capello, a renowned expert on Canon Law who taught at the Gregorian and 'happened' to be related to Luciani, Pope Pius

XII personally granted a dispensation in a letter signed by Cardinal Maglione and dated March 27th, 1941. (The fact that the Second World War was in full flood at the time is not apparent from the Vatican correspondence.) Luciani chose for his thesis, 'The origin of the human soul according to Antonio Rosmini'.

His experiences during the war were an extraordinary mixture of the sacred and the profane. They included improving his German as he listened to the confessions of soldiers from the Third Reich. They included meticulous study of Rosmini's works, or that part of them that was not banned. Later when Luciani became Pope it would be said that his thesis was 'brilliant'. That at least was the view of the Vatican newspaper *L'Osservatore Romano,* which they had not expressed in the pre-conclave biographies. It is not a view shared by teachers at the Gregorian. One described it to me as 'a competent piece of work'. Another said, 'In my opinion it is worthless. It shows extreme conservatism and also lacks scholarly method.'

Many would say that Luciani's interest in and involvement with the works of Rosmini were clear indications of his liberal thinking. The Albino Luciani of the 1940s was far from being a liberal. His thesis attempts to refute Rosmini on each point. He attacks the nineteenth-century theologian for using second-hand and incorrect quotations, for his superficiality, for 'ingenious cleverness'. It is a scathing demolition job and a clear indication of a reactionary mind.

In between establishing that Rosmini had misquoted St Thomas Aquinas, Albino Luciani trod a delicate path when teaching his students at Belluno. He told them not to intervene when they saw German troops rounding up local resistance groups. Privately he was in sympathy with the resistance but he was aware that among the trainee priests in the classroom were many who were pro-Fascist. He was equally aware that the resistance movement was provoking reprisals by the Germans against the civilian population. Houses were destroyed; men were taken out and hanged on trees. In the latter part of the war, however, Luciani's seminary became a haven for members of the resistance. Discovery by the German troops would have resulted in certain death, not only for the resistance fighters but also for Luciani and his colleagues.

On November 23rd, 1946 Luciani defended his thesis. It was finally published on April 4th, 1950. He obtained a *magnum cum laude* and became a Doctor of Theology.

In 1947, the Bishop of Belluno, Girolamo Bortignon, made Luciani Pro-Vicar-General of the diocese and asked him to organize the approaching Synod and inter-diocesan meeting of Feltre and Belluno. The increase in responsibility coincided with a broadening outlook. While still unable to come to terms with Rosmini's 'Origins of the Soul' Luciani had begun to appreciate and agree with Rosmini's view of what ailed the Church. The fact that the same problems still obtained a hundred years later made the factors of social remoteness, an uneducated priesthood, disunion among bishops, the unhealthy interlocking of power between Church and State and most of all the Church's preoccupation with material wealth, even more pertinent.

In 1949, Luciani was made responsible for catechetics in preparation for the Eucharistic Congress that was taking place that year in Belluno. This, plus his own experiences of teaching, prompted his first venture in authorship, a small book embodying his views entitled *Catechsi in Briciole* (Crumbs from the Catechism).

Catechism classes: possibly these are the earliest memory of most adult Catholics. Many theologians would dismiss them but it is precisely this stage of growth that the Jesuits refer to when they talk of 'catching a child for life'. Albino Luciani was one of the best teachers of this subject the Church has had in this century. He had the simplicity of thought that comes only to the highly intelligent, and added to this was a genuine, deep humility.

By 1958, Don Albino, as he was known by all, had a settled life. His mother and father were both dead. He paid frequent visits to his brother, Edoardo, now married and living in the family home, and to his sister, Antonia, also married and living in Trento. As Vicar-General of Belluno he had more than enough work to occupy him. For leisure there were his books. He had little interest in food, eating whatever was put in front of him. His main forms of exercise were cycling around his diocese or climbing the nearby mountains.

This small, quiet man succeeded, apparently without trying, in having an extraordinary and lasting effect on people. Again and again as I talked to those who knew him I could see a remarkable change happen within the person recalling Albino Luciani. Their faces would soften, quite literally relax. They would smile. They smiled a great deal as they recalled the man. They grew gentler before my eyes. He clearly touched something very deep within them. Catholics would call it the soul. Happily oblivious, Albino Luciani was already leaving a unique legacy as he cycled around Belluno.

In the Vatican there was a new Pope, John XXIII, a man born at nearby Bergamo, which was also the birth-place of the man from whom Albino acquired his Christian name. John was busy shuffling episcopal appointments. Urbani to Venice to replace himself, Carraro to Verona. In Vittorio Veneto there was a vacancy for a bishop. The Pope asked Bishop Bortignon for a name. The response made him smile. 'I know him. I know him. He will do me fine.'

Luciani, with that disarming humility that so many would later totally fail to comprehend, declared after his appointment as Bishop of Vittorio Veneto, 'Well, I have taken a couple of train journeys with him, but he did most of the talking. I said so little he could not have got to know me.'

The 46-year-old Luciani was ordained Bishop by Pope John in St Peter's Basilica two days after Christmas, 1958.

The Pope was fully aware of the pastoral activities of the young man from the north and he praised him warmly. Picking up a copy of *The Imitation of Christ* by Thomas à Kempis Pope John read aloud Chapter 23. In it the four elements that bring peace and personal liberty are quoted:

My son, try to do another's will rather than your own. Always choose to have less rather than more. Always choose the lowest place and to be less than everyone else. Always long and pray that the Will of God may be fully realized in your life. You will find that the man who does all this walks in the land of peace and quietness.

Before his ordination, Luciani had written of the coming event in a letter to Monsignor Capovilla, the Pope's private secretary. One phrase he used strikingly demonstrates how closely he was already attempting to lead a life that embraced the ideals of Thomas à Kempis, 'Sometimes the Lord writes his works in dust'.

The first time the congregation gathered to hear their new bishop in Vittorio Veneto, he elaborated on this theme:

With me the Lord uses yet again his old system. He takes the small ones from the mud of the streets. He takes the people of the fields. He takes others away from their nets in the sea or the lake, and he makes them Apostles. It's his old system.

As soon as I became consecrated a priest I started to receive from my superiors tasks of responsibility and I have understood what it is for a man to be in authority. It is like a ball that is pumped up. If you watch the children who play on the grass outside this Cathedral when their ball is punctured they don't even bother to look at it. It can stay with tranquillity in a corner. But when it is pumped up the children jump out from all sides and every one believes that they have the right to kick it. This is what happens to men when they move up. Do not therefore be envious.

Later he talked to the 400 priests who were now answerable to him. A number of them had offered him gifts, food, money. He declined these. When they were all gathered he attempted to explain the reason: 'I come without five lire. I want to leave without five lire.'

He continued:

My dear priests. My dear faithful. I would be a very unfortunate bishop if I didn't love you. I assure you that I do, and that I want to be at your service and put at your disposal all of my poor energies, the little that I have and the little that I am.

He had the choice of living in a luxurious apartment in the city or a more spartan life in the Castle of San Martino. He chose the Castle.

For many bishops their life is a relatively remote one. There is an automatic gulf between them and their flock, accepted by both. The bishop is an elusive figure, seen only on special occasions. Albino Luciani took a different view of his role in Vittorio Veneto. He dressed as a simple priest and took the gospel to his people. With his priests he practised a form of democracy that was at that time extremely rare within the Church. His Presbyterial Council for example was elected entirely without nominations from the bishop.

When that same Council recommended the closure of a particular minor seminary despite the fact that he did not agree with the decision, he went to all his parishes and quietly talked over the issue with the parish priests. As soon as it became clear to him that the majority favoured the closure he authorized it. The pupils were sent on the instructions of this former seminarian to state schools. He later stated publicly that the majority view had been right and his own wrong.

No priest ever had to make an appointment to see his bishop. If one came, he was seen. Some considered his democracy a weakness. Others saw him differently and compared him to the man who had made him bishop.

It was like having your own personal Pope. It was as if Papa Roncalli [John XXIII] was here in this diocese working alongside us. His table usually had two or three priests at it. He simply could not stop giving of himself. One moment he would be visiting the sick or the handicapped. They never knew at the hospitals when he was coming. He would just turn up on a bike or in his old car leaving his secretary to read outside while he wandered the wards. The next moment he would turn up in one of the mountain villages to discuss a particular problem with the local priest.

In the second week of January 1959, less than three weeks after he had ordained Bishop Luciani, Pope John was discussing world affairs with his pro-Secretary of State, Cardinal Domenico Tardini. They discussed the implications of what a young man named Fidel Castro was doing to the Batista regime in Cuba; of the fact that France had a new President, General Charles de Gaulle; of the Russian demonstration of advanced technology in sending a new rocket into orbit around the moon. They discussed the revolt in Algeria, the appalling poverty in many Latin American countries, the changing face of Africa with a new nation seemingly emerging each week. It seemed to John that the Roman Catholic Church was not coming to terms with the problems of the mid-twentieth century. It was a crucial point in history with a significant part of the world turning to things material and away from things spiritual. Unlike many in the Vatican the Pope considered that reform, like charity, should begin at home. Suddenly John had an idea. He was later to say it was an inspiration of the Holy Spirit. Wherever it came from it was an excellent one: 'A Council'.

Thus did the idea for the Second Vatican Ecumenical Council emerge. The first in 1870 had resulted in giving the Church an infallible Pope. The effects of the second, many years after its conclusion, are still reverberating around the world.

On October 11th, 1962, 2,381 bishops gathered in Rome for the opening ceremony of this Second Vatican Council. Among them was Albino Luciani. As the Council meetings progressed Luciani made friendships that would endure for the rest of his life. Suenens of Belgium. Wojtyla and Wyszynski of Poland. Marty of France. Thiandoum of Dakar. Luciani also experienced during the Council his own road to Damascus. It was the Council's declaration *On Religious Freedom*.

Others were less impressed with this new way of looking at an old problem. Men like Cardinal Alfredo Ottaviani, who controlled the Holy Office, were determined to wreck not only the concept of tolerance that was implicit in *On Religious Freedom,* they were fighting a bitter rearguard action against anything that smacked of what Pius X at the beginning of the century had termed 'modernism'. This was the generation which had taught Luciani in the Belluno seminary that religious 'freedom' was confined to Roman Catholics. 'Error has no rights.' Luciani in turn had taught his own pupils this same appalling doctrine. Now at the Second Vatican Council he listened with growing wonder as bishop after bishop challenged the concept.

When Luciani considered the arguments for and against he was over fifty years of age. His response was typical of this prudent man of the mountains. He discussed the problem with others, he withdrew into thought, he concluded that the 'error' had been in the concept he had been taught.

It was also typical of the man that he subsequently published an article explaining how and why he had changed his mind. He began with a recommendation to his readers:

> If you come across error, rather than uprooting it or knocking it down, see if you can trim it patiently, allowing the light to shine upon the nucleus of goodness and truth that usually is not missing even in erroneous opinions.

Other aspects of the various debates caused him less difficulty. When the principle of the poor church – a church lacking political, economic and ideological power – was extolled, the Council was merely seeking something in which Luciani already believed.

Before the Council opened Luciani had issued a pastoral letter, 'Notes on the Council', to prepare his congregations. Now with the Council still in session the changes he had already introduced into the Vittorio Diocese were accelerated. He urged his seminary teachers to read the new theological reviews and discard manuals that still looked back lovingly to the nineteenth century. He sent his teachers on courses to the principal theological universities of Europe. Not only the teachers but the pupils could now be found at his dinner table. He wrote weekly to all his priests, sharing his ideas and plans with them.

In August 1962, a few months before the opening of the Second Vatican Council, Luciani was confronted with an example of error of quite another kind. Two priests in the diocese had become involved with a smooth-talking sales representative who also speculated in property. The priest were tempted to join in. When one of them came to Luciani he confessed that the amount of money missing, much of it belonging to small savers, was in excess of two billion lire.

Albino Luciani had very set ideas about wealth and money, particularly Church wealth. Some of his ideas stemmed from Rosmini; many directly from his own personal experience. He believed in a Roman Catholic Church of the poor, for the poor. The enforced absences of his father, the hunger and the cold, the wooden clogs with the extra nails banged into the soles so that they would not wear out, cutting grass on the mountain sides to augment the family dinners, the long spells in seminary without seeing a mother who could not afford to visit him, this environment produced in Luciani a deep compassion for the poor, a total indifference to the acquisition of personal wealth and a belief that the Church, his Church, should not only be materially poor but should be seen to be so.

Conscious of the damage the scandal would do he went directly to the editor of the Venice newspaper *Il Gazzettino*. He asked the editor not to treat the story in a lurid manner with sensational headlines.

Back in his diocese he called together his 400 priests. Normal practice would have been to have claimed ecclesiastic immunity. To do so would ensure that the Church would not pay a penny. Speaking quietly Luciani told his priests:

> It is true that two of us have done wrong. I believe the diocese must pay. I also believe that the law must run its due course. We must not hide behind any immunity. In this scandal there is a lesson for us all. It is that we must be a poor Church. I intend to sell ecclesiastical treasure. I further intend to sell one of our buildings. The money will be used to repay every single lira that these priests owe. I ask for your agreement.

Albino Luciani obtained their agreement. His morality prevailed. Some who were present at that meeting admired the man and his morality. Some almost ruefully observed that they considered Luciani was too moral in such matters. The property speculator who had involved the two priests was obviously one who considered the Bishop 'too moral'. Before his trial he committed suicide. One of the priests served a one-year prison sentence and the other was acquitted.

Others among the priesthood were less than enchanted with the manner in which Luciani wholeheartedly embraced the spirit of the Vatican Council. Like Luciani their thinking had been shaped in the early, more repressive, years. Unlike him they were not prepared to have that thinking reshaped. This aspect was constantly to occupy Luciani's work during the remainder of his time at Vittorio Veneto. With the same hunger with which he had read book after book in his youth he now, in the words of Monsiguor Ghizzo who worked with him, 'totally absorbed Vatican Council II. He had the Council in his blood. He knew the documents by heart. Further, he implemented the documents.'

He twinned Vittorio Veneto with Kiremba, a small township in Burundi, formerly part of German East Africa. In the mid-1960s when he visited Kiremba he was brought face to face with the Third World. Nearly 70 per cent of the country's three-and-a-quarter million people were Roman Catholics. The faith was flourishing, but so were poverty, disease, a high infant mortality rate and civil war. Churches were full, bellies were empty. It was realities like this that had inspired Pope John to summon the Second Vatican Council, as an attempt to drag the Church into the twentieth century. While the old Curial Palace Guard in Rome were being blinded by the Second Council, Luciani and others like him were being illuminated by it.

John literally gave his life to ensure that the Council he had conceived should not be stillborn. Advised that he was seriously ill, he declined the operation his specialists were insisting upon. They told him that such an operation would prolong his life. He retorted that to leave the Vatican Council at the mercy of the reactionary element within the Vatican during the early delicate stages would be to ensure a theological disaster. He preferred to remain in the Vatican helping the child he had created to grow. In doing so he calmly and with extraordinary courage signed his own death warrant. When he died on June 3rd, 1963, the Roman Catholic Church, through the Second Vatican Ecumenical Council, was finally attempting to come to terms with the world as it was rather than how it would like it to be.

With John dead, replaced by Pope Paul VI, the Church inched its way nearer to one specific reality, to one particular decision, the most important the Roman Catholic Church has taken this century. In the 1960s the question was being asked with increasing urgency; what was the Church's position on artificial birth control?

In 1962 Pope John had set up a Pontifical Commission on the family. Birth control was one of the major issues it was directed to study. Pope Paul enlarged the Commission until its membership reached sixty-eight. He then created a considerable number of 'consultants' to advise and monitor the Commission. While hundreds of millions of Roman Catholics around the world waited and wondered, speculation that a change in the Church's position was imminent grew ever larger. Many began using the Pill or other forms of artificial contraception. While the 'experts' in Rome debated the significance of Genesis 38:7–10 and a man called Onan, everyday life had to go on.

It is ironic that the confusion which prevailed in the Catholic world on this issue was exactly mirrored by the Pope's thinking on the problem. He did not know what to do.

During the first week of October 1965, Pope Paul granted a unique interview to Italian journalist Alberto Cavallari. They discussed many problems facing the Church. Cavallari later observed that he did not raise the issue of artificial birth control because he was aware of the potential embarrassment. His fears were unfounded. Paul raised the subject himself. It should be remembered that this was an era when the Papacy still clung to Royal illusions; personal pronouns were not Paul's style.

Take birth control for example. The world asks what we think and we find ourselves trying to give an answer. But what answer. We can't keep silent. And yet to speak is a real problem. The Church hasn't had to deal with such things for centuries. And it is a somewhat foreign and even humanly embarrassing subject for men of the Church. So, the commissions meet, the reports pile up, the studies are published. Oh, they study a lot, you know. But then we still have to make the final decisions. And in deciding, we are all alone. Deciding is not as easy as studying. We have to say something. But what? God will simply have to enlighten us.

While the Pope waited for God's enlightenment on sexual intercourse his Commission toiled on. While the 68 laboured, their efforts were closely watched by the smaller commission of approximately twenty cardinals and bishops. For any liberalizing recommendation from the group of 68 to reach the Pope it had to pass through this smaller group, which was headed by a man who was the epitome of the reactionary element within the Church, Cardinal Ottaviani. Many considered him the leader of that element.

A crucial moment in the Commission's history came on April 23rd, 1966. By that date the Commission had conducted an exhaustive and exhausting examination of the birth control issue. Those who had maintained their opposition to a change in the Church's position were by now reduced to four priests who stated that they were irretrievably committed to maintaining a position forbidding any form of artificial birth control. Pushed by the other members of the Commission, the four admitted that they could not prove the correctness of their position on the grounds of natural law. Neither could they cite the scriptures or divine revelation to justify their view. They argued that various Papal utterances over the years had all condemned artificial contraception. Their reasoning would appear to be 'once in error, always in error'.

In October 1951, Pius XII (1939–58) had softened the somewhat austere position on birth control he had inherited from his predecessors. During an audience with Italian midwives he gave his approval to the use of the 'rhythm' method by all Catholics with serious reasons for wishing to avoid procreation. In view of the notorious unreliability of what became known as 'Vatican Roulette' it is not surprising that Pius XII also called for further research into the rhythm method. Nevertheless, Pius had moved the Church away from its previous position that had viewed procreation as the sole purpose of sexual intercourse.

After Pius XII came not only a new Pope but also the invention of the progesterone pill. Infallibility had been claimed for certain Papal opinions but no one yet claimed Papal clairvoyance. A new situation required a new look at the problem, but the four dissenting priests on the Commission insisted that the new situation was covered by old answers.

Finally the Commission wrote its report. In essence it advised the Pope that consensus had been reached by an overwhelming majority (64 votes to 4) of theologians, legal experts, historians, sociologists, doctors, obstetricians and married couples, that a change in the Catholic Church's stand on birth control was both possible and advisable.

Their report was submitted in mid-1966 to the commission of cardinals and bishops who were overseeing the Pontifical Commission. These churchmen reacted with some perplexity. Obliged to record their own views on the report, 6 of the prelates abstained, 8 voted in favour of recommending the report to the Pope and 6 voted against it.

Within certain sections of the Roman Curia, that central administrative body of civil servants who control and dominate the Catholic Church, there were widespread reactions. Some applauded the recommendation for change, others saw it as part of the mischievous wickedness that Vatican Council II had generated. In this latter category was Cardinal Ottaviani, Secretary of the Supreme Sacred Congregation of the Holy Office. The motto on his coat-of-arms read *Semper Idem*, 'Always the Same'.

By 1966, Alfredo Ottaviani was, next to the Pope, the most powerful person in the entire Roman Catholic Church. An ex-pupil of the Roman Seminary, he was a man who passed his whole career in the Secretariat of State and the Curia without ever being posted out of Rome.

He had fought a bitter and often successful battle against the liberalizing effects of Vatican Council II. His forehead permanently furrowed, his skull curved back dramatically as if constantly avoiding a direct question, a neck-line hidden by bulging jowls, there was about him an air of sphinx-like immobility. He was a man not merely born old but born out of his time. He exemplified that section of the Curia which has the courage of its prejudices.

He saw himself as defender of a faith that did not accommodate the here and now. To Ottaviani the hereafter was reached by embracing values that were old in medieval times. He was not about to budge on the issue of birth control; more important, he was determined that Pope Paul VI was not going to budge.

Ottaviani contacted the four dissenting priests from the Pontifical Commission. Their views had already been fully incorporated within the Commission's report. He persuaded them to enlarge their dissenting conclusions in a special report. Thus the Jesuit Marcellino Zalba, the Redemptorist Jan Visser, the Franciscan Ermenegildo Lio and the American Jesuit John Ford, created a second document.

No matter that in doing so they acted in an unethical manner; the object of the exercise was to give Ottaviani a weapon to brandish at the Pope. The four men bear an awesome responsibility for what was to follow. The amount of death, misery and suffering that directly resulted from the final Papal decision can to a large degree be laid directly at their feet. An indication of the thought-processess applied by these four can be gauged from one of their number, the American Jesuit, John Ford. He considered he was in direct contact with the Holy Spirit with regard to this issue and that this Divine guidance had led him to the ultimate truth. If the majority view prevailed, Ford declared that he would have to leave the Roman Catholic Church. This minority report represents the epitome of arrogance. It was submitted to Pope Paul along with the official Commission report. What followed was a classic illustration of the ability of a minority of the Roman Curia to control situations, to manipulate events. By the time the two reports were submitted to Paul most of the 68 members of the Commission were scattered to the corners of the earth.

Convinced that this difficult problem had finally been resolved with a liberalizing conclusion the majority of the Commission members waited in their various countries for the Papal announcement approving artificial birth control. Some of them began to prepare a paper that could serve as an introduction or preface to the impending Papal ruling, in which there was full justification for the change in the Church's position.

Throughout 1967 and continuing into early 1968 Ottaviani capitalized on the absence from Rome of the majority of the Commission. Those who were still in the City were exercising great restraint in not bringing further pressure upon Paul. By doing so they played straight into Ottaviani's hands. He marshalled members of the old guard who shared his views. Cardinals Cicognani, Browne, Parente and Samore, daily just happened to meet the Pope. Daily they told him that to approve artificial birth control would be to betray the Church's heritage. They reminded him of the Church's Canon Law and the three criteria that were applied to all Catholics seeking to marry. Without these three essentials the marriage is invalidated in the eyes of the Church: erection, ejaculation and conception. To legalize oral contraception, they argued, would be to destroy that particular church Law. Many, including his predecessor John XXIII, have compared Pope Paul VI with the doubt-racked Hamlet. Every Hamlet has need of an Elsinore Castle in which to brood. Eventually, the Pope decided that he and he alone would make the final decision. He summoned Monsignor Agostino Casaroli and advised him that the problem of birth control would be removed from the competence of the Holy Office. Then he retired to Castel Gandolfo to work upon the encyclical.

On the Pope's desk at Castel Gandolfo, amid the various reports, recommendations and studies on the issue of artificial birth control, was one from Albino Luciani.

While his Commissions, consultants and Curial cardinals were dissecting the problem the Pope had also asked for the opinion of various regions in Italy. One of these was the Veneto diocese. The Patriarch of Venice, Cardinal Urbani, had called a meeting of all the bishops within the region. After a day's debate it was decided that Luciani should draw up the report.

The decision to give Luciani the task was largely based on his knowledge of the problem. It was a subject he had been studying for a number of years. He had talked and written about it, he had consulted doctors, sociologists, theologians, and not least that group who had personal practical experience of the problem, married couples.

Among the married couples was his own brother, Edoardo, struggling to earn enough to keep an ever-growing family that eventually numbered ten children. Luciani saw at first hand the problems posed by a continuing ban on artificial birth control. He had grown up surrounded by poverty. Now in the late 1960s there appeared to him to be as much poverty and deprivation as in the lost days of his youth. When those one cares for are in despair because of their inability to provide for an increasing number of children, one is inclined to view the problem of birth control in a different light from Jesuits who are in direct contact with the Holy Spirit.

The men in the Vatican could quote Genesis until the Day of Judgment but it would not put bread on the table. To Albino Luciani Vatican Council II had intended to relate the Gospels and the Church to the twentieth century, and to deny men and women the right of artificial birth control was to plunge the Church back to the Dark Ages. Much of this he said quietly and privately as he prepared his report. Publicly he was acutely aware of his obedience to the Pope. In this Luciani remained an excellent example of his time. When the Pope decreed then the faithful agreed. Yet even in his public utterances there are clear clues to his thinking on the issue of birth control.

By April 1968, after much further consultation, Luciani's report had been written and submitted. It had met with the approval of the bishops of the Veneto region and Cardinal Urbani had duly signed the report and sent it directly to Pope Paul. Subsequently, Urbani saw the document on the Pope's desk at Castel Gandolfo. Paul advised Urbani that he valued the report greatly. So highly did he praise it that when Urbani returned to Venice he went via Vittorio Veneto to convey directly to Luciani the Papal pleasure the report had given.

The central thrust of the report was to recommend to the Pope that the Roman Catholic Church should approve the use of the anovulant pill developed by Professor Pincus. *That it should become the Catholic birth control pill.*

On April 13th, Luciani talked to the people of Vittorio Veneto about the problems the issue was causing. With the delicacy that had by now become a characteristic Luciani hallmark, he called the subject 'conjugal ethics'. Having observed that priests in speaking and in hearing confessions 'must abide by the directives given on several occasions by the Pope until the latter makes a pronouncement', Luciani went on to make three observations:

1   It is easier today, given the confusion caused by the press, to find married persons who do not believe that they are sinning. If this should happen it may be opportune, under the usual conditions, not to disturb them.

2   Towards the penitent onanist, who shows himself to be both penitent and discouraged, it is opportune to use encouraging kindness, within the limits of pastoral prudence.

3   Let us pray that the Lord may help the Pope to resolve this question. There has never perhaps been such a difficult question for the Church: both for the intrinsic difficulties and for the numerous implications affecting other problems, and for the acute way in which it is felt by the vast mass of the people.

Humanae Vitae was published on July 25th, 1968. Pope Paul had Monsignor Lambruschini of the Lateran University explain its significance to the Press, in itself a rather superfluous exercise. More significantly, it was stressed that this was not an infallible document. It became for millions of Catholics an historic moment like the assassination of President John F. Kennedy. Years later they knew exactly what they were doing and where they were when the news reached them.

On a disaster scale for the Roman Catholic Church it measures higher than the treatment of Galileo in the seventeenth century or the declaration of Papal Infallibility in the nineteenth. This document which was intended to strengthen Papal authority had precisely the opposite effect.

This celibate man, then 71 years of age, having expanded the Commission that was advising him on the problem of birth control, ignored its advice. He declared that the only methods of birth control which the Church considered acceptable were abstinence and the rhythm method '. . . in any use whatever of marriage there must be no impairment of its natural capacity to procreate human life.'

Millions ignored the Pope and continued to practise their faith and use the Pill or whatever other method they found most suitable. Millions lost patience and faith. Others shopped around for a different priest to whom to confess their sins. Still others tried to follow the encyclical and discovered they had avoided one Catholic concept of sin only to experience another, divorce. The encyclical totally divided the Church.

'I cannot believe that salvation is based on contraception by temperature and damnation is based on rubber,' declared Dr Andre Hellegers,

an obstetrician and member of the ignored Pontifical Commission.
One surprising line of the Vatican's defence came from Cardinal
Felici: 'The possible mistake of the superior [the Pope] does not
authorize the disobedience of subjects.'

Albino Luciani read the encyclical with growing dismay. He knew
the uproar that would now engulf the Church. He went to his church
in Vittorio Veneto and prayed. There was no question in his mind but
that he must obey the Papal ruling but, deep as his allegiance to the
Pope was, he could not, would not, merely sing praise to *Humanae
Vitae*. He knew a little of what the document must have cost the Pope;
he knew a great deal of what it was going to cost the faithful who
would have to attempt to apply it to their everyday lives.

Within hours of reading the encyclical Luciani had written his
response to the diocese of Vittorio Veneto. In ten years' time when he
became Pope, the Vatican would assert that Luciani's response was
'Rome has spoken. The case is closed.' It was yet another Vatican lie.
Nothing approaching that sentiment appears in his words. He began by
reminding the diocese of his comments in April, then continued:

> I confess that, although not revealing it in what I wrote, I privately
> hoped that the very grave difficulties that exist could be overcome
> and the response of the Teacher, who speaks with special charisma
> and in the name of the Lord, might coincide, at least in part, with the
> hopes of many married couples after the setting up of a relevant
> Pontifical Commission to examine the question.

He acknowledged the amount of care and consideration the Pope
had given to the problem and said that the Pope knew 'he is about to
cause bitterness in many', but he continued, 'The old doctrine,
presented in a new framework of encouraging and positive ideas about
marriage and conjugal love, better guarantees the true good of man
and family.' Luciani faced some of the problems that would inevitably
flow from *Humanae Vitae*:

> The thoughts of the Pope, and mine, go especially to the
> sometimes grave difficulties of married couples. May they not
> lose heart, for goodness sake. May they remember that for
> everyone the door is narrow and narrow the road that leads to life
> (cf Matt 7:14). That the hope of the future life must illuminate the
> path of Christian couples. That God does not fail to help those
> who pray to Him with perseverance. May they make the effort to

live with wisdom, justice and piety in the present time, knowing
that the fashion of this world passes away (cf 1 Cor 7:31) . . .
'And if sin should still have a hold on them, may they not be
discouraged, but have recourse with humble perseverance to
God's mercy through the sacrament of Penance'.

This last quotation, direct from *Humanae Vitae,* had been one of the
few crumbs of comfort for men like Luciani who had hoped for a
change. Trusting that he had his flock with him in a 'sincere adhesion
to the teaching of the Pope', Luciani gave them his blessing.

Other priests in other countries took a more openly hostile line.
Many left the priesthood. Luciani steered a more subtle course.

In January 1969 he returned yet again to this subject that the Vatican
would have him make a one-line dogmatic pronouncement upon. He
was aware that some of his priests were denying absolution to married
couples using the contraceptive pill and that other priests were readily
absolving what Pope Paul had deemed a sin. Dealing with this
problem Luciani quoted the response from the Italian Bishops'
Conference to *Humanae Vitae*. It was a response he had helped to
draft. In it priests were recommended to show 'evangelical kindness'
towards all married people, but especially, as Luciani pointed out,
towards those 'whose failings derive . . . from the sometimes very
serious difficulties in which they find themselves. In that case the
behaviour of the spouses, although not in conformity with Christian
norms, is certainly not to be judged with the same gravity as when it
derives from motives corrupted by selfishness and hedonism.' Luciani
also admonished his troubled people not to feel 'an anguished,
disturbing guilt complex'.

Throughout this entire period the Vatican continued to benefit from
the profits derived from one of the many companies it owned, the
Istituto Farmacologico Sereno. One of Sereno's best selling products
was an oral contraceptive called Luteolas.

The loyalty Albino Luciani had demonstrated in Vittorio Veneto
was not lost on the Holy Father in Rome. Better than most the Pope
knew that such loyalty had been achieved at a heavy price. The
document on his desk that bore Cardinal Urbani's signature, but was
in essence Luciani's position on birth control, was mute testimony to
the personal cost.

Deeply impressed, Pope Paul VI observed to his Under-Secretary of
State, Giovanni Benelli, 'In Vittorio Veneto there is a little bishop who
seems well suited to me.' The astute Benelli went out of his way to

establish a friendship with Luciani. It was to prove a friendship with far-reaching consequences.

Cardinal Urbani, Patriarch of Venice, died on September 17th, 1969. The Pope remembered his little bishop. To Paul's surprise Luciani politely declined what many saw as a glittering promotion. Entirely without ambition he was happy and content with his work in Vittorio Veneto.

Pope Paul cast his net farther. Cardinal Antonio Samore, as reactionary as his mentor Ottaviani, became a strong contender. Murmurings of discontent from members of the Venetian laity, declaring they would be happier if Samore remained in Rome, reached the Pope's ears.

Pope Paul then gave yet another demonstration of the Papal dance he had invented since ascending to the throne of Peter: one step forward, one step back – Luciani, Samore, Luciani.

Luciani began to feel the pressure from Rome. Eventually he succumbed. It was a decision he regretted within hours. Unaware that its new Patriarch had fought against accepting the position, Venice celebrated the fact that 'local man' Albino Luciani was appointed on December 15th, 1969.

Before leaving Vittorio Veneto, Luciani was presented with a donation of one million lire. He quietly declined the gift and after suggesting that the people should donate it to their own personal charities reminded them what he had told his priests when he had arrived in the diocese eleven years earlier: 'I came without five lire. I want to leave without five lire.' Albino Luciani took with him to Venice a small pile of linen, a few sticks of furniture and his books.

On February 8th, 1970, the new Patriarch, now Archbishop Luciani, entered Venice. Tradition decreed that the entry of a new Patriarch be a splendid excuse for a gaily bedecked procession of gondolas, brass bands, parades and countless speeches. Luciani had always had an intense dislike of such pomp and ceremony. He cancelled the ritual welcome and confined himself to a speech during which he referred not only to the historic aspects of the city but acknowledged that his diocese also contained industrial areas such as Mestre and Marghera. 'This was the other Venice,' Luciani observed, 'with few monuments but so many factories, houses, spiritual problems, souls. And it is to this many-faceted city that Providence now sends me. Signor Mayor, the first Venetian coins, minted as long ago as A.D. 850, had the motto "Christ, save Venice". I make this my own with all my heart and turn it into a prayer, "Christ, bless Venice".'

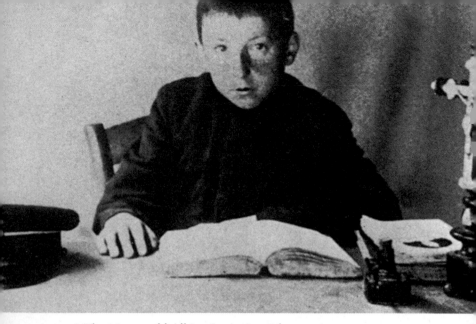

2 The 11-year-old Albino Luciani at Feltre seminary.
3 *(Below left)* Giovanni and Bortola with Pia: the photograph which accompanied Luciani everywhere. 4 *(Below right)* Luciani, the newly ordained priest, July 7th 1935.

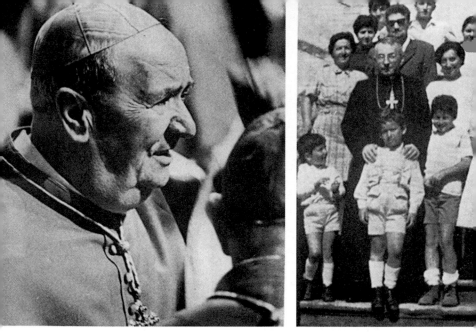

5 (Above left) Cardinal Ottaviani led those who were against reform of the Church's position on birth control. *6 (Above right)* Luciani with his brother Edoardo and sister-in-law and their ten children, took the opposing view. *7* Vatican City State.

8 The Patriarch of Venice with some of his priests, including *(second right)* his secretary, Father (now Monsignor) Senigaglia.
9 Pope Paul VI and Albino Luciani in St Mark's Square, Venice.

10 Pope Paul I with his Secretary of State, Cardinal Villot.
11 Cardinal Cody of Chicago *(in foreground, left)*. Behind Pope Paul VI *(to the left)* is Helen Wilson.

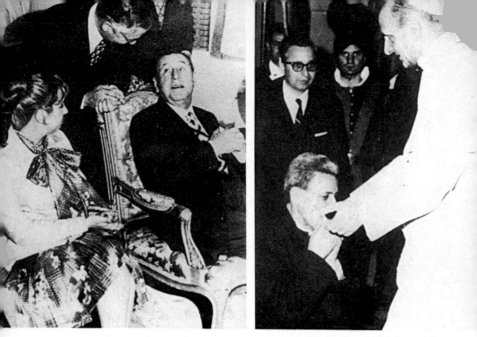

12 and 13 *(Above)* The Puppet Master, Licio Gelli, leaning forward in conversation with General Juan Peron, waiting to be received by Pope Paul VI. 14 *(Below)* President Nixon with Pope Paul VI and Monsignor Macchi, one of the members of the 'The Milan Mafia'.

15 John Volpe, then U.S. Ambassador to Rome, congratulates Sindona *(right)* on being named by the American Club 'Man of The Year.'

16 President Lyndon B. Johnson meets Pope Paul VI, with Paul Marcinkus *(second left)* acting as interpreter.

17 The two leaders of P2 in the company of President Leone of Italy *(centre foreground)*: second and fourth from the President's left are Licio Gelli and Umberto Ortolani.

18 Gelli with the then Prime Minister of Italy, Giulio Andreotti.

The pagan city was in dire need of Christ's blessing. It was bulging with monuments and churches that proclaimed the former glories of an imperial republic, yet Albino Luciani rapidly learned that the majority of the churches within the 127 parishes were continually nearly empty. If one discounted the tourists, the very young and the very old, then church attendance was appallingly low. Venice is a city that has sold its soul to tourism.

The day after his arrival, accompanied by his new secretary, Father Mario Senigaglia, he was at work. Declining invitations to attend various soirées, cocktail parties and receptions, he visited instead the local seminary, the women's prison of Giudecca, the male prison of Santa Maria Maggiore, then celebrated Mass in the Church of San Simeone.

It was customary for the Patriarch of Venice to have his own boat. Luciani had neither the personal wealth nor the inclination for what seemed to him an unnecessary extravagance. When he wanted to move through the canals he and Father Mario would catch a water bus. If it was an urgent appointment Luciani would telephone the local fire brigade, the carabinieri or the finance police and beg the loan of one of their boats. Eventually the three organizations worked out a roster to oblige the unusual priest.

During a national petrol crisis the Patriarch took to a bicycle when visiting the mainland. Venetian high society shook its head and muttered disapprovingly. Many of them enjoyed the pomp and ceremony they associated with the Patriarchship. To them a Patriarch was an important person to be treated in an important manner. When Albino Luciani and Father Mario appeared unannounced at a hospital to visit the sick they would immediately be surrounded by the administrators, doctors, monks and nuns. Father Senigaglia recalled for me such an occasion.

'I don't want to take up your precious time. I can go round on my own.'

'Not a bit of it, Your Eminence, it's an honour for us.'

Thus a large procession would begin to make its way through the wards with an increasingly discomfited Luciani. Eventually he would say, 'Well, perhaps it's better if I come back another time, it's already late.'

He would effect several false exits in an attempt to shake off the entourage; without success.

'Don't worry, Your Eminence. It's our duty.'

Outside he would turn to Father Senigaglia, 'But are they always like this? It's a shame. I am used to something different. Either we shall have to make them understand or I shall lose a good habit.'

Slowly some of the messages got across, but it was never the same as at Vittorio Veneto.

His fresh approach was not confined to his technique for visiting the sick. A considerable number of monsignors and priests whose behaviour did not accord with Luciani's view that 'the real treasures of the Church are the poor, the weak who should not be helped with occasional charity but in such a way that they can really benefit', found themselves parish priests in a far province.

One such priest, a property owner, received from Luciani a personal lesson in social justice that left him bemused. The priest, having increased the rent on one of his houses, discovered that the tenant, an unemployed schoolteacher, could not afford the increase. He promptly served an eviction notice. Luciani, hearing of the incident through his secretary, remonstrated in vain with the priest, who shrugged his shoulders at this whimsical Patriarch who quoted Christ to him. 'My kingdom is not of this earth.' He proceeded with the eviction of the schoolteacher and his family. Luciani immediately wrote out a cheque for 3 million lire, enabling the family to live in a pensione until they found a permanent residence. Today the teacher has a photocopy of the cheque framed and hanging in his living room.

On another occasion Senigaglia inadvertently interrupted a visit Luciani was making to a sick priest. He discovered Luciani emptying his wallet on the priest's bed. Later the secretary gently remonstrated with the Patriarch. 'You can't do this.' Albino Luciani's response sums up much of the man: 'But it was all I had on me at the time.'

Senigaglia explained that the Curia had a special fund so that the Patriarch could help his priests, in silence. This, Senigaglia explained, was how the previous Patriarch had performed these various acts of charity. Luciani listened, then told his secretary to make the same arrangement with the Curia.

He discovered that as Patriarch he had unwittingly acquired a house at San Pietro di Fileto. He attempted to give it to the unfortunate schoolteacher but the Vatican objected. After a battle with the Curia they finally conceded that Luciani could allow the retired Bishop Muchin to live there.

Within a short while of becoming Patriarch his offices were continuously over-flowing with the poor. 'The door of the Patriarch is always open, ask Don Mario and whatever I can do for you I will always willingly do it.' The strongly smelling crowd murmured their thanks.

Don Mario spoke to his superior, gritting his teeth, 'Your Excellency, you are ruining me, they will never leave me in peace.'

Luciani smiled and replied, 'Someone will help us.'

The offices of the Patriarch were frequently filled with ex-prisoners, alcoholics, poor people, abandoned people, tramps, women who could no longer work as prostitutes. One such unfortunate still wears the pyjamas Luciani gave him and writes 'thank you' letters to a man no longer here to read them.

During his first year in the city he showed his concern for those who lived in what he had described on his first day as 'the other Venice'. When strikes and violent demonstrations erupted in Mestre and Marghera he urged workers and management to seek a middle position. In 1971, when 270 workers were made redundant at La Sava factory, he reminded the bosses of the paramount need to remember personal human dignity. Certain sections of the traditional Catholic establishment in Venice could be heard expressing the wish for a Patriarch who would content himself with sermons to uncomprehending tourists. Pope Paul VI, however, was clearly delighted with Luciani. In 1971 he nominated him to attend the World Synod of Bishops. Items on the agenda were priestly ministry and justice in the world. One suggestion of Luciani's at the Synod showed the shape of things to come:

> I suggest, as an example of concrete help to the poor countries, that the more fortunate churches should tax themselves and pay one per cent of their income to the Vatican aid organizations. This one per cent should be called the 'brothers' share' and should not be given as charity, but as something that is owed, to compensate for the injustices being committed by our consumer world against the developing world, and to make up in some way for social sin, of which we should all be aware.

One of the injustices that Luciani continuously worked to eliminate in Venice concerned a widely prevalent attitude towards the subnormal and the handicapped. Not only the mayor and city officials showed indifference, but Luciani found the same prejudice among some of his parish priests. When he went to give First Communion to a large group of handicapped people at St Pius X in Marghera he had to cope with a delegation of protesting priests who argued that he should not do such a thing. 'These creatures do not understand.' He instructed the group that he was personally ordering them to attend the First Communion.

Alter the Mass he picked up a young girl suffering from spina bifida. The congregation was completely silent.

'Do you know whom you have received today?' he asked the little girl.

'Yes. Jesus.'

'And are you pleased?'

'Very.'

Luciani turned slowly and looked at the group of protesting priests. 'You see, they are better than we adults.'

Because of the reluctance of the City Council to contribute to Special Work Centres, Luciani was obliged initially to rely on diocesan funds and the bank known as 'the priests' bank', Banca Cattolica del Veneto. Soon after he had been made a Cardinal he became aware that it was no longer the priests' bank. Joining the regular crowd in his outer office who required help, he now found bishops, monsignors and priests. In the past the bank had always loaned money to the clergy at low interest rates. It was a bank founded for the diocese which had previously contributed to the vital work for that section of society which Luciani described in the following words: 'They have no political weight. They cannot be counted on for votes. For those reasons we must show our sense of honour as men and Christians towards these handicapped people.'

By mid-1972 the low interest loans had stopped. The Venetian clergy were advised that in future they would have to pay the full rate of interest no matter how laudable the work. The priests complained to their bishops. The bishops made a number of discreet enquiries.

Since 1946 the Istituto per le Opere di Religione, the IOR, usually referred to as the Vatican Bank, had held a majority share in Banca Cattolica del Veneto. The various dioceses in the Veneto region also had small shareholdings in the bank amounting to less than 5 per cent of the bank's share.

In the normal commercial world this would make the minority shareholder vulnerable, but this was not the normal commercial world. A clear understanding existed between Venice and the Vatican that the IOR's vast shareholding (by 1972 it was 51 per cent) was an insurance against any potential takeover by a third party. Despite the very low interest rates charged to the Veneto clergy the bank was one of the wealthiest in the country. Where the priest banks the parishioner will follow. (A significant amount of the bank's wealth was derived from real estate holdings in Northern Italy.) This happy arrangement had now been abruptly terminated. The bank that the bishops believed they owned, at least morally, had been sold over their heads without reference to the Patriarch or any person in the Veneto region. The man who had done the selling was Vatican Bank President, Paul Marcinkus. The man who had done the buying was Roberto Calvi, of Banco Ambrosiano, Milan.

The bishops of the region descended en masse on the Patriarch's office in St Mark's Square. He listened quietly as they outlined what had happened. They told him how in the past when they had wished to raise capital they had turned to the Vatican Bank who had loaned money, holding their shares in Banca Cattolica as security. Now these shares, along with a large stake independently acquired by the Vatican Bank, had been sold at a huge profit to Calvi.

The enraged bishops pointed out to Luciani that had they been given the opportunity they could have raised the necessary money to repay the Vatican Bank and thereby re-acquire their shares. What was more pertinent in their eyes was the appalling breach of trust perpetrated by Marcinkus, acting on behalf of the Vatican that claimed to be the moral leader in the world; he had at the very least displayed a total lack of morals. The fact that he had kept the entire profit on the transaction for the Vatican Bank may also have caused some of their anger.

The bishops urged Luciani to go directly to Rome. They wanted Papal intervention. If that intervention took the form of firing Paul Marcinkus it was clear that in the Veneto region at least, not many tears would be shed. Luciani calmly weighed the problem. Ever a prudent man, he considered he needed more facts before laying such a problem before Pope Paul.

Luciani began to probe quietly. He learned a great deal about Roberto Calvi and also about a man named Michele Sindona. What he learned appalled him. It also alerted him to the dangers of complaining directly to the Pope. Based on the information he had obtained it was clear that Calvi and Sindona were highly favoured sons of the Church and were held in great esteem by Paul VI. The man Albino Luciani turned to was one who had become a close friend over the previous five years, Under-Secretary of State Monsignor Giovanni Benelli.

Though Benelli was number two in the Secretariat of State under Cardinal Villot, to all intents and purposes he ran the department. And as Pope Paul's troubleshooter Benelli not only knew where all the bodies were buried – he was responsible for the placement of quite a number of them.

Benelli listened while the Patriarch of Venice told his story. When he had finished the Monsignor gave his Eminence another cup of coffee as Luciani uttered a qualification.

'I have not of course seen any documentary evidence.'

'I have,' responded Benelli. 'Calvi is now the majority shareholder in the Banca Cattolica del Veneto. Marcinkus sold him 37 per cent on March 30th.'

Benelli was a man who enjoyed reeling out facts and figures. He told the wide-eyed Luciani that Calvi had paid 27 billion lire (approximately $45 million) to Marcinkus; how the sale was the result of a scheme hatched jointly by Calvi, Sindona and Marcinkus, of a company called Pacchetti which had been purchased by Calvi from Sindona after its price had been grossly and criminally inflated on the Milan stock exchange, of how Marcinkus had assisted Calvi in masking the nature of this and other operations from the eyes of Bank of Italy officials by putting the Vatican bank facilities at the disposal of Calvi and Sindona.

Luciani was bewildered. 'What does all this mean?' he asked.

'Tax evasion, illegal movement of shares. I also believe that Marcinkus sold the shares in your Venice bank at a deliberately low price and Calvi paid the balance, a separate 31 billion lire deal on Credito Varesino.'

Luciani became angry. 'What has all this to do with the Church of the poor? In the name of God . . .'

Benelli held up a hand to silence him. 'No, Albino, in the name of profit.'

'Does the Holy Father know these things?'

Benelli nodded.

'So?'

'So you must remember who put Paul Marcinkus in charge of our bank.'

'The Holy Father.'

'Precisely. And I must confess I fully approved. I've had cause to regret that many times.'

'Then what are we to do? What am I to tell my priests and bishops?'

'You must tell them to be patient, to wait. Eventually Marcinkus will over-reach himself. His Achilles heel is his greed for Papal praise.'

'But what does he want to do with all this money?'

'He wants to make more money.'

'For what purpose?'

'To make more money.'

'And in the meantime should my priests get out begging bowls and tramp through the Veneto?'

'In the meantime you must counsel patience. I know you have it. Teach it to your priests. I'm having to apply it.'

Albino Luciani returned to Venice and called his fellow bishops to his office. He told them some of what had transpired in Rome, enough to make it abundantly clear that the Banca Cattolica was now for ever lost to the diocese. Later some of them talked about it. They concluded that this would never have happened in the days of Cardinal Urbani. They felt that Luciani's innate goodness had proved a useless weapon against the IOR. Most of them, including Luciani, sold what remaining shares they held in the bank to express their disapproval of the Vatican's conduct. In Milan Roberto Calvi was gratified to note that his brokers had acquired on his behalf another small piece of the priests' bank in Venice.

Albino Luciani and many others in Venice closed their accounts at the Banca Cattolica. For the Patriarch of Venice to move the official diocesan accounts to the small Banco San Marco was an extraordinary step. He confided to one colleague, 'Calvi's money is tainted. The man is tainted. After what I have learned of Roberto Calvi I would not leave the accounts in his bank if the loans they granted to the diocese were totally free of interest.'

Luciani then attempted to get the directors of Banca Cattolica to change the name of the bank. He insisted that for the word Catholic to appear in their title was an outrage and a libel on all Catholics.

In Rome Pope Paul VI was made fully aware of the added burden that had been placed on the Veneto region by the sale of the Banca Cattolica. Giovanni Benelli urged the Holy Father to intervene but by then the sale to Calvi was already a reality. When Benelli argued for the removal of Marcinkus the Pope responded with an agonized helpless shrug of the shoulders but the fact that Luciani had not led an open rebellion left a deep impression on Paul. At the slightest opportunity he would proclaim the goodness of the man he had appointed Patriarch of Venice. In an audience with Venetian priest Mario Ferrarese he declared three times, 'Tell the priests of Venice that they should love their Patriarch because he is a good, holy, wise, learned man.'

In September 1972, Pope Paul stayed at the Patriarch's Palace on his way to a Eucharistic Congress in Udine. In a packed St Mark's Square the Pope removed his stole and placed it over the shoulders of a blushing Luciani. The crowd went wild. Paul was not a man to make insignificant public gestures.

When the two men were being served coffee in the Palace he made a more private one. He indicated to Luciani that 'the little local difficulty over finance' had reached his ears. He had also heard that Luciani was trying to raise money for the creation of a work centre for the sub-normal at Marghera. He told Luciani how much he approved of such work and said that he would like to make a personal donation. Between Italians, that most voluble of races, much is often unsaid but understood.

Six months later during March 1973, the Pope made Albino Luciani a Cardinal. Whatever his deep misgivings about the fiscal policies of the IOR, Luciani considered that he owed the Pope, his Pope, complete and unswerving loyalty. Italian bishops are in a unique position with regard to their relationship to the Vatican. Control of their actions is tighter. Retribution for any failure, real or imagined, is quicker.

When Luciani was made Cardinal he was aware that Ottaviani and other Curial reactionaries, far from demonstrating total obedience, were in fact involved in a long, acrimonious argument with the Pope. They were quite simply trying to destroy any good that had flowed from the historic Vatican Council II series of meetings. Called upon to make a speech in front of not only the other new cardinals and the Pope but also Ottaviani and his clique, Albino Luciani observed, 'Vatican Council I has many followers and so has Vatican Council III. Vatican Council II, however, has far too few.'

Two months later during May 1973, Luciani found himself playing host yet again to a visitor from Rome, Giovanni Benelli. In general Benelli had come to assure him that the problems they had discussed the previous year had not been forgotten. In particular he had an extraordinary story to tell about the American Mafia, nearly one billion dollars' worth of counterfeit securities and Paul Marcinkus.

On April 25th, 1973, Benelli had received some very unusual guests in his offices at the Secretariat of State in Vatican City: William Lynch, Chief of the Organized Crime and Racketeering section of the US Department of Justice, and William Aronwald, Assistant Chief of the Strike Force in the Southern District of New York. Two members of the FBI had accompanied them.

'Having met these gentlemen from the United States,' Benelli told me, 'I made my apologies and left them in the capable hands of three of my staff. They of course subsequently reported to me exactly what had taken place.'

The secret FBI report that I acquired many months after my conversation with Cardinal Benelli confirmed that his account was very accurate. It also told a story which reads like an outline for a Hollywood movie.

Monsignors Edward Martinez, Carl Rauber and Justin Rigali listened while William Lynch told of a police investigation that had begun in the world of the New York Mafia and had led inexorably to the Vatican. He told the priests that a package of 14.5 million dollars' worth* of American counterfeit bonds had been carefully and pain-stakingly created by a network of members of the Mafia in the USA. The package had been delivered to Rome in July 1971 and there was substantial evidence to establish that the ultimate destination of those bonds was the Vatican Bank.

Lynch advised them that much of the evidence, from separate sources, strongly indicated that someone with financial authority within the Vatican had ordered the fake bonds. He pointed out that other evidence also indicated the 14.5 million dollars was merely a down payment, and that the total of counterfeit bonds ordered was 950 million dollars' worth.

The attorney then revealed the name of the 'someone with financial authority' who had master-minded the illegal transaction. On the basis of the evidence in Lynch's hands, it was Bishop Paul Marcinkus.

Displaying remarkable self-control the three priests listened as the two US attorneys outlined the evidence.

At this stage of the investigation a number of the conspirators had already been arrested. One of them who had felt the desire to unburden himself was Mario Foligni, self-styled Count of San Francisco with an honorary doctorate in Theology. A first-class conman, Foligni had on more than one occasion narrowly avoided prison. When he was suspected of having manipulated the fraudulent bankruptcy of a company he controlled, a Rome magistrate had issued a search warrant to the finance police. Opening Foligni's safe, the police had discovered a signed blessing from Pope Paul VI. They had apologized for the intrusion and departed.

Subsequently others had been equally impressed with Foligni's Vatican connections. He had opened the Vatican doors to an Austrian named Leopold Ledl. It was Ledl who had put the Vatican deal together – the purchase of 950 million dollars' worth of counterfeit bonds, the purchase price to be 635 million dollars. 'Commission' of 150 million dollars would be paid back by the gang to the Vatican, leaving the Mafia with 485 million dollars and the Vatican with bonds that had a face value of nearly one billion dollars.

*Here and throughout, monetary figures are expressed in values at the time in question.

The American Mafia had been sceptical about the deal until Ledl produced a letter from the Vatican. Written under the letter-heading of the Sacra Congregazione Dei Religiosi it was confirmation that the Vatican wished to 'buy the complete stock of the merchandise up to the sum of 950 million dollars'.

Foligni had told the American investigators that Marcinkus, ever prudent, had requested that a trial deposit of one-and-a-half million dollars' worth of the bonds be made at Handelsbank in Zürich. According to Foligni, Marcinkus had wanted to satisfy himself that the bonds would pass as genuine. Late in July the 'trial' deposit was duly made by Foligni. He nominated Vatican cleric Monsignor Mario Fornasari as the beneficiary of the account he opened.

A second 'trial' deposit of two-and-a-half million dollars' worth had been made at the Banco di Roma in September 1971. On both occasions the bonds had passed bank scrutiny, a tribute to Mafia skill. Regrettably for the conspirators, both banks had sent samples to New York for physical examination. The Bankers Association in New York ascertained that the bonds were false. Hence the unusual presence of American attorneys and men from the FBI within the Vatican walls.

Apart from a desire to recover the balance of 10 million dollars' worth of the initial delivery, Lynch and his colleagues were anxious to bring all the participants in the crime to justice.

Foligni had told the investigators that the reason the Vatican required the fake bonds was to enable Marcinkus and Italian banker and businessman Michele Sindona to buy Bastogi, a giant Italian company with wide interests including property, mining and chemcals. Bastogi's headquarters were in Milan; so were Sindona's. It was in this city that the then Archbishop Montini, later Pope Paul VI, had met Sindona. When Montini had become Pope, the Vatican gained a new heir to Peter and the Vatican Bank gained a new lay financial adviser, Michele Sindona.

William Lynch, himself a devout Catholic, continued his story. Mario Foligni, it transpired, had fired a series of accusations at Bishop Marcinkus during the US Department of Justice interrogations. Apart from the allegation that Sindona and Marcinkus had planned to buy Bastogi with fake bonds, Foligni also asserted that with Sindona's assistance, the Bishop had several secret numbered bank accounts in the Bahamas for his personal use.

Under interrogation Mario Foligni had claimed that he had been working personally with Benelli's office, the Secretariat of State, and that as a direct result of his cooperation 'the Secretary of State had caused stringent administrative action to be taken against Bishop Marcinkus, which severely restricted the Bishop's enormous financial power within the Vatican.' Foligni had insisted that he had told the Secretariat of State of the trial deposits he had made in Switzerland and Rome and that this information was used by Benelli's office against Marcinkus. He had also advised the Justice Department that he was under orders from the Secretary of State's office not to give the investigators any further details concerning the swindle.

Having put this evidence forward the Americans sat back and waited for a response. As William Lynch and William Aronwald made clear when I interviewed them, this first meeting at the Vatican was not seen by either side as an interrogation. It was informal, an opportunity to lay before members of the Vatican's Secretariat of State some very serious allegations.

The Justice Department was aware that the central thrust of the allegations stemmed from two expert con-men but there was also powerful internal evidence to support the validity of the statements of Foligni and Ledl.

It was because of that evidence that William Aronwald had contacted Cardinal Cooke of New York via the US attorney for the southern district of that city. The Cardinal had been most co-operative and via the Papal delegation in Washington this extraordinary meeting had been arranged. Its real object was not merely to lay information, but ultimately to confront Marcinkus.

While more coffee was served the three monsignors remained silent but thoughtful. Eventually Monsignor Martinez, Assessor of the Secretary of State's office, responded. He assured the Americans that he and Monsignor Rauber had complete knowledge of all the affairs of Archbishop Benelli and categorically denied that Foligni had turned over any evidence to Benelli's office. As for the counterfeit bonds and the trial deposits this was the first time that anyone on the Secretariat of State had heard about the affair. Taking a classic Curial position he remarked that, 'It is not the intention of the Vatican to collaborate with the United States officials in their investigation at this point, since this is considered to be an informal meeting, and our purpose at the present time is only to listen.'

What Lynch and his colleagues were confronted with was a mentality that has defeated many better minds than theirs – that of the Curia, a body of men that gives absolutely nothing away; a Government machine that holds the Roman Catholic Church in a vice-like grip. Lynch reminded the monsignors that to date only four million dollars' worth of the fake bonds had been recovered and continued: 'Since all evidence strongly indicates that the eventual destination for all of the bonds was the Vatican Bank and in view of the fact that the total amount ordered is worth 950 million dollars perhaps I can give you a list of the types of bonds?'

Martinez merely swayed out of the path of that punch. Lynch persisted. 'That way the records of the Istituto per le Opere di Religione can be checked to determine if any of the counterfeit stocks have been "inadvertently" received on deposit at that bank.'

The style of Martinez in the ring was really most impressive.

'I, of course, have no idea if any of these American counterfeit bonds have been received by our bank. I cannot, however, take a list from you to check. That would be the function of Bishop Marcinkus. He handles such matters. Perhaps if you have difficulty in contacting the Bishop you might send a list with a formal letter to the Papal Nuncio in Washington.'

It was obviously time for a change of tactics.

The US attorneys produced a document they had taken from Leopold Ledl after his arrest. The Vatican seal was on the letterhead below which was printed, 'Sacra Congregazione Dei Religiosi'. It was the Vatican order for nearly one billion dollars' worth of counterfeit securities. It had convinced the Mafia. The monsignors examined it carefully. There was much staring and holding up to the light.

Martinez rubbed his chin thoughtfully. The Americans leaned forward eagerly. Perhaps they had finally got one past the redoubtable Martinez.

'The letterhead appears to be identical to the letterhead of one of our sacred congregations which is located here in the Vatican.'

There was a pause. Just time for the Americans to enjoy the moment. Then Martinez continued:

'However, I would note that while the letterhead appears to be legitimate that particular congregation changed its name in 1968 and that as of the date of this letter, June 29th, 1971, the name shown on the letterhead would be incorrect. The new name is Sacra Congregazione per i Religiosi e gli Istituti Secolari.'

The American investigators had, however, succeeded in their main objective. It was agreed that they could see Bishop Paul Marcinkus face to face the following day. This in itself was an extraordinary achievement, for Vatican City fiercely guards its independent statehood.

During my interview with Cardinal Benelli he confirmed that he had indeed received information about the whole affair from Mario Foligni before the Vatican visit of the American investigators. It had seemed to the Cardinal to be a self-serving effort by Foligni, who by that time knew the game was up. As to the validity of the information, Benelli confined himself to the observation that he found the information 'very interesting and useful'.

On the morning of April 26th, 1973, the two American attorneys and the two FBI men were shown into the private office of Bishop Paul Marcinkus. Lynch and Aronwald repeated the story they had told the previous day while Marcinkus puffed on a large cigar. In the light of some of his subsequent omissions his initial remark is of particular interest.

'I am very disturbed by the seriousness of the allegations. In view of them I'll answer each and every question to the best of my ability.' He began with Michele Sindona.

'Michele and I are very good friends. We've known each other for several years. My financial dealings with him, however, have only been very limited. He is, you know, one of the wealthiest industrialists in Italy. He is well ahead of his time as far as financial matters are concerned.'

He extolled the virtues and talents of Michele Sindona at some considerable length. Then, placing the Vatican Bank on a par with the confessional, Marcinkus remarked:

'I would prefer to withhold names in many of the instances I intend to give because although the charges that Foligni makes against me are extremely serious they are so wild that I do not believe it necessary to break banking secrecy laws in order to defend myself.'

While the previous day's meeting had been largely of an informal nature, this confrontation with Marcinkus was an interrogation. On the evidence that the US Department of Justice had carefully and painstakingly acquired over more than two years, Lynch and Aronwald and FBI agents Biamonte and Tammaro had before them the man who had master-minded one of the world's greatest swindles. If the evidence was correct then the Chicago suburb of Cicero's claim for world notoriety would in future be shared by Al Capone and Paul Marcinkus. But as Mrs Beeton observed, 'first catch your hare'.

William Lynch raised the temperature a little.

'If it becomes necessary at some future date will you make yourself available for a face to face confrontation with Mario Foligni?'

'Yes, I will.'

'If it becomes necessary are you also prepared to testify in a United States court?'

'Well, yes, if it's absolutely necessary. I hope it won't be though.'
'Why?'
'Well the only people who would gain anything if I appeared in court would be the Italian Press.'
'How's that?'
'They frequently relish the opportunity to write inflammatory material concerning the Vatican, whether it's true or not.'

Lynch and Aronwald showed a total lack of concern at the Vatican's sensitivity towards the Italian Press.

'Do you have a private numbered account in the Bahamas?'
'No.'
'Do you have an ordinary account in the Bahamas?'
'No, I don't.'
'Are you quite certain, Bishop?'
'The Vatican does have a financial interest in the Bahamas but it's strictly a business transaction similar to many controlled by the Vatican. It's not for any one person's private financial gain.'
'No, we are interested in personal accounts that you have.'
'I don't have any private or public account in the Bahamas or anywhere else.'

How Marcinkus constantly carried his salary and expenses around in cash was not explored. Neither did Marcinkus reveal that he was in fact on the board of directors of Banco Ambrosiano Overseas in Nassau and had been since 1971. He had been invited on to the board by the two men who had set up this Bahamas operation, Michele Sindona and Roberto Calvi. Both men used the Bishop's name frequently in their business deals. Sindona put it bluntly to Marcinkus on one occasion: 'I've put you on the board because your name helps me to raise money.'

Sindona and Calvi showed their gratitude by giving Marcinkus and the Vatican Bank 2.5 per cent of the Nassau Bank's stock. This eventually rose to 8 per cent. Marcinkus frequently attended board meetings and took holidays in the Bahamas. It must have been irksome constantly having to change the large amounts of currency that, according to the statements he made to the American investigators, he would have been obliged to carry – the first President of a Bank in the world's history without a personal bank account.

At this point in the interrogation Bishop Marcinkus observed: 'You know my position within the Vatican is unique.'

One of the world's great understatements was followed by: 'I'm in charge of what many people commonly refer to as the Vatican Bank. As such I have complete control of Vatican financial affairs. One of the things that makes my position completely unique is that I am answerable only to the Pope as to how I handle those financial affairs. In theory my operations are directed by a group of cardinals who meet from time to time and generally act as overseers to the Bank. In reality, however, I virtually have a sole hand in directing the financial affairs of the Vatican.'

The personal testimony did not impress the Bishop's listeners.

'What's the point you're trying to make?'

'Well, this position that I hold has led to, shall we say, certain hard feelings by other men in responsible positions within the Vatican.'

'Really?'

'Oh yes, it's just part of the job I'm afraid. I am the first American ever to have risen to such a position of power within the Vatican and I'm sure that this has also caused a certain amount of hard feelings.'

Whether he was guilty or not of being the mastermind behind this enormous swindle, Paul Marcinkus undoubtedly spoke the truth when he talked about 'certain hard feelings' held by other senior men within the Vatican, and not only there. In Venice, Cardinal Albino Luciani was another whose feelings towards Marcinkus grew somewhat more than 'hard' as Benelli told him of this latest episode in the Marcinkus saga. Ironically what Benelli did not know was that, during that private interview with the American investigators, Paul Marcinkus had attempted to entangle him in the swindle.

To read the statement Marcinkus made, it is clear that in his eyes everyone but himself merited investigation. Of Father Mario Fornasari, who was allegedly deeply involved in the affair, Marcinkus noted:

'Some of the people who work for me at the Bank have pointed Fornasari out to me as an individual to avoid. I'm sure you know that Fornasari was denounced some time ago for writing libellous letters.'

'Really, what happened?'

'I believe the charges were dropped.'

Marcinkus conceded that he had been involved with Mario Foligni, without doubt one of the principal figures in the billion dollar swindle, on at least two business ventures. The first concerned a 100 million dollar investment scheme that did not come to fruition. The second was a 300 million dollar deal involving Foligni and the Italian industrialist Carlo Pesenti. That too had aborted, but as Marcinkus told his convoluted tale he was at pains to drag in Benelli's name. Apart from demonstrating that his ego had been bruised because Benelli had asked Pope Paul to consider the 300 million dollar deal and Marcinkus clearly believed that no one should talk to the Pope about money but him, Marcinkus also attempted to link Benelli and Foligni, presumably working on the law of guilt by association. In view of the subsequent activities of Michele Sindona and Roberto Calvi, both close friends of Marcinkus, it would be interesting to know if Marcinkus still holds to this dubious legal tenet.

What Marcinkus neglected to explain, perhaps because he was not asked to, was why he was even prepared to consider the 300 million dollar deal involving Foligni, some eight months after Foligni had unloaded 1.5 million dollars' worth of fake securities in a Swiss Bank and some six months after he had unloaded 2.5 million dollars' worth of phoney bonds in the Banco di Roma. As President of the Vatican Bank it is inconceivable that Marcinkus was the only head of a bank in Europe not to know of these criminal activities.

At the end of a long interrogation, Marcinkus maintained total innocence and disclaimed all knowledge. He happily accepted a list of the counterfeit bonds and said he would keep his eye open for them.

A variety of people were eventually found guilty of involvement in the billion dollar swindle. With regard to the allegations that Bishop Paul Marcinkus was involved, Attorney William Aronwald told me:

> The most that could be said is that we were satisfied that the investigation had not disclosed sufficiently credible evidence to prove or disprove the allegation. Consequently since we were not morally satisfied ourselves that there was anything wrong, or that Marcinkus or anyone else in the Vatican had done anything wrong, it would have been improper of us to try to grab some headlines.

It is abundantly clear that what seriously restricted this investigation was not the lack of will of the United States investigators. They tried hard, very hard. It would later be alleged that they were themselves part of a giant coverup,* that they had merely gone through the motions of an enquiry. This is nonsense and shows total ignorance of the very real problems that are posed when an investigation which begins in one country has to be continued inside another. The Vatican City is an independent State. That Lynch and Aronwald and the men from the FBI got inside the Vatican gates at all is a tribute to their tenacity. One cannot go rushing over the Tiber like a TV New York

*Richard Hamer, *The Vatican Connection,* Holt, Rinehart and Winston, 1982.

cop, armed with a .45 gun, search warrants, authority to hold and question witnesses and the many other legal devices that can be used within the United States.

If Vatican City were part of the United States then doubtless all members of the Curia working in the Sacra Congregazione Dei Religiosi would have been interrogated in depth. Fingerprints would have been taken. Forensic tests on all typewriters within the Congregation would have been made. If all that could have been done the question of Bishop Marcinkus's guilt or innocence might have been resolved. The fact that the United States Government took the evidence seriously enough to risk a very delicate political situation is illuminating in itself. As William Aronwald said to me, 'We were not about to waste that amount of taxpayers' money unless we took the evidence very seriously indeed. At the end of the investigation the case against Marcinkus had to be filed for lack of evidence that might have convinced a jury.'

The question therefore remains unanswered. Who was the customer who ordered the counterfeit bonds? Based on all the available official evidence it is possible to draw only two conclusions. Each is bizarre. Leopold Ledl and Mario Foligni were planning to steal from the American Mafia a huge fortune in counterfeit bonds, having first conned the Mafia into going to the very considerable expense of creating the bonds. This particular section of the Mafia had a number of members who killed or maimed people who they merely imagined had insulted them. If this is the real reason then Ledl and Foligni were seeking an unusual form of suicide. The other conclusion is that the 950 million dollars' worth of counterfeit bonds were destined for the Vatican.

In Venice, Albino Luciani continued to wear the robes that had been left by his predecessor, Cardinal Urbani. Throughout the entire period of his Patriarchship he refused to buy new ones, preferring instead to have the nuns who looked after him mend and re-mend. Indeed he wore the robes of Cardinal and Patriarch rarely, preferring his simple priest's cassock.

His personal humility often created interesting situations. Motoring through Germany in 1975 with Father Senigaglia, the Cardinal arrived at the town of Aachen. Luciani particularly wanted to pray at a very ancient altar in the main church. Senigaglia watched as Luciani was told in rather a peremptory manner by the Church officials that the altar was closed and he should return another day. Back in the car Luciani translated the conversation he had had for Senigaglia's benefit. Enraged, Senigaglia erupted from the car, ran to the church and gave the dignitaries a burst of Italian. They understood enough to know that he was declaring that the little priest they had turned away was the Patriarch of Venice. It was now Luciani's turn to get angry with his secretary as he was almost dragged from the car by the German priests. As Luciani entered the church one of the still apologetic priests murmured to him, 'Eminence, a little bit of red, at least, could be useful.'

On another occasion in Venice, Luciani was attending a conference on ecology. He became deeply involved in conversation with one of the participants. Wishing to continue the dialogue he invited the ecologist to call on him at his home. 'Where do you live?' asked the ecologist. 'Just next door to St Mark's,' responded Luciani. 'Do you mean the Patriarch's Palace?' 'Yes.' 'And whom do I ask for?' 'Ask for the Patriarch.'

Underneath his humility and gentleness was a man who, by his environment and his vocation, was exceptionally strong. Neither to the left nor the right, he refused to become involved with the warring factions in Rome. The power plays inside the Vatican left Luciani on occasions puzzled as to why some of these men had become priests at all. In an Easter sermon of 1976 he observed:

> Some are in the Church only as troublemakers. They are like the employee who first moved heaven and earth to get into the firm but once he had the job was perpetually restless and became a pestilential hair shirt on the skin of his colleagues and his superiors. Yes, some people seem only to look at the sun in order to find stains on it.

His desire to achieve a new synthesis by taking what in his view was right from both sides led him into considerable conflict in Venice. The issue of divorce is an example.

In Italy in the mid-1970s divorce was legal in the eyes of the State but unacceptable in the eyes of the Church. A move began to test the issue again through a referendum. Luciani was deeply opposed to the referendum simply because he was convinced it would split the Church and result in a majority committing themselves at the polling booths to a decision that the divorce laws should remain unchanged. If that happened it would be an official defeat for the Roman Catholic Church in the country it traditionally claimed as its own.

Benelli took the opposite view. He was convinced that the Church would win if there was a referendum.

The debate, not only within the Church but throughout Italy, reached an intense level. Shortly before the referendum took place, FUCI, a student group organized by a priest in Venice, sent a forty-page document to every bishop in the Veneto region. In it was a powerful argument supporting the pro-divorce position. Albino Luciani read the document carefully, considered for a while, then made national headlines by apparently disbanding the student group. In the Church it was seen by many as an act of courage. In the country commentators seized upon Luciani's action as yet another example of the bigotry of the Catholic hierarchy.

What had outraged Luciani was not the pro-divorce statements but the fact that to buttress their arguments the group had quoted extensively from a wide variety of church authorities, leading theologians and a number of Vatican Council II documents. To use the latter in such a way was to Luciani a perversion of Church teaching. He had been there at the birth of *Lumen Gentium, Gaudium et Spes* and *Dignitatis Humanae*. Error might well have rights in the modern Church but in Venice 1974 for Luciani there was still a limitation to those rights. Thus to see a quotation from *Dignitatis Humanae* that extolled the rights of the individual 'Protecting and promoting the inviolable rights of man is the essential duty of every civil power. The civil power must therefore guarantee to every citizen, through just laws and through other suitable means, the effective protection of religious liberty', followed by the statement:

'On other occasions the Church has found itself confronted by serious situations in society against which the only reasonable possibility was obviously not the use of repressive methods but the adoption of moral criteria and juridical methods which favoured the only good which was then historically possible: the lesser evil. Thus Christian morality adopted the theory of the just war; thus the Church allowed the legalization of prostitution (even in the Papal States), while obviously it remained forbidden on a moral level. And so also for divorce . . .'

To see such statements juxtaposed in a plea that the Church take a liberal view on divorce for the sake of expediency was unacceptable to Luciani. Obviously his beloved Vatican Council II teachings, like the Bible, could be taken to prove and justify any position. Luciani was aware that as he was head of the Bishops' Council for the Veneto region, the Italian public would consider the statement official policy and then be faced with the dilemma of whether they should follow the bishops of the Veneto region or the bishops in the rest of Italy. In fact he did not disband the student group as is generally thought. He used a technique that was central to his philosophy. He firmly believed that you could radically alter power groups by identifying the precise centre of power and removing it. So he simply removed the priest who was advising the student group.

In reality, as Father Mario Senigaglia confirmed to me, Luciani's personal view on divorce would have surprised his critics:

> It was more enlightened than popular comment would have it. He could and did accept divorcees. He also easily accepted others who were living in what the Church calls 'sin'. What outraged him was the biblical justification.

As Luciani had prophesied, the referendum resulted in a majority for the pro-divorce lobby. It left a split Church, a Pope who publicly expressed his amazement and incredulity at the result, and a dilemma for those who had to reconcile the differences between Church and State.

Luciani's own dilemma was that he was committed to an unswerving obedience to the Papacy. Often the Pope would take a different position from that held by the Patriarch of Venice. When that position became public, Luciani felt it his duty publicly to support it. What he did on a one-to-one basis with members of his diocese frequently bore no resemblance to the Vatican line. By the mid-1970s he had moved even further towards a liberal position on birth control. This man, who upon the announcement of *Humanae Vitae* had allegedly declared 'Rome has spoken. The case is closed,' clearly felt that the case was far from closed.

When his young secretary Father Mario Senigaglia discussed with Luciani, with whom he had developed an almost father-son relationship, different moral cases involving parishioners, Luciani always approved the liberal view that Senigaglia took. Senigaglia said to me, 'He was a very understanding man. Very many times I would hear him say to couples. "We have made of sex the only sin when in fact it is linked to human weakness and frailty and is therefore perhaps the least of sins".'

It is clear that Albino Luciani did not want for critics in Venice. Some considered that he revealed a nostalgia for the past rather than a desire for change. Some labelled him to the right, others to the left. Others saw his humility and gentleness as mere weakness. Perhaps posterity should judge the man on what he actually said rather than on what others thought he should have said.

On violence:

Strip God away from the hearts of men, tell children that sin is only a fairy tale invented by their grandparents to make them good, publish elementary school texts that ignore God and scoff at authority, and then don't be surprised at what is happening. Education alone is not enough! Victor Hugo wrote that one more school means one less prison. Would that that were so today!

On Israel:

The church must also think of the Christian minorities who live in Arab countries. She cannot abandon them to fortune . . . for me personally, there is no doubt that a special tie exists between the people of Israel and Palestine. But the Holy Father, even if he wanted to, could not say that Palestine belongs to the Jews, since this would be to make a political judgment.

On nuclear weapons:

People say that nuclear weapons are too powerful and to use them would mean the end of the world. They are manufactured and accumulated, but only to 'dissuade' the enemy from attacking and to keep the international situation stable.

Look around. Is it true or not that for 30 years there has not been a world war?

Is it true or not that serious crises between the two great powers, the USA and the USSR have been avoided?

Let's be happy over this partial result . . . A gradual, controlled and universal disarmament is possible only if an international organization with more efficient powers and possibilities for sanctions than the present United Nations comes into being and if education for peace becomes sincere.

On racism in the USA:

In the United States, despite the laws, Negroes are in practice on the edge of society. The descendants of the Indians have seen their situation bettered significantly only in recent years.

To call such a man a reactionary nostalgic may have validity. He yearned for a world that was not largely ruled by Communist philosophies, a world where abortion was not an every minute event. But if he was a reactionary he had some remarkably progressive ideas.

Early in 1976 Luciani attended yet another Italian Bishops' Conference in Rome. One of the subjects openly discussed was the serious economic crisis Italy was then facing. Linked with this subject was another which the bishops discussed privately: the Vatican's role in that economic crisis and the role of that good friend of Bishop Marcinkus, Michele Sindona. His empire had crashed in spectacular fashion. Banks were collapsing in Italy, Switzerland, Germany and the USA. Sindona was wanted by the Italian authorities on a range of charges and was fighting his extradition from the United States. The Italian Press had asserted that the Vatican had lost in excess of 100 million dollars. The Vatican had denied this but admitted that it had sustained some loss. In June 1975 the Italian authorities, while continuing their fight to bring Sindona to justice had sentenced him *in absentiato* to a prison term of three-and-a-half years, the maximum they could give for the offences. Many bishops felt that Pope Paul VI should have moved Marcinkus from the Vatican Bank when the Sindona bubble burst in 1974. Now, two years later, Sindona's friend was still controlling the Vatican Bank.

Albino Luciani left Rome, a city buzzing with speculation about how many millions the Vatican had lost in the Sindona affair, left a Bishops' Conference where the talk had been of how much the Vatican Bank owned of Banca Privata, of how many shares the Bank had in this conglomerate or that company. He returned to Venice where the Don Orione School for the handicapped did not have enough money for school books.

Luciani went to his typewriter and wrote a letter which was published in the next edition of the diocese magazine. It was entitled 'A loaf of bread for the love of God'. He began by appealing for money to help the victims of a recent earthquake disaster in Guatemala, stating that he was authorizing a collection in all churches on Sunday, February 29th. He then commented on the state of economic affairs in Italy, advising his readers that the Italian bishops and their ecclesiastical communities were committed to showing practical signs of understanding and help. He went on to deplore:

The situation of so many young people who are looking for work and cannot find it. Of those families who are experiencing the drama or prospect of sacking. Those who have sought security by emigrating far away and who now find themselves confronted by the prospect of an unhappy return. Those who are old and sick and because of the insufficiency of social pensions suffer worst the consequences of this crisis . . .

I wish priests to remember and frequently to refer in any way they like to the situation of the workers. We complain sometimes that workers go and seek bad advice from the left and the right. But in reality how much have we done to ensure that the social teaching of the Church can be habitually included in our Catechism, in the hearts of Christians?

Pope John asserted that workers must be given the power to influence their own destiny at all levels, even the highest scale. Have we always taught that with courage? Pius XII while on the one hand warning of the dangers of Marxism, on the other hand reproves those priests who remain uncertain in face of that economic system which is known as capitalism, the grave consequences of which the Church has not failed to denounce. Have we always listened to this?

Albino Luciani then gave an extraordinary demonstration of his own abhorrence of a wealthy, materialistic Church. He exhorted and authorized all of his parish priests and rectors of sanctuaries to sell their gold, necklaces, and precious objects. The proceeds were to go to the Don Orione centre for handicapped people. He advised his readers that he intended to sell the bejewelled cross and gold chain which had belonged to Pius XII and which Pope John had given to Luciani when he had made him a bishop.

It is very little in terms of the money it will produce but it is perhaps something if it helps people to understand that the true treasures of the Church are, as St Lorenzo said, the poor, the weak who must be helped not with occasional charity but in such a way that they can be raised a little at a time to that standard of life and that level of culture to which they have a right.

He also announced that he intended to sell to the highest bidder a valuable pectoral cross with gold chain and the ring of Pope John. These items had been given to Venice by Pope Paul during his September visit of 1972. Later in the same article he quoted two Indians. Firstly, Gandhi: 'I admire Christ but not Christians.'

Luciani then expressed the wish that the words of Sandhu Singh would perhaps one day no longer be true:

One day I was sitting on the banks of a river. I took from the water a round stone and I broke it. Inside it was perfectly dry. That stone had been lying in the water for a very long time but the water had not penetrated it. Then I thought that the same thing happened to men in Europe. For centuries they have been surrounded by Christianity but Christianity has not penetrated, does not live within them.

The response was mixed. Some of the Venetian priests had grown attached to the precious jewels they had in their churches. Luciani also came under attack from some of the traditionalists of the city, those who were fond of recalling the glory and power that was interwoven in the title of Patriarch, the last vestige of the splendour of the Serenissima. This man who was pledged to seeking out and living the essential, eternal truth of the Gospel met a deputation of such citizens in his office. Having listened to them he said:

I am first a bishop among bishops, a shepherd among shepherds, who must have as his first duty the spreading of the Good News and the safety of his lambs. Here in Venice I can only repeat what I said at Canale, at Belluno and at Vittorio Veneto.

Then he phoned the fire brigade, borrowed a boat and went to visit the sick in a nearby hospital.

As already recorded, one of the methods this particular shepherd employed to communicate with his flock was the pen. On more than one occasion Luciani told his secretary that if he had not become a priest he would probably have become a journalist. To judge by his writings he would have been an asset to the profession. In the early 1970s he devised an interesting technique to make a variety of moral points to the readers of the diocesan magazine: a series of letters to a variety of literary and historical characters. The articles caught the eye of the editor of a local newspaper, who persuaded Luciani to widen his audience through the paper. Luciani reasoned that he had more chance of spreading the 'Good News' through the press than he did preaching to half-empty churches. Eventually a collection of the letters was published in book form, *Illustrissimi* – the most illustrious ones.

The book is a delight. Apart from providing an invaluable insight into the mind of Albino Luciani, each letter comments on aspects of modern life. Luciani's unique ability to communicate, unique that is for an Italian Cardinal, is demonstrated again and again. The letters are also a clear proof of just how widely read Luciani was. Chesterton and Walter Scott receive a letter from the Patriarch, as do Goethe, Alessandro Manzoni, Marlowe and many others. There is even one addressed to Christ which begins in typical Luciani fashion.

Dear Jesus,
I have been criticized. 'He's a Bishop, he's a Cardinal,' people have said, 'he's been writing letters to all kinds of people: to Mark Twain, to Péguy, to Casella, to Penelope, to Dickens, to Marlowe, to Goldoni and heaven knows how many others. And not a line to Jesus Christ!

His letter to St Bernard grew into a dialogue, with the Saint giving sage advice, including an example of how fickle public opinion could be.

In 1815 the official French newspaper, *Le Moniteur,* showed its readers how to follow Napoleon's progress: 'The *brigand* flees from the island of Elba'; 'The *usurper* arrives at Grenoble'; '*Napoleon* enters Lyons'; 'The *Emperor* reaches Paris this evening'.

Into each letter is woven advice to his flock, on prudence, responsibility, humility, fidelity, charity. As a piece of work designed to communicate the Christian message it is worth twenty Papal encyclicals.

Spreading the 'Good News' was one aspect of Luciani's years in Venice. Another was the recalcitrance constantly demonstrated by some of his priests. Apart from those who spent their time evicting tenants or complaining about having to sell Church treasures there were others who embraced Marxism as wholeheartedly as yet others were preoccupied with capitalism. One priest wrote in red paint across the walls of his Church, 'Jesus was the first socialist'; another climbed into his pulpit in nearby Mestre and declared to his astonished congregation, 'I shall do no more work for the Patriarch until he gives me a pay rise.'

Albino Luciani, a man with a highly developed sense of humour, was not amused at such antics. In July 1978 from the pulpit of the Church of the Redemptor in Venice he talked to his congregation of clerical error: 'It is true that the Pope, bishops and priests do not cease to be poor men subject to errors and often we make errors.'

At this point he lifted his head from his manuscript and looking directly at the people said with complete sincerity:

'I am convinced that when Pope Paul VI destined me to the See of Venice he committed an error.'

Within days of that comment Pope Paul VI died; at 9.40 pm on Sunday, August 6th, 1978. The throne was empty.

The Empty Throne

Within twenty-four hours of Paul's death, with his body unburied and his Papacy unevaluated, Ladbrokes, the London bookmakers, had opened a book on the Papal election. The *Catholic Herald,* while carrying a front-page article criticizing the action, took care to let its readers know the current odds.

Cardinal Pignedoli was favourite at 5–2. Cardinals Baggio and Poletti were joint second favourites at 7–2, followed by Cardinal Benelli at 4–1. Also strongly fancied was Cardinal Willebrands at 8–1. Cardinal Koenig was quoted at 16–1. England's Cardinal Hume was 25–1. These surprisingly long odds on the Englishman could perhaps be attributed to a statement Hume had made to the effect that he did not have the qualities for the job. Longest odds were quoted for Cardinal Suenens. Albino Luciani did not appear in the list of Papal runners.

Condemned by some for displaying lack of taste, Ladbrokes defended themselves by pointing out that with regard to the empty throne the 'newspapers are full of speculation about front-runners, contenders and outsiders.'

Indeed the speculation had begun even before Pope Paul's death. Peter Hebblethwaite, an ex-Jesuit priest converted to Vatican-watching, had asked in the *Spectator* on July 29th, 'Who is running for Pope?' He picked out three form horses to follow – Pignedoli, Baggio and Pironio. Whether Pope Paul had read Hebblethwaite's comment that he 'cannot be expected to live very much longer' in his last few days, is not known.

The Italian media were a little slower off the mark. On the day after the Pope's death the radio gave out nothing but Beethoven. On day two they relaxed a little with continuous Mozart. On day three there was a diet of light orchestral music. On day four the solemnity eased a little more with vocal renditions of 'Moonlight Serenade' and 'Stardust'. Italian television for the first few days gave its viewers a variety of movies entirely peopled with nuns, Popes and cardinals.

Careful analysis of the English-speaking press covering the first few weeks of August 1978 indicates that if the 111 cardinals were as perplexed as the Vaticanologists then the Church was in for a long, confusing Conclave.

Followers of Hebblethwaite's writings must have had a particularly hard time backing the winner. In the *Sunday Times* of August 13th, Cardinals Felici, Villot, Willebrands, Pellegrino and Benelli were added to his list of tips. The following Sunday he told his readers, 'The new Pope: it could be Bertoli.' The Sunday after that even Luciani got a mention. It was reminiscent of a racing correspondent reviewing the form for the Grand National or the Derby. If he mentioned every horse then after the race his paper could quote his comment about the winner.

A fish-seller in Naples had rather better luck. Using the numbers derived from the date of Pope Paul's death, he won the national lottery.

Despite the pomp and ceremony, the funeral of the Pontiff was a curiously unemotional affair. It was as if his Papacy had ended long ago. After *Humanae Vitae* there had been no more Papal encyclicals and, apart from his courageous comments when his close friend, the former Prime Minister Aldo Moro, had been first kidnapped then murdered, there had been little from Paul over the past decade to inspire an outpouring of grief at his death: a man to respect, not one to love. There were many long and learned articles analyzing his Papacy in depth but if he is remembered at all by posterity it will be as the man who banned the Pill. It may be a cruel epitaph, an unfair encapsulation of a sometimes brilliant and often tortured mind, but what transpires in the marital bed is of more import to ordinary people than the fact that Paul flew in many aeroplanes, went to many countries, waved at many people and suffered agonies of mind.

In October 1975, Pope Paul had issued a number of rules which were to apply upon his death. One of these was that all cardinals in charge of departments of the Roman Curia would automatically relinquish their offices. This ensured that the Pope's successor would have a completely free hand to make appointments. It also ensured during the period of *sede vacante,* between death and election, a considerable amount of nervous agitation. One of the few exceptions to this rule of automatic dismissal was the Camerlengo or Chamberlain. This office was held by Secretary of State Cardinal Jean Villot. Until the throne was filled, Villot became the keeper of the keys of Peter. During the vacancy the government of the Church was entrusted to the Sacred College of Cardinals who were obliged to hold daily meetings or 'General Congregations'.

Another of the late Pope's rules quickly became the subject of furious debate during the early General Congregations. Paul had specifically excluded from the Conclave that would elect his successor all cardinals over the age of eighty. Ottaviani mounted an angry attack on this rule. Supported by the 85-year-old Cardinal Confalonieri and the other over-eighties, they attempted to reverse it. Paul had fought many battles with this group. In death he won the last one. The cardinals voted to adhere to the rules. The General Congregation continued, on one occasion discussing for over an hour whether ballot papers should be folded once or twice.

Rome was beginning to fill, but not with Italians – most of them were at the beaches. Apart from tourists the city was swarming with pressure groups, Vaticanologists, foreign correspondents, and the lunatic fringe. Part of this last group went around the city sticking up posters that proclaimed, 'Elect a Catholic Pope'.

One of the 'experts' breathlessly informed *Time Magazine*, 'I don't know of one Italian cardinal who would feel happy voting for a foreigner'. He obviously did not know many Italian cardinals, certainly not the one who was Patriarch of Venice. Before leaving for Rome, Luciani had made it clear to former secretary Monsignor Mario Senigaglia, now officiating at the church of Santo Stefano, 'I think the time is right for a Pope from the Third World'.

He also left no doubt whom he had in mind. Cardinal Aloisio Lorscheider, Archbishop of Fortaleza, Brazil. Lorscheider was widely regarded as a man possessed of one of the best minds in the modern Church. During his years in Venice, Luciani had come to know him well and as he confided to Senigaglia, 'He is a man of faith and culture. Further than that he has a good knowledge of Italy and of Italian. Most important of all, his heart and mind are with the poor.'

Apart from their meetings in Italy, Luciani had spent a month with Lorscheider in Brazil in 1975. They had conversed in a variety of languages and discovered they had much in common. What was unknown to Luciani was the high regard that Lorscheider had for him.

Lorscheider was later to observe of that month in Brazil, 'On that occasion many people hazarded the guess that one day the Patriarch of Venice could become Pope.'

Driven to Rome by Father Diego Lorenzi, the man who had replaced Senigaglia as Secretary to the Patriarch two years previously, Luciani stayed at the Augustinian residence near St Peter's Square. Apart from his attendance at the daily General Congregations he kept very much to himself, preferring to walk in the Augustinian gardens, quietly contemplating. Many of his colleagues led more strenuous lives: Ladbroke's favourite, for example, Cardinal Pignedoli.

Pignedoli had been a close friend of the late Pope. Some Italian commentators cruelly observed he was the only friend Paul had. Certainly he appeared to be the only one to address him by the intimate 'Don Battista'. In support of Pignedoli Cardinal Rossi of Brazil was at pains to remind the other cardinals of the tradition that Popes indicated who their successor should be and insisted that Pignedoli was 'Paul's best loved son'. Pignedoli was one of the most progressive of the Curial cardinals and hence disliked by most of the other Curial cardinals. He was cultured, well-travelled and, perhaps most important for his candidature, he had influenced either directly or indirectly the appointments of at least 28 of his brother cardinals.

Straightforward and honest running for the Vatican Throne is considered rather bad form in the higher reaches of the Roman Catholic Church. Candidates are not encouraged to stand up and announce publicly what their programme or platform will be. In theory there is no canvassing, no lobbying, no pressure group. In practice there is all of this and much more. In theory, the cardinals gather in secret Conclave and wait for the Holy Spirit to inspire them. As the hot August days went by, phone calls, secret meetings and pre-election promises ensured that the Holy Spirit was being given considerable worldly assistance.

One standard technique is for a candidate to state that he really does not think he measures up to the job. In this election run-up, that was said by a number with total sincerity, for example, Cardinal Basil Hume. Others made similar statements and would have been distressed if they had found their colleagues accepting them at their face value.

Attending afternoon tea on August 17th, Pignedoli declared to a gathering of Italian cardinals which went right across the spectrum of right, centre and left, that in spite of all the urgings and promptings he did not feel that he was suited for the Papacy. He suggested to his colleagues that they should vote instead for Cardinal Gantin. It was an imaginative suggestion.

Gantin, the black Cardinal of Benin, was 56 years of age. There was therefore very little chance of his election because of his relative youth. The ideal age was felt to be late 60s. Pignedoli was 68. Further, Gantin was black. Racialism is not confined to one side of the Tiber. Putting forward Gantin's name could well attract votes for Pignedoli from the Third World whose cardinals held a vital 35 votes.

Pignedoli remarked that whoever was elected it should be done with all possible speed. Voting in the Conclave was to begin on the morning of August 26th, a Saturday. Pignedoli felt that it would be fitting if the new Pope was elected by the morning of Sunday 27th so that he could address the crowds at mid-day in a packed St Peter's Square.

If there was a widespread desire among the cardinals for a quick resolution of the Conclave it would of course work greatly to the advantage of the candidate who entered with the largest following. Cardinals are just as susceptible to bandwagons as lesser mortals. To attain the Papacy Pignedoli knew that he had to look to the non-Curial cardinals to give him the 75 votes (two thirds plus one) essential for election. When the Curia had finished its internal fighting it would eventually focus on a specific candidate, preferably one of its own group. The pundits tossed a variety of Curial candidates into the air like demented jugglers – Bertoli, Baggio, Felici.

In a curious manoeuvre to assist his own candidature, Baggio contacted Paul Marcinkus and assured him that he would be confirmed in his post as Head of the Vatican Bank if Baggio were elected. Bishop Marcinkus, unlike the cardinals who had been dispossessed by the late Pope's rules, was still running the Bank. There was no public indication that he would not continue to do so. The gesture by Baggio mystified Italian observers. If they had been able to persuade any of the cardinals present during the private General Congregations to talk, the move by Baggio would have taken on a deeper significance.

These meetings were giving very serious consideration to the problems facing the Church and to the possible solutions. In this manner Papal candidates emerge who are considered to have the abilities to implement the solutions. The August meetings were inevitably far-ranging. The concerns that emerged included discipline within the Church, evangelization, ecumenism, collegiality and world peace. There was another subject that occupied the minds of the cardinals: Church finances. Many were appalled that Marcinkus was still running the Vatican Bank after the Sindona scandal. Others wanted a full-scale investigation into Vatican finances. Cardinal Villot, as Secretary of State and Camerlengo, was obliged to listen to a long list of complaints which all had one common denominator, the name of Bishop Paul Marcinkus. This had been the reason for Baggio's offer to keep him on in the job, an attempt to maintain the status quo and also a gambit to win the votes of such men as Cardinal Cody of Chicago, who would be perfectly content to let Marcinkus stay in his job.

The Cardinal from Florence, Giovanni Benelli, was another who preoccupied observers. As Paul's troubleshooter he had made many enemies but it was freely acknowledged that he could influence at least fifteen voters.

To muddy the form book even further the fifteen very disgruntled old men who were about to be excluded from the actual Conclave began to bring pressure to bear on their colleagues. Their group, which contained some of the most reactionary men in the Vatican, predictably began to push for the Cardinal who they considered most completely represented their collective point of view, the Archbishop of Genoa Cardinal Giuseppe Siri. Siri had led the fight against many of the Second Vatican Council reforms. He had been the principal right-wing candidate in the Conclave which had elected Paul. Now a number of the over-age cardinals considered he was the ideal man for the chair of Peter. The octogenarians were not unanimous, however – at least one, Cardinal Carlo Confalonieri, was quietly singing the praises of Albino Luciani. Nevertheless the group as a whole thought Siri should be the next Pope.

Cardinal Siri claims that he is a much misunderstood man. During one sermon he had castigated women for wearing trousers and exhorted them to return to dresses, 'so that they could remember their true function on this earth'.

During the series of nine memorial Masses to Pope Paul, homilies were delivered by, among others, Cardinal Siri. The man who had blocked and obstructed Pope Paul at every turn pledged himself to the aims of the late Pontiff. The campaign for Siri went largely unnoticed by the Press. One of the arguments used by Siri's supporters was that the next Pope must be an Italian. To insist that the next Pope be home-grown, even though only 27 of the voting cardinals out of a total of 111 were Italian, was typical of an attitude that abounds throughout the Vatican.

The belief that only an Italian Papacy can control not just the Vatican and the wider Church beyond but also Italy itself is deeply embedded in the thinking of the Vatican village. The last so-called 'foreign' Pope had been Adrian VI from Holland, in 522. This highly talented and scrupulously honest man became fully aware of the many evils that were flourishing in Rome. In an attempt to halt the rising tide of Protestantism in Germany he wrote to his Delegate in that country:

> You are also to say that we frankly acknowledge that . . . for many years things deserving of abhorrence have gathered around the Holy See. Sacred things have been misused, ordinances transgressed, so that in everything there has been a change for the worse. Thus it is not surprising that the malady has crept down from the Head to the members, from the Popes to the hierarchy. We all, prelates and clergy, have gone astray from the right way . . . Therefore in our name give promises that we shall use all diligence to reform before all things, what is perhaps the source of all evil, the Roman Curia.

Within months of making that statement Pope Adrian was dead. Evidence suggests that he was poisoned by his doctor.

Now with Paul VI buried, the Roman Curia minority were yet again attempting to prevail over the majority. In one of the early General Congregation meetings with only 32 cardinals present, most of them Italian, it had been agreed that the 111 cardinals would not go into Conclave until August 25th and that voting would not start until August 26th. The delay of twenty days was just one day short of the longest permissible period laid down by the rules of the late Pope. It was also the longest in modern history. In 1878, sans TWA and Pan Am, the cardinals had waited a mere ten days before going into the Conclave that elected Leo XIII. The three-week period gave the Italian cardinals the maximum time to persuade the 'foreigners' of the wisdom of electing an Italian successor to Paul VI. They met unexpected opposition. Albino Luciani was not alone in thinking the time had come for a Pope from the Third World. Many from the Third World felt the same.

The majority of the cardinals from Latin America attended a secret meeting at the Brazilian College in Rome on August 20th. No major candidate emerged but it was agreed that the need was for a pastoral Pope, for a man who clearly manifested holiness, who recognized the needs of the poor, a man in favour of power sharing, of collegiality, a man who by his very nature and qualities would have world-wide appeal. The group was primarily concerned with what the new Pope should represent rather than who the new Holy Father was, though the qualifications they specified reduced the field of possible winners dramatically.

In Florence,* Giovanni Benelli, wrongly thought by many observers to be running for the Papacy, received the Latin American specification. He smiled as he considered the qualities the Latin Americans were seeking. It read like an accurate biography of exactly the man Benelli considered should be Pope. Picking up the telephone, he dialled a number outside Florence, and moments later was engaged in animated conversation with the Belgian Cardinal, Suenens.

In Rome Pignedoli continued to give lavish dinner parties, Curial cardinals continued to lobby discreetly on behalf of Siri and the Vatican Press Office maintained its policy of giving the world's commentators the minimum of co-operation, as the date of what Peter Nichols of *The Times* called 'The World's Most Secret Ballot' drew nearer.

The Latin American cardinals were not the only group to formulate a document that amounted to a job description. A week earlier, a group of Catholics calling themselves CREP (Committee for the Responsible Election of the Pope) held a Press conference in the Columbus Hotel, Rome. The brave man chosen to field questions from over 400 reporters was Father Andrew Greeley. Not himself a member of CREP, Greeley and a group of theologians had drawn up the job description on behalf of the Committee.

There were to be many critics of the document. Much of the criticism was banal, much was dismissive. Undoubtedly the signatories appeared to be looking for an extraordinary man. It is equally without doubt that the document showed a deep love for the Roman Catholic Church. These men cared desperately about the nature and quality of the new Papacy. To dismiss men of the quality of Hans Kung, Yves Congar and Edward Schillebeeck requires a mentality bordering on spiritual sterility. Professor Kung, for example, is in the view of many who are qualified to judge, the most brilliant Catholic theologian alive today. All the signatories of the press release have impressive records.

*Giovanni Benelli had been manoeuvred out of Rome in 1977. His continuing efforts to have Marcinkus removed from the Vatican Bank had resulted in a cabal, which included in its members Mancinkus and Paul's secretary Monsignor Macchi, having Benelli removed from the Secretariat of State's office. He had been made a cardinal and been given Florence by way of compensation.

HELP WANTED
A hopeful, holy man who can smile.
Interesting work, guaranteed income, residence comes with position. Protection by proven security organization. Apply College of Cardinals, Vatican City.

Thus began the job description. It went on to describe the man they would like chosen by the secret Conclave. It did not matter, they stated, if he was Curial or non-Curial; Italian or non-Italian; whether he was of the First, Second or Third World. It did not matter if he was an intellectual or non-intellectual, whether he was a diplomat or pastor, progressive or moderate, an efficient administrator or lacking in administrative experience . . . What was needed, the theologians said, at this present critical time in history was 'a man of holiness, a man of hope, a man of joy. A holy man who can smile. A Pope not for all Catholics but for all peoples. A man totally free from the slightest taint of financial organizational wheeling and dealing.' It went on to list other vital essentials. Reading the qualifications needed and comparing it with the list of leading candidates, the overriding impression is one of deep, urgent need bordering on desperation.

Greeley was given a rough ride which got rougher when he had the temerity to suggest that perhaps a Pope of the female gender might not be a bad idea. To suggest this in a room largely full of macho Italian male reporters, showed enormous courage. Eventually the meeting ended in some disorder with a young Italian woman screaming at Father Greeley that he was evil and had sexual problems.

A few days later Professor Hans Kung indicated in an interview with the Italian news magazine *Panorama* that in his view the entire Roman Catholic Church had and would continue to have sexual problems until something was done about *Humanae Vitae*. He put birth control at the head of the problems facing the new Pope. 'It is a fundamental question for Europe and the United States but above all, for the Third World . . . A revision of *Humanae Vitae* is necessary. Many theologians and also bishops would have no difficulty in consenting to birth control, even by artifical means, if the idea could be accepted that rules established in the past by Popes could be corrected.'

On August 21st, Cardinal Lorscheider of Brazil made public through an interview exactly what was on the Latin American 'wanted' list. They sought a Pope who was a man of hope with a positive attitude towards the world. They wanted a man who would not seek to impose Christian solutions on non-Christians; who was sensitive to social problems and open to dialogue, with a commitment to the search for unity; a good pastor, a good shepherd in the way that Jesus was; a man who sincerely believed that the Bishops' Conference should be an influencing factor on the Papacy rather than a mere charade. He must be open to finding a new solution to birth control, which, while it would not contradict *Humanae Vitae,* would go beyond it.

Cardinals Benelli and Suenens, still avoiding the heat of Rome, were quietly building the candidature of a man who measured up to the desires of the Latin American cardinals, Father Greeley, and Professor Kung: Albino Luciani.

When Luciani's name surfaced in the Italian Press during the pre-Conclave period his candidature was dismissed as a gambit. One Italian Vatican expert, Sandro Magister, referred to 'the uncolourful Patriarch of Venice'. Another, who should have known better, was Giancarlo Zizola. A few days before the Conclave, Zizola – who had interviewed Albino Luciani in depth nine years earlier – wrote a dismissive little biography entitled 'With the poor (not on the left)'. Zizola quoted an un-named source who had observed, 'The least you can say is that he is now the recognized leader of the ecclesiastical right, a Venetian replica of Cardinal Ottaviani.'

Luciani, when questioned by the Press about the spasmodic emergence of his name among the contenders, dismissed the suggestion with a laugh. 'I am at best on the C List for Pope.' Content, the news media left him alone. His name was quickly forgotten.

Remaining aloof from the wheeling and dealing, Luciani walked in the gardens of the Augustinian residence which overlook St Peter's, where he engaged Brother Clemente in conversation. Clemente was perspiring as he laboured among the flower beds. Luciani recalled that when he was a boy he had worked in the fields. 'Then I had callouses on my hands. Now I have callouses in my brain.'

As the day of the Conclave drew nearer Albino Luciani had other concerns. The five-year-old Lancia 2000 had developed engine trouble. He told his secretary, Father Lorenzi, that he must get it repaired quickly. The voting in the Conclave was due to start on Saturday, August 26th. Luciani insisted that the car must be ready for their return journey to Venice on Tuesday 29th. He wanted to make an early start. There was much to do upon their return home.

On August 25th Luciani wrote to his niece, Pia:

Dear Pia,

I am writing to let you have the new stamps of the Sede Vacante and also to congratulate you for your first exam which went well. Let us hope the Lord will help you also for the rest. Today we finished the pre-Conclave with the last General Congregation. After which, having drawn lots for a cell, we went to see them. I've got number 60, a drawing room converted into a bedroom; it is like being in the seminary in Feltre in 1923. An iron bed, a mattress, a basin to wash in.

In 61 is Cardinal Tomasek of Prague. Further on, Cardinals Tarancon, Madrid; Medeiros, Boston; Sin, Manila; Malual, Kinshasa. The only one missing is Australia and we would have a concentration from the whole world. I don't know how long the Conclave will last, it is difficult to find the right person to confront so many problems which are very heavy crosses. Fortunately I am out of danger. It is already a very heavy responsibility to cast one's vote in these circumstances. I am sure that as a good Christian you will pray for the Church in these moments. Say 'hello' to Francesco, Father and Mother. I am not writing to these last two as I am rather busy at the moment.
Your very affectionate
Albino Luciani

The following day a few hours before the Conclave he wrote to his sister, Antonia:

Dear Sister,

I am writing to you shortly before going into the Conclave. These are heavy moments of responsibility, even if there is no danger for me, despite the gossip in the papers. Casting one's vote for a Pope in these moments is a heavy weight. Pray for the Church, and an affectionate greeting also to Errere, Roberto and Gino.
Albino Luciani

Handing his letter to the Augustinians to be posted, he advised them that he had left most of his belongings in his room. That morning he had celebrated a Mass 'for the Election of a Pope' with his brother cardinals. Clemente had already taken an overnight bag for Luciani to the Sistine Chapel. Now the cardinal joined his colleagues in the Pauline Chapel with its frescoes by Michelangelo. Fussed over by Monsignor Virgilio Noe, the Papal Master of Ceremonies, and preceded by the Sistine Chapel Choir singing the hymn to the Holy Spirit, they walked through the Sala Ducale, beneath Bernini's cherubs and into the Sistine Chapel.

When Monsignor Noe called 'Extra omnes' ('All out'), the choir, altar servers, television crews and all extraneous personnel departed. With Cardinal Villot standing just inside and Noe just outside, the door slowly closed on the 111 cardinals. It would not open until a Pope had been elected. The world's most secret ballot would continue until puffs of white smoke told the waiting crowds in St Peter's Square and the many millions of world-wide observers that the Vatican throne had been filled.

Inside the Conclave

❦

Whatever Pope Paul's failings might have been, he certainly knew how to organize a secret Conclave. He had left very clear instructions about the proceedings to elect his successor.

One of Paul's preoccupations had been secrecy. Two days before the Conclave, the cardinals were obliged to swear a solemn oath. Under pain of excommunication they were forbidden subsequently to discuss the balloting 'either by signs, word or writing, or in any other manner'. To drive home the point, the cardinals also had to promise and swear 'not to use devices designed in any way for taking pictures'. Obviously Pope Paul did not entirely trust these princes of the Roman Catholic Church.

In case any of the cardinals might have suffered a memory lapse between taking the Oath of Secrecy and entering the Conclave, they were obliged to take it again when those extraneous to the proceedings had left the Sistine Chapel.

To make triply sure, after the cardinals had gone to their assigned rooms, or 'cells' as Paul preferred to call them, Cardinal Villot, helped by a number of colleagues and two technicians, made a search of the entire Conclave area looking for anyone who had hidden himself hoping for the scoop of a lifetime. Then in a manner reminiscent of Stalag Five or Colditz, all the various personnel were physically checked and a roll call of them taken in the Chapel.

To ensure that nobody without was trying to get within, Paul had also instructed that a large retinue of Vatican personnel, including the Swiss Guard and Vatican architects, were to make a careful check outside the Sistine Chapel. Whether Paul was fearful that the banned octogenarians might attempt to climb the outer wall is not stated within the rules!

Villot and his assistants plus the two technicians certainly earned their lire during the Conclave. Yet another of their tasks was to make random searches of the entire Conclave area, looking for tape recorders, video equipment and all forms of bugging device.

With all this searching, body counting and double checking, the late Pope clearly appreciated that there would be very little time on the first day to get down to the actual task of voting for a Pope.

While Rome basked in a heatwave, the temperature within the Sistine Chapel must have been close to unbearable for those mainly elderly men. The late Pope had not forgotten the windows. Under his instructions all of them had been sealed and boarded up. In this environment 111 cardinals would on the morrow make the most important decision of their lives.

If outside the walls the hopes, needs and desires of millions concerning the new Papacy were myriad, then they accurately mirrored the cross-section of views contained within the Conclave. The right wing was reflected in the aspirations of those who desired a return to the pre-Vatican Council II world, where ecclesiastical discipline of a rigid nature was the keystone. The left wing sought a Pope who understood and related the Church to the poor, a Pope who would rule in a democratic manner and acknowledge that his bishops should influence the direction in which the Church moved. They yearned for a John XXIII, while the right wing longed for a Pius XII. In the middle were men grappling with both points of view, attempting to go backwards and forwards simultaneously. There was also Albino Luciani, a man with a simplicity that is rarely given to a person of such high intelligence; a simplicity that sprang from a sophisticated and complex mind. He saw his task as the need to acknowledge the unfulfilled aspirations of the Third World. Hence his decision to vote for the Archbishop of Fortaleza, Brazil, Aloisio Lorscheider, a man with glittering intellectual gifts who knew all about the problems of the poor. To elect such a man as Pope would be an inspired choice with or without the aid of the Holy Spirit.

Giovanni Benelli and Leon Joseph Suenens had an equally inspired choice. Before the Conclave Benelli had watched with wry amusement when media speculation identified him as a possible Pope. He had remained silent when subjected to snide attacks by Curial cardinals such as Pericle Felici, the Administrator of the Patrimony for the Holy See, who had said of him, 'His vote will go only to himself.'

Felici was soon to discover that Benelli had different plans for his vote and, more important, for the votes of others. When news of some of the quiet, discreet lobbying being done by Benelli and `Suenens reached the Curia, they were as dismissive of Albino Luciani as were the men and women of the media. Of the many pre-Conclave biographies issued by the Vatican, that on Luciani was the shortest. Clearly those in power agreed with his own assessment, that he was no more than a C List candidate. Like the world's Press, the Curia did not know the man. Unfortunately for the Curia the other cardinals did. After the election many of the world's Press and the Vatican experts would excuse their inability to pick the winner by stating that he was 'unknown, has not travelled outside Italy, does not speak any languages'.

Albino Luciani was fluent in German, French, Portuguese and English, as well as his native Italian and Latin. Apart from being well known by the non-Curial Italian cardinals he had a wide range of friendships. The Poles, Wojtyla and Wyszynski, had stayed with him in Venice. Wojtyla had shaped Luciani's thinking with regard to the problem of Marxism. He had stayed with Lorscheider during a trip to Brazil in 1975. Cardinal Arns, also from Brazil, was another close friend. Suenens of Belgium, Willebrands of Holland, Marty of France, Cooke of New York, Hoeffner and Volk of Germany, Manning of Los Angeles, Medeiros of Boston, were just a few of the cardinals who enjoyed friendships with Luciani. In addition to Brazil he had also been to Portugal, Germany, France, Yugoslavia, Switzerland and Austria, as well as Africa where he had created the link between Vittorio Veneto and Kiremba, a town in Burundi.

He had formed friendships with many non-Catholics. The black Phillip Potter, Secretary of the World Council of Churches, had been his house guest. Others included Jews, Anglicans, and Pentecostal Christians. He had exchanged books and letters with Hans Kung. If the Roman Curia had known that, alarm bells would have rung all over Vatican City.

This then was the man who now merely wished to cast his vote, see a new Pope elected, climb into his repaired Lancia and go home to Venice. He had already considered the possibility that by some absurd twist of fate his name might emerge from the pack. When Mario Senigaglia had wished him luck and urged him to take some of his speeches 'just in case', Luciani had dismissed the suggestion. 'There is always a way out of it. You can always refuse.'

In Rome Diego Lorenzi, Luciani's secretary since 1976, had also expressed the wish that this man, whom like Senigaglia before him – he regarded as a father, should be the next Pope. Again Luciani dismissed the suggestion. He reminded Lorenzi of the rules which the late Pope had drawn up. He referred to that supreme moment which occurs when one of the cardinals has received two thirds plus one of the votes, in this case 75. The cardinal in question is then approached and asked, 'Do you accept?' Luciani smiled at his secretary. 'And if they elect me I will say, "I'm sorry. I refuse".'

On Saturday morning, August 26th, after they had celebrated Mass and breakfasted, the cardinals walked to their allotted chairs in the Sistine Chapel. The rules urged that each cardinal disguise his handwriting on the voting card which was so designed that when folded in two it was reduced in size to about one inch. After scrutineers were appointed to check the votes, three more cardinals were appointed to scrutinize the scrutineers. The two-thirds plus one was Pope Paul's safeguard against a cardinal voting for himself.

Eventually, with the temperature as well as the tension mounting, the first ballot began.*

After the ballot cards had been counted, checked, checked again and then checked for a third time to ensure that no cardinal had voted twice, the cards were then carefully threaded together, recounted, rechecked and placed in a designated box for subsequent burning. The voting on the first ballot produced the following result:

Siri 25 votes
Luciani 23 votes
Pignedoli 18 votes
Lorscheider 12 votes
Baggio 9 votes

The remaining 24 were scattered. The Italians, Bertoli and Felici, the Argentinian, Pironio and the Polish cardinal, Karol Wojtyla received votes, as did Cardinals Cordeiro of Pakistan and Franz Koenig of Austria.

*The only official record of what transpired is buried deep in the Vatican archives. What follows is the result of evidence I have acquired from a variety of informed sources. The figures did not always agree and consequently I fully acknowledge that there must be a margin of error. This also applies to the names of the cardinals who voted for Luciani on the first ballot. Though there will inevitably be variances I am satisfied that the general shape and pattern of voting recorded here is accurate.

Albino Luciani had listened with growing incredulity as the scrutineer called out his name twenty-three times. When a number of the cardinals sitting nearby had turned and smiled at him he merely shook his head, bemused. How could it be that he had obtained so many votes?

Cardinals Benelli, Suenens and Marty could have supplied the answer. They had created what they considered to be a successful base from which to promote Luciani. Apart from these three, also voting for Luciani on the first ballot was an international cross-section of cardinals. From France, Renard and Gouyon; from Holland, Willebrands and Alfrink; Koenig of Austria; Volk and Hoeffner of Germany; Malula of Zaire; Nsubuga of Uganda; Thiandoum of Dakar; Gantin from Benin; Colombo of Milan; Pelligrino of Turin; Ursi of Naples; Poma of Bologna; Cooke of New York; Lorscheider of Brazil; Ekandem of Nigeria; Wojtyla of Cracow; Sin of Manila.

Unaware of the identities of his supporters, Luciani concluded that this aberration would correct itself at the second vote, and, reaching for another voting card, again wrote the name of Aloisio Lorscheider upon it.

The Curial cardinals were eyeing Luciani with renewed interest. Their first task had been to halt the Pignedoli campaign for the Papacy. The second ballot confirmed they had achieved that object.

Siri 35 votes
Luciani 30 votes
Pignedoli 15 votes
Lorscheider 12 votes

The remaining 19 votes were again scattered.

The voting papers together with those from the first ballot were stuffed into the antiquated stove, the 'nero' handle was pulled and black smoke, instead of emerging outside on the roof promptly filled the Sistine Chapel. Despite the fact that the funeral of Pope Paul and the Conclave were costing the Church several million dollars, some Vatican official decided to save a lira or two and had decreed that the chimney should not be swept. The result, with all windows sealed, threatened to bring the Conclave to a sudden and dramatic end. The late Pope had not foreseen the possibility of all 111 cardinals being suffocated to death but he had provided for several members of the Vatican fire brigade to be locked in the area. They promptly risked excommunication by opening several windows.

Eventually some of the black smoke made its way out of the Sistine Chapel chimney and Vatican Radio confirmed that the morning had not produced a Pope. Many Vatican experts had predicted a long Conclave, reasoning that it would take a great deal of time for 111 men from around the world to arrive at any form of relative unanimity. Seeing the black smoke, the pundits nodded sagely and continued in their attempts to prise from the Vatican Press office such vital details as the lunch menu in the Conclave.

The biggest and most diverse Conclave in the Church's entire history moved hastily out of the Sistine Chapel to the temporary canteen.

The third ballot would be crucial. Siri and Luciani were finely balanced. While a very troubled Patriarch of Venice picked at his food, others were busy. Giovanni Benelli talked quietly to the cardinals from Latin America. They had made their point, he assured them, but clearly a Pope from the Third World was not going to emerge during this Conclave. Did they want a man like Siri with his reactionary views on the throne? Why not a man who, if not from the Third World, clearly loved it? It was no secret, Benelli told them, that Luciani was voting for their own Aloisio Lorscheider.

In fact Benelli was in danger of gilding the lily. The cardinals from Latin America had done their homework to a far greater degree than any other geographical group. Aware that their chances of electing Lorscheider were not great they had, before the Conclave, prepared a short list of non-Curial Italians. One of the men with whom they discussed the list was Father Bartolomeo Sorge, a Jesuit priest based in Rome. During a two-hour discussion Sorge pointed out the various aspects for and against each of the possibles. The name that had emerged was Albino Luciani. Father Sorge recalled for me his final words of advice to the group of cardinals:

> If you want to elect a Pope who will help to build up the Church in the world, then you should vote for Luciani. But remember he is not a man who is accustomed to governing, consequently he will need a good Secretary of State.

As the quiet buzz of conversation continued, Cardinals Suenens, Marty and Gantin, less flamboyantly but with equal effectiveness, spoke to others who were still wavering. Koenig of Vienna quietly remarked to those sitting near him that non-Italians should have no objection to another Italian as their spiritual leader.

The Curia were also considering their options over lunch. It had been a good morning for them. They had stopped Pignedoli. Siri, their candidate that morning, had clearly reached his maximum position. Despite all the pressure they had exerted before the Conclave it was now obvious to Felici and his clique that the left and the centre could not be drawn in sufficient numbers to Siri. Luciani, the quiet man from Venice, would surely be easy to control in the Vatican. Those who yearned for a pre-Vatican II Papacy were not convinced. They pointed out that Luciani more than any other Italian cardinal had put into practice the spirit of Pope John's Vatican Council.

In England everything stops for tea. In Italy the same state of suspended animation is achieved during siesta. While some lingered in the dining hall, talking quietly, others retired to their rooms to sleep. In cell 60, Albino Luciani knelt and prayed.

'You can't make gnocchi out of this dough,' Luciani had remarked to several well-wishers before the Conclave. It now appeared that a significant number of his fellow cardinals disagreed with this self-evaluation.

Through prayer he sought the answer, not to the ultimate result of the balloting, but to what he should do if elected. Luciani, who had never wanted to be anything other than a parish priest, stood on the threshold of the most powerful position in the Roman Catholic Church and went down on his knees earnestly to entreat his God to choose someone else.

Emerging from his cell at 4.00 p.m. Luciani was warmly embraced by Cardinal Joseph Malula from Zaire. Full of joy Malula offered his congratulations.

Luciani shook his head sadly. 'A great storm is troubling me,' he said as the two men made their way back for the third ballot.

Luciani 68 votes
Siri 15 votes
Pignedoli 10 votes

The remaining 18 votes on the ballot were scattered. Albino Luciani was now within seven votes of the Papacy. With a hand to his forehead he was heard to murmur, 'No. Please no.'

It was Cardinals Willebrands and Riberio, seated either side of Luciani, who heard the entreaty. Both men instinctively reached out and gripped Luciani. Willebrands spoke quietly. 'Courage. If the Lord gives the burden, he also gives the strength to carry it.'

Riberio nodded and then added, 'The whole world prays for the new Pope.'

There was no doubt whatsoever in the minds of many present that the Holy Spirit was manifest on that hot afternoon. Others took a more cynical view of what was inspiring the Conclave. Taofina'y of Samoa was heard to murmur, 'Power in the form of man, or rather a cardinal of the Curia.' His eyes were fastened on Felici when he made this observation.

Felici, who had spent the morning voting for Siri, now approached Albino Luciani. He handed him an envelope with the remark, 'A message for the new Pope'. The piece of paper within contained the words 'Via Crucia', a symbol of the way of the Cross.

There was great excitement in the Conclave. Many were now convinced that they were acting by Divine inspiration. Dispensing with the late Pope's instructions that each cardinal should swear a solemn oath each time before voting, the fourth ballot began.

Luciani 99 votes
Siri 11 votes
Lorscheider 1 vote (that of Albino Luciani)

As the final vote was announced there was a tremendous burst of applause from the gathering. The time was 6.05 p.m. A clique of Siri supporters, members of the intransigent right, had held out to the end. The doors of the Chapel opened and various Masters of Ceremonies came, accompanying the Camerlengo Villot, to where Albino Luciani sat. Villot spoke.

'Do you accept your canonical election as Supreme Pontiff?'

All eyes were upon Luciani. Cardinal Ciappi described for me that moment. 'He was sitting three rows behind me. Even at the moment of his election he was hesitating, Cardinal Villot put the question to him and he continued to hesitate. Cardinals Willebrands and Ribeno were clearly encouraging him.'

Luciani eventually responded. 'May God forgive you for what you have done in my regard.' Then he added, 'I accept.'

'By what name do you wish to be called?' asked Villot.

Luciani hesitated again. Then for the first time he smiled: 'John Paul the First'.

There were murmurs of delight from some of the listening cardinals. The name was an innovation, the first double name in the history of the Papacy. Tradition holds that by the choice of name a Pope gives an indication of the direction his reign may take. Hence the choice of Pius would have delighted the right wing, indicating perhaps a return to a pre-conciliar Church. What message Luciani was sending out with his choice of name depended on what message his listeners wanted to receive.

Why had Luciani, a man without ambition, accepted this position that for a number of other cardinals present would have been the realization of their life's ambition?

The answer, like much about this simple man, is complex. Research indicates that he was overwhelmed by the speed and size of the vote. Many spoke to me of this aspect. It is perhaps best summarized by a member of the Curia who had a close, twenty-year friendship with Albino Luciani.

> He was distressed by it. If he had not been so overwhelmed by the sheer quantity, if events had moved more slowly, taken the Conclave into a second day, he would have had time to gather himself and refuse; and yet, if he had decided in that Conclave that he was not the man to become Pope he would have refused. He was one of the strongest men I have known in thirty years in the Curia.

There is also the vital element of Luciani's personal humility. Describing the acceptance of the Papacy as an act of humility may appear to be contradictory. To equate the taking of supreme power with meekness is, in fact, entirely consistent if the last thing you want on earth is supreme power.

Inside the Conclave, as the new Pope was led to the Sacristy, all was joy. Outside all was confusion. While the Gammarelli brothers, tailors to the Vatican, tried to find a Papal white cassock that fitted, the cardinals were merrily burning their voting papers with the special chemical that was designed to ensure white smoke for the watching world. The watching world saw first white smoke, then a short while later, puffs of black (indicating that the Church was still without a Pope) emerge from the small chimney. The smoke had begun to emerge at 6.24 p.m. As it continued to belch out in a variety of hues, the Gammarelli brothers inside were not having any better luck with the white cassocks. Normally before a Conclave they made three: small, medium and large. This time, working from a list of twelve *papabili*, they had produced four, including an extra large one. The slightly-built Luciani had obviously not featured on their short-list of fancied cardinals. Eventually, nearly drowning in his new cassock, he emerged from the Sacristy and, sitting on a chair in front of the altar, received each cardinal who, having kissed Luciani's hand, was then warmly embraced by the new Pope.

Suenens, one of the cardinals largely responsible for this election, observed 'Holy Father, thank you for saying "yes".

Luciani smiled broadly at him. 'Perhaps it would have been better if I had said "no".'

The cardinals in charge of the stove were still happily throwing on voting papers and a large bundle of chemical candles which were supposed to produce the elusive white smoke. Vatican Radio manifestly knew less about what was going on than anyone else and uttered the remarkable statement: 'We can now say with total certainty that the smoke is either black or white.' In fact at that moment it was grey.

Vatican Radio telephoned the home and office of the Gammarelli brothers and obtained no answer. The brothers meanwhile were in the Sacristy attempting to fasten the blame on someone else over the fiasco of the white cassocks. It was rapidly becoming one of those operas that only Italians can stage.

Meanwhile, inside the Sistine Chapel, the cardinals had started to sing the Te Deum, the Hymn of Thanksgiving.

Outside, Father Roberto Tucci, the Jesuit director of Vatican Radio, was observed hurtling towards the bronze door of the Papal Palace across the Piazza. The Captain of the Swiss Guard, who was obliged to greet the new Pope with a loyal salute of his men, was interrogating the guard who said there had been a burst of clapping when, to his astonishment, he heard the Te Deum. That meant but one thing – whoever he was, they had a Pope. The problem was he did not have a retinue of guards ready.

Assuming the multi-coloured smoke indicated a deadlocked Conclave, the crowds in the Square had largely dispersed, when a voice boomed out on the massive loudspeaker address.

'Attenzione.'

People began to hurry back into the Square. The large door behind the balcony of St Peter's swung open. Figures could be seen emerging on the balcony itself . . . It was now 7.18 p.m., over an hour since the election. Senior Cardinal Deacon Felici appeared on the balcony and suddenly the crowd below was still.

Among that crowd was Luciani's secretary, Don Diego Lorenzi. He was standing next to a family from Sweden who had asked him what work he did. Young Lorenzi remarked, 'I am in Rome for a few days.

I work in Venice.' Then he turned his gaze to the figure of Felici on the balcony.

'Annuncio vobis gaudium magnum: Habemus Papam' – 'I bring you news of great joy! We have a Pope' – 'Cardinalem Albinum Luciani.'

At the mention of the name 'Albinum' Lorenzi turned back to the Swedish family. Tears were running down his face. He smiled then said proudly, 'I am the secretary of the newly-elected Pope.'

The roar from the crowd had almost drowned the 'Luciani'. When Felici continued, 'who has chosen the name John Paul the First,' there was a bedlam of noise. Many, indeed most, had never heard of Luciani but what mattered was that they had a Pope. The personal reaction came a short while later when Albino Luciani stepped on to the balcony. The enduring memory is of that smile. It touched the very soul. The man exuded delight and joy. Whatever else this Papacy was going to be it was going to be fun. After the gloom and agonizing of Paul the contrast was an extraordinary shock. As the new Pope intoned the blessing 'Urbi et Orbi', to the city and the world, the effect was similar to a burst of bright dazzling sun after an eternity of dark days.

In a moment he was gone, only to return. The Captain of the Swiss Guard had finally assembled a battalion. Albino Luciani waved and smiled. That smile reached out to everyone. The man from the mountains of northern Italy, who as a small boy had wanted more than anything to be a parish priest, stood on St Peter's balcony on the evening of Saturday, August 26th, 1978 as Pope John Paul I.

Luciani kept the Conclave in session that night. Having sat down to dinner in his previously assigned place, one of his first thoughts was for the over-age excluded cardinals. They had already been given the election result by telephone. Now Luciani invited them into the Conclave for the following morning's Mass.

The Secretariat of State had already prepared a speech which in theory was intended to indicate the direction of the new Papacy, any new Papacy. Luciani took the speech and, retiring to cell 60, altered and amended what had initially been vague statements about love, peace and war to a number of specifics.

The speech was delivered at the end of the Mass of Thanksgiving celebrated the following morning. Luciani pledged his pontificate to the teachings of the Second Vatican Council. He placed a high value on collegiality, the sharing of power with his bishops. He declared that he intended to bring back into force the great discipline of the Church and to this end he gave high priority to the revision of the two codes of Canon

Law. Union with other denominations would be pursued without compromise to the Church's teachings but equally without hesitation.

The central thrust of the speech revealed that this man who described himself in Venice as 'a poor man accustomed to small things, and silence' had a dream: a revolutionary dream. He gave notice of his intention to pursue the pastoralization of the entire Church, indeed of the entire world.

> The world awaits this today; it knows well that the sublime perfection it has attained by research and technology has already reached a peak, beyond which yawns the abyss, blinding the eyes with darkness. It is the temptation of substituting for God one's own decisions, decisions that would prescind from moral laws. The danger for modern man is that he would reduce the earth to a desert, the person to an automaton, brotherly love to planned collectivization, often introducing death where God wishes life.

With the text of *Lumen gentium* (the Light of Nations), Vatican Council's Dogmatic Constitution of the Church, in his hand, Albino Luciani gave notice that he intended to put the Church back where it belonged: back to the world and the words of Christ; back to the simplicity and honesty of its origins. If Christ returned to earth, Luciani wanted him to find a Church he would recognize – one free of political interests, free of the big business mentality which had corroded the original vision.

At noon the new Pope appeared on the central balcony of the Basilica. The square below was packed tight with some 200,000 people. Millions more around the world watched on television as Luciani's smile broadened in response to the thunderous applause. He had come out to say the Angelus but before giving the mid-day prayer he had decided to give his listeners a glimpse into the secret Conclave. When the applause and cheering had died down he promptly broke two Papal rules, the paranoiac secrecy that Paul had sternly insisted upon concerning the Conclave, and the use of the majestic 'we' that for nearly two thousand years had demonstrated Papal aspirations to territory. He smiled at the crowd and then began.

'Yesterday,' the word was followed by an almost imperceptible shrug of the shoulders, as if to say, 'a funny thing happened to me on my way to the Conclave.' The crowd roared with laughter. Luciani joined in the merriment, then began again.

'Yesterday morning I went to the Sistine Chapel to vote peacefully.

Never could I have imagined what was about to take place. As soon as it began to be a danger for me, two of my colleagues who were sitting near me whispered words of encouragement.' Simply and without trace of pomposity he recalled the words of Willebrands and Ribeno. He told the crowd why he had chosen his particular name.

> My thoughts were like this. Pope John had wanted to consecrate me with his own hands here in the Basilica of St Peter's. Then, though unworthy, I succeeded him in the Cathedral of St Mark, in that Venice which is still filled with the spirit of Pope John. The gondoliers remember him, the sisters, everyone. On the other hand Pope Paul not only made me a cardinal, but some months before that, on the wide footbridge in St Mark's Square, he made me blush to the roots of my hair in front of twenty thousand people, because he took off his stole and placed it on my shoulders. I was never so red-faced. Furthermore, in the fifteen years of his pontificate, this Pope showed not only me but the whole world how he loved the Church, how he served it, worked for it, and suffered for this Church of Christ. And so I took the name John Paul.
>
> Be sure of this. I do not have the wisdom of heart of Pope John, nor do I have the preparation and culture of Pope Paul. However, I now stand in their place. I will seek to serve the Church and I hope that you will help me with your prayers.

With those simple, everyday words followed by the Angelus and his Blessing, Pope John Paul I announced his arrival to the world. The warm, enthusiastic response of the Rome crowd was an accurate reflection of the larger, watching world.

Vatican watchers puzzled over the clues to the new Papacy contained in the choice of names. Is he John or is he Paul? One of those who was asked was Cardinal Suenens: 'He will be both in his own way. His manner is closer to John's but it is like mixing oxygen and hydrogen – you get water, two different elements producing a third substance.'

His chosen names hint at a continuity, but the fact that John Paul included the designation 'The First', a convention that is never applied until there is a second of the same name, should have told the Vatican watchers something. What they and the rest of the Church were about to experience related to neither of the new Pope's immediate predecessors. It was unique.

He had not spelled out to the listening world on this his first day, exactly how he intended to make his dream of a poor Church a reality but within hours he embarked on a course of action that was of vital importance if his vision was to be realized.

In the evening of Sunday, August 27th, 1978 he had dinner with Cardinal Jean Villot and asked him to continue, at least for a while, as Secretary of State. Villot accepted. The new Pope also reconfirmed the various cardinals in charge of the departments of the Roman Curia. Having entered the Conclave without any aspirations to become Pope it would have been extraordinary if he had emerged with a prepared list of new Cabinet members.

On August 31st Italy's leading and highly respected economic periodical, *Il Mondo,* addressed a long, open letter to Albino Luciani. The letter asked for Papal intervention to impose 'order and morality' on the Vatican's financial dealings which included 'speculation in unhealthy waters'. The letter, entitled 'Your Holiness, Is It Right?', made a series of slashing attacks on what it saw to be the state of affairs inside the Vatican's financial operations. Accompanying the open letter was a long analysis entitled 'The Wealth of Peter'.

Il Mondo asked Albino Luciani a number of highly relevant questions:

> Is it right for the Vatican to operate in markets like a speculator?
> Is it right for the Vatican to have a Bank whose operations help the illegal transfer of capital from Italy to other countries? Is it right for that Bank to assist Italians in evading tax?

Financial editor Paolo Panerai attacked the Vatican links with Michele Sindona. He attacked Luigi Mennini and Paul Marcinkus of the Vatican Bank and their relationships with 'the most cynical financial dealers in the world, from Sindona to the bosses of the Continental Illinois Bank in Chicago (through which, as Your Holiness's advisers can tell you, all of the Church's investments in the United States are handled)'.

Panerai asked:

> Why does the Church tolerate investments in companies, national and multi-national, whose only aim is profit; companies which, when necessary, are ready to violate and trample upon the human rights of millions of the poor, especially in that Third World which is so close to Your Holiness's heart?

Of Marcinkus the open letter observed:

He is, however, the only Bishop who is on the Board of a Lay Bank, which incidentally has a Branch in one of the great tax havens of the capitalistic world. We mean the Cisalpine Overseas Bank at Nassau in the Bahamas. Using tax havens is permitted by earthly Law, and no lay banker can be hauled into court for taking advantage of that situation (they all do); but perhaps it is not licit under God's Law, which should mark every act of the Church. The Church preaches equality but it does not seem to us that the best way to ensure equality is by evading taxes, which constitute the means by which the Law state tries to promote the same equality.

There was no official reaction from the Vatican, but inside Vatican City the responses ranged from quiet satisfaction felt by those who objected to the activities of the Vatican Bank and the Extraordinary Section of the Administration of the Patrimony of the Holy See (APSA), to anger and resentment from those who considered that the only problem with the Vatican's financial speculations was that they should make even bigger profits.

The Italian newspaper, *La Stampa*, weighed in with another piece entitled 'The Wealth and Powers of the Vatican'. Journalist Lamberto Furno took a largely sympathetic look at Vatican finances and discounted some of the accusations that had been published over the years alleging massive Vatican wealth. But Furno did see a number of pressing problems facing the new Pope, including verification that the Church reforms to achieve a state of poverty, which in Furno's mind had been implemented by Pope John and continued by Pope Paul, had become a reality. This could be achieved only by 'publishing the Vatican budgets'.

Furno concluded:

The Church does not have riches or resources that exceed its needs. But it is necessary to give proof of this. Bernanos has his country Curate observing, 'on sacks of money our Lord has written in his own hand, "Danger of death"'.

The new Pope read these articles with interest. They confirmed in his mind the wisdom of a course he had *already* embarked upon.

Before his election, Luciani had been aware of the many complaints about Vatican finances which had been aired to Cardinal Villot: complaints about the way that Bishop Marcinkus ran the Vatican Bank; complaints about his involvement with Michele Sindona; complaints about the links between the APSA and Sindona. Luciani had personal experience of the manner in which Marcinkus operated the Vatican Bank; experience dating from 1972, when Marcinkus had sold the controlling interest in Banca Cattolica del Veneto to Calvi, without reference to the Patriarch of Venice.

He knew as early as 1972 that there was something terribly wrong with the whole structure and philosophy of Vatican finance but he had been powerless. Now he had the power. On Sunday, August 27th, 1978, as he sat eating dinner with Cardinal Villot, he instructed his newly confirmed Secretary of State to initiate an investigation immediately. There was to be a review of the entire financial operation of the Vatican; a detailed analysis of every aspect. 'No department, no congregation, no section is to be excluded,' Luciani told Villot.

He made it clear that he was particularly concerned with the operation of the Istituto per le Opere di Religione, the Institute for Religious Works, generally known as the Vatican Bank. The financial review was to be done discreetly, quickly, and completely. The new Pope advised his Secretary of State that once he had considered the report he would decide on appropriate courses of action.

Clearly Luciani was a firm believer in practising what he preached. In one of his 'letters' to St Bernard he had discussed the virtue of prudence.

I agree that prudence should be dynamic and urge people to action. But there are three stages to consider: deliberation, decision, and execution.

Deliberation means seeking the means that lead to the end. It is made on the basis of reflection, of advice that has been asked for, of careful examination.

Decision means, after examining the various possible methods, make up your mind to choose one of them . . . Prudence isn't an everlasting see-saw, suspending everything and tearing the mind apart with uncertainty; nor is it waiting in order to decide for the best. It is said that politics is the art of the possible, and in a way that is right.

Execution is the most important of the three: prudence, linked with strength, prevents discouragement in the face of difficulties and impediments. This is the time when a man is shown to be a leader and guide.

Thus Albino Luciani, a man totally committed to the belief that the Roman Catholic Church should be the Church of the poor, set in motion an enquiry into the wealth of the Vatican. He would deliberate, decide, then execute.

Vatican Incorporated

꧁꧂

When Albino Luciani became Head of the Roman Catholic Church in August 1978 he was in command of a truly unique organization. Over 800 million people, nearly one-fifth of the world's population, looked to Luciani as their spiritual leader. Nearer to hand, within Vatican City, was the structure that controlled not only the faith, but the fiscal policy of the Church.

'Vatican Incorporated' is a vital part of this structure. It exists in bricks and mortar. It exists within certain philosophies. Paul Marcinkus of the Vatican Bank is credited with the observation that, 'You can't run the Church on Hail Marys'. Obviously the power of prayer has been devalued along with many of the world's currencies in recent years.

Marcinkus should not be condemned for what might appear to be a materialistic observation. The Church plays many roles in many countries. It needs money. How much money is a different question. What it should be doing with that money is another. That it does much that is good is beyond doubt. That it does much that is highly questionable is also beyond doubt. There is a large quantity of published works which give details of the many charities financed by the Church, of the aid it gives to famine relief, to alleviate suffering of every kind. Education, medicine, food, shelter – these are some of the benefits that derive from the work of the Church. What is lacking is information on how much is acquired and how it is acquired. On these matters the Vatican is and always has been very secretive. That secrecy has inevitably given rise to one of the world's great unsolved mysteries. How much is the Roman Catholic Church worth?

In mid-1970, commenting on a Swiss newspaper article which declared, 'the productive capital of the Vatican can be reckoned at between 50 and 55 billion Swiss francs' (a figure approaching 13 billion dollars), *L'Osservatore Romano* said: 'It is a simply fantastic figure. In reality, the productive capital of the Holy See, including both Deposits and Investments placed both in Italy and outside Italy, is far from reaching one hundredth of this sum.' That would place a ceiling figure on Vatican wealth on July 22nd, 1970, of £46 million or 111 million dollars.

The first falsehood contained in the Vatican newspaper's statement is the exclusion of the assets of the Vatican Bank. It is comparable to asking ICI or Du Pont for complete disclosure and being favoured with the total in the petty cash box. Even excluding the annual profits of the Vatican Bank, the figure quoted by the Vatican is an outrageous lie. It was a lie that over the years was to be heard again. In April 1975 Lamberto Furno of *La Stampa* asked His Eminence Cardinal Vagnozzi: 'If I were to put forward the sum of 300 billion lire for the productive patrimony of the five administrations,* would I be close to the mark?'

Furno was deliberately excluding the Vatican Bank in his question. He drew from Vagnozzi the assertion, 'I tell you, the productive patrimony of the Holy See, in Italy and in the world, is less than a quarter of the sum you mention.'

If that were true it would follow that on April 1st, 1975 the productive wealth† of the Holy See, excluding the Vatican Bank, was a figure lower than 75 billion lire or approximately 113 million dollars. One single administration, the Extraordinary Section of the Administration of the Patrimony of the Holy See, or the APSA, is treated as a central bank by the World Bank, the International Monetary Fund and the Bank of International Settlements at Basle. Every year the staff at Basle publish annual figures which show what the world's central banks have deposited or borrowed from other banks in the Group of Ten. Their figures for 1975 indicate that the Vatican had 120 million dollars on deposit in foreign banks and that, uniquely, the Vatican was debtless, the only bank in the entire world to be in such a position. This was just one administration

---

*1 The ordinary Section of the Administration of the Patrimony of the Holy See (APSA) and the extraordinary Section of the Administration of the Patrimony of the Holy See, again usually abbreviated to APSA. 2 The Governorship of the Vatican City State. 3 The Prefecture for Economic Affairs. 4 St Peter's Workshop. 5 Propaganda Fide.

†I.e. income-producing assets. The Vatican makes a distinction between productive and non-productive wealth, an example of the latter being the Vatican art treasures.

In God's Name

within the Vatican and to ascertain the entire actual wealth of just that one section a great many other tangible assets must be added.

Like Rome itself, Vatican wealth was not built in a day. The problem of a wealthy Church – and all who aspire to follow the teachings of Jesus Christ must regard that wealth as a problem – has its roots as early as the fourth century. When the Roman Emperor Constantine converted to Christianity and gave colossal wealth to the then Pope, Silvester I, he created the first rich Pope. Dante ends the *Inferno* with the lines:

> Alas! Constantine, how much misfortune you caused,
> Not by becoming Christian, but by the dowry
> Which the first rich Father accepted from you.

The Catholic faith's claim to uniqueness is valid. It is the only religious organization in the world which has as its headquarters an independent State, Vatican City, which is a law unto itself. At 108.7 acres it is smaller than many of the world's golf courses, is the size of St James's Park in London and approximately one eighth the size of Central Park in New York City. A leisurely stroll right round Vatican City takes something over an hour. To count the wealth of the Vatican would take rather longer.

The modern wealth of the Vatican is based on the generosity of Benito Mussolini. The Lateran Treaty which his government concluded with the Vatican in 1929 gave the Roman Catholic Church a variety of guarantees and measures of protection.

The Holy See obtained recognition of itself as a Sovereign State. It was exempted from paying taxes both for its properties and its citizens, exempted from paying duty on imported goods; it had diplomatic immunity and accompanying privileges for its own diplomats and those accredited to it by foreign powers. Mussolini guaranteed the introduction of Catholic religious teaching in all State High Schools and the entire institution of marriage was placed under Canon Law, which ruled out divorce. The benefits for the Vatican were many, not least the fiscal ones.

> Article one. Italy undertakes to pay the Holy See, on the ratification of the Treaty, the sum of 750 million lire and to hand over at the same time Consolidated 5 per cent State Bonds to the bearer for the nominal value of one billion lire.

At the 1929 rate of exchange this package represented 81 million dollars. A 1984 equivalent figure is approximately 500 million dollars. Vatican Incorporated was in business. It has never looked back.

To handle the windfall, Pope Pius XI created on June 7th, 1929 The Special Administration. He appointed to run the Department the layman Bernardino Nogara. Apart from having many millions of dollars to play with, Nogara had another very important asset. One hundred years earlier the Roman Catholic Church had completely reversed its position on money lending. The Church can rightfully claim to have changed the meaning of the word usury.

In the classic sense usury means *all* gains from money lending. For over eighteen hundred years the Roman Catholic Church had dogmatically stated that the charging of any interest on a loan was absolutely forbidden as being contrary to Divine Law. The prohibition was restated in various Church Councils: Arles (AD 314), Nicea (325), Carthage (345), Aix (789), Lateran (1139) – at this Council usurers were condemned to excommunication – various State Laws made the practice legal. It was still heresy, that is, until 1830. Thus, by courtesy of the Roman Catholic Church, usury now means lending money at exorbitant rates of interest.

Self-interest produced a total reversal on the Church's teaching with regard to money lending. Perhaps if celibacy was no longer the rule for priests it might move the Roman Catholic Church's teaching on birth control.

Nogara was a member of a devout Roman Catholic family; many of its members made in a variety of ways significant contributions to the Church. Three of his brothers became priests, another became director of the Vatican Museum but Bernardino Nogara's contribution was by any standards the most profound.

Born in Bellano, near Lake Como, in 1870, he achieved early success as a mineralogist in Turkey. In 1912 he played a leading role in the peace treaty of Ouchy between Italy and Turkey. In 1919 he was again a member of the Italian delegation that negotiated the peace treaty between Italy, France, Britain and Germany. He subsequently worked on behalf of the Italian Government as a delegate to the Banca Commerciale in Istanbul. When Pope Pius XI was seeking a man capable of administering the fruits of the Lateran Treaty, his close friend and confidant Monsignor Nogara suggested his brother Bernardino. With that selection Pius XI struck pure gold.

Nogara was reluctant to accept the job and did so only when Pope Pius XI agreed to certain conditions. Nogara did not wish to be trammelled by any traditional views the Church might still hold about making money. The ground rules Nogara insisted upon included the following:

1 Any investments he chose to make should be totally and completely free of any religious or doctrinal considerations.
2 He would be free to invest Vatican funds anywhere in the world.

The Pope agreed, and opened the doors to currency speculation, and to playing the market in the Stock Exchange, including the buying of shares in companies whose products were inconsistent with Roman Catholic teaching. Items such as bombs, tanks, guns, and contraceptives might be condemned in the pulpit but the shares Nogara bought for the Vatican in companies which manufactured these items helped to fill the coffers in St Peter's.

Nogara played the gold market and the futures market. He bought Italgas, sole supplier of gas in many of Italy's cities, placing on the Board on behalf of the Vatican Francesco Pacelli. Pacelli's brother became, in time, the next Pope (Pius XII) and the nepotism which stemmed from that Papacy was manifest throughout Italy. The rule became 'if there is a Pacelli on the Board, six to four it belongs to the Vatican'.

Among the banks that came under Vatican influence and control through Nogara's purchases were Banco di Roma, Banco di Santo Spirito and Cassa di Risparmio di Roma. The man clearly not only had a way with money, he was fairly gifted in the art of persuasion. When Banco di Roma was floundering and threatening to take with it a large amount of Vatican money, Nogara persuaded Mussolini to take over the bank's largely worthless securities and transfer them to a Government holding company, IRI. Mussolini also agreed that the Vatican should he reimbursed, not at the current market value of the securities, which was virtually nil, but at their original purchase price. IRI paid Banco di Roma over 630 million dollars. The loss was written off by the Italian treasury, which is another way of saying the ordinary people picked up the bill, just as they had been doing for the clerics since the Middle Ages.

Much of the speculation Nogara indulged in on behalf of the Vatican certainly contravened Canon Law and probably Civil Law, but as his client was the Pope, who was not asking questions, Nogara remained untroubled by such niceties.

Using Vatican capital, Nogara acquired significant and often controlling shares in company after company. Having acquired a company he rarely sat on the Board, preferring to nominate one of the trusted Vatican elite to look after the Church's interests.

The three nephews of Pius XII, Princes Carlo, Marcantonio and Giulio Pacelli, were among the inner elite whose names began to appear as directors on an ever-growing list of companies. These were the Church's 'uomini di fiducia', men of trust.

Textiles. Telephone communications. Railways. Cement. Electricity. Water. Bernardino Nogara was everywhere. When Mussolini needed armaments for his invasion of Ethiopia in 1935, a substantial proportion was supplied by a munitions plant which Nogara had acquired on behalf of the Vatican.

Realizing, before many, the inevitability of the Second World War, Nogara moved part of the assets then at his disposal into gold. He bought 26.8 million dollars' worth of gold at 35 dollars per ounce. Later he sold 5 million dollars' worth on the free market. The profit on the sale was in excess of the 26.8 million dollars he had paid for the entire original quantity. His speculations in gold continued throughout his control of Vatican Incorporated: 15.9 million dollars' worth bought between 1945 and 1953; 2 million dollars' worth sold between 1950 and 1952. My research indicates that 17.3 million dollars' worth of that original purchase is still held on deposit on behalf of the Vatican at Fort Knox. At the current market price that 17.3 million dollars, originally purchased at 35 dollars per ounce, is now worth a figure approaching 230 million dollars.

In 1933 Vatican Incorporated again demonstrated its ability to negotiate successfully with Fascist governments. The Concordat of 1929 with Mussolini was followed with a Concordat between the Holy See and Hitler's Reich. Solicitor Francesco Pacelli had been one of the key figures in the Mussolini agreement; his brother Cardinal Eugenio Pacelli, the future Pius XII, had a leading role as the Vatican's Secretary of State in concluding a treaty with Nazi Germany.

Hitler saw many potential benefits in the treaty, not least the fact that Pacelli, a man already displaying marked pro-Nazi attitudes, might prove a useful ally in the approaching World War. History was to prove that Hitler's assessment was accurate. Despite a great deal of world pressure, Pope Pius XII declined to excommunicate either Hitler or Mussolini. Perhaps his refusal was based on an awareness of just how irrelevant he was. His was a Papacy which affected neutrality, which talked to the German episcopate about 'just wars' and did precisely the same to the French bishops. This resulted in the French bishops supporting France and the German bishops supporting Germany. His was a Papacy which declined to condemn the Nazi invasion of Poland because, he said, 'We cannot forget that there are forty million Catholics in the Reich. What would they be exposed to after such an act by the Holy See?'

For the Vatican, one of the major assets to emerge from the very lucrative deal with Hitler was confirmation of the 'Kirchensteuer', Church Tax. This is a State tax which is still deducted at source from all wage-earners in Germany. One can opt out by renouncing one's religion. In practice few choose to. This tax represents between 8 and 10 per cent on income tax collected by the German Government. The money is handed over to the Protestant and Catholic Churches. Substantial amounts derived from the Kirchensteuer began to flow to the Vatican in the years immediately preceding the Second World War. The flow continued throughout the war, 100 million dollars in 1943, for example. In the Vatican Nogara put the German revenue to work alongside the other currencies which were pouring in.

On June 27th, 1942, Pope Pius XII decided to bring another part of the Vatican into the modern world and into the ambit of Bernardino Nogara. He changed the name of the Administration of Religious Works to the Institute for Religious Works. The change did not capture the front pages of the world's newspapers; they were rather preoccupied with the Second World War. The IOR, or the Vatican Bank as it is known by all but the Vatican, was born. 'Vatican Incorporated' had sired a bastard child. The original function of the Administration, set up by Pope Leo XIII in 1887, had been to gather and administer funds for religious works; it was in no sense a bank. Under Pius, its function became 'the custody and administration of monies (in bonds and cash) and properties transferred or entrusted to the Institute itself by fiscal or legal persons for the purposes of religious works, and works of Christian piety'. It was, and is, in every sense a bank.

Nogara took to reading the terms of the Lateran Treaty very closely, particularly Clauses 29, 30 and 31 of the Concordat. These dealt with tax exemptions and the formation of new, tax-exempt 'ecclesiastical corporations' over which the Italian State would have no control. Interesting discussions began about the meaning of the phrase 'ecclesiastical corporations'. Doubtless distracted by other events of the time, Mussolini took a liberal view. On December 31st, 1942, the Finance Ministry of the Italian Government issued a circular stating that the Holy See was exempt from paying the tax on share dividends.

It was signed by the then Director General of the Ministry, who was called quite appropriately Buoncristiano (Good Christian). The circular specified the various organizations within the Holy See which were exempt from the tax. The list was long and included The Special Administration and the Vatican Bank.

The man whom Nogara selected to control the Vatican Bank was Father, later Cardinal, Alberto di Jorio. Already functioning as Nogara's assistant in The Special Administration, he kept a foot in both sections by retaining that position and assuming the role of First Secretary, then President, of the Vatican Bank. Apart from the controlling interests in many banks outside the Vatican walls which Nogara acquired, he now had two in-house banks to play with.

Nogara, applying his mind to the task of increasing the Vatican's funds, went from strength to strength. The tentacles of 'Vatican Incorporated' spread world wide. Close links were forged with an array of banks. Rothschilds of Paris and London had been doing business with the Vatican since the early nineteenth century. With Nogara at the Vatican's helm the business increased dramatically: Crédit Suisse, Hambros, Morgan Guarantee, The Bankers Trust Company of New York – useful when Nogara wanted to buy and sell stock on Wall Street – the Chase Manhattan, and Continental Bank of Illinois among others, became Vatican partners.

Nogara was evidently not a man with whom to play Monopoly. Apart from banks, he acquired for the Vatican controlling interests in companies in the fields of insurance, steel, financing, flour and spaghetti, mechanical industry, cement and real estate. With regard to the last named his purchase of at least 15 per cent of the Italian giant Immobiliare gave the Church a share of an astonishing array of property. Società Generale Immobiliare is Italy's oldest construction company. Through its ownership of the building firm SOGENE, Immobiliare, and therefore to a significant degree the Vatican, owned after its 15 per cent acquisition: the Rome Hilton; Italo Americana Nuovi Alberghi; Alberghi Ambrosiani, Milan; Compagnia Italiana Alberghi Cavalieri; and Soc. Italiani Alberghi Moderni. These are just the major hotels in Italy. The list of major buildings and industrial companies also owned is twice as long.

In France they built a huge block of offices and shops at 90 Avenue des Champs Elysées, another at 61 Rue de Ponthieu, and another at 6 Rue de Berry.

In Canada they owned the world's tallest skyscraper – the Stock Exchange Tower situated in Montreal – the Port Royal tower, a 224-apartment block, a huge residential area in Greensdale, Montreal . . .

In the United States they had five huge apartment blocks in Washington, including the Watergate Hotel, and in New York a residential area of 277 acres situated at Oyster Bay.

In Mexico they owned an entire satellite city of Mexico City called Lomas Verdes.

This list of properties is by no means exhaustive. Nogara also bought into General Motors, Shell, Gulf Oil, General Electric, Bethlehem Steel, IBM and TWA. If the shares moved, and moved upwards, it was men like Nogara who created the movement.

Although Nogara retired in 1954, he continued to give the Vatican his unique brand of financial advice until his death in 1958. Scant mention was made of the man's passing by the Press, as the majority of his activities on behalf of the Roman Catholic Church had been cloaked in secrecy. This one man who demonstrated that, wherever Christ's Kingdom might be, that of the Catholic Church was most assuredly of this world, was given a memorable epitaph by Cardinal Spellman of New York. 'Next to Jesus Christ the greatest thing that has happened to the Catholic Church is Bernardino Nogara.'

Starting with 80 million dollars, less the 30 million dollars that Pius XI and his successor Pius XII held back to spend on regional seminaries and parish houses in South Italy, the building of Santa Maria and the massive building projects in Rome, including the setting up of the Vatican library and art gallery, Nogara had created Vatican Incorporated. Between 1929 and 1939 he had also had access to the annual world-wide collection of Peter's Pence. With the 'pennies' of the faithful plus the lire from Mussolini and the Deutschemarks from Hitler, he handed on to his successors a complex array of financial interests worth at a very conservative estimate 500 million dollars controlled by the Special Administration, 650 million dollars controlled by the Ordinary Section of the APSA, and assets in the Vatican Bank in excess of 940 million dollars, with an annual profit from the Bank averaging 40 million dollars going directly to the Pope. In capitalistic terms, Nogara's service in the cause of the Roman Catholic Church was an incredible success. Viewed in the light of the message contained in the Gospels it was an unmitigated disaster. The Vicar of Christ was now Chairman of the Board.

Four years after Nogara's death in 1958 the Vatican had urgent need of his expertize. The Italian Government of the day had raised the spectre of taxing share dividends again. What followed has a direct bearing on a sequence of disasters for the Vatican, including Mafia involvement, financial mayhem and murder. That would begin in 1968.

In any list of years purporting to be the worst in the Church's history, 1968 should feature very near the top. It was the year of *Humanae Vitae*. It was also the year when The Gorilla and The Shark, as they were known, were let loose on the two Vatican banks. The Gorilla is Paul Marcinkus; the Shark, Michele Sindona; and the events which led to their control of Vatican finances make salutary reading.

Benjamin Franklin said, 'But in this world nothing can be said to be certain except death and taxes.' Not many have chosen to argue with that statement. Among the few who have are the men who control the Vatican's finances. They have made strenuous attempts to eliminate taxes.

In December 1962 the Italian Government passed legislation taxing the profits on share dividends. Initially the tax was set at 15 per cent. Then it went the way of all taxes and was doubled.

The Vatican at first raised no objection to paying the tax, at least not publicly. Privately, through diplomatic channels, it advised the Italian Government that: 'In the spirit of our Concordat and considering the Law of 2nd October 1942, it would be desirable that a favourable treatment be granted to the Holy See.' Negotiations had begun.

The secret letter from Vatican Secretary of State, Cardinal Cicognani, to the Italian Ambassador to the Holy See, Bartolomeo Mignone, goes on to detail exactly what the 'favourable treatment' should be: tax exemption for a list of departments as long as a cardinal's arm, including of course the two Vatican banks, The Special Administration and the IOR.

The Vatican wanted to play the market but not to pay for the privilege. The minority Vatican-backed Christian Democrat Government of the day touched its forelock, kissed the Papal ring and agreed to the Vatican's request. No reference was made to the Italian Parliament or to public opinion. When the minority Government fell, to be replaced by Christian Democrat Aldo Moro with a coalition of Christian Democrats and Socialists, the post of Finance Minister went to Socialist Roberto Tremelloni. He was disinclined to approve what was clearly an illegal agreement made by his predecessor, made furthermore without being ratified by Parliament and, even more important, made eight days after the government had resigned.

Aldo Moro, confronted with a Finance Minister threatening to resign on the one hand and an intransigent Vatican on the other, sought a compromise. He asked the Vatican to submit a statement of its share-holdings as a prelude to obtaining exemption. Not unreasonably, the Prime Minister felt that the Italian nation should know of just how much money they were being deprived. The Vatican refused to reveal the details and talked loudly about being a Sovereign State. Apparently it is perfectly permissible to exploit the stock market of another Sovereign State and make profits from the exploitation, but the exploited State is not allowed to know by just how much it is being exploited.

Various governments came and went. The issue was discussed from time to time in the Italian Parliament. At one point in 1964 the Vatican indicated just how far they had abandoned Christ's dictum 'my kingdom is not of this earth' and had embraced instead the teachings of Bernardino Nogara: 'Increase the size of your Company because fiscal controls on the part of Government become advantageously difficult.' The 'Company' to which Nogara was referring was Vatican Incorporated, the 'Government' those unfortunates across the Tiber, who were obliged to deal with an off-shore tax-haven in the middle of Rome.

In June 1964, with Aldo Moro yet again in power, the Church of the poor threatened to bring down the entire Italian economy. During negotiations Vatican officals told the Italian Government that if they did not get their way they would throw on to the market every single share they held in Italy. They picked their moment well. The Italian Stock Market was going through a particularly bad period, with shares dropping daily. Suddenly to place on the market the enormous share-holdings of the Vatican would have destroyed the entire Italian economy. The Italian Government, faced with this reality, capitulated. In October 1964 a draft Bill was prepared which would ratify the illegal agreement.

The draft Bill was never put before Parliament, mainly because Governments were collapsing quicker than various Finance Ministers could discover what was in their pending trays. Meanwhile the Vatican continued to enjoy tax exemption. It had not paid tax on its shares since April 1963. In 1967 the Italian Press, specifically the left-wing Press, went on to the attack. They wanted to know why. They also wanted to know how much. They also wanted to know how many shares the Vatican held in their country. Figures began to fly. They ranged from estimates that put the worth of the Vatican investment on the Italian Stock Exchange at 160 million dollars to others that put it at 2.4 billion dollars.

In March 1967, the then Italian Finance Minister, Luigi Preti, in response to questions in the Italian Senate, threw some official light on the Vatican's shareholdings in Italy. His breakdown showed that by far the biggest Vatican investor was the IOR, followed by The Special Administration. Various other Vatican Departments with high-sounding names such as The Fabric of St Peter's, The Pontifical Society for St Peter Apostle, the Administration of the Holy See Patrimony, and Propaganda Fide were also revealed as players of the Stock Market. Finance Minister Preti stated that the Vatican owned shares worth approximately 100 billion lire, 104.4 million dollars, at the then rate of exchange. The actual total figure was undoubtedly much higher. Preti's figures did not take account of the large Vatican investment in State Bonds and Debentures which are completely exempt from any form of taxation. He was dealing only with shares that were liable for the tax levy.

Neither did the Finance Minister concern himself with the fact that under Italian Stock Exchange regulations, the holder of shares is allowed to leave the dividends uncollected for five years. Evidence indicates that the Vatican investments covered by these two aspects were, at the very least, as great as those that had come under the Minister's province. The real value, therefore, of the Vatican investment in 1968 in Italian shares alone is at the very minimum 202.2 million dollars. Added to that should be the value of the Vatican's real estate holdings, particularly in Rome and the surrounding districts, and also all non-Italian investments.

Eventually Italy decided to call the Vatican's bluff: the Roman Catholic Church should, at least in Italy, render unto Caesar what was Caesar's. In January 1968 yet another transitory Government led by Giovanni Leone declared that at the end of the year the Vatican would have to pay up. With considerable ill grace and comments about its investments being a wonderful stimulus for the Italian economy, the Vatican agreed – but in typical Vatican fashion. Like the prisoner in the dock found guilty, it asked for time to pay in easy instalments.

The whole affair had a number of unfortunate results for the Vatican. Whatever the actual total, everyone in Italy was now aware that the Church of the poor had very large investments producing millions of dollars of annual profit. Further, the six-year-old argument had resulted in many companies being identified as Vatican owned or controlled. The wide portfolio might indicate shrewd capitalism, but it was bad public relations to let the man who complained that his phone/water/electricity/gas were not working, know that he had the

Church to thank for it. Then, most important of all, if the Vatican maintained its heavy investment in Italy it was going to face very large tax bills. Pope Paul VI had a problem. The men he turned to for the solution were The Gorilla and The Shark.

If Sigmund Freud's conclusion that a man's entire personality is formed in the first five years of life is correct, then Paul Marcinkus merits particularly close study by the experts. Even if one disputes Freud's opinion few would argue with the view that environment is certainly a major influence in the formative years.

Marcinkus was born into a city ruled by the Mafia, where gangland murder was an everyday event; where corruption reached from the Mayor to the pre-pubescent youth. It was a city riddled with every conceivable type of crime, in which, between 1919 and 1960, 976 gangland murders were committed and only two of the murderers convicted. It was a city where in the autumn of 1928 the President of the Crime Commission appealed to one man to ensure that the forth-coming November elections were conducted in an honest, democratic manner. The man in question was Al Capone; the city, Chicago. Capone boasted, 'I own the police'. A more accurate statement would have been, 'I own the city'. Capone responded to the plea for fair elections. He told the police of America's second largest city what to do and the police obeyed. The President of the Crime Commission later observed: 'It turned out to be the squarest and the most successful election day in forty years. There was not one complaint, not one election fraud and no threat of trouble all day.'

Paul Marcinkus was born in the suburb of Cicero, Illinois on January 15th, 1922. The following year Al Capone, confronted with the extraordinary spectacle of an honest Mayor and an equally honest Chief of Police in Chicago, moved his headquarters to Cicero. The population of some 60,000, mainly first and second generation Poles, Bohemians and Lithuanians, became accustomed to the sight of the Mafia in their midst. Capone set up headquarters at the Hawthorne Inn at 4833 Twenty-second Street. Along with Capone came such gentlemen as Jake 'Greasy Thumb' Guzik, Tony 'Mops' Volpi, Frank 'The Enforcer' Nitti, Frankie 'The Millionaire Newsboy' Pope.

This was the Cicero in which Paul Casimir Marcinkus grew up. His parents were Lithuanian immigrants. His father earned a living cleaning those windows that were not being smashed by machine gun bullets, and his mother worked in a bakery. Their grasp of the English language was poor. In the classic manner of many of the poor immigrants who sought a better life in the land of the free, they determined that their children through honest endeavour and hard work should have better lives. Marcinkus, the youngest of their five children, succeeded beyond their wildest dreams. His is the story of local boy makes God's banker.

Guided by his parish priest, Marcinkus developed a vocation for the priesthood. He was ordained in 1947, the year Al Capone died of syphilis. The Catholic burial of America's all-time Public Enemy Number One in Chicago was officiated by Monsignor William Gorman, who explained to reporters: 'The Church never condones evil, nor the evil in any man's life. This very brief ceremony is to recognize his (Capone's) penitence and the fact that he died fortified by the Sacraments of the Church.'

Marcinkus went to Rome and studied at the same Catholic University, the Gregorian, at which Albino Luciani had obtained his degree. Marcinkus was equally successful and obtained his doctorate in Canon Law. During his seminarian days, he had used his 6 ft 3 ins of height and his 16-stone of brawn with considerable success on the playing fields. When he went in for the ball during a football match, he usually came out with it. His physical strength was to prove a decided asset in his rise to the top. Clearly some of the lessons learned on the streets of Cicero paid off.

Returning to Chicago he worked as a parish priest, then became a member of the Ecclesiastical Court of the Diocese. One of the first to be impressed with Marcinkus was the then Head of the Archdiocese of Chicago, Cardinal Samuel Stritch. After a recommendation from the Cardinal, Marcinkus was transferred to the English section of the Vatican Secretary of State's office in 1952. Tours of duty attached to the Papal Nuncios of Bolivia and Canada followed, then in 1959 he returned to Rome and the Secretary of State's Department. His fluency in Spanish and Italian ensured his constant employment as an interpreter.

In 1963 the Cardinal of New York, Francis Spellman, advised Pope Paul during one of his frequent trips to Rome that Marcinkus was a priest with an excellent potential. In view of the fact that Spellman headed the wealthiest diocese in the world at that time, and was frequently referred to as 'Cardinal Moneybags' – a tribute to his financial genius – the Pope began quietly to monitor Paul Marcinkus.

In 1964, during a visit to down-town Rome, the over-enthusiastic crowds were in danger of trampling the Vicar of Christ underfoot. Suddenly Marcinkus appeared. Using shoulders, elbows and hands he physically clove a path through the crowds for the frightened Pope.

The following day the Pope summoned him for personal thanks. From then on he became the unofficial bodyguard to the Pope and his nickname, The Gorilla, was born.

In December 1964 he accompanied Pope Paul to India; the following year to the United Nations. By now Marcinkus had taken over the duties of security adviser on such trips. Personal bodyguard. Personal security adviser. Personal translator. The boy from Cicero had come far. He was by now a close friend of the Pope's personal secretary, Father Pasquale Macchi. Macchi was a key member of the Papal entourage, which the Roman Curia referred to as 'The Milan Mafia'. When the Archbishop of Milan, Montini, was elected Pope in 1963 he had brought with him a whole train of advisers, financiers, clerics. Macchi was one of the entourage. All roads may lead to Rome; a number go via Milan. The dependence that the Pope placed upon men like Macchi was out of all proportion to their official positions. Macchi would berate the Pope when he considered him morbid or depressed. He would tell him when to go to bed, who should be promoted, who should be punished with an uncomfortable transfer. Having tucked His Holiness up at nights Macchi could invariably be found in an excellent restaurant just off the Piazza Gregono Settimo. His usual companion for dinner was Marcinkus.

Further trips abroad with 'The Pilgrim Pope' to Portugal in May 1967 and to Turkey in July of the same year cemented the friendship of Pope Paul and Marcinkus. Later that year Pope Paul VI created a Department called the Prefecture of the Economic Affairs of the Holy See. A more comprehensible title would have been Chancellor of the Exchequer or Auditor General. What the Pope sought was a department that would be able to produce an annual summary of the exact state of Vatican wealth and the progress of all assets and liabilities of every Administration of the Holy See, with a view to obtaining figures in black and white which would give a final balance or estimate for each year. From its creation the Department has struggled under two very serious handicaps. Firstly, on Pope Paul's express instructions the Vatican Bank was specifically excluded from the economic exercise. Secondly, there was Vatican paranoia.

After the Department had been established by a trio of cardinals, the man subsequently appointed to run it was Cardinal Egidio Vagnozzi. In theory he should have been able after a maximum of one year in the job to provide the Pope with the exact state of Vatican finances. In practice Vagnozzi found that the manic desire for financial secrecy which the various Vatican departments frequently demonstrate to enquiring journalists, was extended to him. The Congregation of the Clergy wanted to keep its figures to itself. So did the APSA. So did they all. In 1969 Cardinal Vagnozzi observed to a colleague: 'It would take a combination of the KGB, the CIA and Interpol to obtain just an inkling of how much and where the monies are.'

To assist Bernardino Nogara's aging colleague, the 84-year-old Cardinal Alberto di Jono, who was still functioning as Head of the Vatican Bank, Pope Paul consecrated as bishop, Paul Marcinkus. The morning after Marcinkus had prostrated himself at the feet of the Pope he took over as the Vatican Bank's Secretary. For all practical purposes he was now running the Bank. Interpreting for President Johnson when he talked to the Pope had been relatively easy but, as Marcinkus freely admitted, 'I have no banking experience'. The virgin banker had arrived. From being an obscure priest in Cicero, Paul Marcinkus had risen higher and further in terms of real power than any American before him.

One of the men who had assisted the rise of Paul Marcinkus was Giovanni Benelli. His initial assessment to Pope Paul of the golf-playing, cigar-chewing, extrovert from Cicero was that Marcinkus would be a valuable asset to the Vatican Bank. Within two years Benelli concluded that he had made a disastrous misjudgement and that Marcinkus should be removed immediately. He discovered that in that brief period Marcinkus had built himself a power base stronger than his own. When the final showdown came in 1977 it was Benelli who left the Vatican.

The extraordinary promotion of Marcinkus was part of a carefully planned change of Vatican policy. Paying large amounts of tax on share profits and having a high profile as an owner of countless Italian companies was now decidedly passé for Vatican Incorporated, particularly when those companies made embarrassing little items such as the contraceptive pill, on which Pope Paul had just invoked the wrath of God. The Pope and his advisers had taken the decision to reduce their commitments in the Italian money markets and transfer the bulk of Vatican wealth to the foreign markets, particularly the USA. They also wished to move into the highly lucrative world of Eurodollar blue chips and off-shore profits.

Marcinkus was selected as an essential component in this strategy. The Pope used another part of his 'Milan Mafia' to complete the team. He chose a man who actually was Mafia, not from Milan, which was merely his adopted city. 'The Shark' was born in Patti near Messina, Sicily. His name – Michele Sindona.

Like Albino Luciani, Michele Sindona knew poverty as a child and like Luciani he was deeply affected and influenced by that environment. While the former grew to manhood determined to relieve the poverty of others, the latter resolved to relieve others of their wealth.

Born on May 8th, 1920 and educated by the Jesuits, Sindona demonstrated early in life a marked proclivity for mathematics and economics. Having graduated from Messina University with an excellent Law degree, in 1942 he avoided conscription in Mussolini's armed forces with the aid of a distant relation of his fiancée who worked in the Vatican Secretariat of State, one Monsignor Amleto Tondini.

During the last three years of the Second World War, Sindona put his Law degree to one side and earned a very lucrative living doing what he would ultimately become world famous for: buying and selling. He bought food on the Black Market in Palermo and smuggled it with the aid of the Mafia to Messina, where it was sold to the starving population.

After June 1943 and the Allied landings, Sindona turned to the American Forces for his supplies. As business expanded so did his Mafia connections. In 1946 he left Sicily for Milan, taking with him his young wife Rina, invaluable lessons in the law of supply and demand, and a number of even more invaluable letters of introduction from the Archbishop of Messina, whose friendship Sindona had carefully cultivated.

In Milan he lived in the suburbs at Affori, and worked for a business consultancy and accounting firm. Sindona's speciality, as American capital began to flow into Italy, was to show would-be investors how to dance their way through Italy's complex tax laws. His Mafia associates were suitably impressed with his progress. He was talented, ambitious, and, more important in the eyes of the Mafia, he was also ruthless, totally corruptible and one of their own. He knew the importance of Mafia traditions like 'omertá', the rule of silence. He was Sicilian.

The Mafia family Gambino were particularly taken with the young Sindona and his dexterity at placing dollar investments without reference to tiresome tax regulations. The Gambino family has global interests but its two main power centres are New York and Palermo. The former is controlled by the Gambinos, the latter by their Sicilian cousins the Inzerillos. On November 2nd, 1957 there was a 'family' reunion in the Grand Hotel des Palmes, Palermo. Also invited to enjoy the wine and food was Michele Sindona.

The Gambino family made Sindona an offer he accepted with enthusiasm. They wanted him to manage the family's re-investment of the huge profits just beginning to accrue from the sales of heroin. They needed a laundryman. Sindona, with his proven abilities at moving amounts of money in and out of Italy without disturbing the tranquillity of the Government's taxation departments, was an ideal choice. Added to this ability was the fact that he was by the time of this Mafia summit conference already a director of an increasing number of companies. He frequently said to grateful clients, 'No, I'll take payment in some shares in your company'. He had also begun to perfect the technique of acquiring troubled companies, dividing them up, selling off pieces, merging other pieces, shuffling everything sideways and then selling at a large profit. It was dazzling to behold, particularly if you were not paying the conjuror.

Within seventeen months of the Mafia summit conference Sindona bought his first bank, aided by Mafia funding. Sindona had already discovered one of the cardinal rules of theft: the best way to steal from a bank is to buy one.

Sindona created a Liechtenstein holding company, Fasco AG. Shortly afterwards Fasco acquired the Milanese Banca Privata Finanziaria, usually called BPF. Founded in 1930 by a Fascist ideologist, the BPF was a small, very private, exclusive institution which served as a conduit for the illegal transfer of funds from Italy on behalf of a favoured few. It was doubtless this proud heritage that won Sindona's heart. Though disdaining to fight for Mussolini Michele Sindona was a natural Fascist. It would have appealed to him to acquire such a bank.

In 1959, the same year in which he acquired BPF, Sindona made another very shrewd investment. The Archbishop of Milan was trying to raise money for an old people's home. Sindona stepped in and raised the entire amount: 2.4 million dollars. When Cardinal Giovanni Battista Montini opened the Casa della Madonnina, Sindona was by his side. The two men became firm friends, with Montini relying more and more on Sindona's advice on problems other than diocesan investments.

What Cardinal Montini may not have known is that the 2.4 million dollars were supplied to Sindona very largely from two sources: the Mafia and the CIA. Former CIA agent Victor Marchetti was later to reveal:

In the 1950s and the 1960s the CIA gave economic support to many activities promoted by the Catholic Church, from orphanages to the missions. Millions of dollars each year were given to

a great number of Bishops and Monsignors. One of them was
Cardinal Giovanni Battista Montini. It is possible that Cardinal
Montini did not know where the money was coming from. He
may have thought it was coming from friends.

'Friends', who as part of their determination to stop Italy voting into
power a Communist Government, not only poured many millions of
dollars into the country but were also prepared to smile benignly upon
men like Michele Sindona. He might well be a criminal of growing
significance but at least he was a right-wing criminal.

The Shark began to swim faster. The Milanese, who as a breed are
inclined to be dismissive about the Romans, let alone the Sicilians, had
initially disregarded this quietly spoken, polite man from the South.
After a while the financial circles of the city which is the financial
capital of Italy conceded that Sindona was a fairly bright tax
consultant. When he began to acquire a company here and there they
put it down to beginner's luck. By the time he had become a bank
owner and confidant of the man many were tipping as the next Pope,
it was too late to stop him. His progress was irresistible. Again through
his holding company, Fasco, he acquired the Banca di Messina. This
move particularly pleased the Mafia families Gambino and Inzerillo,
giving them as it did, unlimited access to a bank in Sicily, in Sindona's
own home province.

Sindona forged close links with Massimo Spada, one of the
Vatican's trusted men, Administrative Secretary of the Vatican Bank
and on the Board of twenty-four companies including Banca Cattolica
del Veneto on behalf of the Vatican. Luigi Mennini, another top
Vatican bank official, also became a close friend. Father Macchi,
Montini's secretary, yet another. Banca Privata began to flower. In
March 1965, Sindona sold 22 per cent to Hambros Bank of London.
Hambros, with their long-standing close links with Vatican finances,
considered Sindona's direction of the funds flowing into BPF
'brilliant'. So did the Gambino and Inzerillo families. So did
Continental Bank of Illinois, who also bought 22 per cent of the bank
from Sindona. Continental were by now the major conduit for all USA
investment by the Vatican. The bonds Sindona was placing around
himself and the various Vatican elements were now multi-layered. He
became a close friend of Monsignor Sergio Guerri. Guerri had taken
over the responsibility of running Nogara's monolithic creation, The
Special Administration.

In 1964, Sindona had acquired yet another bank, this time in

Switzerland, the Banque de Financement in Geneva, Finabank. Largely owned by the Vatican it was, like his first bank, little more than an illegal conduit for the flight of money from Italy. After Sindona's purchase of the controlling block of shares the Vatican still retained a 29 per cent share of the bank. Hambros of London and Continental Illinois of Chicago also had a stake in Finabank.

For three such august institutions as Vatican Incorporated, Hambros and Continental to be involved so closely with Sindona must surely indicate that Sindona ran his banks in an exemplary manner. Or does it?

Carlo Bordoni discovered a different reality. Bordoni first met Sindona in the latter half of November 1964 at Studio Sindona, Via Turati 29, Milan. Previously Bordoni had worked as Manager of the Milan Branch of First National Citibank of New York. Shortly before his meeting with Sindona, Bordoni had been fired by Citibank for exceeding his limits on foreign exchange deals. Sindona could be counted on to look kindly at such a man. He offered Bordoni the opportunity of handling the foreign exchange of BPF. In view of the fact that the bank's entire deposits were less than 15 billion lire (approximately 15 million dollars), Bordoni declined. Compared with the billion dollar turnover at Citibank this was small change. Further, at that stage, the bank was not even an agent bank and therefore was not authorized to deal in foreign currency. It was unknown internationally, with, in Bordoni's view, 'no possibility of inserting itself in the noble club of international banks'.

Bordoni had a better idea. Why not create an international brokerage company? With hard work and Bordoni's excellent contacts, such a company could earn large commissions. It would, again in Bordoni's words, 'increase the lustre of the then modest Sindona Group and after a while there would be the near certainty of consistent foreign currency credits in favour of BPF and Finabank.'

As Bordoni recalled later in a sworn deposition to Milan magistrates, when he turned State evidence against his former boss, Sindona became visibly excited and gave his approval for the project without hesitation. It is easy to understand Sindona's delight. The aptly named Moneyrex went into operation on February 5th, 1965. Initially run in an ethical manner, it made significant profits. By 1967 it was dealing in a volume of 40 billion dollars per year with net profits in excess of 2 million dollars – profits which in Sindona's hands promptly disappeared before the tax authorities had time to blink. But Sindona wanted more than honest profit. He urged Bordoni to channel the maximum possible amount of foreign currency towards his two banks. Bordoni pointed out that there were several very serious difficulties which made the idea impractical. The Shark began to get angry and shouted that Bordoni should remember his 'force of conviction' and his 'power'. Bordoni shouted back that these were precisely the difficulties he had been talking about. In case Sindona was in any doubt, Bordoni elaborated: 'Your "force" is the Mafia and your "power" is Freemasonry. I don't intend to risk my good name and the success of Moneyrex just because a Mafioso asks me to.'

Eventually Bordoni's discretion overcame his valour, and he agreed to look over the banking operations of BPF and Finabank. What he found tells as much about the Vatican, Hambros and Continental Illinois as it does about Sindona. Twelve years later, in his sworn affidavit from a prison hospital in Caracas to the Milan magistrates, he recalled his discoveries:

> When I started to go to BPF during the summer of 1966, I was deeply affected by the chaos which reigned in the various sectors. It was a tiny bank which was able to survive only thanks to the margins that emanated, duly masked of course, from a myriad of 'black operations' which BPF effected on behalf of Credito Italiano, Banca Commerciale Italiana and other important national banks. These foreign currency black operations, a vast illegal export of capital, took place daily and large figures were involved. The technique was really the most coarse and criminal which can be imagined.

He found numerous overdrawn accounts without any real guarantees and for amounts far in excess of the legal limit of a fifth of capital and reserves. He also found massive theft. The staff were transferring large amounts of money from the accounts of depositors without their knowledge. These sums were then moved to the account held by the Vatican Bank. The Vatican Bank then transferred the amounts, less their 15 per cent commission, to Sindona's account at Finabank in Geneva. The account name in Finabank was MANI. MA stood for Marco, NI for Nino: the names of Sindona's sons. The amount of 15 per cent commission paid to the Vatican was a variable figure depending on the current exchange rate operating on the Black Money Market.

If a client of BPF Milan remonstrated that a cheque he had made out in good faith had bounced or that his account should contain more than was shown he was initially told to take his business elsewhere. If he persisted, then the Manager would appear, and full of Milanese sincerity, apologize and offer the explanation, 'it is all a big accounting error – you know – these modern computers'.

Bordoni's discoveries at Finabank, Geneva were as bad. The Managing Director, one Mario Olivero, knew nothing about banking. The General Manager spent all day playing the share, commodity and currency markets. If he lost, the loss was transferred to a client's account. If he won the profit was his. The heads of the various divisions followed the example of the General Manager, as did the Vatican Bank.

The IOR, apart from being part owner of the bank, also had a number of accounts there. Bordoni discovered that these accounts 'reflected exclusively, gigantic speculative operations which resulted in colossal losses'. These losses, like everyone else's, were financed by a shell company called Liberfinco (Liberian Financial Company). At the time of Bordoni's inspection, this shell company was showing a loss of 30 million dollars. When the Swiss bank inspectors hove into view in 1973, the loss this phantom company was showing had grown to 45 million dollars. The Swiss told Sindona, the Vatican, Continental Illinois and Hambros they had 48 hours to close Liberfinco or they would declare Finabank bankrupt. Another Sindona aide, Gian Luigi Clerici di Cavenago, then demonstrated he had as many bright ideas as names. By means of a counter account for 45 million dollars, a device that did not use any actual cash, he closed Liberfinco and opened another company, Aran Investment of Panama, with an immediate deficit of 45 million dollars.

When Sindona had asked Bordoni to look into Finabank, he had observed in one of the great understatements of all time: 'Strange things are happening there'. When Bordoni told him just how strange these things were, Sindona insulted him and threw him out of his office. Business continued as usual at both banks. Bordoni tried to extricate himself, Sindona used one of his classic techniques: blackmail. Bordoni too had transgressed in his foreign speculations. His transgressions would be reported to the President of the Bank of Italy. Bordoni stayed.

Carlo Bordoni should have seen the writing on the wall before he put his hand in the till. During one of their initial confrontations, Sindona had shouted at him: 'You will never be a real banker because not only are you unable to lie, you are also a man with principles. You would never know how to use the valid weapon of blackmail.'

Sindona's respect for his colleague might have increased immeasurably if he had known that Bordoni had begun to siphon off money into secret accounts in Switzerland. Before the end, Bordoni would relieve Sindona of over 45 million dollars. It was hardly on a par with Sindona's own criminal activities but then he lacked Sindona's schooling.

Sindona was a master when it came to blackmail. Apart from an innate ability in this direction, he had his Mafia training and he also had available to him the talents of the most skilled blackmailer then practising the art in Italy, Licio Gelli. When Bordoni had contemptuously thrown Sindona's Mafia and Masonic connections in his face, he was playing with double fire. Sindona was not a member of a Masonic Lodge that could claim to trace its origin back to the stonemasons of Solomon. His was no Lodge inspired by the Italian patriot Garibaldi. There was no Duke of Kent as the Grand Master. The Lodge was 'Propaganda Due' or P2 and its Grand Master was Licio Gelli.

Gelli was born in Pistoia, central Italy on April 21, 1919. His formal education ceased when he was expelled from school in his mid-teens. A story from Gelli's school days indicates that a peculiar kind of cunning came early to him. There was a youth in one particular class attended by Gelli who was bigger and stronger than the rest. He was admired by many and feared by all. One day Gelli stole the youth's lunch and during the ensuing uproar said to him, 'I know who stole your food but I have no wish to get the boy into trouble. You'll find it hidden under the third bench.' The youth became Gelli's friend and protector from that day and Gelli had learned the art of manipulation. By the age of 17 he had already acquired a hatred of Communism comparable to King Herod's attitude towards the first born. As members of the Italian Black Shirt Division, Gelli and his brother fought alongside Franco's army against the Communists in Spain. Of this period in his life Gelli observes: 'Only I returned alive.'

During the early stages of the Second World War Gelli fought in Albania. Subsequently, he obtained the rank of Oberleutnant in the SS in Italy and worked for the Nazis as a 'liaison officer'. His work involved spying on the partisans and betraying them to his German masters. Some of his early wealth was derived from his presence in the Italian town of Cattaro, where, during the war, the national treasures of Yugoslavia were hidden. A significant proportion of those treasures have never been returned to Yugoslavia but were stolen by Gelli. Gelli's early devotion to a hatred of all things Communist lessened in direct proportion to the defeats suffered by the Axis powers as the war progressed. He began to collaborate with the partisans, who were very largely Communists. Thus he would locate a partisan hideout, dutifully tell the Germans, then advise the partisans to move before the raid.

He continued to play both ends against the middle throughout the remainder of the war and was one of the last of the Fascists to surrender in Northern Italy, close to where a young priest Albino Luciani had been hiding partisans in Belluno.

Gelli's agreement to continue to spy for the Communists after the war was instrumental in saving his life when he faced an anti-Fascist Commission sitting in Florence. The evidence that he had tortured and murdered patriots was deemed, after discreet intervention by the Communists, to be insufficient.

Having been cleared of these charges he immediately organized a 'rat line' for Nazis wishing to flee to South America. His fee was 40 per cent of their money. Another organizing member of the 'rat line' was the Catholic priest from Croatia, Father Krujoslav Dragonovic. Among the men who escaped was the Gestapo Chief Klaus Barbie, usually referred to as The Butcher of Lyons. Barbie was not obliged to pay either Father Dragonovic or Gelli. The cost was borne by the US Counter Intelligence Corps which employed Barbie in espionage work until February 1951.

While continuing to assist Vatican officials and US Intelligence, Gelli also continued spying for the Communists until 1956. The termination of his espionage work for the Communists coincided with the commencement of his work for the Italian secret service. Part of his fee for spying for his own country was the closure of the file the secret service had on him. This also occurred in 1956. Two years earlier he had followed the same path on which he had sent so many members of the Third Reich to South America, aligning himself with extreme right-wing elements in Argentina, where he became a close friend and confidant of General Juan Peron. When Peron was excommunicated by the Catholic Church, Gelli experienced one of his few failures in attempting to intercede with the Vatican. Peron's anti-clerical campaign, which had led to his excommunication, weighed more heavily with the Church than Gelli's assurances that the General was a greatly misunderstood genius. When Peron left the country after a military coup in 1956, Licio Gelli promptly set about befriending the incoming junta. Slowly and carefully Gelli set about building a power base that began to stretch through much of South America. It was always the rich and powerful, or the potentially rich and powerful whom Gelli courted. In terms of political philosophies or ideals, Gelli was a whore. If you could afford him he would perform for you. While helping the right-wing junta of Argentina, he simultaneously recommenced spying on behalf of the Soviet Union, through his links with Rumania. He carried a recommendation from the Communists of Italy which had saved his life after the war, and the phone numbers of the CIA contacts to whom he also sold information. In addition he continued to work for SID, Italian Army Intelligence.

While Sindona was moving upwards through the financial jungles of post-war Milan, Gelli was ascending the complex power structure of South American politics. A general here, an admiral there, politicians, senior civil servants – while Sindona cultivated contacts in the belief that power lay in money, Gelli, through his new friends, aspired to the source of real power: knowledge. Information, the personal file on this banker, the secret dossier on that politician – his network spread from Argentina into Paraguay, into Brazil, Bolivia, Colombia, Venezuela, and Nicaragua. In Argentina he acquired dual nationality and became that country's economic adviser to Italy in 1972. One of his principal tasks was to negotiate and arrange the purchase of quantities of arms for Argentina. These included tanks, planes, ships, radar installations, and ultimately the deadly Exocet missile. Before that he held less exalted positions. In Italy, they included the post of General Manager to Permaflex, a company making mattresses, and a spell as Manager of Remington Rand in Tuscany. Among the directors listed at that time on the board of Remington Rand was Michele Sindona.

Ever anxious to increase his circle of power and influence Gelli saw the rehabilitated Masonic movement as the perfect vehicle. Ironically it had been his beloved leader Mussolini who had banned the Freemasons. Mussolini had considered them 'a state within a state'. It was equally ironic that the democratic Italian Government Gelli held in such total contempt restored the freedom of Masons, though they retained an aspect of the Fascist Law that made it a punishable offence to create a secret organization. Consequently the reformed Masons were obliged to deposit lists of their members with the Government.

Gelli joined a conventional Masonic Lodge in November 1963. He rapidly rose to third degree membership, which made him eligible to lead a Lodge. The then Grand Master Giordano Gamberini urged Gelli to form a circle of important people, some of whom might eventually become Masons but all of whom could be useful to the growth of legitimate Freemasonry. Gelli leapt at the opportunity. What he in fact conceived was an illegal secret organization. This group was given the name Raggruppamento Gelli – P2. The P stood for Propaganda, the name of an historic lodge of the nineteenth century. Initially he brought into it retired senior members of the Armed Forces. Through them he obtained the entrée to the active Service Heads. The web he spun was gradually to cover the entire power structure of Italy. The ideals and aspirations of genuine Freemasonry were rapidly abandoned, though not officially. Gelli's aim was somewhat different: extreme right-wing control of Italy. Such control would function as a secret state within a state, unless the unthinkable happened and the Communists were elected to power. If that happened then there would be a coup. The right wing would take over. Gelli was confident that the Western Powers would accept the situation. Indeed, from the early formation of P2, he had the active support and encouragement of the CIA operating in Italy. It may sound like the scenario of a madman, doomed to the fate of all such schemes, but it should be noted that within the membership of P2 in Italy alone (there were, and still are, powerful branches in other countries) were the Armed Forces Commander Giovanni Torrisi, the Secret Service Chiefs Generals Giuseppe Santovito and Giulio Grassini, the Head of Italy's Financial Police, Orazio Giannini, cabinet ministers and politicians of every political shade (except of course the Communists), thirty generals, eight admirals, newspaper editors, television executives, top industrialists, and bankers, including Roberto Calvi and Michele Sindona. Unlike conventional Freemasonry, the list of members of P2 was so secret that only Gelli knew all the names.

Gelli used a variety of techniques to increase the power of P2. One of them was the innocuous method of personal contact and introduction from an already existing member. Others were less tasteful. Blackmail was the most prevalent. When a 'target' joined P2 he was obliged to demonstrate loyalty by placing at Gelli's disposal documents that would compromise not only the new member but other possible targets. Confronted with the evidence of their own misdeeds the targets joined P2. This technique was used for example on the President of ENI, the State oil company, Giorgio Mazzanti. Shown the evidence of his own corruption concerning proposed huge bribes and pay-offs on a pending Saudi oil deal, Mazzanti caved in and joined P2, bringing to Gelli even more compromising information.

Another technique Gelli used to seduce a new member was to ascertain from already corrupted sources the shortlist of three on a top job. He would then telephone all three applicants and announce that he intended to fix it for them. Next day he would have one very grateful new member of P2.

On the surface P2 was, and still is, a fanatical insurance policy against potential Communist governments. Excluding Italy there are still branches functioning in Argentina, Venezuela, Paraguay, Bolivia, France, Portugal and Nicaragua. Members are also active in Switzerland and the USA. P2 interlocks with the Mafia in Italy, Cuba and the USA. It interlocks with a number of the military regimes of Latin America, and with a variety of groups of neo-Fascists. It also interlocks very closely with the CIA. It reaches right into the heart of the Vatican. The central common interest of all these elements is apparently a hatred and fear of Communism.

In fact, P2 is not a world conspiracy with the aim of preventing the spread of Marxism or its many variations. It is an international grouping with a number of diverse aims. It combines an attitude of mind with a community of self interest, its main goals being not the destruction of a particular ideology but an insatiable greed for power and wealth and the furtherance of self, hiding behind the acceptable face of 'defenders of the free world'. In the world of P2, however, nothing is free. Everything has a price.

Licio Gelli's contacts and associates spread far and wide. They included Stefano Delle Chiaie, Pierluigi Pagliani and Joachim Fiebelkorn, all members of the private army set up in Bolivia by ex-Gestapo Chief Klaus Barbie. The group took the name 'Fiancés of Death'. Political assassinations were performed to order, including that of Bolivian Socialist leader Marcelo Quiroga Cruz. The 'Fiancés of Death' were also instrumental in bringing to power in Bolivia in 1980 General Garcia Meza. Klaus Barbie used his Nazi training as 'security adviser' to Colonel Gomez, a man with a great deal of Bolivian blood on his hands.

The group that Barbie controlled with the blessing of the Bolivian junta expanded its activities after a coup of 1980. The murders of political opponents, investigating journalists, labour leaders and students increased. Added to this work was the task of 'regulating' the cocaine industry – destroying the small dealers to ensure that the big drug traffickers could flourish with the junta's protection. From 1965, Barbie's activities in Bolivia had included arms deals not only on behalf of Bolivia but also for other right-wing South American regimes and Israel. It was through such arms deals that Klaus Barbie, an unrepentant member of the SS, and Licio Gelli became business partners: Barbie, who between May 1940 and April 1942 was responsible for the liquidation of all known Freemasons in Amsterdam, and Licio Gelli, the Grand Master of Masonic Lodge P2. The two men had much in common, including the mutual high regard they had for men like Stefano Delle Chiaie. The Italian Delle Chiaie has been involved in at least two attempted coups in his own country. When a civilian Government returned to office in Bolivia in October 1982, Delle Chiaie fled to Argentina. There he was given comfort and aid by P2 member José Lopez Rega, the creator of the notorious Triple A death squads.

Rega had also created a large cocaine-smuggling connection between Argentina and the USA. Clearly Licio Gelli is as skilful at selling his particular vision of the world as he once was selling mattresses. To have a range of close friends and associates that includes a man like José Lopez Rega, Klaus Barbie and the esoteric Cardinal Paolo Bertoli is a considerable achievement. Like Gelli, the Cardinal is a Tuscan. His career includes forty years in the Vatican diplomatic service. Bertoli was not without support in the Conclave that elected Albino Luciani.

Cardinal Bertoli was only one of the many doors to Gelli's entry into the Vatican. He dined with Bishop Paul Marcinkus. He had a number of audiences with Pope Paul. Many a cardinal, archbishop, bishop, monsignor and priest, who today would deny all knowledge of Licio Gelli, was only too pleased to be seen in his company in the 1960s and the 1970s.

One of Gelli's closest P2 associates was Italian lawyer and businessman Umberto Ortolani. Like 'The Puppet Master', Ortolani learned early in life the value of secret information. During the Second World War he became head of two large operational units of SISMI, the military intelligence agency in Italy. His speciality was counter-espionage. A Roman Catholic, he appreciated while still a young man that one of the real centres of power was across the Tiber within Vatican City. Consequently his penetration of the Vatican and its corridors of influence was total.

Vatican dignitaries were frequent dinner guests at Ortolani's Rome house in Via Archimede. An indication of how far back Ortolani's excellent Vatican contacts reached can be gauged from the fact that he was first introduced to Cardinal Lercaro in 1953. Lercaro had immense influence within the Church and was destined to become one of the four 'moderators' of the Second Vatican Council. He was widely regarded as one of the liberal enlightened influences which helped to ensure that many of the reforms which flowed from the

Council became realities. Ortolani was generally known as the Cardinal's 'cousin', a misconception he actively encouraged.

In the run-up to the Conclave which elected Paul VI, the central issue was whether the work of Pope John XXIII would continue or whether the Papacy should revert to the reactionary ethos of Pius XII. The 'liberals' needed a safe house to debate strategy. Lercaro, one of the liberal front-runners, asked Ortolani to host the meeting. It was held at Ortolani's villa in Grottaferata, near Rome, a few days before the Conclave. A large number of Cardinals attended, including Suenens of Brussels, Doepfner of Munich, Koenig of Vienna, Alfrink of Holland and 'Uncle' Giacomo Lercaro.

This highly secret meeting was the single most important factor in what subsequently occurred in the Conclave. It was agreed that if Lercaro's very considerable support should prove insufficient then his votes should swing to Giovanni Battista Montini. Thus on the third ballot Montini suddenly found himself twenty additional votes nearer to the Papacy he eventually acquired.

Within months the new Pope bestowed upon Umberto Ortolani the Vatican award of 'Gentleman Of His Holiness'. He subsequently received many more Vatican honours and awards. He even succeeded in affiliating Licio Gelli, a non-Catholic, to the Knights of Malta and the Holy Sepulchre. A close friend of Casaroli, the man usually referred to as the Vatican's Kissinger because of his major involvement in foreign policy, lawyer Ortolani provided his P2 master with an unrivalled access to any Vatican dignitary. Like his master, Ortolani is a man who, on paper at least, is the citizen of many countries. Born in Viterbo in Italy, he has since become a Brazilian national. A useful by-product of that arrangement is that no extradition treaty exists between Italy and Brazil.

The list of P2 members grew ever larger. In 1981 when a huge quantity of Gelli's secret documents were seized in Tuscany, they revealed that the secret society had nearly 1,000 members in Italy alone. But that 1,000 is merely the tip of the iceberg. SISMI, Italy's military intelligence agency, puts the membership at nearly 2,000. Gelli himself puts the figure at 2,400. In either event a number of Europe's intelligence agencies are agreed that the identity of the majority of P2 members has yet to be revealed and that within their ranks are nearly 300 of the most powerful men in what it pleases the twentieth century to call the free world.

When the Italian exposure of nearly 1,000 members of this illegal secret society occurred in 1981, one P2 member, Senator Fabrizio

Cicchitto, stated a fundamental truth: 'If you wanted to make it to the top in Italy in the 1970s the best way was Gelli and P2.'

The close relationship between P2 and the Vatican was, like all relationships formed by Gelli, self-serving to both parties. Gelli played on the almost paranoid fear of Communism existing within the Vatican. He was particularly given to quoting pre-Second World War statements that had justified Fascism, including one by Cardinal Hinsley of Westminster who had told Catholics in 1935: 'If Fascism goes under, God's cause goes under with it.'

The most bizarre factor in the close and continuous contacts that existed between P2 and the Vatican is that various cardinals, bishops and priests could smile so benevolently on this bastard child of orthodox Masonry. The Roman Catholic Church has viewed Freemasons for many hundreds of years as sons of evil. The organization has been repeatedly condemned and has inspired at least six Papal bulls that have been specifically directed against it; the earliest being 'In eminenti' from Pope Clement XII, in 1738.

The Church regards this secret society of self-interest as an alternative religion controlled by the godless. It considers that one of Freemasonry's principal aims is the destruction of the Catholic Church. Consequently any Catholic discovered to be a member has been subjected to automatic excommunication from the Church.

There can be little doubt that many historical revolutionary movements utilized Freemasonry in their quarrels with the Church. A classic example is the Italian patriot Garibaldi, who forged the Masons of the country into a force that aroused the general populace, overthrew Papal domination, and resulted in a unified Italy.

Today Freemasonry means different things in different countries. All Masons contend that it is a force for good. Non-Masons view this self-serving, secret society with varying degrees of hostility and suspicion. But until very recently the Roman Catholic Church has maintained an entirely consistent position: Freemasonry is a profound evil and all who belong to it are in the eyes of the Church anathema. If this was the thinking of the Church on conventional Freemasonry, then it makes the close ties between P2 and the Vatican even more extraordinary: one of the smallest but most powerful States on earth embracing a state within a state. The overwhelming majority of P2 members were, and are, practising Roman Catholics.

Though the complete Italian Lodge of P2 never met in its entirety (they would have needed to hire La Scala for that), there were undoubtedly meetings of selected groups. Discussions were not confined merely to lamenting the evils of Communism. Active steps were planned to combat and contain what Gelli and his friends saw as the ultimate disaster, a Communist Government democratically elected to power.

There have been over the past two decades a number of bomb outrages in Italy which remain unsolved. If the Italian authorities ever catch Gelli they will be in a position, if he chooses to talk and tell the truth, to solve some of those mysterious attacks. These include: Milan 1969, the Piazza Fontana bomb attack – 16 people killed; Bologna 1974, bomb attack on the Rome–Munich express, 'The Italicus', near Bologna – 12 people killed; Bologna 1980, railway station bombing – 85 people killed, 182 injured. According to a disenchanted follower of Gelli, a neo-Fascist called Elio Ciolini, this last outrage was planned at a P2 meeting held in Monte Carlo on April 11th, 1980. Licio Gelli was the Grand Master at that meeting. Again, according to the sworn testimony of Ciolini, three of the men allegedly responsible for the railway station bombing are Stefano Della Chiaie, Pierluigi Pagliani and Joachim Fiebelkorn.

The purpose of this series of appalling attacks was to direct public outrage towards Italian Communists by making it appear that they were responsible.

In July 1976 Italian magistrate Vittorio Occorsio was in the middle of an investigation into the links between a neo-Fascist movement called National Vanguard and P2. On July 10th the magistrate was murdered by an extended burst of machine-gun fire. The neo-Nazi group New Order subsequently claimed responsibility. New Order, National Vanguard – the names become academic. What mattered was that Vittorio Occorsio, a man who could not be bought, lay dead and the investigation into P2 had been halted.

By the late 1960s Michele Sindona was a member of P2 and also a close friend of Licio Gelli. He had much in common with Gelli, not least the close attention they were both paid by the CIA and Interpol. The functions of these two organizations do not always run in tandem. Interpol's investigation of Sindona is a perfect illustration of this. In November 1967 Interpol, Washington, telexed the following message to the Rome Police Headquarters:

Recently we have received unverified information that the following individuals are involved in the illicit movement of depressant, stimulant and hallucinogenic drugs between Italy, the United States and possibly other European countries.

Top of the list of four names was Michele Sindona. The Italian Police replied that they had no evidence to link Sindona with the drug trade. A copy of the Interpol request and the response were in Sindona's hands the same week. A similar request by Interpol, Washington to the CIA operating out of the Rome Embassy and the Milan Legation, if answered honestly, would have produced confirmation that the information Interpol had was entirely correct.

The CIA file on Sindona was by this time extensive. It details Sindona's link with the New York Mafia family Gambino, with its 253 members and its 1,147 'associates'. It tells how the five New York Mafia families, Colombo, Bonanno, Gambino, Lucchese and Genovese were interlocked in a range of crimes that included drug refining, smuggling and dealing, the drugs in question being heroin, cocaine and marijuana. Further criminal activities of these Mafia families which are annotated on the CIA files include prostitution, gambling, pornography, usury, protection, racketeering, fraud, and large-scale thefts from banks and pension funds.

The files are full of details of how the Sicilian Mafia families Inzerillo and Spatola moved the refined heroin from Sicily to their colleagues in New York; of their infiltration of the Italian airline Alitalia, and of how 50,000 dollar contracts were awarded by the New York families to 'associates' to collect unaccompanied baggage from Palermo – baggage that contained heroin which had been refined at one of the five Inzerillo narcotics laboratories in Sicily. By the late 1960s the profits from heroin sales to these two Sicilian families were in excess of 500 million dollars per year.

The files detail the journeys of nearly thirty ships per year which until very recently left Lebanese ports with cargoes of both unrefined and refined heroin, destined for a variety of ports in Southern Italy.

The most serious question this information raises is why did such incriminating evidence lie dormant and unused throughout the 1960s and the 1970s? The CIA never initiates policy, it merely implements or attempts to implement Presidential instructions. Did a succession of Presidents take the view that the Mafia's activities were to be tolerated if they helped to ensure that NATO member Italy did not fall to the Communists through the polling booths?

The Mafia families themselves desperately needed men like Michele Sindona. The extraordinary growth of bank deposits and the array of new banks and branches in Sicily, one of the poorest regions in the country, is mute testimony to the size of the Mafia's problem. Enter Michele Sindona. On one occasion Sindona was asked where he obtained the money for his grandiose schemes. He replied: Ninety-five per cent of it is other people's money.' It was a response that was 95 per cent true.

Michele Sindona was the man chosen by Pope Paul VI to act as financial adviser to the Vatican; the man chosen, after a long friendship with the Pope, to relieve the Church of its high-profile business position in Italy. The plan was to sell Sindona some of the major assets acquired under Nogara. Vatican Incorporated was about to distance itself from the unacceptable face of capitalism. Theoretically it was going to embrace the philosophy contained in the message Pope Paul VI gave the world in his 1967 encyclical *Populorum Progressio*:

> God has destined the earth and all it contains for the use of all men and of all peoples, so that the goods of creation must flow in just proportion into the hands of everybody, according to the rule of justice which is inseparable from charity. All other rights, of whatever kind, including those of private property and of free trade, must be subordinated to it: they must not obstruct, but on the contrary foster its achievement, and it is a grave and urgent social duty to restore them to their original aims.

Pope Paul in the same encyclical quoted St Ambrose, 'You never give to the poor what is yours; you merely return to them what belongs to them. For what you have appropriated was given for the common use of everybody. The land is given to everybody, and not only to the rich.'

When that statement was uttered the Vatican was the biggest owner of private real estate in the world. *Populorum Progressio* also contained the memorable observation that even when entire populations are suffering massive injustice revolutionary insurrection is not the answer. 'One cannot fight a real evil at the cost of a greater evil.'

Confronted with the problem of the evil of a wealthy Roman Catholic Church when he apparently desired a poor Church for the poor, the Pope and his advisers decided to liquidate a sizeable proportion of their Italian assets and re-invest in other countries. Thus they would avoid heavy taxation, and the yield on the investment would be better. When Pope Paul proclaimed the magnificent aspirations of *Populorum Progressio* in 1967, Vatican Incorporated had already for a number of years been a close working partner of Michele Sindona. Through the illegal flight of currency from Sindona's Italian banks via the Vatican Bank to the Swiss Bank which they jointly owned,

Sindona and the Vatican, if not making the goods of creation flow to the poor, were certainly making them flow out of Italy. By early 1968 another Vatican-controlled bank, the Banca Unione, was in trouble. The Vatican Bank owned approximately 20 per cent. It was represented on the Board of Directors by Massimo Spada and Luigi Mennini. By 1970, two years after Sindona bought control and with the Vatican still substantial part-owners, the bank in theory had become an astonishing success. Aiming at the small saver and offering superior rates of interest the bank's deposits rose from 35 million dollars to over 150 million dollars – in theory.

In practice during the same period, the bank was robbed of over 250 million dollars by Sindona and his associates. Most of this fortune was poured through yet another Sindona bank, the Amincor Bank of Zürich. Much was lost in wild speculation on the Silver Market. One of the men who was deeply impressed with Sindona at this time was David Kennedy, Chairman of Continental Illinois, soon to be appointed Treasury Secretary in the President Nixon Cabinet.

In 1969 it was clear to Vatican Incorporated that it had lost the long battle with the Italian Government over taxation of its share dividends. Realizing that to unload its entire stock on the market would result in the possible collapse of the Italian economy, it occurred to the Vatican that such an action would be self-defeating. A collapse of that magnitude would result in Vatican losses.

The Pope, in conjunction with Cardinal Guerri, Head of the Special Administration of the APSA, decided to unload from the Italian portfolio a major asset, the Vatican's share in the giant Società Generale Immobiliare. With assets in excess of half a billion dollars scattered around the world, that was certainly highly visible wealth. They again sent for The Shark.

The shares of Società Generale Immobiliare were selling at around 350 lire. The Vatican held directly and indirectly some 25 per cent of the 143 million shares. Would Sindona like to buy? The question was put by Cardinal Guerri. Sindona's response was immediate and positive. He would take the lot – at double the market price. Guerri and Pope Paul were delighted. The agreement between Sindona and Guerri was signed at a secret midnight meeting in the Vatican, in the spring of 1969.

For the Vatican this was a particularly good meeting. It also wished to unload its majority shares in Condotte d'Acqua, Rome's Water Company, and its controlling share of Ceramica Pozzi, a chemical and porcelain company which was losing money. The Shark smiled, agreed a price, and snapped up both holdings.

Precisely who had conceived this entire operation? Who was the man who collected a handsome commission from Sindona and high praise from Pope Paul VI and Cardinal Guerri? The answer is powerful evidence of not only how far P2 had penetrated the Vatican but also how the interests of P2, the Mafia and the Vatican were often identical. Licio Gelli's number two, Umberto Ortolani, was the man responsible for arranging the mammoth transaction. All Sindona had to do now was to pay for it.

It is easy to purchase massive companies if you are using other people's money. Sindona's initial payment was made entirely with money illegally converted from the deposits of Banca Privata Finanziaria. In the last week of May 1969 Sindona transferred 5 million dollars to a small Zürich bank, Privat Kredit Bank. The Zürich bank was instructed to send the money back to BPF for the account of Mabusi Beteiligung. Mabusi resided in a Post Office Box in the Liechtenstein capital of Vaduz, and was a company controlled by Sindona. From there it was transferred again to another Sindona-controlled company, Mabusi Italiana. From there the 5 million dollars were paid to the Vatican. Further money was raised to pay for the huge acquisitions by bringing in Hambros and the American giant Gulf and Western.

Sindona obviously has a highly developed sense of humour. One company owned by Gulf and Western was Paramount and one of its most successful films of the period was the adaptation of Mario Puzo's book *The Godfather*. Thus a film taking a highly glamorous and amoral look at the world of the Mafia produced enormous profits, some of which went to sustain Michele Sindona, financial adviser to the Mafia families Gambino and Inzerillo. They in turn were channelling the multi-million profits acquired largely from heroin dealing into Sindona's banks. The circle was complete. Life was imitating Art.

By the early 1970s the massive illegal flight of money from Italy was having a serious effect upon the economy. Sindona and Marcinkus might be making significant profits through their efforts at diverting this money out of Italy, but the effect on the lira was devastating. Unemployment rose. The cost of living increased. Uncaring, Sindona and his associates continued to play the markets. By pushing up share prices to a much inflated level, the Sindona banks went through millions of dollars of other people's money.

Sindona and his close friend Roberto Calvi of Banco Ambrosiano openly boasted that they controlled the Milan Stock Market at this time. It was a control which they criminally exploited again and again.

Shares went up and down like yoyos. Games were played with companies for the amusement and financial benefit of Sindona and his associates. The manipulation of a company called Pacchetti gives an example of the everyday activities of these men.

Pacchetti began as a small, insignificant, leather-tanning company. Sindona acquired it in 1969 and decided to transform it into a conglomerate. He took as his model the Gulf and Western, an American giant with a wide spread of interests ranging from Paramount studios through publishing to airlines. Sindona's acquisitions for Pacchetti were more modest. In fact it became a commercial dustbin containing interests in unprofitable steelworks and commercially unsuccessful household cleaners. There was, however, one jewel in it: he had acquired from Bishop Marcinkus an option to purchase Banca Cattolica del Veneto. Doubtless the fact that the Administrative Secretary of the Vatican Bank, Massimo Spada, was also the President of Pacchetti and President of Banca Cattolica helped Marcinkus forget the prior claims of the Veneto clergy and Patriarch Luciani.

Roberto Calvi, who was a party to these negotiations, agreed to buy on a specified date a Sindona company called Zitropo. The scenario was now ready to manipulate the Milan Stock Market illegally yet again.

The book value of the Pacchetti shares was about 250 lire per share. Sindona instructed the Stock Exchange department of the Banca Unione to purchase Pacchetti shares. By using nominees the shares were then illegally parked in Sindona-owned companies. The price of the shares began to surge dramatically, eventually reaching 1,600 lire on the Exchange. In March 1972 the day for Calvi's purchase of Zitropo duly arrived. Simultaneously all the parking companies dumped their Pacchetti shares into Zitropo. The effect was to inflate artificially the value of Zitropo. Calvi paid an astronomically higher price than the company was worth. Sindona, having funded the entire operation with fictitious guarantees, made a huge illegal profit. An indication of just how much profit he made on this one operation can be appreciated from the fact that in 1978 a Government-appointed liquidator, Giorgio Ambrosoli, discovered incontrovertible evidence that Sindona had paid an illegal kick-back to Calvi of 6.5 million dollars, and that Calvi shared this criminal payment fifty-fifty with Bishop Paul Marcinkus.

Why would Calvi pay so much over the odds for Zitropo? There are three reasons. Firstly, he used money belonging to others to effect the purchase. Secondly, there was a 3.25 million dollars profit for him. Thirdly, at the conclusion of the Pachetti/Zitropo deal he acquired an option to buy Banca Cattolica del Veneto. Sindona had acquired the option from Marcinkus earlier. The fact that no one had consulted Albino Luciani, the Patriarch of Venice, or the members of his diocese who had lodged their shares with the Vatican Bank, was considered an irrelevance by Bishop Marcinkus.

Sindona and Calvi became very adept at this form of robbery. Never in the history of banking has so much been paid for so little. In 1972 Calvi pocketed a further 5 million dollars from Sindona when Bastogi shares changed hands, and an additional 450 million Swiss francs when Sindona sold him 7,200 shares in Finabank. Each time Sindona paid the kick-back to Calvi through his MANI account in Finabank. These huge amounts were paid into Calvi's secret Swiss accounts which he held jointly with his wife. At the Union de Banques Suisses and Credit Bank of Zürich the Calvis held four secret accounts: Account number 618934; Account number 619112; Account number Ralrov/G21; and Account number Ehrenkranz. The very minimum that Sindona himself would have made on each deal was equivalent to the amount he was kicking back to Calvi.

Roberto Calvi developed an insatiable appetite for this particular game and on occasions played it as a solo performer. Hence he obliged one of his own banks, Centrale, to buy a large block of Toro Assicurazioni shares in 1976 for 25 billion lire more than they were worth. The 25 billion ended up in one of the Swiss accounts previously noted. So did a further 20 billion lire after Calvi played the game again with over one million shares in Centrale. These huge sums of money were not just items on a balance sheet. The money physically moved from a variety of shareholders' pockets directly into the pockets of the Calvis and Sindona. What Bishop Marcinkus did with his 3,250,000 dollar kick-back from the Pacchetti swindle has yet to be established.

The shares in the Banca Cattolica were also subjected to this treatment. Sindona was aware that Calvi was negotiating with Marcinkus to acquire control of the bank – hence the share push. At the end of that exercise everyone except the Veneto Diocese was immeasurably richer.

Calvi had been introduced to Marcinkus by Sindona in 1971. Thus Bishop Marcinkus, the man who on his own admission 'knew nothing about banking', had two excellent tutors. Meanwhile Marcinkus had been promoted by Pope Paul and was now President of the Vatican Bank.

The various Vatican departments continued to unload a wide variety of companies on Sindona and then on Calvi. In 1970, for example, they finally sold Serono, a pharmaceutical works which featured among its more successful lines an oral contraceptive pill.

An additional source of profit for the Sindona/Vatican-owned Finabank was another part of the cause of Italy's faltering economy: double invoicing. As Bordoni observed: 'It was less succulent than the kick-backs earned through the illegal exportation of black money but it still reached a high figure.'

Exports would be invoiced at costs that were much lower than the real ones. Thus the bent invoice would be officially paid via the Bank of Italy which, of course, would pass the information on to the Taxation Department. The exporter would be taxed on this low figure.

The balance was paid by the receiver of the goods abroad direct to Finabank. In many instances Italian exporters actually showed a loss which was converted into tax credits by the Government.

The large number of Sindona-owned exporting companies showed such losses. Sindona would bribe various Government politicians to allow this situation to continue. He would also argue that by doing so the Government was helping to keep down unemployment.

A similar crime was worked on imports. Then the invoice would be for a much higher figure than the actual cost of the goods. When the goods passed through customs, payment of the artificially high figure would be made by the company to the foreign supplier. The foreign supplier in turn would assign the balance to a numbered account at Finabank or occasionally one of the other Swiss banks.

Pope Paul's poor Church for the poor grew instead immeasurably richer. The Vatican divestment of Italian wealth had resulted in men like Sindona and Calvi robbing the world to pay St Peter and Pope Paul.

Finabank was also a part of the giant laundry for Mafia/ P2/criminal money. With the Vatican retaining a 5 per cent of Società General Immobiliare it owned part of that laundry. With the further use by the Mafia of the Vatican Bank to move money both into and out of Italy, the Vatican ultimately owned the entire laundry. Use by Sindona and his staff of the Vatican Bank's accounts at BPF has already been explained. That was one of the methods of getting dirty money out of the country and cleaning it at Finabank, but this was a two-way operation. Dirty money from the Mafia operating in Mexico and Canada and the USA was also being cleaned as it flowed into Italy. The operation was very simple. To quote again from Carlo Bordoni:

These companies in Canada and Mexico were used to bring into the USA over the Canadian and Mexican borders dollars from the Mafia, from the Freemasons and from numerous illegal and criminal operations; the money arrived in suitcases and was then invested in US State Bonds. These were then sent to Finabank. Clean and easily negotiable.

The USA Mafia obviously had no problems with borders. Their money was converted to State Bonds directly by Edilcentro of Washington, a subsidiary of SGI; then the Bonds also found their way to Finabank. If the Mafia wished to bring some of their clean money into Italy they used Vatican Bank channels.

In the early 1970s Sindona extolled his own virtues to Bordoni. 'My operating philosophy is based on my personality which is unique in the world, on well-told lies and on the efficient weapon of blackmail.'

Part of the blackmail technique was to bribe. A bribe in Sindona's view was 'merely an investment. It gave you a hold over the individual bribed'. Thus he unofficially 'financed' the ruling Italian political party, the Christian Democrats: 2 billion lire to ensure the promotion of party nominee Mario Barone to the position of Managing Director of Banco di Roma; 11 billion lire to finance the same party's campaign against the divorce referendum. He arranged for the Christian Democrats to 'earn' billions of dollars. He opened an account for the party at Finabank, account no SIDC. Throughout the early 1970s three-quarters of a million dollars were transferred to this account. Sindona, the self-proclaimed hero of anti-communism, was also a man to hedge his bets. He opened another account at Finabank for the Italian Communist Party. Into this he also poured three-quarters of a million dollars per month, of other people's money, account no SICO.

He speculated against the lira, the dollar, the German Mark and the Swiss franc. With regard to his massive speculation against the lira (a 650 million dollar operation entirely created by Sindona), he told Italian Prime Minister Andreotti that he was aware of the existence of heavy speculation against the lira, and in order to learn more about the size of the operation and the source, he had instructed Bordoni through Moneyrex to join in in a 'symbolic' manner. Having reaped enormous profits by attacking the lira, he was hailed by Andreotti as 'The Saviour of the Lira'. It was during this period that he received a citation presented by the American Ambassador to Rome. He was named 'Man of the Year for 1973'.

A year earlier, at a reception given to celebrate his purchase of the

Rome *Daily American*, Sindona had announced that he intended to expand his interests and move a further 100 million dollars into the USA. Among those listening to his speech was his close friend Bishop Paul Marcinkus. In reality, by purchasing the *Daily American* Sindona was already expanding his USA interests. The paper had been backed by the CIA. American Congress was pressing the CIA to make precise disclosures of exactly what they did with the millions allocated to them. Like Pope Paul, they thought the moment seemed propitious to jettison a few embarrassing investments. Sindona insists that he bought the paper at the specific request of Ambassador Martin, who feared that it would 'fall into the hands of the leftists'. Martin in decidedly undiplomatic language has denied this. He called Sindona 'a liar'.

Whoever asked him, there is no doubt that the paper had been previously subsidized by the CIA. There is equally no doubt that this was not the first favour Sindona did for The Company. In 1970 the CIA had asked him to buy a 2 million bond issue from the National Bank of Yugoslavia. Sindona obliged. The CIA placed the bonds in Yugoslavia in what they considered 'friendly hands'. Sindona also moved money on behalf of the CIA into the hands of right-wing groups in Greece and Italy.

Thwarted in his attempt to take over Bastogi, the large Milan-based holding company, by the Italian Establishment, who were motivated partially by fear of an ever-increasingly powerful Sindona and partially by racialism towards a Sicilian, The Shark turned his attention to the USA. There this man, who already owned more banks than many men have shirts, bought another bank, the Franklin National Bank of New York.

The Franklin was the twentieth largest bank in the country. Sindona paid 40 million dollars for one million shares in it, representing 21.6 interest. He paid 40 dollars per share at a time when the share price was 32 dollars. More important, this time he had bought a very sick bank. It was tottering on the edge of bankruptcy. The fact that he used 40 million dollars of other people's money from his Italian banks without reference to the owners should not hide from us that, for once, a few people in New York saw the boy from Patti coming.

The true megalomania of Sindona can be gauged from the fact that, having realized what he had acquired, he did not give a damn. To him dealing with tottering banks was an everyday event as long as huge deposits could be kept whirling around on paper – as long as the Telex machine was there to transfer A to B and then to C and then back to A again.

Within twenty-four hours of his purchase and before he had even had an opportunity to try out the boardroom for size, the Franklin Bank announced its trading figures for the second quarter of 1972. They showed a 28 per cent drop from the same period for 1971. Sindona The Shark, the saviour of the lira and the man Marcinkus considered to 'be well ahead of his time as far as banking matters are concerned', took the news in typical Sindona manner. 'I have important connections in all important financial centres. Those who do business with Michele Sindona will do business with Franklin National.' The previous owners meanwhile were laughing all the way to another bank.

As to the 'important connections', none could deny the truth of that. They ranged from the Mafia families Gambino and Inzerillo in Sicily and New York to Pope Paul VI, Cardinals Guerri and Caprio and Bishop Marcinkus in the Vatican. They covered the political spectrum from Andreotti and Fanfani in Italy to President Nixon and David Kennedy in the White House. They included intimate banking relationships with some of the most powerful institutions in the world – the Vatican Bank, Hambros of London, Continental of Chicago and Rothschilds of Paris. Through Gelli's P2 he had forged close links with the men who ruled in Argentina, Paraguay, Uruguay, Venezuela, and Nicaragua. Of the Nicaraguan dictator, Somoza, he told a Rome lawyer:

> I prefer to deal with men like Somoza. Doing business with a one man dictatorship is much easier than doing business with democratically elected Governments. They have too many committees, too many controls. They also aspire to honesty, that's bad for the banking business.

This is a perfect illustration of the P2 philosophy given to its members by its founder Licio Gelli: 'The doors to all bank vaults open to the Right.' While Sindona was doing business with Somoza and looking for a United States equivalent, Gelli had not been idle in Argentina. Sensing the nation's disenchantment with the ruling junta, he began to plot the return of General Peron from exile. In 1971 he convinced the then President Lanusse that the only way Argentina could regain political stability was through the return of Peron. The General returned in triumph. One of his first actions was to kneel in gratitude at the feet of Licio Gelli, a gesture witnessed by, among others, Italian Prime Minister Andreotti. By September 1973, Peron had become President of Argentina.

19-23 Some contenders for the empty throne. *(Above left)* Cardinals Siri and Felici. *(Above right)* Cardinal Pignedoli in conversation with Cardinal Gantin. *(Below left)* Luciani's choice, Cardinal Aloisio Lorscheider. *(Centre)* Cardinal Bertoli, a good friend of Gelli. *(Far right)* Cardinal Baggio.

24 'We have a Pope!'
25 Cardinal Felici places the woollen pallium over the shoulders of the new Pope.

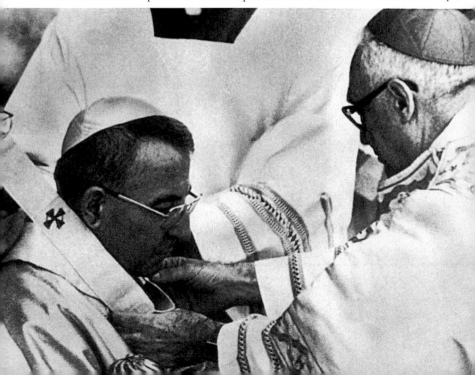

26 and 27 Lucian's impact was immediate with young and old alike.

28 *(Above left)* Between the Pope and his secretary, Father Diego Lorenzi, sits a member of the Curial old guard, Monsignor Martin.

29 *(Above right)* Luciani exchanges greetings with the Communist Mayor of Rome; Giuilo Argan, on the only occasion on which he went outside the Vatican City during his reign. 30 *(Below)* Members of the Curia attempted to monitor the Pope's every movement.

31 The Swiss Guard acknowledges the arrival of Paul Marcinkus at the
Vatican.

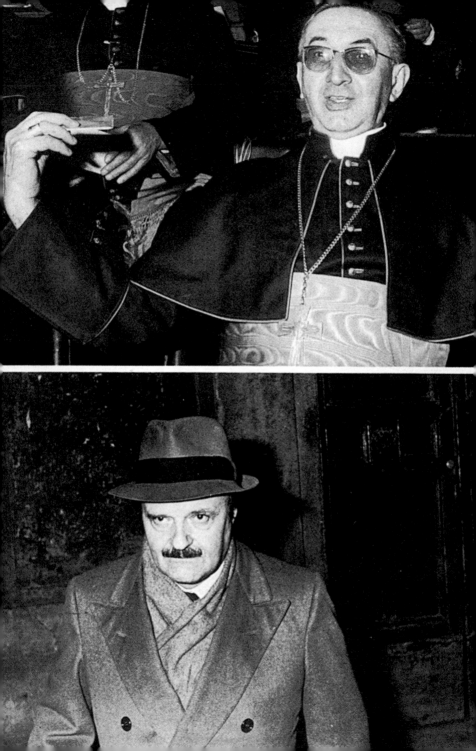

Like Marcinkus, all of these men stood to gain by the death of Luciani.
32 *(Opposite above)* Cardinal Jean Villot.
33 *(Opposite below)* Roberto Calvi.
34 *(Above)* Cardinal Cody.
35 *(Above right)* Umberto Ortolani.
36 *(Right)* Michele Sindona.

37 Licio Gelli stood to lose his grip on a whole empire through Luciani's proposed reforms.

While Gelli was busy making one President, Sindona, having surveyed the political arena. in the United States, focused on the man who to his mind was closest to the political ideals of Somoza and Peron, Richard Millhouse Nixon.

To help along his good connections, Sindona arranged a meeting with Maurice Stans, Nixon's chief fund raiser in the 1972 Presidential Campaign. He took with him to the meeting a very large suitcase. It contained one million dollars in cash. Sindona offered it to Stans for the Campaign Fund to 'show his faith in America'. His faith was clearly limited, as he insisted the gift to assist Nixon back into the White House must remain a secret. According to later statements, Stans declined the gift because under a new Federal Law anonymous election gifts were no longer allowed.

At about the time that Bishop Marcinkus was extolling the banking brilliance of The Shark to the USA attorneys investigating the billion dollar counterfeit securities operation, he was also writing out a cheque for 307,000 dollars. It was the amount Sindona had cost the Vatican as a result of illegal dealings on the American Stock Exchange in the shares of a company called Vetco Industries. In violation of SEC regulations a Los Angeles investment broker had acquired on behalf of Sindona and Marcinkus some 27 per cent of Vetco. The Vatican paid the fine, then sold its shares at a profit.

By mid-1973 the hole in Sindona's banks had reached enormous proportions. It is one thing to move large amounts of money on paper from bank to bank, contravening all kinds of laws and committing countless offences (provided the bribes are placed in the right hands it is a game that is endless). It is something else when you syphon off capital in large amounts to third parties. A hole begins to appear. It fills up with the declaration of false and nonexistent profits, but that is only on paper. The hard cash meanwhile is continuing to pour out to the third parties. The hole grows bigger and the false and non-existent profits needed to fill it have to be proportionally greater. Sindona was pouring out other people's money in a variety of directions. P2, The Christian Democrats, The Vatican, right-wing juntas in South America – these were just a few of the major beneficiaries. Many of his staff were creating their own personal fortunes too.

Appropriately The Shark sat at his desk practising the Japanese art of Origami. The executive suite in his Sixth Avenue office in New York was littered with countless examples of his paper-folding expertise – just like so many of his companies, empty little boxes piled one upon another. The Shark was now involved in a wild, intercontinental juggling act – the merging of this company with that finance house, the transfer of those shares for that company. Merge. Divide. Re-merge.

Il Crack Sindona, the Italians called it. When it came, the collapse of the monument to greed and corruption that Sindona had erected was not unimpressive. He had talked grandly of not knowing what his personal wealth was, but accepted that it was in the order of half a billion dollars. Sindona was a trifle confused. The reality was somewhat different: but then a grasp of reality had never been one of The Shark's attributes. His self-delusions were fed by the illusions of others, as the meteoric pattern of his career shows:

September 1973: at the Waldorf Astoria in New York the Prime Minister of Italy, Giulio Andreotti, rises to his feet at a luncheon and, delivering a eulogy to The Shark, hails him as 'the Saviour of the Lira'.

January 1974: Grand Hotel, Rome. American Ambassador John Volpe awards The Shark, 'The Man of the Year' citation.

March 1974: prices on the Milan Stock Exchange are flying high, as is the exchange rate against the dollar at 825 lire. If Sindona were to close down the huge currency operations now he would emerge with a profit of at least 100 billion lire. Anna Bonomi, a rival in the Milan financial world, makes an excellent offer for Sindona's holding in Immobilaire. Sindona refuses to sell.

April 1974: the Stock Market goes into decline and the exchange rate falls dramatically. It is the beginning of Il Crack Sindona. The Franklin Bank in New York announces a net operating income for the first quarter of 2 cents per share compared with the previous year's 68 cents per share. Even this is a falsified figure. The reality is that the bank had suffered a 40 million dollar loss.

May 1974: Franklin has the brakes put on its massive currency speculation. National Westminster of London object to the volume of Franklin's sterling clearings through its account. In the previous week they have averaged £50 million per day. Franklin now announce that they will not declare a quarterly dividend, the first time since the Depression that a major American bank has been forced to omit a payment to shareholders. The Shark tells tbe Board of Società Generale Immobilaire that the balance sheet is the best in the company's history.

July 1974: the holes are showing in Italy and the USA. In an attempt to fill the Italian hole, The Shark merges Banca Unione and Banca Privata Finanziaria. He calls the new creation Banca Privata. Instead of two medium-size bent banks in Milan, he now has one very large bent bank in Italy's financial centre. Instead of two large holes, one gigantic hole is revealed: a 200 billion lire hole.

August 1974: it is time for the Establishment to rally round. In Italy Banco di Roma, having taken a large part of the Sindona empire as collateral, pushes 128 million dollars into Banca Privata in an attempt to fill the hole. In the United States the Government, fearing the collapse of Franklin will trigger off a capitalistic Armageddon, give the Franklin unlimited access to Federal funds. Over two billion dollars flow from the reserve into the Franklin.

September 1974: Banca Privata goes into compulsory liquidation. Estimated losses are in excess of 300 million dollars. This includes 27 million dollars of Vatican money plus their share of the Bank.

October 3rd: Licio Gelli repays a little of the huge investment that Sindona has made in P2. By courtesy of P2 members planted in the judiciary and the police force, he is advised that Sindona will be arrested the following day. Gelli tips off Sindona.

October 4th: an arrest warrant for Michele Sindona is issued. Sindona has fled the country. Ever a man of vision, he has previously changed his nationality. He is now a citizen of Switzerland. The boy from Sicily flies to his homeland in Geneva.

October 8th: the Franklin Bank collapses. Losses to the Federal Deposit Insurance Corporation – 2 billion dollars. It is the biggest bank crash in American history.

October 1974/January 1975: Europe resounds to the noise of crashing banks that are either Sindona-controlled or -linked – Bankhaus Wolff A.G. of Hamburg, Bankhaus I.K. Herstatt of Cologne, Amincor Bank of Zürich, and Finabank of Geneva. With regard to Finabank, Swiss banking sources estimate Vatican losses at 240 million dollars. The Finabank's losses on foreign exchange dealings alone are a minimum of 82 million dollars.

The Italian authorities, or rather that section of Italian authority not controlled by P2, had by this stage become very agitated. Sindona, having eventually surfaced in the USA, showed a marked disinclination to return to Italy. From October 1974 a long battle began to extradite him. This battle was destined to have a direct influence on the ultimate fate of the man who, at that time, was preoccupied in Venice with trying to raise money to help a group of mentally handicapped people. It would be difficult to find a greater contrast between two men than the values which separated Albino Luciani from The Shark.

Though Sindona's presence was urgently required in Italy, he had most certainly become *persona non grata* inside the Vatican. As Secretary of State Cardinal Villot brought Pope Paul news of each new aspect of The Crack. His Holiness grew more distressed. It has been said that Pope Paul had aspired to be the first poor Pope in modern times. This is a fallacy. The divestment of the majority of the Vatican's Italian holdings had but one aim: more profit. Prompted by the desire to avoid Italian taxes on share profits and for a lower profile in Italy, Vatican Incorporated had been seduced by Sindona and his clan with the prospect of greater wealth through investment in the USA, Switzerland, Germany and other countries.

The story that the Vatican would have one believe today is that Pope Paul alone was responsible over nearly a decade for the Vatican's deep and continuing involvement with Michele Sindona. It is yet another Vatican fallacy. Significantly this particular lie never floated to the surface during Pope Paul's lifetime. Persuaded by his secretary Monsignor Pasquale Macchi, by his advisers Cardinals Guerri and Benedetto Argentieri from the Special Administration, by his Secretary of State Cardinal Villot and by Umberto Ortolani, that Sindona was the answer to the Vatican's prayers, the Pope undoubtedly opened the bronze doors to The Shark and beckoned. Once inside he did not want for company. Indeed, the Pope might have been alerted if his advisers had exercised elementary caution. Close study of the events already described lead to the irresistible conclusion that many within the Vatican walls were ready, willing and eager to join in the criminal activities of Michele Sindona. Were Macchi, Argentieri, Guerri and Villot all honourable men? Were Marcinkus, Mennini and Spada of the Vatican Bank all honourable men? Was His Holiness Pope Paul VI an honourable man?

Bishop Marcinkus was obliged to suffer the indignity of several sessions of intensive questioning by the Italian authorities about his personal and business relationship with Sindona. Marcinkus, who sat at the behest of Sindona and Roberto Calvi as a director in the Bahamas tax haven of Nassau, Marcinkus, the close friend of Sindona, in April 1973, during another intensive interrogation, had told the USA Government attorneys:

> Michele and I are very good friends. We've known each other for several years. My financial dealings with him, however, have only been very limited. He is, you know, one of the wealthiest industrialists in Italy. He is well ahead of his time as far as financial matters are concerned.

Less than two years later the honourable Bishop Marcinkus was questioned by the Italian magazine, *L'Espresso* about his relationship with Sindona. On the morning of February 20th 1975, the Bishop said: 'The truth is that I don't even know Sindona. How can I have lost money because of him? The Vatican has not lost a cent, the rest is fantasy.'

For a bank president, Bishop Marcinkus constantly displayed an alarmingly poor memory. He had told the USA Government attorneys in 1973: 'My financial dealings with Michele Sindona have only been very limited'. On the contrary, his financial dealings with the Mafia's banker were large and continuous from the late 1960s until shortly before Il Crack Sindona in 1975. Less than two years before his interrogation by the US attorneys and the FBI Sindona had played a crucial role in Marcinkus's sale of Banca Cattolica to Roberto Calvi for 46.5 million dollars, a deal that resulted in Sindona paying an illegal kickback to Calvi and Marcinkus of 6.5 million dollars. This, like the later losses inflicted on the Vatican by Sindona, was no 'fantasy'.

Dr Luigi Mennini, Secretary Inspector of the Vatican Bank, was arrested as a result of the Sindona crash and his passport was withdrawn. Mennini, who worked directly under Marcinkus, denied everything and knew nothing. Possibly one of his sons, Alessandro, who held a high executive position in the foreign affairs section of Banco Ambrosiano, the nerve centre of much of the currency speculation, would have been equally mystified if questioned about the criminal activities of both Sindona and Calvi.

Before Il Crack Sindona, Mennini speculated, on behalf of the Vatican Bank, in foreign currencies alongside Sindona's colleague, Carlo Bordoni. Over the years Bordoni got to know him well.

Despite the fact that he acted like a prelate he was a seasoned gambler. He tormented me in every sense of the word because he wanted to earn money in ever-increasing quantities. He speculated in Finabank, in shares, in commodities. I recall one day he gave me a short letter from Paul VI which gave me his benediction for my work as consultant to the Holy See. Mennini was virtually a slave to Sindona's blackmail. Sindona had often threatened to make public information about Mennini's illegal operations carried out with Finabank.

Massimo Spada, administrative secretary to the Vatican Bank, again directly under Bishop Marcinkus, although officially retired from the Bank in 1964, continued to represent a wide cross-section of Vatican interests. Like Mennini, Spada opened his front door at dawn one morning to find the Italian Finance Police there armed with search warrants. His personal bank accounts were frozen by Court Order, his passport was withdrawn. Three separate legal cases were started against him, all alleging a wide range of banking law violations and fraudulent bankruptcy.

Spada, who on Carlo Bordoni's sworn statements was another slave to Sindona's blackmail, who was fully acquainted with all of Sindona's illegal operations, expressed the classic Vatican Bank position when questioned by *L'Espresso* in February, 1975: 'Who would have thought that Sindona was a madman?' Spada asked. This man who was a director of three of Sindona's banks, for which he was very highly paid, continued, 'In 45 years I have never found myself in a situation of this kind. I have lived through the most difficult periods, but I have never seen anything like it. Raving lunatics started to buy billions of dollars with European currencies. All the losses come from that. Who could have known that every day Mr Bordoni was selling 50 or 100 million dollars against Swiss francs or Dutch guilders? What does a Board of Directors know of the mad operations which took place between January and June 1974?'

At the time Spada made these observations he was considered, at the age of 70, to be so brilliant as a business man that he was still on the board of directors of 35 companies.

And so it went on. No one in Vatican Incorporated knew Sindona or anything about his criminal activities. The trusting Men of God had been 'conned' by the Devil.

Is it possible that they were indeed all honourable men who were betrayed by Michele Sindona? Is it possible that Vatican representatives like Mennini and Spada could sit on the boards of Sindona's banks and remain ignorant of the crimes Sindona and Bordoni were perpetrating? Massimo Spada gave the game away during his interview with *L'Espresso*. He was asked if it was indeed only Sindona and Bordoni who were guilty of currency speculation.

You must be joking. Using hundreds and hundreds of billions in currency operations has become a habit for the banks. When an average-sized dealer on the Milan market moves an average value of 25–30 billion lire and a small Milanese bank moves 10–12 billion a day in currency, one has to conclude that if the entire Italian banking system did not go up in smoke we have to thank Providence, God, St Ambrose, St George and above all St

Januarius. I would say in this respect that they should have sent legal letters to all Italian banks warning them they were being investigated.

So, according to Spada, a man whose name was synonymous with Vatican Incorporated, a man who was born into the business dynasty of the Spada family – his great grandfather banker to Prince Torlonia, his grandfather a director of the Bank of Italy, his father Luigi an exchange agent, he himself having worked for Vatican Incorporated since 1929 – according to a man with that illustrious record, the entire Italian banking industry was up to its neck in criminal activity, yet he claimed to be ignorant of what was going on in the very banks where he sat as a director.

After the crash estimates of the size of the Vatican losses were many and varied. They ranged from the Swiss banking estimate previously referred to of 240 million dollars to Vatican Incorporated's own estimate: 'We have not lost a cent'. The truth can probably be found in the region of 50 million dollars. When the multi-national across the Tiber talked of not losing a cent they were no doubt allowing into the calculation the previous massive profits made through their association with The Shark, but a reduction of overall profit from 300 million dollars to 250 million is a loss in any language, including Latin.

Added to that 50 million dollars, Sindona-created loss, was a further 35 million dollar loss sustained by Vatican Incorporated in the curious affair of Banco di Roma per la Svizzera in Lugano (Svirobank). The Vatican Bank held the majority 51 per cent share in the Swiss bank – the Bank President was Prince Giulio Pacelli, the Executive Director, Luigi Mennini. Like other Vatican-linked banks, Svirobank speculated with the black funds which it held on behalf of the illegal exporters of lire and sections of the criminal fraternity of Italy. Gold and foreign exchange speculation was an everyday occurrence. In 1974 a hole began to appear. The blame was fastened upon Deputy Manager Mario Tronconi which, in view of the fact that the person who materially transacted the deals was another Svirobank employee Franco Ambrosio, is odd.

In the autumn of 1974 Mario Tronconi was 'suicided' – his body was found on the Lugano–Chiasso railway line. In his pocket was a farewell letter to his wife. Before his death, doubtless for the sake of tranquillity, Pacelli, Mennini and the other Svirobank directors had obliged Tronconi to sign a confession in which he assumed full responsibility for the 35 million dollar hole. No one denounced

Ambrosio, the man who had actually created the hole. Indeed, Ambrosio was given the task of recovering the loss. The truth came to light only two years later when Mario Barone, one of Banco di Roma's joint chairmen of the board (Banco di Roma held the other 49 per cent of Svirobank), was arrested and questioned about Il Crack Sindona. Clearly Italian banking has many attendant risks. Mario Tronconi was only one member of the fraternity whose death was made to look like suicide. In the following decade the list would grow alarmingly. The Italian Solution would be applied to a growing number of problems.

While Michele Sindona fought his extradition from New York and plotted revenge, Vatican Incorporated was already back speculating again through his successor, Roberto Calvi. Calvi was known in Milan business circles as 'Il Cavaliere', The Knight; a curious nickname for the man who was paymaster to P2. It originated in 1974 when Giovanni Leone, the then President of Italy, made him a Cavaliere del Lavoro (Knight of Labour) for his services to the economy. Calvi was to be Sindona's replacement as laundryman for the Mafia, and the man who carried out the biggest theft in the history of banking.

Roberto Calvi was born in Milan on April 13th, 1920, but his family roots are in the Valtellina, a long alpine valley near the Swiss border and near the home of Albino Luciani. They were both men of the mountains. After studying at the prestigious Bocconi University he fought for Mussolini on the Russian front in the Second World War. Then he followed his father into banking. In 1947 he went to work for Banco Ambrosiano in Milan. Deriving its name from St Ambrose, the bank exuded religiosity. Like Banca Cattolica del Veneto it was known as 'The Priests' Bank'. Baptismal certificates establishing the holder was Catholic were obligatory before a bank account could be opened. Prayers thanking God for the annual figures were offered at the end of board meetings. In the early 1960s there was a greater air of reverence inside the bank than in a number of the nearby churches. The Knight with the ice-cold eyes had other plans for this sleepy diocesan bank which included among its customers the Cardinal Archbishop of Milan, Giovanni Montini. By the time Montini became Pope Paul VI in 1963 Calvi had advanced within the bank to Central Manager. When Pope Paul decided to call Sindona into the Vatican to relieve the Church of its embarrassingly large Italian holdings, The Shark and The Knight were close friends. They were already plotting to gain control of Banco Ambrosiano and transform it into a very special kind of international banking institution. In 1971, Calvi became Managing Director of the Bank. At fifty-one years of age he had risen far above his father's humble clerical position. The average man might have been content to rest on his laurels for a while and enjoy leading the prayers at the board meeting. The only thing that was average about Roberto Calvi was his height. His ability to dream up crooked schemes for laundering Mafia money, exporting lire illegally, evading tax, concealing the criminal acts of buying shares in his own bank, rigging the Milan Stock Market, for bribery, for corruption, for perverting the course of justice, arranging a wrongful arrest here, a murder there – his ability to do all of this and more puts The Knight in a very special criminal class. Calvi was prone to advise all and sundry that if they really wanted to understand the ways of the world then they should read Mario Puzo's novel *The Godfather*. He carried a copy everywhere, rather like a priest with his Bible.

Calvi was introduced to Bishop Marcinkus by Sindona in 1971 and instantly joined the very select Vatican clan of 'uomo di fiducia', men of trust: that small elite group of laymen who worked with and for Vatican Incorporated; men such as Sindona, Spada, Mennini and Bordoni; men chosen with the greatest possible care.

In 1963 he formed a Luxembourg company called Compendium – the name was later changed to Banco Ambrosiano Holdings SA. This shell company was the keystone to Calvi's schemes. Millions of borrowed eurodollars were destined to flow through the Luxembourg holding company. The number of banks world-wide which would be conned into lending money direct to this small shell company is in excess of 250. The amount of money is in excess of 450 million dollars.

The Knight's empire grew rapidly. Already in the early 1960s Banco Ambrosiano had acquired Banca del Gottardo in Lugano, Switzerland. This became the main conduit for washing Mafia money after the collapse of Sindona's Amincor in Zürich. Other foreign assets were to follow. One of these was Banco Ambrosiano Overseas Ltd, Nassau. This branch in the Bahamas tax haven was founded in 1971 and had from its inception on its board of directors Bishop Paul Marcinkus. It was originally called Cisalpine Overseas Bank to deflect further any inquiring members of Italy's Finance Police.

The profits being channelled into the coffers of the Vatican Bank grew proportionally with Calvi's empire. To understand many of the very complicated and often deliberately over-complicated financial convolutions in which Calvi indulged throughout the 1970s, one fact has to be grasped: essentially, Banco Ambrosiano of Milan and the Vatican Bank were interlocked. Many of the crucial operations were joint operations. The reason that Calvi was able to break the law again and again was because of the ready assistance given to him by the Vatican Bank. Thus when on November 19th, 1976 Calvi wished to acquire 53.3 per cent of Banco Mercantile SA of Florence, the purchase appeared to be on behalf of the Vatican Bank. The shares found their convoluted way on December 17th to Milan stockbrokers Giammei and Company, who frequently acted on behalf of the Vatican. By dexterous paperwork the shares were 'parked' on the same day at the Vatican Bank. The fact that the Vatican did not have adequate funds in a particular account to pay for the shares was overcome by crediting on December 17th to the Vatican Bank, in a newly opened account, number 42801, 8 billion lire. The following summer, on June 29th 1977, Giammei bought the shares back from the Vatican Bank through Credito Commerciale of Milan. As the shares followed this snake-like path they were undergoing, at least on paper, a dramatic price increase. The original purchase had been made at 14,000 lire per share. By the time the shares found their way back to Giammei they were deemed to be worth 26,000 lire per share. On June 30th 1977 the shares were then sold by Credito Commerciale to Immobiliare XX Settembre SA, which was controlled by Calvi. On paper the Vatican Bank had made a profit of 7,724,378,100 lire as the price of the shares was hiked. The reality was that Calvi paid the Vatican Bank 800 million lire for the privilege of using their name and facilities. The Vatican Bank, situated in the independent State of Vatican City, was beyond the reach of the Italian Bank Inspectors. By selling himself shares he already owned at twice the original purchase price Calvi vastly increased the worth, on paper, of Banco Mercantile and stole 7,724,378,100 lire, less, of course, the kick-back he gave to the Vatican Bank. Subsequently Calvi sold his shares to Milan business rival Anna Bonomi for 33 billion lire.

With the close and continuous co-operation of the Vatican Bank, Calvi was able to dance an illegal and criminal path through the Italian laws again and again. Operations such as that described above could not take place without the full knowledge and approval of Marcinkus.

With regard to the Sindona/Calvi/Marcinkus scheme concerning Banca Cattolica del Veneto all the available evidence suggests a criminal conspiracy involving all three men.

Marcinkus wanted to keep the operation secret, even from Pope Paul VI. Some years afterwards Calvi recalled the deal to friend and business associate Flavio Carboni:*

*Carboni secretly tape-recorded this and many other conversations with Calvi between October 1981 and May 1982.

Mercinkus, who is a rough type, born in a suburb of Chicago of poor parents, wanted to carry out the operation without even telling the boss. That is the Pope. I had three meetings with Marcinkus regarding Banca Cattolica del Veneto. He wanted to sell it to me. I asked him: 'Are you sure? Is it available to you? Is the boss in agreement with it?' It was I who insisted and told him, 'Go to the boss, tell him'. Marcinkus took my advice. Later Marcinkus told me, yes, he had spoken with Paul VI and had his assent. Some time later Marcinkus got me an audience with Paul VI, who thanked me because in the meantime I had sorted out some problems of the Ambrosiano Library. In reality I understood he was thanking me for buying Banca Cattolica del Veneto.

If anyone seeks confirmation that by the early 1970s the Pope had acquired the new title of Chairman of the Board it can be found in Calvi's description. The Holy Father and Vicar of Christ is reduced to 'the boss'. Equally illuminating are Roberto Calvi's anxious questions to Bishop Marcinkus. 'Are you sure? Is it available to you?' The Milanese banker was obviously fully aware of the close ties that bound the bank to the Vicenza clergy. The fact that Marcinkus wished to keep the Pope ignorant of the transaction is a further indication of just how dubious the sale to Calvi was. Cardinal Benelli's advice to Albino Luciani that the Pope would not intercede on behalf of the Patriarch, his bishops and his priests, is demonstrated as being wise. There was not much point in complaining about the sale to the man who had given it his personal blessing. What Pope Paul VI, with the aid of Calvi, Marcinkus and Sindona, had created was a time bomb which would continue to tick until September 1978.

Fearful of a hostile reaction from Venice, all news of the sale of the bank was suppressed by Marcinkus and Calvi. On March 30th, 1972 Calvi's group announced that they had acquired 37.4 per cent of Banca Cattolica, but the documentary evidence I have acquired tells another story.

On July 27th, 1971 Calvi wrote to Marcinkus:

With this letter we wish to inform you of our firm offer to buy up to 50 per cent of the shares of the Banca Cattolica del Veneto, Vicenza, at a price of 1,600 lire each share with normal usufruct to take place through the following steps:
1   For 45 per cent of the shares making up the aforesaid company, that is 16,254,000 shares with the application

depending on your acceptance of our firm offer and against a
payment by us of $42 million.

2   For the remaining shares, that is up to a further 5 per cent of
the capital, 1,806,000 shares, to take effect from the date of the
'declaration of intent' concerning the aforementioned Banca
Cattolica del Veneto, to take place before October 31, 1971, and
against a payment of $4,500,000 on 29.10.1971.

The Vatican Bank received 46.5 million dollars, at the 1971 value.
A comparable figure today would be 115,000.00 million dollars.

Calvi, who was aware that, at his insistence, this offer would be
shown to the Pope, continued in his letter:

We inform you that we formally assume the responsibility of
maintaining unchanged from the point of view of the high social,
moral and Catholic religious purposes the conduct of Banca
Cattolica del Veneto's activities.

The Vatican copy of this letter is officially stamped and signed by
Marcinkus. Thus the secret sale of 1971 became known to Venice
nearly one year later.

The 'high social, moral and Catholic religious purposes' were so
rapidly dispensed with by Calvi at the Banca Cattolica that the entire
clergy of the region had been up in arms and besieging Luciani's
residence in Venice by mid-1972. Luciani had hurried to Rome, but
1972 was clearly not the time for remedial action, with Paul VI
blessing the transaction. The time for action was to be September
1978.

During the intervening years a curious situation pertained. The
shares never left the Vatican Bank. On October 29th, 1971, the date on
which the final 5 per cent was sold to Calvi, the shares – which were
still held in their entirety by the Vatican Bank – were re-assigned to
Zitropo, a company owned at that time by Sindona. Later Zitropo
became firstly a Calvi-owned asset and subsequently a Vatican Bank
asset. And the shares of Banca Cattolica continued to remain in the
Vatican safe. It is little wonder that as late as March 1982 the then
Archbishop Paul Marcinkus would talk of 'our investments in Banca
Cattolica, which are going very well.'

When the Milan Stock Exchange began to fall in 1974, among those
to be hurt was Banco Ambrosiano. Calvi was particularly vulnerable.
The main ingredient in international banking is confidence. It was

known that he was a close associate of Sindona. When Il Crack occurred, the banking world began to take a more cautious view of The Knight. Credit limits to Ambrosiano were cut back. Loans on the international market became difficult to obtain and, most ominous of all, the demand by small investors for the Bank's shares began to diminish, with a consequent drop in the price. Magically, at what was fast becoming the eleventh hour for Ambrosiano, a company called Suprafin SA with a registered office in Milan, entered the market. This finance house began to display supreme confidence in Signor Calvi. It bought shares in his bank daily and before there was time for the name Suprafin to be written on the list of shareholders, the shares were resold to companies in Liechtenstein and Panama. Confidence in Calvi began to return and Suprafin kept on buying. In 1975, 1976, 1977 and 1978, throughout all of these years Suprafin continued to display massive faith in the future of Calvi's bank – 50 million dollars' worth of faith.

Suprafin clearly knew something no one else did. Between 1974 and 1978 Ambrosiano shares continued to fall, yet Suprafin acquired over 15 per cent of the bank. Suprafin was officially owned by two Liechtenstein companies, Teclefin and Imparfin. In theory these were technically owned by the Vatican Bank. That was the technical theory. In practice Suprafin was owned by Calvi. Consequently, with the complete knowledge of the Vatican Bank, he was supporting the market value of Ambrosiano shares by massive purchases – a totally illegal activity. The money to finance the fraud came from international loans made to the Luxembourg subsidiary and from the parent bank in Milan.

The Vatican Bank received huge annual payments for providing the facilities for The Knight to operate a gigantic international fraud. This money was paid in a variety of ways. All Vatican deposits with Ambrosiano banks received interest payments of at least 1 per cent higher than other depositors. Another method was for Ambrosiano to 'buy' shares from the Vatican. On paper the Vatican Bank would sell a block of shares to a Panamanian company at a price approaching 50 per cent more than the shares were actually worth. The shares would never leave the Vatican portfolio and the bank that Marcinkus controlled would be millions of dollars better off. The Panamanian company, usually with a capital of only a few thousand dollars, would borrow the millions from Banco Ambrosiano Overseas in Nassau where Marcinkus was a director. The Nassau branch would have been loaned the money initially by the Luxembourg company, who in turn had borrowed the money from international banks.

Calvi was obviously hoping against hope that the price of Banco Ambrosiano shares would eventually pick up so that he could offload them. By 1978 he was walking on a knife-edge. As if this entire operation was not enough to keep the banker awake at nights, he was also contending with the problems of laundering Mafia money. Allied to that were the constant demands being made by P2 for funds. This involved further embezzlement. He was also suffering from the after-effects of a blackmail campaign by Michele Sindona.

While The Knight was busy embezzling millions of dollars to maintain fraudulently the share price of Ambrosiano, The Shark had been far from inactive. Sindona reminds one forcibly of a character from a Pirandello play where all expectations may prove to be illusion. The man exudes theatre. A fiction writer would baulk at such a creation. Only real life could create Michele Sindona.

Licio Gelli continued to repay Sindona's commitment to P2. When the Milan public prosecutor's office applied for The Shark's extradition in January 1975, the American judicial authorities asked for more information, including a photograph of Sindona. They also demanded that the extradition papers be translated into English. The Milan office completed a new request running to 200 pages and sent it to the Ministry of Justice in Rome, for translation and dispatch to Washington. It was eventually returned with the observation that the Justice Department in Rome could not manage the translation. This despite the fact that they have one of the largest translation departments in Italy. The American Embassy in Rome declared that it had no knowledge of the extradition request. Licio Gelli had friends in many places.

Sindona meanwhile was living in his luxurious Hotel Pierre apartment in New York. He retained the Richard Nixon/John Mitchell law firm to help him fight extradition. He dismissed his Italian problems when questioned by reporters:

The Governor of the Bank of Italy and other members of the Italian establishment are plotting against me. I have never done a single foreign exchange contract in my life. My enemies in Italy have swindled me and I hope that one day justice will be done.

In September 1975, when photographs of the dinner-jacketed Shark shaking hands with New York's Mayor Abraham Beame appeared in the Italian Press, there was outrage from at least some quarters in Italy. *Corriere della Sera* observed:

Sindona continues to release statements and interviews and continues, in his American exile-refuge, to frequent the jet set. The laws and mechanisms of extradition are not equal for all. Someone who steals apples can languish in prison for months, perhaps years. An emigrant working abroad who does not reply to his call-up papers is forced to come back and face the rigours of the military tribunal. For them, the twists and turns of the bureaucracy do not exist.

In Italy small savers appointed lawyers in an attempt to salvage some of their money from the Sindona wreckage and the Vatican declared a 'serious budget deficit'. In the USA The Shark hired a public relations man and went on the University lecture circuit.

Whilst senior executives of the Franklin National Bank were arrested and charged with conspiring to misapply millions of dollars by speculating on the foreign exchange, Sindona was telling the students of Wharton Graduate School in Philadelphia;

The aim, perhaps an ambitious one, of this brief talk is to contribute to restoring the faith of the United States in its economic, financial and monetary sectors, and to remind it that the free world needs America.

Whilst he was being sentenced by a Milan court to three-and-a-half years' imprisonment, having been found guilty on 23 counts of misappropriating 10 million pounds, he was moralizing to the students of Columbia University.

When payments are made with the intent of evading the law in order to obtain unfair benefits, a public reaction is clearly called for. Both the corrupted and the corrupter should be punished.

Whilst he planned the blackmail of his fellow P2 member and close friend Roberto Calvi, he painted a visionary image to students who yearned to emulate him.

I hope in the not too distant future, when we will have been in contact with other planets and new worlds in our myriad galaxies, the students of this University will be able to suggest to the companies they represent that they expand to the cosmos creating 'cosmos-corporations' which will bring the creative spirit of the private entrepreneur throughout the universe.

Sindona was clearly in earnest. He arranged a number of meetings of the American Mafia, Cosa Nostra and the Sicilian Mafia and attempted to persuade them and Licio Gelli that they should organize the secession of Sicily from Italy. He had previously, in 1972, been a conspirator in the so-called 'White Coup' – a plot to take over Italy. The Mafia were sceptical and Gelli contemptuous. He called the idea 'mad' and told Sindona that secession of Sicily could only take place with the support of the military and political members of P2, and that the members were biding their time. He advised Sindona: 'Put the plan in the "Pending" File.'

In September 1976 the Italian authorities finally succeeded in having Sindona arrested in New York. It was the first significant breakthrough they had achieved in the long fight for his extradition. Sindona expressed surprise that 'the United States chose now, some two years after the false charges were lodged against me in Italy, to begin these extradition proceedings. I want to emphasize that the charges were made in Italy on the basis of little or no investigation and, on their face, are false.' He was subsequently released on 3 million dollars bail but by 1977 the net was finally beginning to close. A Federal Grand Jury began investigating alleged violations by Sindona involving the collapse of the Franklin Bank.

Sindona used all the weapons at his disposal. Important people went to court to speak for The Shark as he fought extradition. Carmelo Spagnuolo, President of a division of the Supreme Court in Rome, swore an affidavit testifying that the charges against Sindona were a Communist plot. He also swore that Sindona was a great protector of the working class, that the people investigating Sindona in Italy were at best incompetent and were controlled by political persecutors. For good measure he advised the United States Court that many members of the Italian judiciary were left-wing extremists and that if The Shark was returned to Italy he would be murdered. Carmelo Spagnuolo was a member of P2.

Licio Gelli also swore an affidavit on behalf of Sindona. He noted that he himself had been accused of being a 'C.I.A. agent; the chief of the Argentine Death Squad; a representative of the Portuguese secret service; the co-ordinator of the Greek, Chilean and West German secret services; the chief of the international movement of underground Fascism, etc.'

He made no attempt to deny these various allegations, and offered no evidence that all of them or any of them were ill-founded. He attributed them to 'the rise of Communist power in Italy'. On oath he then went on to make a few allegations of his own including: 'Communist influence has already reached certain sectors of the Government, particularly the Justice Department, where during the last five years there has been a political shift from the centre towards the extreme left'. Again he offered no evidence. Gelli asserted that because of 'left-wing infiltration' Sindona would not receive a fair trial in Italy and would probably be murdered. He continued: 'The Communists' hatred of Michele Sindona is due to the fact that he is an anti-Communist and that he has always been favourable to the free enterprise system in a democratic Italy.'

On November 13th, 1977, Sindona gave a demonstration of his version of the free enterprise system at work in democratic Italy. The planned blackmail of Calvi was activated and posters and pamphlets began to appear all over Milan. They accused Calvi of fraud, exporting currency, falsifying accounts, embezzlement, tax evasion. They quoted secret Swiss Bank Account numbers belonging to Calvi. They detailed illicit deals. They referred to his Mafia links. It became more interesting to read the walls of the city than *Corriere della Sera*. Sindona, who had orchestrated this public washing of Calvi's dirty laundry, had come to the conclusion that his fellow P2 member and former protégé Roberto Calvi was not taking a sufficiently active interest in The Shark's predicament. Sindona had appealed to Licio Gelli, who agreed that Calvi should make a 'substantial contribution' to Sindona's war chest. Gelli offered himself as an intermediary between his two masonic friends. This ensured that they both paid Gelli a commission.

Roberto Calvi dipped into his pocket yet again, or more accurately dipped into the pockets of those who banked with him. Half-a-million dollars were paid by Calvi into Banca del Gottardo, Lugano in April 1978. It was placed in a Sindona account.

The man who had organized the poster and pamphlet campaign on behalf of Sindona, Luigi Cavallo, had gone about his task with enormous relish. Cavallo had operated for some time in Italy as a one-man smear campaign unit that, like all professional whores, sold itself to the highest bidder. The posters were followed on November 24th, 1977, with a letter to the Governor of the Bank of Italy, Paolo Baffi, listing all the accusations which had appeared on the walls of Milan. It also referred to an earlier communication which had given photocopies of Calvi's Swiss Bank accounts. Cavallo concluded his letter to the Governor with the threat to sue the Bank of Italy for failure to carry out its legal duties unless they began to investigate the Banco Ambrosiano.

This letter shows the fundamental difference between a first-division criminal like Sindona and a third-division crook like Cavallo. The letter was Cavallo's idea and was written without reference to Sindona, who would never have authorized such action. You may steal eggs from the golden goose but you do not kill it, at least not while it is still capable of laying.

The same week in April 1978 in which Sindona received his half-a-million-dollar pay-off, officials from the Bank of Italy who, for a number of years had retained the gravest reservations about Banco Ambrosiano and Roberto Calvi, moved into the bank in force. The twelve men had been carefully chosen by Paolo Baffi and his senior colleague Mario Sarcinelli. The man selected to head the inspection was Giulio Padalino. Unfortunately for Calvi, Padalino was incorruptible.

The poster and pamphlet attack by Sindona was a flea-bite compared with the problems now facing Calvi. News of the massive investigation leaked around Milan's business world. The price of Ambrosiano shares plummeted further, forcing Calvi to divert even more money to prop up the price. By now the tangled empire he controlled had a branch in Nicaragua; another was planned for Peru. There were Calvi companies in Canada, Belgium and the USA.

The Achilles heel was Suprafin. If the bank inspectors discovered the truth about Suprafin then the collapse of Banco Ambrosiano and the arrest and imprisonment of Calvi were inevitable. Equally the long-desired extradition of Sindona would become a much simpler operation. Both men stood to lose everything, including their liberty, if the inspectors could crack the Suprafin puzzle. In Milan Calvi became agitated. In New York Sindona stopped gloating about the half-a-million dollars he had just extorted from The Knight. The one hope for both men was Bishop Paul Marcinkus. Marcinkus duly obliged. When the Bank of Italy inspectors asked Ambrosiano's General Manager Carlo Olgiati who owned Suprafin, he told them it was owned by the Instituto per le Opere di Religione, the Vatican Bank.

Calmly the Bank inspectors continued probing, working their way through the maze of share purchases, transfers, cross transfers, buy backs, parking. They were severely limited by Italian law. The information they could insist upon with regard to the foreign associates left much to be desired. If for example they had been able to obtain detailed information on Calvi's Luxembourg holding company and had realized that millions of dollars borrowed on the European market had been funnelled to Nassau where Marcinkus sat on the Board with Calvi and Managua and that these two Ambrosiano-owned banks had then loaned millions to small Panamanian shell companies *without security*, the game would have been up there and then. But full information on the Luxembourg holding company was denied to the inspectors. Calvi stalled; he grew evasive. 'It was so difficult, you know what these foreigners are like? I cannot breach their rules on "confidentiality"'. The Bank inspectors continued to dig. They discovered that on May 6th, 1975 Luigi Landra, a former chief executive of Banco Ambrosiano, and Livio Godeluppi, brother of Ambrosiano's chief accountant, had been made directors of Suprafin. Had these two men clearly in the trust of Ambrosiano also joined the elite ranks of the Vatican's 'uomini di fiducia' – men of trust?

The inspectors established that Suprafin had been created in Milan in November, 1971 by two of Calvi's closest associates, Vahan Pasargiklian, who by the time of the 1978 investigation had become Managing Director of Banca Cattolica, and Gennaro Zanfagna. Perhaps they too had become men of trust for the Vatican? Suprafin had 'owned by Calvi' written all over it.

The probe continued. Careful analysis of the current accounts held by Suprafin convinced the inspectors that the company was indeed owned by Banco Ambrosiano and not the Vatican. Why would the Bank buy La Centrale shares from Suprafin at 13,864 lire as against a market price of 9,650 and then sell the shares back to Suprafin at 9,340? To obtain a letter of thanks from Pope Paul? A pat on the back from Marcinkus?

In July 1978 they tackled Calvi's executive colleague, Carlo Olgiati, again. Olgiati consulted Calvi. He returned bearing a letter. With great Milanese charm Olgiati gave the letter to Padalino to read. It was from the Vatican Bank to Roberto Calvi. It was dated January 20th, 1975.

It read:

This is to refer to the portfolio of shares as per December 31st 1974, held by the company Suprafin SA. A company pertaining to our Institute. You are herewith requested to manage and administer the said portfolio in the most appropriate form and to arrange for all suitable and divestment operations. Will you please keep us periodically up to date as regards the position of the above named portfolio and related transactions.

The letter was signed by Luigi Mennini and the Vatican Bank's Chief Accountant, Pellegrino De Strobel. It might well be dated January 1975 but the bank inspectors strongly suspected that it had been written after their investigation had begun in April 1978, and was written with the full approval of Bishop Marcinkus.

If Marcinkus and his colleagues at the Vatican Bank were to be believed then the Holy See had given a new definition to the phrase 'Christian charity'. It now embraced entering the Milan stock market and spending millions merely to defend the price of Banco Ambrosiano shares. It seemed unlikely to the Bank of Italy officials that the offerings of the poor in churches around the world had been given with quite this course of action in mind. Nevertheless, Calvi, by courtesy of Bishop Marcinkus, was off the hook, at least temporarily. Here was the apparent proof that Suprafin was indeed owned by the Vatican Bank. The normally cold and aloof Calvi became almost affable in the eyes of some of his more senior colleagues at the Milan headquarters. Confident that he had blocked the bank investigation in what was potentially his most vulnerable area, he finalized the arrangements for a trip to South America with his wife Clara. The trip was planned to be part business, part pleasure. There was to be some sightseeing of potential sites for branches on the South American continent plus the inevitable business meetings associated with such a development, then sightseeing of a more plebeian nature.

Once in South America Calvi began to relax. Then Pope Paul VI died. The lines between Calvi's hotel suite in Buenos Aires and various parts of Italy became busy. When he heard the name of the new Pope, Albino Luciani, Calvi was shocked. Virtually any of the other 110 Cardinals would have been preferable.

Calvi was fully aware of the anger his takeover of the Banca Cattolica Veneto had generated in Venice; aware that Luciani had gone to Rome in an attempt to regain diocesan control over the bank. He was equally aware that Luciani was a man with a formidable reputation for personal poverty and intransigence towards clerical wheeler dealing. The episode of the two priests and the speculating salesman in Vittorio Veneto was legendary in northern Italy. From Buenos Aires Calvi phoned instructions to sell some of the shares in the bank that Suprafin held. With bank inspectors looking over their shoulders his staff had to move cautiously. Nevertheless in the first three weeks of September, 1978, they unloaded 350,000 shares. Then Calvi heard the news he had been dreading. Bishop Paul Marcinkus's days were numbered. If Marcinkus went, total exposure of the entire fraud was inevitable. He recalled what Marcinkus had said to him by telephone within days of Luciani's election: 'Things are going to be very different from now on. This Pope is quite a different man.'

Albino Luciani represented a very serious threat to both Michele Sindona and Roberto Calvi. Subsequently events were to demonstrate powerfully what happened to people who represented serious threats to these two.

The new Pope also clearly represented a major threat to Bishop Paul Marcinkus, President of the Vatican Bank. If Luciani dug into the Bank there were likely to be quite a number of vacancies. Mennini and De Strobel who had put their names to the Suprafin letter were also on borrowed time. Both had been involved over the years with the criminal activities of Sindona and Calvi. If Marcinkus was in any doubt whatsoever about the capacity of Luciani to take vigorous effective action he had but to confer with De Strobel, a lawyer from near Venice who was fully conversant with the affair of the embezzling priests in Vittorio Veneto.

Bernardino Nogara may well have had a purely capitalistic mentality but compared with what came after him in Vatican Incorporated, the man was a saint. The company had come a long way since Mussolini gave it its modern impetus in 1929.

By September, 1978 the Pope sat at the head of massive multi-national corporation. As Albino Luciani looked out of the windows of his third-floor nineteen-room apartment this man who was dedicated to a poor Church for the poor had a task that was as supreme as his position.

If his dream to be the last 'rich Father' was to become a reality then Vatican Incorporated would have to be dismantled. The Papal States might have been lost for ever but in their place was an extraordinary money-making machine.

There was the Administration of the Patrimony of the Holy See (APSA), with its President Cardinal Villot, secretary Monsignor Antonetti, and its ordinary and extraordinary sections. The ordinary section administered all the wealth of the various congregations, tribunals and offices. It specifically administered a great deal of the real estate of the Papacy. In Rome alone this amounted to over 5,000 rented apartments. In 1979, its gross assets were in excess of 1 billion dollars.

The extraordinary section, the Vatican's other bank was as active in its daily stock speculations as the IOR controlled by Marcinkus. It specialized in the currency market and worked closely with Crédit Suisse and the Société des Banques Suisses. Its gross assets in September 1978 were in excess of 1.2 billion dollars.

The Vatican Bank, which Marcinkus was running, had gross assets of over 1 billion dollars. Its annual profits by 1978 were over 120 million dollars; 85 per cent of this went directly to the Pope to use as he saw fit. Its number of current accounts were over 11,000. Under the terms by which the Bank was created by Pius XII during the Second World War these accounts should have belonged very largely to religious orders and religious institutes. When Albino Luciani became Pope only 1,047 belonged to religious orders and institutes, 312 to parishes and 290 to dioceses. The remaining 9,351 were the property of diplomats, prelates and 'privileged citizens'; a significant number of this last category were not even Italian citizens. There were four who were: Sindona, Calvi, Gelli and Ortolani. Other accounts were held by leading politicians of every shade and major industrialists. Many of the account holders used the facility as a conduit through which to export currency out of Italy illegally. Any deposits made were not subjected to any taxation.

The two departments of APSA and the Vatican Bank were Albino Luciani's major problems which had to be overcome before the Church could revert to its early Christian origins. There were many others, not least the wealth that had been acquired over many centuries. This took many forms, including a multitude of art treasures.

Vatican Incorporated, like all multi-nationals which aspire to respectability, was not negligent in matters of art. Vatican patronage is there for all to see, opening times permitting: the Caravaggios, the Raphael tapestries, the Farnese gold altar cross and candlesticks by Gentile da Fabriano, the Belvedere Apollo, the Belvedere Torso, the paintings of Leonardo da Vinci, Bernini's sculptures. Would the words of Jesus Christ be heard less clearly in somewhere more modest than the Sistine Chapel with its majestic Last Judgment by Michelangelo? The Vatican classifies all of these as non-productive assets. What the founder of Christianity would classify them as can be gauged from his own comments about wealth and property.

What would Jesus Christ have felt if he had returned to earth in September 1978 and been allowed into the Vatican City State?

What would the man who declared, 'My Kingdom is not of this earth', have felt if he had wandered through the departments of APSA with its teams of clerical and lay stock analysts, each an expert in his own field, following the day-by-day and often minute-by-minute fluctuations of the shares, securities and investments that APSA owns throughout the world? What would the carpenter's son have made of the IBM equipment that functions both in APSA and the Vatican Bank? What would the man who compared the difficulty of a rich man entering the Kingdom of Heaven with a camel passing through the eye of a needle have said about the latest stock market quotations of London, Wall Street, Zürich, Milan, Montreal and Tokyo that chatter endlessly into the Vatican?

What would the man who said 'Blessed are the poor', have said about the annual profit from the sale of Vatican stamps? Profit in excess of 1 million dollars. What would have been his opinion of the annual collection of Peter's Pence that went directly to the Pope? This annual collection, considered by many to be an accurate barometer of the popularity of the Pope, had under the charismatic John XXIII produced between 15 and 20 million dollars per annum. Under Paul VI this had dropped after *Humanae Vitae* to an average of 4 million dollars per annum.

What would the Founder of the Faith have felt about these few examples of how far his teaching had been perverted? The question is of course rhetorical. If Jesus Christ had returned to earth in September 1978, or if he came now and attempted to enter the Vatican, the result would be the same. He would not get as far as the doors of the Vatican Bank. He would be arrested at the Saint Anne Gate and handed over to the Italian authorities. He would never have the opportunity to learn at first hand about Vatican Incorporated, the multi-national conglomerate that is fed from so many directions. He would not hear, for example, how it derives vast sums from the USA and West Germany; how in 1978, through the State tax of 'Kirchensteuer', the Roman Catholic Church of West Germany received 1.9 billion dollars, of which it then subsequently passed on to the Vatican a significant proportion.

If Albino Luciani was to succeed with his dream of a poor Church for the poor, it was going to be a Herculean task. The modern monster created by Bernardino Nogara had by 1978 become self-generating. When the cardinals elected Albino Luciani to the Papacy on that hot August day in 1978 they set an honest, holy, totally incorruptible Pope on a collision course with Vatican Incorporated. The irresistible market forces of the Vatican Bank, APSA and the other money-making elements were about to be met by the immovable integrity of Albino Luciani.

The Thirty-three Days

🙦🙤

When Albino Luciani threw open the windows of the Papal Apartments within twenty-four hours of his election, the gesture personified his entire Papacy. Fresh air and sunlight rushed into a Roman Catholic Church which had grown increasingly dark and sombre during the last years of Paul VI.

Luciani, the man whose self-description during his Venice days had been, 'I am just a poor man accustomed to small things and silence', now found himself obliged to confront the Vatican grandeur and the Curial babble. The son of a bricklayer was now Supreme Head of a religion whose founder was the son of a carpenter.

Many of the Vatican experts who had failed even to consider the possibility of Luciani's election hailed him as 'The Unknown Pope'. He had been well enough known by ninety-nine cardinals to be entrusted with the Church's future, this man without any diplomatic training or Curial experience. The considerable number of Curial cardinals had been rejected. In essence the entire Curia had been rejected in favour of a quiet, humble man who promptly announced that he wished to be called Pastor rather than Pontiff. Luciani's aspirations quickly became clear: total revolution. He was intent on taking the Church back to its origins, back to the simplicity, honesty, ideals and aspirations of Jesus Christ. Others before him had had the same dream only to have the reality of the world as perceived by their advisers impinge upon the dream. How could this small, unassuming man accomplish even the beginnings of the transformation, both material and spiritual, that would be required?

In electing Albino Luciani, his fellow cardinals had made a number of profound statements about what they wanted and what they did not want. Clearly they did not want a reactionary Pope who might make his mark upon the world with dazzling examples of incomprehensible intellectualism. It would seem they had sought to make an impact on the world by electing a man whose goodness, wisdom and exemplary humility would be manifest to all. In the event that was what they got. A shepherd intent upon pastoral care.

His new name was considered a bit of a mouthful by the Romans and they quickly abbreviated it to the more intimate 'Gianpaolo', a corruption the Pope happily accepted and used to sign letters, only to have them returned by Secretary of State Villot for correction to the formal title. One such letter written in his own hand was to thank the Augustinians for their hospitality during his stay before the Conclave. This simple act was typical of the man. Two days after being elected Pope to over eight hundred million Catholics Luciani made time to thank his former hosts.

Another letter, written on the same day, struck a more sombre note. Writing to an Italian priest whose work he admired, Luciani revealed his awareness of the burden that was now uniquely his. 'I don't know how I could have accepted. The day after I already regretted it, but by then it was too late.' One of his first acts upon entering the Papal Apartments had been to phone his homeland in the north. He spoke to an astonished Monsignor Ducoli, a long-time friend and working associate, now Bishop of Belluno. He told the Bishop he was 'lonely for my people'. Later he spoke to his brother Edoardo, 'Now look what's happened to me.' These acts were private; others of a more public nature caught the world's imagination.

To begin with there was his smile. With just that facial expression of joy he touched many. It was impossible not to warm to the man, and as one warmed the feeling was good. Paul VI with his agonizing had turned people off in millions. Albino Luciani dramatically reversed the trend. He recaptured world interest in the Papacy. When the world listened to what was behind the smile the interest quickened. His smile cannot be found in any book that claims to make its reader a better Christian but it effectively caught the joy that this man had discovered in Christianity. What Luciani demonstrated in a manner and to a degree never before seen from a Pope, any Pope, was the ability to communicate, whether directly or through radio, Press and television. It was an undreamed-of asset to the Roman Catholic Church.

Luciani was an object lesson in how to win the battle for mankind's heart, mind and soul. For the first time in living memory a Pope was talking to his people in a manner and a style they could understand. The sigh of relief from the faithful was almost audible. The murmurs of delight continued through the Indian summer of 1978. Luciani began to take the Church on the long walk back to the Gospel.

The public rapidly judged this charismatic man a huge success. Vatican observers simply did not know what to make of him. Many had given instant and learned opinions about the choice of Papal name, they had talked of 'symbolic continuity'. Luciani had unwittingly demolished all of that on the first Sunday with, 'John made me a bishop, Paul made me a cardinal'. Not much symbolic continuity there. The experts wrote speculative articles about what the new Pope might or might not do on a range of issues. A large amount of that speculation was rendered superfluous by one comment in Pope John Paul's very first speech when he had stated, 'As the Second Vatican Council, to whose teachings I wish to commit my total ministry, as priest, as teacher, as pastor . . .' There was no need to speculate; all they had to do was to refer to the various conclusions of the Council.

Luciani, speaking to a packed St Peter's Square on Sunday September 10th, talked of God and said, 'He is our Father; even more he is our Mother'. The Italian Vatican experts, in particular, were beside themselves. In a country noted for its macho image to suggest that God was a woman was deemed by some to be confirmation of the end of the world. There were many anxious debates about this fourth member of the Trinity until Luciani gently pointed out that he had been quoting Isaiah. The male-dominated Mother Church relaxed.

Earlier, on September 6th, during a General Audience, members of the Papal entourage, fussing around the Holy Father in a manner reminiscent of irritating flies around a horse, publicly displayed embarrassment as Luciani held over 15,000 people spellbound. Entering almost at a trot into the Nervi Hall, which was filled to overflowing, he talked about the soul. There was nothing remarkable in that. What was unusual was the manner and the style.

Once a man went to buy a new motor car from the agent. The salesman gave him some advice. 'Look, it's an excellent car, make sure you treat it correctly. Premium petrol in the tank, the best oil in the engine.' The customer replied, 'Oh no, I can't stand the smell of petrol or oil. Fill the tank with champagne, which I like very much and I'll oil the joints with jam.' The salesman shrugged, 'Do what you like: but don't come and complain if you end up in a ditch with your car.'

The Lord did something similar with us: he gave us this body, animated by an intelligent soul, a good will. He said, 'This machine is a good one, but treat it well.'

While the Vatican elite shuddered at such profanity Albino Luciani knew full well that his words were being carried around the earth. Scatter enough seed, some will grow. He had been presented with the most powerful pulpit on earth. His use of the gift was deeply impressive. Many within the Church talk *ad nauseam* of the 'Good News of the Gospel', while giving the impression that they are informing the listeners of unmitigated disasters. When Luciani talked of the Good News, it was clear from his whole demeanour that the news was very good indeed.

Several times he brought a young boy out of the choir to share the microphone with him, to help him work not only the audience inside the Nervi Hall but the wider audience outside. Other world leaders were adepts at picking up the young and kissing them. Here was a man who actually talked to them and even more remarkably listened and responded to what they had to say.

He quoted Mark Twain, Jules Verne and the Italian poet Trilussa. He talked of Pinocchio. Having already compared the soul to a car he now drew an analogy between prayer and soap. 'Prayer well used, would be a marvellous soap, capable of making us all saints. We are not all saints because we have not used this soap enough.' The Curia, particularly certain bishops and cardinals, winced. The public listened.

A few days after his election he faced over one thousand members of the world's Press and, gently chiding them for concentrating excessively on Conclave trivia rather than on its true significance, he acknowledged that theirs was not a new problem by recalling the advice an Italian editor had given to his reporters: 'Remember, the public does not want to know what Napoleon III said to William of Prussia. It wants to know whether he wore beige or red trousers and whether he smoked a cigar.'

Luciani obviously felt at home with the reporters. He was a man who more than once in his life had remarked that if he had not become a priest he would have become a journalist. His two books and numerous articles indicate a talent that could have held its own with many of the listening correspondents. Recalling the late Cardinal Mercier's observations that if the Apostle Paul were alive today he would have been a journalist, the new Pope showed a keen awareness of the importance of the various news media by enlarging on the

Apostle's possible modern role: 'Not only a journalist. Possibly Head of Reuters. Not only Head of Reuters, I think he would have also asked for airtime on Italian television and NBC.'

The correspondents loved it. The Curia were less amused. All the above remarks to the reporters were censored out of the official records of the speech. What remains for posterity is a drab, unctuous, prepared speech, written by Vatican officials – though in fact the Pope had continually departed from it – mute, inaccurate testimony to the wit and personality of Albino Luciani. This Vatican censorship of the Pope became a constant feature during September 1978.

Illustrissimi, the collection of his letters to the famous, had been available in book form in Italy since 1976. It had proved to be highly successful. Now with its author the leader of 800 million Roman Catholics, the commercial potential was not lost on the publishing world. High-powered executives began appearing at the office of *Il Messaggero di San Antonio* in Padua. The Catholic monthly was sitting on the proverbial gold mine, less author's royalties. For the author, the real pay-off was that the ideas and observations in the letters would be read by a world-wide audience. The fact that they would be read only because he had now become Pope mattered not one jot to Luciani. More seed was being scattered. More would grow.

One of the truly delightful results that became apparent in the days following the August Conclave was that as long as Luciani was in charge, Vatican interpreters, watchers, experts and seers had all been made redundant. What was needed was verbatim reporting. Given that, the new Pope's intentions were very clear.

On August 28th the beginning of his Papal revolution was announced. It took the form of a Vatican statement that there was to be no coronation, that the new Pope refused to be crowned. There would be no *sedia gestatoria*, the chair used to carry the Pope, no tiara encrusted with emeralds, rubies, sapphires and diamonds. No ostrich feathers, no six-hour ceremony. In short the ritual with which the Church demonstrated that it still lusted after temporal power was abolished. Albino Luciani had been obliged to engage in long, tedious argument with the Vatican traditionalists before his wishes prevailed. Luciani, who never once used the royal 'we', the monarchical first person plural, was determined that the royal Papacy with its appurtenances of worldly grandeur should be replaced by a Church which resembled the concepts of its founder. The 'coronation' became a simple Mass. The absurdity of a swaying Pontiff reminiscent of a Caliph from the Arabian Nights was supplanted by a supreme Pastor quietly walking up the steps of the altar. With that gesture Luciani abolished a thousand years of history and moved the Church a little farther back down the road towards Jesus Christ.

The triple-decked, bee-hive-shaped tiara was superseded by the pallium, a white woollen stole around the Pope's shoulders. The monarch had made way for the shepherd. The era of the poor Church had officially begun.

Among the twelve Heads of State and other representatives of their countries at the ceremony were men whom the Pope had been anxious to avoid meeting. In particular he had asked his Secretariat of State not to invite the leaders of Argentina, Chile and Paraguay to his inaugural Mass, but Cardinal Villot's department had already sent out the invitations before checking with Albino Luciani. They had assumed there would be the traditional coronation and the invitation list reflected that assumption.

Consequently taking part in the Mass in St Peter's Square were General Videla from Argentina, the Chilean Foreign Minister and the son of the President of Paraguay – representatives from countries where human rights were not considered pressing priorities. Italian protestors demonstrated against their presence and there were nearly 300 arrests. Later Albino Luciani would be criticized for the presence of such men at the Mass. The experts who criticized were unaware that the blame should be laid at Cardinal Villot's door. When the critical comments appeared Luciani was in no position to respond and Villot remained silent.

At the private audience which followed the Mass, Luciani, the son of a Socialist who had abhorred all aspects of Fascism, left General Videla in no doubt that he had inherited his father's views. He talked particularly of his concern over 'Los Desaparecidos', people who had vanished off the face of Argentinian earth in their thousands. By the conclusion of the 15-minute audience the General began to wish that he had heeded the eleventh-hour attempts of Vatican officials to dissuade him from coming to Rome.

The audience with Vice-President Mondale of the USA was a happier affair. Mondale gave the new Pope a book containing the front page of over fifty US newspapers recording Luciani's election. A more thoughtful present was a first edition copy of Mark Twain's *Life on the Mississippi*. Someone in the State Department had evidently done his homework.

Thus the Papacy of John Paul I began; a Papacy with clear aims and aspirations. Immediately Luciani set cats among a variety of Vatican pigeons. Before the inaugural Mass he had addressed the Diplomatic Corps accredited to the Vatican. His own diplomatic staff visibly blanched when he observed on behalf of the entire Roman Catholic Church:

> We have no temporal goods to exchange, no economic interests to discuss. Our possibilities for intervention are specific and limited and of a special character. They do not interfere with purely temporal, technical and political affairs, which are matters for your government.
>
> In this way, our diplomatic missions to your highest civil authorities, far from being a survival from the past, are a witness to our deep-seated respect for lawful temporal power, and to our lively interest in the humane causes that the temporal power is intended to advance.

'We have no public goods to exchange . . .' It was a public sentence of death upon Vatican Incorporated. All that remained uncertain was the number of days and months during which it would continue to function. The men of the international money markets of Milan, London, Tokyo, and New York pondered Luciani's words with interest. If he really meant what he said then clearly there were going to be changes. Those changes would not be confined to the movement of people out of the Vatican Bank and the APSA, but would inevitably include a curtailment of a number of Vatican Incorporated's activities. For the men in the world's money markets there were billions to be made if they could correctly guess the direction this new Vatican philosophy would take. Albino Luciani wanted a poor Church for the poor. What did he plan to do with those who had created a wealthy Church? What did he plan to do with the wealth?

Luciani's humility was responsible for the birth of several misconceptions. Many observers concluded that this demonstrably holy man was a simple, uncomplicated person who lacked the cultural talents of his predecessor, Paul VI. The reality was that Luciani had a far richer cultivation and a good deal more sophistication than Paul. His gifts were such that this extraordinary man could appear completely plebeian. His was a simplicity that is acquired only by a very few; a simplicity stemming from a deep wisdom.

One of the peculiarities of this age is that humility and gentleness are inevitably taken to be indications of some form of weakness. Frequently they indicate precisely the opposite, great strength.

When the new Pope remarked that he had been leafing through the Vatican Year Book to find out who did what, many in the Curia smirked and concluded that he would be a pushover, a man they could control. There were others who knew better.

Men who had known Albino Luciani over many years watched and waited. They knew the steel within; the strength to take difficult or unpopular decisions. Many spoke to me of these hidden attributes. Monsignor Tiziano Scalzotto, Father Mario Senigaglia, Monsignor Da Rif, Father Bartolomeo Sorge and Father Busa were just five of those who talked of the inner strength of Pope John Paul I. Father Busa observed:

> His mind was as strong, as hard and as sharp as a diamond. That was where his real power was. He understood and had the ability to get to the centre of a problem. He could not be overwhelmed. When everyone was applauding the smiling Pope, I was waiting for him 'tirare fuori le unghie', to reveal his claws. He had tremendous power.

Without an entourage – no Venetian Mafia followed the Milan clique into the Papal Apartments – Albino Luciani would need every scrap of inner strength he could muster if he was to avoid becoming the prisoner of the Vatican Curia.

In the early days after the August Conclave the Vatican Government machine had not been idle. On Sunday, August 27th, after his noon speech to the crowds, Luciani lunched with Cardinal Jean Villot. As Pope Paul's Secretary of State since April 1969, Villot had built a reputation for quiet competence. During the run-up to the Conclave Villot, as chamberlain, had virtually functioned as a caretaker Pope aided by his committees of cardinals. Luciani asked Villot to continue as Secretary of State for 'a little while, until I have found my way'. Villot, 73 years of age, had been hoping that the moment had come when he might retire. In the event Luciani appointed Villot as his Secretary of State and reconfirmed all the Curial heads in their previous positions but the Curia were made aware that this was merely a temporary measure. Ever the prudent man of the mountains, the new Pope preferred to bide his time. 'Deliberation. Decision. Execution.' If the Curia wanted to know how their new Pope would act they had merely to read his letter to St Bernard. A great many did. They also did much deeper research on Pope John Paul I. What they discovered caused consternation in many Vatican departments and a deep pleasure of anticipation in others.

The death of Pope Paul VI brought bubbling to the surface many animosities that existed in the Vatican village. The Roman Curia, the central administrative body of the Church, had been engaging in internecine warfare for many years; only Paul's expertise had kept the majority of the battles from public view. Now after the rebuff within the Conclave the Curial warfare reached the Papal Apartments. Albino Luciani complained bitterly about the situation to a number of friends who came to see him. 'I want to learn quickly the trade of Pope but almost no one explains problems and situations in a thorough and detached manner. Most of the time I hear nothing but bad spoken about everything and everyone.' To another friend from the north he observed: 'I have noticed two things that appear to be in very short supply in the Vatican. Honesty and a good cup of coffee.'

There were as many Roman Curial factions as choirboys in the Sistine Chapel Choir. There was the Curia of Pope Paul VI committed to ensuring that the memory of the late Pope was constantly and continually honoured and also that there would be no deviation from the late Pope's views, opinions and pronouncements.

There was the Curia which favoured Cardinal Giovanni Benelli and the Curia which wished he was in Hell. Pope Paul VI had made Benelli his Under-Secretary of State, number two to Cardinal Villot. He rapidly became the Pope's muscle, ensuring that policy was adhered to. Paul had moved him to Florence and promoted him in order to protect him during Paul's last years. Now his protector was dead but the long knives remained sheathed. Luciani was Pope because of men like Benelli.

There were Curial factions which favoured or opposed Cardinals Baggio, Felici, and Bertoli. There were Curia factions wanting more central power and control, others wanting less.

Throughout his life Albino Luciani had avoided visits to the Vatican. He had kept his contact with the Roman Curia to a minimum. As a result, before his election, he probably had fewer Curial enemies than any other cardinal. It was a situation which quickly changed. Here was a Pope who considered 'mere execution' as the basic function of the Curia. He believed in greater power-sharing with the bishops throughout the world and planned to decentralize the Vatican structure. By refusing to be crowned he had distressed the traditionalists. Another innovation hardly likely to endear Luciani to the more materially-minded members of the Curia was his instruction that the extra month's salary paid automatically upon the election of a new Pope should be cut by half.

Obviously there were many within the 3,000 or so members of the Curia who would loyally serve and love the new Pope; but the way of the world is to ensure that negative forces often predominate. As soon as the result of the election was known the Curia, or certain sections of it swung into action. Within hours a special edition of *L'Osservatore Romano* was available with a full biography of the new Pope. Vatican Radio was already broadcasting similar details.

As an example of how to influence the world's thinking about a hitherto unknown leader, *L'Osservatore Romano*'s treatment of Albino Luciani is definitive. Because it deliberately portrayed a person who existed only in the reactionary, oppressive mind of whoever wrote the biographical details, this particular edition of *L'Osservatore Romano* is also an excellent example of why the Vatican's semi-official newspaper has been compared unfavourably with *Pravda*. Using the 'official facts', many journalists fighting deadlines filed copy which portrayed a man who did not exist. *The Economist*, to take one of several hundred examples, said of the new Pope, 'He would not be much at home in the company of Dr Hans Kung.' Research would have revealed that Luciani and Hans Kung had exchanged very friendly letters as well as sending one another books. Further research would have shown that Luciani had several times quoted Kung favourably in his sermons. Virtually every newspaper and periodical in the world that carried profiles of the new Pope made similar totally erroneous assertions.

To read the special edition of *L'Osservatore Romano* is to read of a new Pope who was even more conservative than Pope Paul VI. The distortion covered a wide range of Luciani's views but one in particular is highly relevant when considering the life and death of Albino Luciani: birth control.

The Vatican newspaper described a man who was an intrepid and unquestioning supporter of *Humanae Vitae*.

He made a meticulous study of the subject of responsible parent-hood and engaged in consultations and talks with medical specialists and theologians. He warned of the grave responsibility of the Church (the ecclesiastical Magisterium) in pronouncing on such a delicate and controversial question.

That was entirely accurate and truthful. What followed was completely inaccurate.

With the publication of the Encyclical *Humanae Vitae* there could be no room for doubt, and the Bishop of Vittorio Veneto was among the first to circulate it, and to insist with those who were perplexed by the document, that its teaching was beyond question.

When the Curia moves it is a formidable machine. Its efficiency and speed would make other Civil Services breathless. Men from the Roman Curia appeared at the Gregorian College and removed all notes and papers that referred to Luciani's period of study for his degree. Other members of the Curia went to Venice, Vittorio Veneto, Belluno. Wherever Luciani had been the Curia went. All copies of the Luciani document on birth control were seized and immediately placed in the Vatican's Secret Archives along with his thesis on Rosmini and a large quantity of other writings. It could be said that the beatification process for Albino Luciani began the day he was elected Pope. It would be equally accurate to observe that the Curial cover-up of the real Albino Luciani began the same day.

What certain sections of the Curia had realized with a profound shock was that in electing Albino Luciani, the cardinals had given them a man who would not let the issue of birth control rest with *Humanae Vitae*. Careful study by members of the Curia of what Luciani had actually said, not only to his parishioners in public but to his friends and colleagues in private, quickly established that the new Pope favoured artificial birth control. The inaccurate and false picture *L'Osservatore Romano* painted of a man who rigorously applied the principles *of Humanae Vitae* was the opening shot in a counter-attack designed to hem Albino Luciani inside the strictures of his predecessor's encyclical. It was quickly followed by another blast.

The Press Agency UPI discovered that Luciani had been in favour of a Vatican ruling which would allow artificial birth control. Italian newspapers also carried stories referring to the Luciani document sent to Pope Paul by Cardinal Urbani of Venice in which the strong recommendation in favour of the contraceptive pill had been made. The Curia speedily located Father Henri de Riedmatten who had been secretary to the Papal Birth Control Commission. He described the reports that Luciani had been opposed to an encyclical that condemned artificial birth control as 'a fantasy'. Riedmatten also asserted that Luciani had never been a member of the Commission, which was accurate. He then went on to deny that Luciani had ever

written a letter or a report on the subject that had been sent to Pope
Paul.

This denial and the manner of it is an example of the duplicity that
abounds in the Curia. The Luciani document went to Rome via
Cardinal Urbani and therefore had the Cardinal's imprimatur upon it.
To deny that a document existed, actually signed by Luciani, was
technically correct. To deny that Luciani on behalf of his fellow
bishops in the Veneto region had not forwarded such a document to
the Pope via the then Patriarch of Venice was an iniquitous lie.

Ironically, within the first three weeks of his Papacy, Albino
Luciani had already taken the first significant steps towards reversing
the Roman Catholic Church's position on artificial birth control.
While those steps were being taken the world's Press, by courtesy of
L'Osservatore Romano, Vatican Radio, and off the record briefings by
certain members of the Roman Curia, had already firmly established a
completely false image of Luciani's views.

During his Papacy Luciani referred to and quoted from a number of
the pronouncements and encyclicals that had come from Pope Paul VI.
Notably absent was any reference to *Humanae Vitae*. The defenders of
the encyclical had first been alerted to the new Pope's views when
they learned with consternation that the draft acceptance speech,
which had been prepared for Paul's successor by the Secretariat of
State's office, containing glowing references to *Humanae Vitae,* had
had all such references excised by Luciani. The anti birth control
element within the Vatican then discovered that in May 1978, Albino
Luciani had been invited to attend and speak at an International
Congress being held in Milan on June 21st–22nd. The main purpose
of the Congress was to celebrate the 10th Anniversary of the
encyclical *Humanae Vitae*. Luciani had let it be known that he would
not speak at the Congress and that further he would not attend. Among
those who did attend and speak in glowing terms about *Humanae
Vitae* was the Polish Cardinal Karol Wojtyla.

Now in September, while the world's Press unquestioningly
repeated the lies of *L'Osservatore Romano*, Albino Luciani was heard
in the Papal Apartments talking to his Secretary of State, Cardinal
Villot: 'I will be happy to talk to this United States delegation on the
issue. To my mind we cannot leave the situation as it currently stands.'

The issue was world population. The 'situation' was *Humanae
Vitae*. As the conversation progressed Villot heard Pope John Paul I
express a view that many others, including his private secretary Father
Diego Lorenzi, had heard many times before. Father Lorenzi is only

one of a number of people who have been able to quote to me
Luciani's exact words:

> I am aware of the ovulation period in a woman with its range of
> fertility from twenty-four to thirty-six hours. Even if one allows
> a sperm life of forty-eight hours the maximum time of possible
> conception is less than four days. In a regular cycle this means
> four days of fertility and twenty-four days of infertility. How on
> earth can it be a sin to say instead of twenty-four days, twenty-
> eight days?

What had prompted this truly historic conversation had been a
tentative approach to the Vatican from the American Embassy in
Rome. The American Embassy had been contacted by the State
Department in Washington and also by US Congressman James
Scheuer. The Congressman headed a House Select Committee on
Population and was also Vice-Chairman of the UN fund for popula-
tion activities, inter-parliamentary working group. The story of the
Luciani document to Pope Paul VI on birth control had alerted
Scheuer and his Committee to the possibility of change in the
Church's position on birth control. It seemed to Scheuer that it was
unlikely that his group would obtain an audience with Luciani so
soon in his Papacy but he still considered it worth the effort of putting
pressure on the State Department and also, through the Embassy in
Rome, on the Vatican. Scheuer was destined to hear some good news.

Villot, like many of the men who surrounded Luciani, was having
considerable difficulty in adjusting to the new Papacy. He had
developed over the years a close working relationship with Paul VI.
He had grown to admire the Montini style. Now the world-weary
81-year-old Hamlet had been replaced by an optimistic Henry VI
who at 65 years of age was a relative stripling.

The relationship between Luciani and his Secretary of State was an
uneasy one. The new Pope found Villot cold and aloof, full of observations about how Paul VI would have approached this problem or
what Paul VI would have said about this particular issue. Paul VI was
dead but it became apparent that Villot and a significant section of the
Curia had not accepted that the Montinian approach to problems had
died with him.

The speech that the new Pope had delivered twenty-four hours after
the Conclave had been largely a generalized statement. The real
programme began to be formulated only during the early days of

September 1978. He was fired with the inspiration of Pope John XXIII's first 100 days.

John had been elected Pope on October 28th, 1958. Within the first 100 days he had made a number of crucial senior appointments including filling the post of Secretary of State with Cardinal Domenico Tardini, a post that had been vacant since 1944. Most significant of all had been his decision to call the Second Vatican Council. That decision was made public on January 25th, 1959, eighty-nine days after his election.

Now that Albino Luciani was wearing the shoes of the fisherman he determined to follow John's example of a revolutionary 100 days. At the top of his list of priorities of reform and change were the need to alter radically the Vatican's relationship with capitalism and the desire to alleviate the very real suffering he had personally witnessed that had stemmed directly from *Humanae Vitae*.

According to Cardinal Benelli, Cardinal Felici and other Vatican sources, the austere Villot listened askance as the new Pope elaborated on the problems the encyclical had caused. It was clear from his attitude during my interviews with him that on this issue Felici was heavily in sympathy with Villot.

Only a few weeks earlier Villot had been extolling the encyclical on the tenth anniversary of its publication. In a letter to Archbishop John Quinn of San Francisco, Villot reaffirmed Paul's opposition to artificial contraception. The Secretary of State had stressed how important Paul had considered this teaching to be, that it was 'according to God's Law'.

There was much more in a similar vein. Now, less than two months later, he was obliged to listen to Paul's successor taking a reverse position. The coffee grew cold as Luciani, rising from his desk, began to pace his study and quietly talk of some of the effects that *Humanae Vitae* had produced over the past decade.

The encyclical which had been designed to strengthen Papal authority by denying that there could be any change in the traditional teaching on birth control, had had precisely the opposite effect. The evidence was irrefutable. In Belgium, Holland, Germany, Britain, the United States and in many other countries there had not only been marked opposition to the encyclical, there had also been marked disobedience. The maxim had rapidly become that if one priest did not take a tolerant attitude within the confessional the sinner shopped around for a more liberated priest. Luciani cited examples of that contradiction he knew of personally in the Veneto region.

The theory of *Humanae Vitae* might well look like an ideal moral viewpoint when proclaimed from within the all-male preserve of the Vatican. The reality Luciani had observed in northern Italy and abroad clearly demonstrated the inhumanity of the edict. In that decade world population had increased by over three-quarters of a billion people.

When Villot demurred to point out that Pope Paul had stressed the virtues of the natural method of contraception Luciani merely smiled at him, not the full beaming smile that the public knew; it was more of a sad smile. 'Eminence, what can we old celibates really know of the sexual desires of the married?'

This conversation, the first of a number the Pope had with his Secretary of State on the subject, took place in the Pope's study in the Papal Apartments on Tuesday, September 19th. They discussed the subject for nearly forty-five minutes. When the meeting ended and Villot was about to leave, Luciani walked to the door with him and said:

Eminence. We have been discussing birth control for about forty-five minutes. If the information I have been given, the various statistics, if that information is accurate, then during the period of time we have been talking over one thousand children under the age of five have died of malnutrition. During the next forty-five minutes while you and I look forward with anticipation to our next meal a further thousand children will die of malnutrition. By this time tomorrow thirty thousand children who at this moment are alive, will be dead – of malnutrition. God does not always provide.

The Secretary of State for the Vatican was apparently unable to find an adequate exit line.

All details of the possible audience with a United States delegation, on the subject of population, were kept a carefully guarded secret both by the Vatican and the State Department. Such a meeting coming so early in Luciani's Papacy would rightly be seen as highly significant if it became known publicly.

Even greater significance would have been attached to this by world opinion if it had become known that this was one reason why Pope John Paul I was not going to attend the Puebla Conference in Mexico. This Conference was to be the follow-up to a most important conference that had taken place in Medellin, Colombia in 1968.

At Medellin, the cardinals, bishops and priests of Latin America had injected new life into the Roman Catholic Church in the South American continent. Their declaration contained within the 'Medellin Manifesto' included the statement that the central thrust of their Church in the future would be to reach out and relate to the poor, the neglected and impoverished. It was a revolutionary change in a Church that had previously been identified with the rich and powerful. The 'Theology of Liberation' which came out of Medellin put the various juntas and oppressive regimes in South America on clear notice that the Church intended to work towards an end of financial exploitation and social injustice. It had, in effect, been a call to arms . . . Inevitably, resistance to this liberal philosophy came not only from the various regimes but also from the reactionary element within the Church. The Puebla meeting, a decade later, promised to be crucial. Would the Church continue farther down the same path or would there be a retrenchment to the old invidious position? For the new Pope to decline the invitation to attend the conference underlies just what importance he placed on his meeting with Scheuer's Committee. He certainly knew the implications of the Puebla meeting,

In the Conclave, less than an hour after he had been elected Pope, Cardinals Baggio and Lorscheider, two key figures in the projected series of meetings in Mexico, had approached Luciani. Puebla had been postponed as a result of the death of Pope Paul VI. The Cardinals were anxious to know if the new Pope was prepared to sanction a new date for the Mexico meeting.

Luciani discussed the issues which would be raised at Puebla, in depth, less than an hour after his election. He agreed that the Conference should take place and the dates of October 12th to 28th were decided upon. During his discussion with Baggio and Lorscheider he astonished both Cardinals with his knowledge and grasp of the central issues which would be explored at Puebla. With regard to his own attendance, he declined to committ himself so early in his Papacy. When Villot advised him that Scheuer's Committee would like an audience on October 24th he told Baggio and Lorscheider that he would not he attending Puebla. He also told Villot to confirm the meeting with the US delegation. It had been for Luciani the final confirmation that for the next few weeks his place was in the Vatican. There were other very cogent reasons for the decision to stay in Rome. Pope John Paul I had concluded by mid-September that his first priority should be to put his own house in order. The problem of the Vatican Bank and its entire operating philosophy had become of paramount importance to him.

Luciani moved with an urgency that had been noticeably lacking in his immediate predecessor's last years. The new broom was not minded to sweep right through the Vatican in his first 100 days but he was anxious that within that time the Church should begin to change direction, particularly with regard to Vatican Incorporated.

Within his first week the new Pope had given an indication of the shape of things to come. He 'assented' to the desire of Cardinal Villot to be relieved of one of his many posts, the Office of President of the Pontifical Council, 'Cor Unum'. The job went to Cardinal Bernard Gantin. Cor Unum is one of the great funnels through which pass monies collected from all over the world to be distributed to the poorest nations.

To Luciani, Cor Unum was a vital element in his philosophy that Vatican finance, like every other factor, should be inspired by the Gospel. Villot was gently replaced, but replaced nonetheless, by Gantin, a man of great spirituality and transparent honesty.

The Vatican village buzzed with speculation. Some proclaimed that they had never met Sindona or Calvi or any of the Milan Mafia who had infested the Vatican during Pope Paul's reign. Others in their individual bids for survival began to filter information to the Papal Apartment.

A few days after the Gantin appointment the new Pope found a copy of an Italian Office of Exchange Control (UIC) circular on his desk. There was no doubt that the circular was a direct response to *Il Mondo*'s long, open letter to the Pope outlining an untenable situation for a man committed to personal poverty and a poor Church.

The circular, signed by the Minister of Foreign Trade Rinaldo Ossola, had been sent to all Italian banks. It reminded them that the IOR, the Vatican Bank, is 'to all effects a non-residential banking institute', in other words foreign. As such, relationships between the Vatican Bank and Italian credit institutes were governed by precisely the same rules that applied to all other foreign banks.

The Minister was particularly concerned with currency abuses involving the illegal flight of money from Italy. His circular was a clear Ministerial admission that these abuses were a reality. It was seen in Italian financial circles as an attempt to curb at least one of the Vatican Bank's many dubious activities. In the Vatican City it was generally regarded as further confirmation that the death knell for Bishop Paul Marcinkus's presidency of the Bank was ringing loudly.

A story which I believe to be apocryphal, but which many within the Vatican and within the Italian media have assured me is true, began to circulate around the Vatican village in early September 1978. It concerned the sale of Banca Cattolica del Veneto and Albino Luciani's trip to the Vatican seeking to stop the sale of the bank to Roberto Calvi. In reality Luciani had the meeting with Benelli recorded earlier in this book. The version that buzzed through the village introduced elegant Italian variations. Luciani had confronted Paul VI who had responded: 'Even you must make this sacrifice for the Church. Our finances have still not recovered from the damage caused by Sindona. But do explain your problem to Monsignor Marcinkus.'

A short while later Luciani presented himself in Marcinkus's office and repeated the list of diocensan complaints concerning the bank sale. Marcinkus heard him out then said, 'Your Eminence, have you nothing better to do today? You do your job and I'll do mine.' At which point Marcinkus showed Luciani the door.

Any who have seen Marcinkus in action will know that his manners match his nickname of The Gorilla. To the bishops, monsignors, priests and nuns in the Vatican City the general feeling was that the confrontation had happened. Now out of the blue, the small quiet man from Belluno could remove Marcinkus at a moment's notice.

Members of the Curia organized a lottery. The object was to guess on which day Marcinkus would be formally removed from the Bank. Apart from the investigation being conducted on the Pope's behalf by Cardinal Villot, the smiling Pope, with typical mountain shrewdness, opened up other lines of enquiry. He began to talk to Cardinal Felici about the Vatican Bank. He also telephoned Cardinal Benelli in Florence.

It was from Giovanni Benelli that the Pope learned of the Bank of Italy investigation into Banco Ambrosiano. It was typical of the way the Roman Catholic Church operated. The Cardinal in Florence told the Pope in Rome what was happening in Milan.

The former number two in the Secretary of State's Department had built a strong network of contacts throughout the country. Licio Gelli of P2 would have been suitably impressed at the range and the quality of information to which Benelli had access. It included very well placed sources within the Bank of Italy. These were the sources which had informed the Cardinal of the investigation taking place within Roberto Calvi's empire, an enquiry which was moving to its climax in September 1978. What particularly concerned Benelli, and subsequently Luciani, was the part of the investigation that was probing Calvi's links with the Vatican. The Bank of Italy contact was certain that the investigation would be followed by serious criminal charges against Roberto Calvi and possibly against some of his fellow directors. Equally certain was the fact that the Vatican Bank was deeply implicated in a considerable number of deals that broke a variety of Italian laws. The men at the top of the investigating team's list of potential criminals inside the Vatican Bank were Paul Marcinkus, Luigi Mennelli and Pellegrino De Strobel.

Benelli had learned over nearly a decade that one did not influence Luciani by strenuously urging a particular course of action. He told me:

> With Pope Luciani, you laid out the facts, made your own recommendation, then gave him time and space to consider. Having absorbed all the available information, he would decide and when Pope Luciani decided, nothing, and understand me on this, nothing would move or shift him. Gentle, yes. Humble, yes. But when committed to a course of action, like a rock.

Benelli was not alone in having access to the thoughts of senior Bank of Italy officials. Members of P2 were feeding precisely the same information to Licio Gelli in Buenos Aires. He in turn was keeping his travelling companions Roberto Calvi and Umberto Ortolani fully briefed.

Other P2 members planted inside Milan's magistrates' offices advised Gelli that upon completion of the investigation into Banco Ambrosiano the papers would be passed to Judge Emilio Alessandrini. A few days after this information became available to Gelli a left-wing terrorist group based in Milan, Prima Linea, received word from their contact within the magistrates' offices about the man whom the contact recommended as their next potential victim. The terrorist leader pinned a photograph of the target on his apartment wall: Judge Emilio Alessandrini. P2 moved in many directions, including the Vatican.

In early September Albino Luciani found that in some mysterious way he had been added to the exclusive distribution list of an unusual news agency called L'Osservatore Politico (OP). It was run by journalist Mino Pecorelli and invariably carried scandalous stories that subsequently transpired to be highly accurate. Now, along with top politicians, journalists, pundits and others with a need to know first, the Pope read about what OP called 'The Great Vatican Lodge'. The article gave the names of 121 people who were alleged to be members of Masonic Lodges. A number of laymen were included in the list but it largely comprised cardinals, bishops, and high-ranking prelates. Pecorelli's motives for publishing the list were simple. He was involved in a struggle with his former Grand Master, Licio Gelli. Pecorelli was a member of P2: a disenchanted member.

He believed that the publication of lists of Vatican Masons would cause the Grand Master of P2 maximum embarrassment, particularly as a considerable number of them were good friends of Gelli and Ortolani.

If the information was authentic then it meant Luciani was virtually surrounded by Masons and to be a Mason meant automatic excommunication from the Roman Catholic Church. Before the Conclave there had been various murmurings that several of the leading *papabili* were Masons. Now on September 12th, the new Pope was presented with the entire list. With regard to the issue of Freemasonry, Luciani held the view that it was unthinkable for a priest to become a member. He was aware that a number of the lay Catholics he knew were members of various Lodges – in much the same way that he had friends who were Communists. He had learned to live with that situation but for a man of the cloth there was in Luciani's view a different criterion. The Roman Catholic Church had decreed long ago that it was implacably opposed to Freemasonry. The new Pope was open to discussion on the issue, but a list of 121 men who were confirmed members hardly constituted discussion.

Secretary of State Cardinal Villot, Masonic name Jeanni, Lodge number 041/3, enrolled in a Zürich Lodge on August 6th, 1966. Foreign Minister Monsignor Agostini Casaroli. Cardinal Vicar of Rome Ugo Poletti. Cardinal Baggio. Bishop Paul Marcinkus and Monsignor Donato de Bonis of the Vatican Bank. The disconcerted Pope read a list that seemed like a Who's Who of Vatican City. Noting with relief that neither Benelli nor Cardinal Felici appeared on the list, which even included Pope Paul's secretary, Monsignor Pasquale Macchi, Albino Luciani promptly telephoned Felici and invited him over for coffee.

Felici advised the Pope that a very similar list of names had been passed quietly around the Vatican over two years earlier in May 1976. The reason for its re-emergence now was obviously an attempt to influence the new Pope's thinking on appointments, promotions and demotions.

'Is the list genuine?' Luciani asked.

Felici told the Pope that in his view it was a clever mix. Some on the list were Masons, others were not. He elaborated. 'These lists appear to have emerged from the Lefebvre faction . . . Not created by our rebel French brother but certainly used by him.'

Bishop Lefebvre had been a thorn in the side of the Vatican and particularly of Pope Paul VI for a number of years. A traditionalist who considered the Second Vatican Council to be the ultimate heresy, he largely ignored the Council's conclusions. He had obtained world-wide notoriety by his insistence that the Mass should be celebrated only in Latin. His right-wing views on a variety of subjects had resulted in his public condemnation by Pope Paul VI. With regard to the Conclave that had elected Pope John Paul I Lefebvre's supporters had initially stated that they would refuse to recognize the new Pope because he had been elected by a Conclave which excluded cardinals over the age of eighty. They had subsequently bemoaned the choice of names as being 'ominous'.

Luciani considered for a moment. 'You say lists like this one have been in existence for over two years.'

'Yes, Holiness.'

'Have the Press got hold of them?'

'Yes, Holiness. The full list has never been pubiished, just a name here, a name there.'

'And the Vatican's reaction?'

'The normal one. No reaction.'

Luciani laughed. He liked Pericle Felici. Curial to his finger-tips, traditional in his thinking, he was nevertheless a witty, sophisticated man of considerable culture. 'Eminence, the revision of Canon Law that has preoccupied so much of your time, did the Holy Father envisage a change in the Church's position on Fremasonry?'

'There have been over the years various pressure groups. Certain interested parties who urged a more "modern" view. The Holy Father was still considering the arguments when he died.'

Felici went on to indicate that among those who strongly favoured a relaxation of the canon rule that declared that any Roman Catholic who became a Freemason was automatically excommunicated, was Cardinal Jean Villot.

In the days that followed their discussion the Pope took to looking carefully at a number of his visitors. The trouble was that Freemasons look uncommonly like the rest of the human race. While Luciani considered this unforeseen problem, several members of the Roman Curia who were strongly sympathetic to Licio Gelli's right-wing view of the world were channelling information out of the Vatican. The information eventually reached its destination, Roberto Calvi.

The news from the Vatican was grim. The Milanese banker was convinced the Pope was seeking revenge for the takeover of Banco Cattolica del Veneto. He could not envisage that Luciani's probe into the Vatican Bank was other than personally directed and inspired by his desire to attack Roberto Calvi. Calvi recalled the anger among the clergy in Venice and Luciani's protests, the closure of the many diocesan accounts and their transfer to a rival bank. What should he do? A substantial gift to the Vatican perhaps? A lavish endowment for charitable works? Everything he had learned of Luciani, however, would have told Calvi that he was dealing with a type of man he had met only rarely in his business, someone who was completely incorruptible.

As the days of September ticked by, Calvi moved around the South American continent, Uruguay, Peru, Argentina. Close by him at all times was either Gelli or Ortolani. If Marcinkus fell, a new man would soon discover the state of affairs and the true nature of the relationship between the Vatican Bank and Banco Ambrosiano. Mennini and De Strobel would be removed. The Bank of Italy would be informed and Roberto Calvi would spend the rest of his life in prison.

He had covered every eventuality, considered every potential danger, blocked every loophole. What he had created was perfect: not *one* theft – not even one *big* theft. His was continuing theft, on a scale hitherto undreamed of. By September 1978 Calvi had already stolen over 400 million dollars. The off-shore concerns, the foreign associates, the dummy companies – most thieves would feel a sense of triumph at pulling off one bank robbery. Calvi was simultaneously engaged in robbing banks by the dozen. They were queueing up to be robbed, fighting each other for the privilege of lending money to Banco Ambrosiano.

Now in the midst of his irresistible success, he already had to contend with officials from the Bank of Italy who could not be corrupted and who were every day moving closer to the conclusion of their investigation. Gelli had assured him that the problem could and would be handled, but how could even Gelli, with the massive power and influence that he controlled, handle a Pope?

If by some miracle Albino Luciani were to drop dead before Marcinkus was removed, then Calvi would have time. Only a month, it was true. But much can happen in a month. Much could happen in the next Conclave. Surely to God it would not produce another Pope who wanted to reform Vatican finances? He turned as he always did to Licio Gelli and confided his worst fears. As they conversed in a variety of South American cities, Roberto Calvi felt some relief. Gelli had reassured him. The 'problem' could and would be resolved.

Meanwhile the daily routine within the Papal Apartments rapidly settled down to a pattern around the new incumbent. Maintaining the habit of a lifetime Luciani rose very early. He had chosen to sleep in the bed used by John XXIII in preference to that used by Paul VI. Father Magee told Luciani that Paul had declined to sleep on John's bed 'because of his respect for Pope John'.

Luciani responded: 'I will sleep in his bed because of my love for him.'

Though his bedside alarm clock was habitually set for 4.45 a.m. in case he overslept, the Pope would be awakened by a knock on his bedroom door at 4.30 a.m. The knock informed him that Sister Vincenza had left a flask of coffee outside. Even this simple act had been subjected to Curial interference. In Venice the nun had been accustomed to knock on the door, call out a 'Good morning' and bring the coffee directly into Luciani's bedroom. The busy monsignors in the Vatican considered this innocent gesture to be a breach of some imaginary protocol. They remonstrated with a baffled Luciani, who agreed that the coffee could be left in his adjoining study. The habit of a coffee consumed immediately upon waking derived from a sinus operation performed many years previously. The operation had left Luciani with an unpleasant taste in his mouth when he awoke. When travelling, if coffee was not available, he would suck a sweet.

Having drunk his coffee, he would shave and take a bath. From five to five-thirty he practised his English with the aid of a cassette course of instruction. At five-thirty, Luciani would leave his bedroom and go to the small private chapel nearby. Until 7.00 a.m. he prayed, meditated, and said his Breviary.

At 7.00 a.m. he would be joined by the other members of the Papal Household, particularly secretaries Father Lorenzi and Father Magee. Lorenzi, like himself a new boy within the Vatican, had asked the Pope if Magee, previously one of Pope Paul's secretaries, could stay on at his post. The Pope, who had been particularly impressed with Father Magee's ability in procuring cups of coffee during the first two days of his Papacy, readily agreed. The three men would be joined for Mass by the nuns from the Congregation of Maria Bambina, whose duties were to clean and cook for the Pope. The nuns, Mother Superior Elena, Sisters Margherita, Assunta, Gabriella and Clorinda were augmented, at Father Lorenzi's suggestion, by Sister Vincenza from Venice.

Vincenza had worked for Luciani since his Vittorio Veneto days and she knew his ways, his habits. She had accompanied him to Venice and had been the Mother Superior of the Community of four nuns who looked after the Patriarch. In 1977 she suffered a heart attack and had been hospitalized. The doctors told her she must never work again, that she should sit and merely give instructions to the other nuns. She had ignored the advice and continued to supervise Sister Celestina's cooking and had fussed over the Patriarch, reminding him to take his medicine for his low blood pressure.

For Albino Luciani, Vincenza and Father Lorenzi represented his only link with the homelands of northern Italy, a home he would now see but rarely, and never live in again. It is a sobering thought that when a man is elected Pope he immediately begins to live where he will, in all probability, die and, in all certainty, be buried. Premature residence in one's own cemetery.

Breakfast of *café latte*, a roll and fruit, was taken immediately after Mass at 7.30 a.m. As Vincenza was to tell the other nuns, feeding Albino Luciani was a considerable challenge. He was usually oblivious to what he ate and his appetite was like a canary's. Like many who had known acute poverty he abhorred waste. The remnants of a special dinner for invited guests would form one of his meals for the following day.

At breakfast, Luciani would read a variety of Italy's morning papers. He had the Venice daily *Il Gazzettino* added to the list. Between 8.00 a.m. and 10.00 a.m. the Pope would work quietly in his study preparing for the first of his audiences. Between 10.00 a.m. and 12.30 p.m., with men such as Monsignor Jacques Martin, the prefect of the Pontifical Household, attempting to keep people moving in and out on time, the Pope met visitors and conversed with them on the Second Floor of the Apostolic Palace.

Martin and other members of the Curia soon discovered that Luciani had a mind of his own. Despite muttered objections, the Pope's conversations with his guests had a habit of over-running and throwing the schedule into confusion. Men like Monsignor Martin epitomize a very prevalent attitude within the Vatican which runs along the lines that, if it were not for the Pope, they could all get on with their jobs.

A lunch of minestrone or pasta, followed by whatever Vincenza had created for a second course, was served at 12.30 p.m. Even this was cause for comment. Pope Paul had always lunched at 1.30 p.m. That such a trivial event could inspire excited comment within the Vatican is indicative of just how much a village the place is. Tongues wagged even faster when the word went around that the Pope had introduced members of the female sex to his dinner table. Pia his niece and his sister-in-law probably entered the Vatican record books.

Between 1.30 p.m. and 2.00 p.m., Luciani took a short siesta. This would be followed by walks on the roof garden or in the Vatican gardens. Occasionally he was accompanied by Cardinal Villot; more frequently Luciani read. Apart from his Breviary he found light relief with works by authors as diverse as Mark Twain and Sir Walter Scott. Shortly after 4.00 p.m. he would be back at his office, studying the contents of a large envelope received from Monsignor Martin, containing a list of the following day's visitors with a full briefing.

At 4.30 p.m., while sipping a cup of camomile tea, the Pope received in his office 'The Tardella', the various cardinals, archbishops, secretaries of Congregations, his inner cabinet. These were the key meetings ensuring that the nuts and bolts of running the Roman Catholic Church were all in place.

The evening meal was at 7.45 p.m. At 8.00 p.m., while still eating, Luciani would watch the news on television. His dinner companions, unless augmented by guests, were Fathers Lorenzi and Magee.

After dinner there was further preparation for the audiences of the following day, then with the final part of the daily Breviary said, the Pope would retire for the night at approximately 9.30 p.m.

Dinner, like the lunch that had preceded it, would be a simple unsophisticated meal. On September 5th he entertained a Venetian priest, Father Mario Ferrarese. Luciani's excuse for inviting the priest to the Papal Apartments was that he wished to repay the hospitality that Father Mario had shown to him in Venice. The fact that the rich and the powerful of Italy were attempting to get Albino Luciani to their dinner tables was an irrelevance; he preferred the company of an ordinary parish priest. That particular meal was served by two members of the Papal staff, Guido and Gian Paolo Guzzo. The Pope asked his guest for news of Venice, then quietly remarked, 'Ask the people there to pray for me because it's not easy being a Pope.'

Turning to the Guzzo brothers the Pope said, 'As we have a guest we must serve him a dessert.' After some delay bowls of ice cream arrived on the Papal table. For others at the table wine was freely available. Luciani was content with mineral water.

This was the daily routine of Pope John Paul I – a routine that he took delight in occasionally disturbing. Without reference, he would go for walks in the Vatican gardens. A simple diversion, one might think, but an impromptu stroll threw Vatican protocol and the Swiss

Guards into total confusion. He had already caused consternation within the ranks of the senior officers of the Guards by talking to men on sentry duty and also requesting that they should refrain from kneeling at his every approach. As he observed to Father Magee: 'Who am I that they should kneel to me?'

Monsignor Virgilio Noe, the Master of Ceremonies, begged him not to talk to the Guards and to content himself with a mute nod. The Pope asked why. Noe spread his hands wide in amazement. 'Holy Father, it is not done. No Pope has ever spoken to them.'

Albino Luciani smiled and continued to talk to the Guards. It was a far cry from the early days of Paul's reign when priests and nuns would still drop to their knees to converse with the Pope even when they were carrying on a telephone conversation with him.

Luciani's attitude towards telephones also provoked alarm among many of the Curial traditionalists. They now had to contend with a Pope who considered he was capable of dialling numbers and answering phones. He phoned friends in Venice. He phoned several Mothers Superior, just for a chat. When he advised his friend Father Bartolomeo Sorges that he would like the Jesuit priest Father Dezza to hear his confession, Father Dezza phoned within the hour to arrange his visit. The voice on the telephone informed him, 'I'm sorry the Pope's secretary isn't here at the moment. Can I help?'

'Well, to whom am I speaking?'

'The Pope.'

It simply was not done this way. It never had been and perhaps never will be again. Both of the men who functioned as Luciani's secretaries strenuously deny it ever happened. It was unthinkable. Yet it definitely happened.

Luciani began to explore the Vatican with its 10,000 rooms and halls, with its 997 stairways, 30 of them secret. He would suddenly take off from the Papal Apartments, either alone, or with Father Lorenzi for company. Equally suddenly he would appear in one of the Curial offices. 'Just finding my way about the place', he explained on one occasion to a startled Archbishop Caprio, the Deputy Head of the Secretariat of State.

They did not like it. They did not like it at all. The Curia were accustomed to a Pope who knew his place, one who worked through the bureaucratic channels. This one was everywhere, into everything, and worse he wanted to make changes. The battle over the wretched *sedia gestatoria*, the chair on which previous Popes had always been carried during public appearances, began to assume extraordinary

proportions. Luciani had it banished to the lumber room. The traditionalists began a fight to have it brought back. That issues so petty should
take up a Pope's time is an illuminating comment on the perspectives
of certain sections of the Roman Curia.

Luciani attempted to reason with men like Monsignor Noe as one
does with a child. Their world was not his and he was clearly not about
to join theirs. He explained to Noe and to others that he walked in
public because he considered that he was no better than any other man.
He detested the chair and what it epitomized. 'Ah but the crowds
cannot see you,' the Curia said. 'They are demanding its return. All
should be able to see the Holy Father.' Luciani doggedly pointed out
that he was frequently on television, that he came to the balcony every
Sunday for the Angelus. He also said how much he detested the idea
of being carried virtually upon the backs of other men.

'But Holiness', the Curia said, 'if you seek an even deeper humility
than you already clearly have, what could be more humiliating than to
be carried in this chair which you detest so much?' Faced with this
argument the Pope conceded defeat. At his second public audience he
was carried into the Nervi Hall on the *sedia gestatoria*.

While some of Luciani's time was occupied on Curia trivia, the
majority of his waking hours were given to more serious problems. He
had told the diplomatic corps that the Vatican renounced all claims to
temporal power. Notwithstanding, the new Pope rapidly discovered
that virtually every major world problem passed through his in-tray.
The Roman Catholic Church, with over 18 per cent of the world's
population owing spiritual allegiance to it, represents a potent force; as
such, it was obliged to take a position and have an attitude on a wide
range of problems.

Apart from his attitude towards Argentina's General Videla, what
would be Albino Luciani's response to the plethora of dictators who
presided over large Catholic populations? What would be his response
to the Marcos clique in the Philippines with its 43 million Catholics?
To the self-elected Pinochet in Chile with its over 80 per cent Catholic
population? To General Somoza of Nicaragua, the dictator so much
admired by Vatican financial adviser Michele Sindona? How would
Luciani restore the Roman Catholic Church to a home for the poor and
underprivileged in a country like Uganda where Amin was arranging
fatal accidents for priests as an almost daily event? What would be his
response to the Catholics of El Salvador, where some members of the
ruling junta considered that to be a Catholic was to be the 'enemy'?
This, in a country with a 96 per cent Catholic population, promised to

be a recipe for genocide, and a problem slightly more serious than the Vatican debate about the Pope's chair.

How would the man who had uttered harsh words about Communism from his pulpit in Venice speak to the Communist worlds from St Peter's balcony? Would the Cardinal who had approved of a 'balance of terror' with regard to nuclear weapons hold to the same position when the world's unilateral disarmers came seeking an audience?

Within his own ranks there was a multitude of problems inherited from Pope Paul. Many priests were urging the end of the vow of celibacy. There was pressure to allow women into the priesthood. There were groups urging reform of the Canon Laws covering divorce, abortion, homosexuality, and a dozen other issues – all reaching up to one man, demanding, pleading, urging.

The new Pope very quickly demonstrated, in the words of Monsignor Loris Capovilla, the former secretary of Pope John XXIII, that 'there was more in his shop than he put in the window'. When Foreign Minister Monsignor Agostino Casaroli came to the Pope with seven questions concerning the Church's relationship with various Eastern European countries, Albino Luciani promptly gave him answers on five of them and asked for a little time to consider the other two.

A dazed Casaroli returned to his office and told a colleague what had occurred. The priest enquired: 'Were they the correct solutions?'

'In my view, totally. It would have taken me a year to get those responses from Paul.'

Another of the problems tossed into the new Pope's lap concerned Ireland and the Church's attitude towards the IRA. Many considered that the Catholic Church had been less than forthright in its condemnation of the continuing carnage occurring in Northern Ireland. A few weeks before Luciani's election the then Archbishop O'Fiaich had hit the headlines with his denunciation of the conditions in the Maze prison, Long Kesh. O'Fiaich had visited the prison and later talked of his 'shock at the stench and filth in some of the cells, with the remains of rotten food and human excreta scattered around the walls'. There was much more in a similar vein. Nowhere in his very long statement, released to the news media with considerable professionalism, did the Archbishop acknowledge that the prison conditions were self-created by the prisoners.

Ireland was without a cardinal; a great deal of pressure was exerted by a variety of people attempting to influence Luciani. Some elements were for O'Fiaich, others felt his previous promotion to the arch-diocese of Armagh had proved an unmitigated disaster.

Albino Luciani returned the dossier on O'Fiaich to his Secretary for State with a shake of the head and a one-line epitaph: 'I think Ireland deserves better.' The search for a cardinal was extended. It ended when Luciani's successor gave O'Fiaich a cardinal's hat.

In September 1978 the troubles in Lebanon were not considered to rank particularly high in the list of the world's major problems. For two years there had been a kind of peace, interspersed with sporadic fighting between Syrian troops and Christians. Long before any other Head of State, the quiet little priest from the Veneto saw the Lebanon as a potential slaughterhouse. He discussed the problem at consider-able length with Casaroli and told him that he wished to visit Beirut before Christmas 1978.

On September 15th, one of the men whom Luciani saw during his morning audiences was Cardinal Gabriel-Marie Garrone, Prefect of the Sacred Congregation for Catholic Education. This particular audience is an excellent example of just how remarkable were the talents of Luciani. Garrone had come to discuss a document called *Sapienta Christiana*, which dealt with the apostolic constitution and with the directives and rules governing all Catholic faculties through-out the world. As long ago as the early 1960s, Vatican Council II had revised the guidelines for seminarians. After two years of internal discussion the Roman Curia had sent its proposals to the world's bishops for their recommendations. All the relevant documents had then been submitted to two more Curial meetings attended by non-Curial consultants. The results were then examined by at least six Curial departments and the final document had been handed to Pope Paul VI in April 1978, sixteen years after the proposed reforms had first been discussed. Paul had wanted to issue the document on June 29th, the Feast Day of St Peter and St Paul, but a document with a gestation period of some sixteen years could not be rushed so quickly through the Curia's department of translation. By the time they had the document prepared, Pope Paul was dead. Any initiative unproclaimed at the time of a Pope's death falls, unless his successor approves it. Consequently, Cardinal Garrone approached his audience with the new Pope with considerable trepidation. Sixteen years of long, hard work could be tossed into the waste-paper basket if Luciani rejected the document. The former seminary teacher from Belluno told Garrone that he had spent most of the previous day studying the document. Then without referring to a copy of it he began to discuss it at length and in great detail. Garrone sat astonished at the Pope's grasp and understanding of such a highly complex document. At the end of the audience, Luciani advised him that the document had his approval and that it should be published on December 15th.

Like Casaroli, Baggio, Lorscheider and a number of other men, Garrone left a discussion with Luciani in complete awe. Returning to his office he chanced to meet Monsignor Scalzotto of Propaganda Fide and remarked: 'I have just met a great Pope.'

The 'great Pope' meanwhile continued to work his way through the mountain of problems left by Paul. One such was Cardinal John Cody, Cardinal of one of the world's wealthiest and most powerful dioceses, Chicago.

For a cardinal, any cardinal, to be considered by the Vatican to be a major problem was unusual, but then Cody was a very unusual man. The allegations made about Cardinal Cody in the ten years before Luciani's Papacy began were extraordinary. If even 5 per cent of them were true then Cody had no business being a priest, let alone Cardinal of Chicago.

Before his promotion to the Chicago Archdiocese in 1965 he had run the diocese of New Orleans. Many of the priests who attempted to work with him in New Orleans still have the scars to prove it. One recalled: 'When that son of a bitch was given Chicago, we threw a party and sang the "Te Deum" (Hymn of Thanksgiving). As far as we were concerned our gain was Chicago's loss.'

When I discussed the Cardinal's subsequent career in Chicago with Father Andrew Greeley, a noted Catholic sociologist, author and long a critic of Cody, I observed that another Chicago priest had compared Cardinal Cody with Captain Queeg, the paranoid, despotic naval captain in *The Caine Mutiny*. Father Greeley's response was: 'I think that's unfair to Captain Queeg.'

In the years that followed Cardinal Cody's appointment to Chicago it became fashionable in the Windy City to compare him with Mayor Richard Daley, a man whose practices in running the city were democratic only by accident. There was one basic difference. Every four years Daley was, at least in theory, answerable to the electors. If they could overcome his political machine, they could vote him out of office. Cody had not been elected. Short of very dramatic action from Rome he was there for life. Cody was fond of observing: 'I am answerable to no one except Rome and God.' Events were to prove that Cody declined to be answerable to Rome. That left God.

When Cody arrived in Chicago he had the reputation of being an excellent manager of finances, a progressive liberal who had battled long and hard for school integration in New Orleans, and a very demanding prelate. He soon lost the first two attributes. In early June, 1970, whilst treasurer of the American Church he put 2 million dollars in Penn Central stocks. A few days later the shares collapsed and the company went bankrupt. He had illegally invested the money during the administration of his duly elected successor to whom Cody refused to hand over the account books until well after the loss. He survived the scandal.

Within weeks of his arrival in Chicago, he had demonstrated his own particular brand of progressive liberalism towards some of his priests. In the files of his predecessor, Cardinal Albert Meyer, he discovered a list of 'problem' priests, men who were alcoholic, senile, or unable to cope.

Cody began to spend Sunday afternoons arriving at their rectories. He then personally dismissed the priests, giving them two weeks to leave their homes. There were no pension funds, no retirement schemes or insurance policies for priests in Chicago in the mid 1960s. Many of the men were over seventy. Cody simply tossed them out on to the street.

He began to move priests from one part of the city to another, without consultation. He took similar action with regard to closing convents, rectories and schools. On one occasion, by order of Cody, a wrecking crew began to demolish a rectory and a convent while the occupants were bathing and having breakfast.

Cody's basic problem would appear to have been a profound inability to recognize the Second Vatican Council as a fact of life. There had been endless talk at the Council of power sharing, of a collegial style of decision making. The news never reached the Cardinal's mansion.

In a diocese with 2.4 million Catholics, the battle lines began to be drawn between factions for and against Cody. The majority of Catholics in the city were in the meantime wondering what was going on.

The priests formed a Trade Union of sorts, the ACP (Association of Chicago Priests). Cody very largely ignored their requests. Letters asking for meetings were not answered. Phone calls found the Cardinal constantly 'unavailable'. Some stayed to continue the fight for a more democratically run Church. Many left. In a decade, one third of Chicago's clergy left the priesthood. Throughout these massive demonstrations proving that there was something very rotten in the State of Illinois, Cardinal Cody continued to insist that his opponents were 'merely the highly vocal minority'.

The Cardinal also pilloried the local Press, declaring them hostile. In truth the Chicago news and television media were extraordinarily fair and tolerant during most of Cody's reign.

The man who fought for integration in New Orleans became known in Chicago as the man who closed the black schools, claiming that the Church could no longer afford to run them; this in a diocese with an annual revenue approaching 300 million dollars.

Like much else that Cody did, many of the school closures were effected without reference to anyone, including the school board. When a cry of 'racist' went up, Cody defended himself by stating that many of the blacks were non-Catholics and that he did not consider the Church had a duty to educate middle-class black Protestants. But the label of racism was a hard one for him to throw off.

As the years passed, the charges and allegations against Cody increased tenfold. His conflict with large sections of his own clergy grew bitter. His paranoia blossomed.

He began to tell tales of how he had been employed on secret espionage work for the US Government. He recounted his contributions to the FBI. He told priests that he had also undertaken special assignments on behalf of the CIA which included flying into Saigon. The details were always vague but if Cody was telling the truth he had been involved in secret service activities on behalf of the Government since the early 1940s. It would seem that John Patrick Cody, the son of a St Louis fireman, had lived many lives.

The reputation for financial astuteness which he had brought to Chicago, a reputation which was rather dented by the 2 million dollar Penn Central debacle, took a further knock when some of Cody's opponents began to dig into his earlier, highly colourful career. In between his real or imaginary flights over enemy territories he had unwittingly succeeded in bringing some of the Church to a state of poverty, though not quite in the manner envisaged by Albino Luciani. He had left the diocese of Kansas City, St Joseph, 30 million dollars in debt. He had performed the same feat in New Orleans, which gave added significance to the Te Deum of thanks when he departed. At least he left a permanent memento of his stay in Kansas City, having spent substantial amounts of money to gild the dome of the restored down-town cathedral.

He began to monitor the day-by-day movements of priests and nuns he suspected of disloyalty. Dossiers were assembled. Secret interrogations of friends of 'suspects' became the norm. What all of this had to do with the Gospel of Christ is unclear.

When some of the activities described above became cause for complaint to Rome by the Chicago clergy, Pope Paul VI worried and agonized.

It would seem abundantly clear that the most senior member of the Roman Catholic Church in Chicago had demonstrated by the early 1970s that he was unfit to preside over the diocese, yet the Pope, with a strange sense of priorities, hesitated. Cody's peace of mind seemed to weigh more heavily than the fate of 2.4 million Catholics.

One of the most extraordinary aspects of the Cody affair is that the man controlled, apparently without reference to anyone, the entire revenue of the Catholic Church in Chicago. A sane, highly intelligent man would be stretched to control with total efficiency an annual sum of between 250 and 300 million dollars. That it should be placed in the hands of a man like Cody defies explanation.

The total assets of the Roman Catholic Church in Chicago were by 1970 in excess of one billion dollars. Because of Cardinal Cody's refusal to publish an annual certified account, priests in various parts of the city took to holding back sums of money, which in happier days would have been destined for control by the Cardinal. Eventually in 1971, six years after his despotic rule had begun, Cody deigned to publish what passed for a set of annual accounts. They were a curious affair. They did not reveal real estate investments. They did not include the share portfolio investments. With regard to the revenue from cemeteries they did give, at last, some evidence of a life after death. The movement of the profit was very lively. Six months before the figures had been published, Cody had confided to an aide that the figure was 50 million dollars. When the accounts were made public this had dropped to 36 million dollars. Perhaps for a man who could simultaneously be in Rome, Saigon, the White House, the Vatican and the Cardinal's mansion in Chicago, misplacing some 14 million dollars' worth of cemetery revenue was child's play.

Sixty million dollars' worth of parish funds were on deposit with the Chicago chancery. Cody declined to tell anyone where the money was invested, or who was benefiting from the interest.

One of the Cardinal's most notable personal assets was the large number of influential friends he assiduously acquired within the power structure of the Church. His pre-war days in the Roman Curia, working initially in the North American College in Rome and subsequently in the office of the Secretariat of State, reaped rich dividends in times of need. Cody was from a very early age a man with both eyes to the main chance. Ingratiating himself with Pius XII and the future Paul VI, he established a formidable power base in Rome.

The Vatican's Chicago connection was by the early 1970s one of its most important links with the USA. The bulk of Vatican Incorporated's share investment on the US Stock Market was funnelled through Continental Illinois. On the Board of the bank along with David Kennedy, a close friend of Michele Sindona, was the Jesuit priest Raymond C. Baumhart. The large amounts of money that Cody funnelled to Rome became an important factor in Vatican fiscal policy. Cody might not be able to handle his priests, but he undoubtedly knew how to turn his hand to a dollar. When the Bishop controlling the diocese of Reno made some 'unfortunate investments' and the finances totally collapsed, the Vatican asked Cody to bail him out. Cody telephoned his banking friends and the money was quickly found.

Over the years the Cody-Marcinkus friendship became particularly close. They had so much in common, so many invested interests. In Chicago, with its very large Polish population unwittingly aiding him, Cody began to divert hundreds of thousand of dollars via Continental Illinois to Marcinkus in the Vatican Bank. Marcinkus would then divert the money to the cardinals in Poland.

The Cardinal took out further insurance by spreading Chicago's wealth around certain sections of the Roman Curia. When Cody was in town, and he made over one hundred trips to Rome, he distributed expensive presents where they would do him most good. A gold cigarette lighter to this monsignor, a Patek Philippe watch to that bishop.

Complaints continued to flood into Rome and outnumber Cody's expensive gifts. In the Sacred Congregation for the Doctrine of Faith, which acts as the Vatican's policeman on matters of doctrinal orthodoxy and clerical morality, the pile of letters grew. They came not only from priests and nuns in Chicago, they came from men and women in many walks of life. Archbishop Jean Hamer, OP, in charge of the Congregation, pondered the problem. Moving against a priest is a relatively easy matter. After due investigation, the Congregation would merely lean on the relevant bishop requesting that the priest be removed from the area of contention. Whom do you lean on when the man you want to move is the Cardinal?

The Priests' Union publicly condemned Cody and stated that he was lying to it. Eventually it passed a vote of censure on him. Despite this Rome remained silent.

By early 1976, Archbishop Hamer was not the only senior member of the Roman Curia who knew the problems that the Chicago connection was causing. Cardinals Benelli and Baggio had independently, and then jointly, decided that Cody must be replaced.

After long consultation with Pope Paul VI a formula was evolved. When Cody made one of his numerous journeys to Rome in the spring of 1976 Benelli offered him a post in the Roman Curia. He would have a wonderful title, but absolutely no power. It was known that Cody was ambitious and believed he had the talent to climb higher than controlling Chicago. What the Cardinal had in mind was to become Pope. It is indicative of Cody's arrogance, that a man who had caused such mayhem in Chicago could seriously consider his chances of the Papacy. With this ambition in mind, he would have been happy to exchange Chicago for control of one of the Curia Congregations which gave out money to needy dioceses throughout the world. Cody reasoned that he could buy enough bishops' votes to place himself on the throne of Rome when the opportunity arose. Benelli was aware of this, hence the job offer, but it was not the job Cody was seeking. He declined. Another solution was needed.

In January 1976, a few months before the Benelli/Cody confrontation, a delegation of priests and nuns from Chicago visited Jean Jadot, the Apostolic Delegate in Washington. Jadot had told them that Rome had the situation in hand. As the year progressed without any resolution, the battle in Chicago recommenced. Cody's public image was by now so appalling that he hired a public relations firm, at the Church's expense, in an attempt to obtain favourable media coverage.

The irate priests and nuns began to complain again to Jadot in Washington. He counselled patience. 'Rome will find the solution,' he promised. 'You must stop this public attack. Let the issue calm down. Then Rome will handle the problem quietly and discreetly.'

The clergy understood. The public criticism abated, only to be provoked to new heights by Cody himself, when he decided to close a number of inner city schools. Baggio seized this issue in yet another attempt to persuade Pope Paul VI to act decisively. The Pope's concept of decisiveness was to write a stiff letter to Cody asking for an explanation of the school closures. Cody ignored the letter and boasted openly that he had ignored it.

Back in Chicago, goaded by the Vatican inactivity, more letters were sent to Italy. Among them were new allegations supported by depositions, affidavits and financial records. There was evidence which indicated that Cody's behaviour in another area left something to be desired. These allegations concerned his friendship with a woman called Helen Dolan Wilson.

Cody had told his staff in the Chancery that Helen Wilson was a relative. The exact nature of the relationship varied; usually he described her as a cousin. To explain her very stylish mode of life, the fashionable clothes, her frequent travelling, her expensive apartment, the Cardinal let it be known that his cousin had been left very 'well fixed' by her late husband. The allegations made to Rome were that Cody and Helen Wilson were not related, that her husband, whom she had divorced long ago, was very much alive at the time Cody had him in the next world, and that further, when the ex-husband did die in May 1969, he left no will and his only worldly goods were an eight-year-old car worth 150 dollars, which went to his second wife.

These allegations, made in the strictest confidence to the Vatican, continued with proof that Cody's friendship with Helen Wilson had lasted from a very early age, that he had taken out a 100,000 dollar life policy on which he paid the premiums, with Helen Wilson as the beneficiary, that her employment records of work done at the Chicago Chancery had been falsified by Cody to enable her to obtain a larger pension. The pension was based on 24 years' work for the diocese which was demonstrably false. Evidence was also produced which showed that Cody gave his woman friend 90,000 dollars to enable her to buy a residence in Florida. The Vatican was reminded that Helen Wilson had accompanied Cody to Rome when he was made Cardinal – but then many other people came with Cody. Unlike Helen Wilson, however, they did not have the run of the Chicago Chancery or decide on the furnishings and fabrics for the Cardinal's residence. It was also alleged that Cody had diverted hundreds of thousands of dollars of Church funds to this woman.

As if this was not enough, the allegations went on to itemize the large amounts of diocesan insurance business put the way of Helen's son David. David Wilson had first benefited from 'Uncle' John's largesse back in St Louis in 1963. As the Cardinal had moved, so had the insurance business. It was alleged that the commissions David Wilson had earned, by apparently monopolizing Church insurance business which Cody controlled, were in excess of 150,000 dollars.

Baggio carefully studied the long, detailed list. Enquiries were made. The Vatican is unrivalled in the business of espionage: consider how many priests and nuns there are in the world, each one owing allegiance to Rome. The answers came back to Cardinal Baggio, indicating that the allegations were accurate. It was now late June 1978.

In July 1978 Cardinal Baggio again discussed the problem of Cardinal Cody with Pope Paul VI, who eventually accepted that Cody should be replaced. He insisted, however, that it must be done with compassion, in a manner that would enable Cody to retain face. Most important, it must be done in a way that would minimize any possible scandalous publicity. It was agreed that Cody was to be told he must accept a co-adjutor – a bishop who would for all practical purposes run the diocese. Officially it would be announced that this was due to Cody's failing health, which in reality was not good. Cody would be permitted to stay on as titular Head of Chicago until he reached the retirement age of 75 in 1982.

Armed with the Papal edict, Cardinal Baggio quickly made his travel arrangements, packed his suitcase and departed for Rome's Fiumicino Airport. Arriving at the airport, he was advised that the Pope wished to speak to him before he flew to Chicago.

Paul had danced yet again, backwards. He told Baggio that the plan for a co-adjutor to strip Cody of power could only proceed if Cody agreed.

Dismayed, Baggio pleaded with the Pope: 'But Holy Father, can I insist?'

'No, no, you must not order him. The plan is to go forward only if His Eminence agrees.'

A very angry and frustrated Cardinal Baggio flew to Chicago.

Spy networks are a two-way conduit for information and Cardinal Cody had his own sources within the Roman Curia. The element of surprise that Baggio had hoped would catch Cody off balance, had, unbeknown to Baggio, been lost within a day of his crucial meeting with the Pope. Cody was ready and waiting.

Most men in Cody's position would subject themselves to a little self-examination, a consideration, perhaps, of events over the years that had led this most sensitive of Popes to the agonizing conclusion that the power Cody wielded must, in the interests of all, be handed to another. Ever considerate of the feelings of the man he wished to replace, the Pope had arranged matters so that Baggio's stop-over in Chicago would be a secret. Officially he was flying direct to Mexico to finalize arrangements for the Puebla Conference. Such gestures were entirely lost on Cardinal Cody.

The confrontation took place at the Cardinal's villa in the grounds of the seminary at Mundelein. Baggio laid out the evidence. He established that, in making gifts of money to Helen Wilson, the Cardinal had certainly intermingled money he was entitled to dispose of with

Church funds. In addition, the pension he had awarded his friend was improper. The Vatican investigations had clearly established a wide variety of indiscretions which would certainly bring the Roman Catholic Church into disrepute if they became public knowledge.

Cody was far from contrite as the confrontation rapidly developed into a shouting match. He began to rant about his massive contributions to Rome; about the vast amounts of money he had poured into the Vatican Bank to be used in Poland; about the gifts of money he had bestowed on the Pope during his *ad limina* visits (obligatory 5-yearly visits and reports) – not the pitiful few thousand dollars that others brought but hundreds of thousands of dollars. The two Princes of the Church could be heard shouting at each other all over the seminary grounds. Cody was adamant. Another bishop would come in and run his diocese 'over my dead body'. Eventually, like the stuck needle in a long-playing record, his tongue could only utter continuously in a single phrase: 'I will not relinquish power in Chicago.'

Baggio departed, temporarily defeated. A defiant Cody who refused to accept a co-adjutor was in total breach of Canon Law but for it to become public knowledge that the cardinal of one of the most powerful dioceses in the world was openly defying the Pope was, for Pope Paul, unthinkable. The Pope would tolerate Cody to the end of his days rather than face the alternative. For Paul, the days of toleration were few. Within one week of receiving Baggio's reports the Pope was dead.

By mid-September, Albino Luciani had studied the Cody file in depth. He met Cardinal Baggio and discussed it. He talked of the implications of the Cody affair with Villot, Benelli, Felici and Casaroli. On September 23rd he had another long meeting with Cardinal Baggio. At the end of it he advised Baggio that he would tell him of his decision within the next few days.

In Chicago, for the first time in his long turbulent history Cardinal Cody began to feel vulnerable. After the Conclave he had privately been dismissive of this quiet Italian who had followed Paul. 'It's going to be more of the same', Cody had declared to one of his close Curial friends. More of the same was what Cody wanted; it would enable him to go on ruling the roost in Chicago. Now the news from Rome indicated that he had seriously underrated Luciani. As September 1978 drew to an end John Cody became convinced that Luciani would act where Paul had not. Cody's friends in Rome advised him that whatever course of action this new Pope decided upon, one thing was certain, he would see it through. They cited many examples from Luciani's life to indicate an unusual inner strength.

On Luciani's desk in his study was one of the few personal possessions he treasured. A photograph. Originally it had been contained within a battered old frame. During his time in Venice a grateful parishioner had had the photograph remounted in a new silver frame with semi-precious jewels. The photograph showed his parents against a background of the snow-covered Dolomites. In his mother's arms was the baby Pia, now a married woman with her own children. During September 1978 his secretaries observed the Pope on a number of occasions lost in thought as he studied the photograph. It was a reminder of happier times, when such men as Cody, Marcinkus, Calvi and the others did not disturb his tranquillity. There had been time for silence and small things then. Now it seemed to Luciani that there was never enough time for such important facets of his life. He was cut off from Canale and even from his family. There were the occasional telephone conversations, with Edoardo, with Pia, but the impromptu visits were now gone for ever. The Vatican machine saw to that. Even Diego Lorenzi attempted to turn Pia away when she telephoned. She had wanted to bring him some little presents, reminders of the north. 'Leave them at the gate,' Lorenzi said, 'The Pope is too busy to see you.' Luciani overheard this conversation and took the telephone.

'Come and see me. I haven't got time but come all the same.'

They lunched together. Uncle Albino was in excellent health and good spirits. As the meal progressed he commented on his new role: 'Had I known I was going to become Pope one day, I would have studied more.' Then in a superb understatement he remarked, 'It's very hard being Pope.'

Pia saw just how hard the job could be – made harder by the obduracy of the ever-watchful Curia. Luciani wished to treat Rome as his new parish, to wander through the streets as he had in Venice and his other dioceses. For a Head of State to behave in such a manner presented problems. The Curia flatly declared the idea not only unthinkable, but unworkable. The city would be thrown into constant chaos if the Holy Father went on walkabouts. Luciani abandoned the idea but only for a modified version. He told the Vatican officials that he wished to visit every hospital, church and refuge centre in Rome and gradually work his way round what he regarded as his parish. For a man bent on being a pastoral Pope the reality on his own doorstep presented a powerful challenge.

Rome has a Catholic population of two-and-a-half million. It should have been producing at least seventy new priests per year. When Luciani became Pope it was producing six. The religious life of Rome was being maintained by enormous importations of clergy from outside. Many parts of the city were, in reality, pagan, with Church attendances of less than 3 per cent of the population. Here, in the heart of the Faith, cynicism abounded.

The city that was now home to Luciani was also home to the Communist Mayor Carlo Argan – a Communist Mayor in a city whose major industry, religion, is rivalled only by the crime rate. One of the new titles Luciani had acquired was Bishop of Rome, a city that had been without a bishop, in the sense that Milan, Venice, Florence and Naples had a bishop, for over a century. It showed.

As Pia lunched with the Pope, Don Diego was involved in a loud, lengthy argument with a Curial official who refused even to consider the Papal wish to visit various parts of Rome. Luciani interrupted his conversation with Pia.

'Don Diego. Tell him it must be done. Tell him the Pope wishes it.'

Lorenzi conveyed the Papal instruction, only to be met with a refusal. He turned to the Pope. 'They say it can't be done, Holy Father, because it's never been done before.'

Pia sat, fascinated, as the game of Vatican tennis continued. Eventually Luciani apologized to his niece for the interruption and told his secretary he would instruct Villot. Smiling at Pia, he observed: 'If the Roman Curia permits, your Uncle hopes to visit the Lebanon before Christmas.'

He talked at length about that troubled country and his desire to intercede before the powder keg exploded. After lunch, as she was leaving, he insisted on giving her a medal presented to him by the mother of the President of Mexico. A few days later on September 15th he entertained his brother Edoardo to dinner. These two family meetings were destined to be the last Albino Luciani would have.

As the Papacy of Albino Luciani progressed, the gulf between the Pope and the professional Vatican watchers increased, in direct proportion to the ever closer bonds and relationship between the new Pope and the general public. The bewilderment of the professionals was understandable.

Confronted with a non-Curial Cardinal, who apparently lacked an international reputation, the experts had concluded that they were observing the first of a new breed of Pope, a man deliberately selected to ensure that there would be a reduction of power, a less significant role for the Papacy. There can be little doubt that Luciani himself saw his role in these reduced terms. The essential problem in this vision of a less significant Papacy was the man himself. The very essence of

Albino Luciani, his personality, intellect and extraordinary gifts, meant that the general public promptly gave the new Pope a position of greater importance, held what he had to say as being of deeper significance. The public reaction to Luciani clearly demonstrated a deep need for an enlarged Papal role, exactly the reverse of that intended by many cardinals. The more Luciani was self-dismissive, the more exalted he became for the faithful.

Many who had known Luciani only in his days in Venice were profoundly surprised by what they considered to be the change in the man. In Vittorio Veneto, Belluno and Canale there was no surprise. This was the real Luciani. The simplicity, the sense of humour, the stress on catechism these were integral elements within the man.

On September 26th, Luciani could look back with satisfaction on his first month in the new job. It had been a month full of powerful impact. His investigations into corrupt and dishonest practices had thrown the perpetrators into deep fear. His impatience with Curial pomposity had caused outrage. Again and again he had abandoned officially written speeches, publicly complaining: 'This is too Curial in style.' Or, 'This is far too unctuous.'

His verbatim words were rarely recorded by Vatican Radio or *L'Osservatore Romano,* but the public heard them and so did the other news media. Borrowing a phrase from St Gregory, the Pope observed that, in electing him, 'The Emperor has wanted a monkey to become a lion'. Lips tightened within the Vatican as mouths parted in smiles among the public. Here was a 'monkey' who during the course of his first month spoke to them in Latin, Italian, French, English, German and Spanish. As Winston Churchill might have remarked, 'some monkey'.

On September 7th, during a private audience with Vittore Branca at 8.00 a.m., an hour that caused Curial eyebrows to shoot even higher, his friend Branca expressed concern about the weight of the Papacy. Luciani responded:

Yes, certainly I am too small for great things. I can only repeat the truth and the call of the Gospel as I did in my little church at home. Basically all men need this, and I am the keeper of souls above all. Between the parish priest at Canale and me there is a difference only in the number of faithful but the task is the same, to remember Christ and his word.

Later the same day he met all the priests of Rome and, talking to them of the need for meditation, his words had a deeply poignant significance when one considers how little time and space a new Pope has for meditation.

I was touched at Milan Station to see a porter sleeping blissfully with his head on a bag of coal and his back against a pillar. Trains were whistling as they left and their wheels were screeching as they arrived. Loudspeakers constantly interrupted. People came and went noisily. But he, sleeping on, seemed to say, 'Do what you must but I need some peace'. We priests must do the same. Around us there is continual movement. People talking, newspapers, radio and TV. With the discipline and moderation of priests we must say, 'Beyond certain limits you do not exist for me. I am a priest of the Lord. I must have a little silence for my soul. I distance myself from you to be with my God for a while.'

The Vatican recorded his speeches in the General Audiences when on successive Wednesdays he spoke on Faith, Hope and Charity. Luciani's pleas that these virtues be shown towards, for example, drug addicts went unrecorded by the Curia who controlled the Vatican media.

When on September 20th he uttered the memorable phrase that it is wrong to believe 'Ubi Lenin ibi Jerusalem' (where Lenin is, there is Jerusalem), the Curia announced that the Pope was rejecting 'liberation theology'. He was not. Further, Vatican Radio and *L'Osservatore Romano* neglected to record Luciani's important qualification, that between the Church and religious salvation, and the world and human salvation, 'There is some coincidence but we cannot make a perfect equation.'

By Saturday September 23rd, Luciani's investigation into Vatican Incorporated was well advanced. Villot, Benelli and others had provided the Pope with reports which Luciani had reflected upon. That day he left the Vatican for the first time, to take possession of his cathedral as Bishop of Rome. He shook hands with Major Argan and they exchanged speeches. After the Mass that followed, with the majority of the Curia present, the Pope touched several times on the inner problems with which he was grappling. Referring to the poor, that section of society closest to Luciani's heart, he remarked:

These, the Roman deacon Lawrence said, are the true treasures of the Church. They must be helped, however, by those who can, to have more and to be more, without becoming humiliated and offended by ostentatious riches, by money squandered on futile things and not invested, in so far as is possible, in enterprises of advantage to all.

Later in the same speech he turned and, looking directly at the gentlemen of the Vatican Bank gathered together, he began to talk of the difficulties of guiding and governing.

Although already for twenty years I have been Bishop of Vittorio Veneto and at Venice, I admit that I have not yet learned the job well. At Rome I shall put myself in the school of St Gregory the Great who writes '[the pastor] should, with compassion, be close to each one who is subject to him: forgetful of his rank he should consider himself on a level with the good subiects, but he should not fear to exercise the rights of his authority against the wicked . . .'

Without a knowledge of events within the Vatican, the members of the public merely nodded wisely. The Curia knew precisely to what the Pope was alluding. This was in Vatican style an elegant, oblique pronouncement of coming events.

Changes were in the air and within the Vatican village there was frenetic speculation. Bishop Marcinkus and at least two of his closest associates. Mennini and De Strobel, were going. That was known to be a fact. What exercised Curial minds were the rumours of other replacements.

When on Sunday, September 25th a private visitor to the Papal Apartments was identified by one sharp-eyed monsignor as Lino Marconato, excitement within the village reached new heights. Marconato was a director of the Banco San Marco. Did his presence in the Papal Apartments indicate that a successor to Banco Ambrosiano had been found already?

In fact the meeting dealt with far less exotic banking matters. Banco San Marco had been made the official bank of the diocese in Venice by Luciani after he had angrily closed all accounts at Banca Cattolica del Veneto. Now Luciani needed to clear up his personal accounts at San Marco, knowing he would never return to live in the city. Marconato found his soon-to-be former client in the best of health. They chatted happily about Venice as Luciani gave instructions that the money in his Patriarch's account should be passed on to his successor.

The preoccupation with the forthcoming changes was intense. In many cities. By many people.

Another with a direct vested interest in what Luciani might be about to do was Michele Sindona. Sindona's four-year battle to avoid extradition from the USA to Italy was moving to a climax in September 1978. Earlier that year, during May, a Federal judge had ruled that the Sicilian, who had transformed himself into a citizen of Switzerland, should be returned to Milan to face the highly expensive music he had previously orchestrated. In his absence he had been sentenced to three-and-a-half years, but Sindona was fully aware that that particular sentence would seem lenient when the Italian courts had finished with him. Despite Federal investigation, he still remained free of any charges in the United States. The Franklin Bank collapse had been followed by a number of men being arrested on various charges but in September 1978 The Shark remained untouched. His major problem at that time was in Italy.

Sindona's million-dollar battery of lawyers had persuaded the courts to withhold activating the extradition until the United States prosecutors had proved that there was well-founded evidence against Sindona with regard to the variety of charges he faced in Milan.

From May onwards, the prosecutors had been working hard to obtain that evidence. Sindona, helped by the Mafia and his P2 colleagues, had been working equally hard to make that evidence vanish. As September 1978 drew to a close he still had a number of outstanding 'problems'.

The first was the evidence given at the extradition proceedings by a witness named Nicola Biase. Biase was a former employee of Sindona and his evidence was deemed to be dangerous. Sindona set about making it 'safe'. After discussing the problem with the Mafia Gambino family a small contract was put out. It was to be nothing particularly sinister. Biase, his wife, family and lawyer were to have their lives threatened. If they succumbed to the threats and Biase withdrew his evidence, the matter would rest there. If Biase refused to co-operate with the Mafia, then the Gambino family and Sindona planned to 'review' the situation. The review did not augur well for the continued good health of Biase. The contract for less than 1,000 dollars would be amended to a more appropriate one. The contract was given to Luigi Ronsisvalle and Bruce McDowall. Ronsisvalle is by profession a hired killer.

Another contract was also discussed with Ronsisvalle. The Mafia advised him that Michele Sindona required the death of Assistant United States District Attorney, John Kenney.

Nothing so clearly illustrates the mentality of Michele Sindona as the contract that was put out on John Kenney. The attorney was the chief prosecutor in the extradition hearings, the man leading the US Government's attack on Sindona's continued presence within the United States. Sindona reasoned that if Kenney were eliminated the problem would disappear. It would act as a warning to the Government that he, Michele Sindona, was objecting to the heat. The investigation should cease. There should be no more irritating court appearances, no more absurd attempts to get him sent back to Italy. The thought processes at work here are 100 per cent Sicilian Mafia. It is a philosophy that works again and again in Italy. It is an essential part of the Italian Solution. The authorities can be cowed, and are. Investigators replacing a murdered colleague will move very slowly. Sindona reasoned that what was effective in Palermo would work in New York.

Luigi Ronsisvalle, although a professional murderer, baulked at accepting the contract. The fee of 100,000 dollars looked good but Ronsisvalle, with a deeper appreciation of the American way of life than Sindona, did not envisage having much opportunity to spend it. If Kenney were murdered there would be waves, big ones. Ronsisvalle began to seek someone, on behalf of the Gambino family, who fancied his chances of survival after killing a district attorney.

Sindona and his associates then turned to the next problem, Carlo Bordoni, former business associate and close friend of Sindona. Bordoni was already facing a number of charges concerning the collapse of the Franklin Bank and Sindona was aware that he could give lethal testimony against The Shark as part of a deal to reduce his own punishment. It was decided that the treatment that was about to be given to Nicola Biase and his family and attorney should be extended to Carlo Bordoni.

The remaining problems for Sindona lay in Italy, particularly within the Vatican. If Marcinkus fell, then Calvi would go. If Calvi went, then Sindona would be pulled down with him. The four-year fight to avoid extradition would be over. Might a man who considered he could solve his problems in the USA with the murder of a United States attorney feel that the major threat facing him in Italy could be eliminated by the death of a Pope?

Sindona, Calvi, Marcinkus and Cody: by September 28th, 1978 each of these men stood to lose much if Albino Luciani were to decide on specific courses of action. Others who stood to be directly affected were Licio Gelli and Umberto Ortolani: for these P2 leaders to lose

Calvi would be for the masonic lodge to lose its paymaster general. By September 28th, another name was added to the growing list of people who were about to be seriously affected by the proposed action of Luciani. The new name was that of Cardinal Jean Villot, the Pope's Secretary of State.

The same morning, after a light breakfast of coffee, croissant and rolls, Luciani was at his desk before 8 a.m. There was much to be done.

The first problem he tackled was *L'Osservatore Romano*. In the previous month, he had been given cause to complain about the paper on numerous occasions. After the battle had been won about the regal use of 'we' and 'our', which the paper had initially insisted on substituting for the Pope's use of the humbler first person, each day's edition had produced further irritations for the Pope. The paper had adhered rigidly to the Curial-written speeches and ignored his own personal comments. It even complained when Italian journalists had accurately reported what the Pope had said rather than what *L'Osservatore Romano* deemed he should have said. Now there were fresh problems of a far more serious nature.

A number of Curial cardinals had discovered to their horror that shortly before the Conclave Albino Luciani had been asked for his opinion on the birth of Louise Brown, known as 'the first test tube baby', an English girl recently born with the aid of artificial fertilization. Luciani had been interviewed on the subject three days before the death of Pope Paul VI but his views were not generally known until the article carried in *Prospettive nel Mondo* after his election. The hardliners on birth control read with growing dismay the views of the man who was now Pope.

Luciani had begun cautiously, making it clear that what he was expressing were his own personal views, because he, like everyone else, 'waited to hear what the authentic teaching of the Church would be when the experts had been consulted'. His surprise election had produced a situation in which the authentic teaching of the Church on this as on any other subject was now totally within Luciani's province.

In the interview Luciani expressed qualified enthusiasm about the birth. He was concerned about the possibility of 'baby factories', a prophetic concern in view of current events in California where women are queueing to be impregnated with the sperm of Nobel prize winners.

On a more personal note to the parents of Louise Brown, Luciani said:

Following the example of God, who desires and loves human life, I too send my best wishes to the baby. As for her parents, I have no right to condemn them; subjectively, if they acted with good intentions and in good faith, they may even have great merit before God for what they have decided and asked the doctors to do.

He then drew attention to a previous pronouncement by Pius XII which might put the act of artificial fertilization in conflict with the Church. Then, considering the view that every individual has the right to choose for him or herself, he expressed an opinion that lay at the heart of his attitude towards many moral problems. 'As for the individual conscience, I agree, it must always be followed, whether it commands or forbids; the individual though must seek always to develop a well-formed conscience.'

The element within the Vatican who believe that the only well-formed conscience is one formed exclusively by them began to mutter. Discreet meetings began to take place. It was clear to those who attended these meetings that Luciani had to be stopped. They talked airily of 'the betrayal of Paul', which to certain refined Roman minds is an elegant way of saying, 'I disagree'.

When news of the cautious dialogue between the Secretariat of State's office and the US State Department began to leak to this group they determined on action. The subsequent information that a delegation of officials concerned with birth control had been granted an audience with the Pope gave added urgency to those within the Vatican who considered *Humanae Vitae* should remain the last word on this subject.

On September 27th there appeared on the front page of *L'Osservatore Romano* a long article entitled '*Humanae Vitae* and Catholic morality'. It was written by Cardinal Luigi Ciappi, OP, theologian to the Papal household. Cardinal Ciappi had been personal theologian to Paul VI and Pius XII. Coming from such an authority, the article would appear to carry the personal imprimatur of the new Pope. It had previously been published in *Laterano* to 'celebrate' the tenth anniversary of *Humanae Vitae*. Its re-publication was a deliberate attempt to forestall any change on the issue of birth control that Albino Luciani might wish to make. The article is a long eulogy extolling the virtues of *Humanae Vitae*. There are copious quotations from Paul VI, but from Luciani not a single word affirming he shared either Paul's or Ciappi's views. The reason for that is simple. Ciappi had not discussed the article with Luciani. Indeed as of September 27th, 1978, Cardinal Ciappi was still awaiting a private audience with the new Pope. The first Luciani knew of the article and the views it contained was when he read it in the paper on September 27th. With rising anger he turned to page two to continue reading the article; it was, as previously noted, very long. On page two he was confronted with yet another of the Curia's efforts to undermine his position. Running over three entire columns was another article entitled 'The Risk of Manipulation in the Creation of Life'. This was a blunt, dogmatic condemnation of the birth of test tube baby Louise Brown and of all artificial fertilization.

Again there had been no reference to Luciani. The Curia knew full well that, for all *L'Osservatore Romano* claims to be only semi-official, such an article would be clearly seen by the world as being the views of the new Pope. The battle was well and truly joined.

On September 28th, therefore, shortly after 8.00 a.m., the Pope telephoned his Secretary of State, Villot. He demanded a full explanation of how the two articles had appeared; then he phoned Cardinal Felici in Padua where he was about to attend a spiritual retreat.

He had taken to using Felici more and more as a sounding board for his ideas. Aware that their views differed on a large range of subjects, Luciani was equally aware that Felici would respond with total honesty. The Pope also knew that, as Dean of the Sacred College, few knew their way through the machinations of the Curia better than Felici.

Luciani expressed his anger at the two articles. 'You recall some days ago advising me that the Curia wished me to restrain my natural exuberance?'

'It was merely a suggestion, Holiness.'

'Perhaps you would be kind enough to return the compliment on my behalf. Tell that little newspaper to restrain its views on such issues. Editors are like Popes. Neither is indispensable.'

After arranging to meet Felici upon his return from Padua, Luciani moved on to the next problem, the Dutch Church. Five of the seven Dutch bishops were planning to take moderate positions on the issues of abortion, homosexuality and the employment of married priests. The five included Cardinal Willebrands, the man who had offered words of comfort to Luciani during the Conclave. The five were opposed by two extremely conservative bishops, Gijsens of Roermond and Simonis of Rotterdam. A meeting in The Netherlands in

November 1978 promised to be the battle arena that would expose the deep divisions to the Dutch public. There was a further problem, which was covered in the detailed report that had been submitted to the late Pope, Paul VI.

The Jesuits were in pursuit of the world famous theologian and Dominican Professor, Edward Schillebeeckx. As with his Swiss contemporary, Hans Kung, the conservatives wished to silence what seemed to them to be the radical ideas of Schillebeeckx. The feared Index of banned and prohibited books had been abolished by Paul VI. His death had left unresolved the problem of how the Roman Catholic Church would control its forward thinkers. In the past Luciani had borrowed a phrase from Kung to condemn 'sniper theologians' but men such as Kung and Schillebeeckx were not sniping; they articulated a deep desire to return the Church to its origins, something of which Albino Luciani wholeheartedly approved. At a few minutes to ten, Luciani placed the report to one side and immersed himself in happier aspects of his job. A series of audiences.

First to be received was a group which included the man whom Luciani had promoted to the Presidency of Cor Unum, Cardinal Bernardin Gantin. The Pope beamed at the strong, youthful figure of Gantin, who for him represented the Church's future. During their conversation, Luciani remarked: 'It is only Jesus Christ whom we must present to the world. Apart from this we would have no reason, no purpose, we would never be listened to.'

Another who was granted an audience that morning was Henri de Riedmatten. When the news had flown around Rome shortly after the Conclave that Luciani had written to Pope Paul before *Humanae Vitae*, urging him not to reaffirm the ban on artificial contraception, it had been Riedmatten who called such a report 'a total fantasy'. His discussion with the Pope on September 28th concerned his work as secretary of Cor Unum but Luciani gave Riedmatten a clear warning against any further 'denials'.

'I understand that my report on birth control passed you by?'

Riedmatten mumbled something about possible confusion.

'One should take care, Father Riedmatten, not to speak publicly until all confusion has cleared. Should you need a copy of my report I'm sure it can be found for you.'

Riedmatten thanked the Pope profusely. Thereafter he maintained a wise silence while Luciani discussed the problems of Lebanon with Cardinal Gantin. He advised Gantin that the previous day he had discussed his projected visit to the Lebanon with Patriarch Hakim

whose Greek Melkite-rite dioceses covered not only the invaded
Lebanon but the invading Syria.

Also received in audience that morning was a group of bishops from
the Philippines who were making their *ad limina* visit. Confronted
with men who had to contend with the day-to-day reality of President
Marcos, Luciani talked to them on a subject very close to his heart:
evangelization. Aware of the difficulties facing these men if he spoke
out directly about Marcos, the Pope chose instead to make his points
through urging the importance of evangelization. He reminded them of
Pope Paul's trip to the Philippines.

> At a moment when he chose to speak about the poor, about
> justice and peace, about human rights, about economic and social
> liberation, at a moment when he also effectively committed the
> Church to the alleviation of misery, he did not and could not
> remain silent about the 'higher good', the fullness of life in the
> Kingdom of Heaven.

The message was clearly understood, not only by the bishops, but
subsequently also by the Marcos family.

After the morning audiences Luciani had a meeting with Cardinal
Baggio. He had arrived at a number of decisions and was now about
to impart two of them to Baggio.

The first was the problem of Cardinal John Cody of Chicago. After
weighing every consideration Luciani had decided that Cody must
be removed. It was to be done in a classic Vatican manner, he hoped
without undue publicity. He told Baggio that Cody was to be given
the opportunity to resign because of ill health. There should be little
adverse Press comment about this because Cody's health was indeed
far from good. If Cody declined to resign, rather than suffer the
uproar of publicly removing him against his will a co-adjutor was
to be appointed. Another bishop would be brought in to take over
all effective power and to run the diocese. Luciani felt sure that faced
with the alternative, Cody would choose to go with dignity. If he
insisted upon staying then so be it. He would be relieved of all
responsibility. Luciani was crystal clear on all of this. There was to
be no asking, no request. A co-adjutor would be appointed.

Baggio was delighted; finally the situation had been resolved. He
was less than pleased with the next decision at which Luciani had
arrived. Venice was without a Patriarch. Baggio was offered the job.

Many men would have felt honoured at such an offer. Baggio was not; he was angry. He saw his future in the short term as dominating the Puebla conference in Mexico. He believed that the Church's future lay in the Third World. In the long term he saw his place in Rome, at the heart of the action. In Venice he would be out of sight and, more important, out of mind when it came to formulating future plans. The manner of his refusal to accept Venice astonished Luciani. Obedience to the Pope and to the Papacy had been instilled into Luciani from his earliest days in the seminary at Feltre and the obedience that Luciani had acquired had been of an unquestioning nature. Through the years as his career had progressed he had begun to question, most notably over the issues of Vatican Incorporated and *Humanae Vitae,* but it would have been unthinkable for Luciani publicly to lead a call to arms even on issues as important as these. This was the man who at Paul's request had written article after article that supported the Papal line, whom when writing such an article on divorce, gave it to his secretary Father Mario Senegaglia with the wry comment, 'This will bring me many headaches I am sure, when it is published, but the Pope has requested it.' To refuse a direct request from the Pope in the arrogant way Baggio was now doing was beyond belief. The two men were functioning with two quite different sets of values. Luciani was considering what was best for the Roman Catholic Church. Baggio was considering what was best for Baggio.

There were several reasons why the Pope had concluded that Baggio should move from Rome to Venice. Not least of these was one particular name on the list of Masons which Luciani had received – Baggio, Masonic name Seba, Lodge number 85/2640. Enrolled on August 14th, 1957.

Luciani had made further enquiries after his conversation with Cardinal Felici. A remark of Felici's had nagged away at him. 'Some on the list are Masons. Others are not.' Luciani's problem was to resolve the genuine from the false. The enquiries had helped by producing some clarifications.

The meeting between Baggio and Luciani has been described to me as 'a very violent argument with the violence and anger entirely deriving from His Eminence. The Holy Father remained calm.'

Calm or otherwise, Luciani had an unresolved problem at lunch time. Venice was still without a leader and Baggio was insisting his place was in Rome. A thoughtful Luciani began his soup.

The Indian summer that Rome had been enjoying throughout the month gave way to cooler weather on that Thursday. After a short siesta Luciani decided to confine his exercise for the day to indoor

walking. He began to stroll alone through the corridors. At 3.30 p.m.
the Pope returned to his study and made a number of telephone calls.
He talked to Cardinal Felici in Padua and Cardinal Benelli in Florence.
He discussed the events of the morning, including the Baggio
confrontation, and then they moved on to talk of his next appointment,
which was to see Villot. The various decisions Luciani had arrived at
were about to be given to the Secretary of State.

Luciani and Villot sat sipping their camomile tea. In an attempt to
get closer to his Secretary of State, the Pope had from time to time
during their numerous meetings spoken to Villot in his native French.
It was a gesture the Cardinal from St Amande-Tallende appreciated.
He had been deeply impressed at how quickly Luciani had settled into
the Papacy. The word had gone out from the Secretariat of State's
office to a number of Luciani's friends and former colleagues.
Monsignor Da Rif, still working at Vittorio Veneto, was one of many
to be given a progress report.

> From Cardinal Villot down they all admired Papa Luciani's way
> of working. His ability to get to the root of problems, to make
> decisions quickly and firmly. They were very struck with his
> ability to carry out his tasks. It was clear that he was a man who
> took decisions and stuck to them. He did not give way to
> pressure. In my own personal experience this ability to stick to
> his own line was a very remarkable feature of Albino Luciani.

During the late afternoon of September 28th Jean Villot was given
an extended demonstration of this ability that had so impressed him
during the previous month. The first problem to be discussed was the
Istituto per le Opere di Religione, the Vatican Bank. Luciani was by
now in possession of a great deal of highly detailed information. Villot
himself had already submitted a preliminary report. Luciani had also
obtained further information from Villot's deputy Archbishop
Giuseppe Caprio, and from Benelli and Felici.

For Bishop Paul Marcinkus, who had initiated the plan and played
such an active helping role for Calvi in the takeover of the Banca
Cattolica, that chicken and a great many others were now going to
come home to roost. Villot advised the Pope that inevitably word had
leaked on the investigation into the Bank. The Italian Press were
becoming very curious and one major story had just been published.

Newsweek magazine clearly had some excellent Vatican sources. It
had learned that before the Conclave a considerable number of

cardinals had requested a full report on the Vatican Bank from Villot. It had also, through its 'knowledgeable source', picked up the fact that there were moves afoot to oust Marcinkus. The magazine quoted its Curial source: 'There's some movement to get him out of there. He'll probably be made an auxiliary bishop.'

Luciani smiled. 'Does *Newsweek* tell me with whom I am replacing Marcinkus?'

Villot shook his head.

As their conversation progressed, Luciani made it clear that he had no intention of leaving Marcinkus in Vatican City, let alone the Vatican Bank. Having personally assessed the man during a 45-minute interview earlier in the month Luciani had concluded that Marcinkus might be more gainfully employed as an auxiliary bishop in Chicago. He had not indicated his thinking to Marcinkus but the cool politeness he had shown to the man from Cicero had not passed unnoticed.

Returning to his bank offices after the interview, Marcinkus later confided to a friend, 'I may not be around here much longer.'

To Calvi via the telephone and to his colleagues in the bank he observed: 'You would do well to remember that this Pope has different ideas from the last one. There are going to be changes around here. Big changes.'

Marcinkus was right. Luciani advised Villot that Marcinkus was to be removed immediately. Not in a week's or a month's time. The following day. He was to take leave of absence. A suitable post in Chicago would be found for him once the problem of Cardinal Cody had been resolved.

Villot was told that Marcinkus was to be replaced by Monsignor Giovanni Angelo Abbo, secretary of the Prefecture of Economic Affairs of the Holy See. As a key figure in the financial tribunal of the Vatican, Monsignor Abbo would demonstrably be bringing to his new job a great deal of financial expertise.

The inspiration of Pope John's first 100 days had certainly galvanized Albino Luciani. The claws of the lion which his intimates had waited to see revealed, were on full display to Villot on the evening of September 28th. Luciani, a man so unassuming and gentle, had, before his Papacy, seemed much smaller than his 5 ft 9 ins. To many observers over the years he had seemed to melt into the wallpaper. His manner was so quiet and calm that after a large gathering many were unaware that he had been present. Villot was left in no doubt of his presence on this evening. Luciani told him:

There are other changes within the Istituto per le Opere di Religione that I wish to be implemented immediately. Mennini, De Strobel and Monsignor De Bonis are to be removed. At once. De Bonis is to be replaced by Monsignor Antonetti. The other two vacancies I will discuss with Monsignor Abbo. I wish all of our links with the Banco Ambrosiano Group to be cut and the cut must happen in the very near future. It will be impossible, in my view, to effect this step with the present people holding the reins.

Father Magee remarked to me, in terms of a general observation, 'He knew what he wanted. He was very clear indeed about what he wanted. The manner in which he went about his aims was very delicate.'

The 'delicacy' lay in his explanation to Villot. Both men knew that Marcinkus, Mennini, De Strobel and De Bonis were all men with inextricable links not only with Calvi but also with Sindona. What was not said could not be misquoted at a later date.

Cardinal Villot noted these changes without much comment. He had been aware of a great deal over the years. Many within the Vatican considered him ineffectual but for Villot it had often been a case of deliberately looking the other way. In the Vatican village it was called survival technique.

Luciani moved to the problem of Chicago and his discussion with Baggio concerning the ultimatum that was to be given to Cardinal John Cody. Villot voiced approval. Like Baggio he regarded Cody as a running sore in the American Church. That the problem was finally to be solved gave the Secretary of State deep gratification. Luciani stated that he wished soundings to be taken via the Papal Nuncio in Washington about a possible successor to Cody, and observed, 'There has been a betrayal of trust in Chicago. We must ensure that whoever replaces His Eminence has the ability to win the hearts and minds of all within the diocese.'

Luciani discussed Baggio's refusal to accept the See of Venice and his continued determination that Baggio should go where he was told to go. 'Venice is not a tranquil bed of roses. It needs a man of Baggio's strength. I wish you to talk with him. Tell him that we all have to make some sacrifice at this time. Perhaps you should remind him that I had no desire for *this* job.' The argument would have limited value for Baggio who himself had earnestly desired to be Paul's successor but Villot diplomatically neglected to make this point.

Luciani then advised Villot of the other changes he planned to make. Cardinal Pericle Felici was to become Vicar of Rome, replacing Cardinal Ugo Poletti, who would replace Benelli as Archbishop of Florence. Benelli was to become Secretary of State. He would take over Villot's job.

Villot considered the proposed changes that included his own 'resignation'. He was old and tired. Further, he was also seriously ill. An illness not helped by the two packs of cigarettes he smoked daily. Villot had made it plain in late August that he sought early retirement. Now it had come somewhat sooner than he had bargained for. There would be a period of handover of course but to all intents and purposes his power was now ceasing. The fact that Luciani proposed to replace him with Benelli must have been particularly vexing to Villot. Benelli had been his number two in the past and it had not been the happiest of relationships.

Villot studied the notes he had made of the proposed changes. Albino Luciani, placing his own handwritten notes to one side, poured out more tea for both of them. Villot said, 'I thought you were considering Casaroli as my replacement?'

'I did, for a considerable time. I think much of his work is brilliant but I share Giovanni Benelli's reservations about some of the policy initiatives that have been made in the recent past towards Eastern Europe.'

Luciani waited for some sign or word of encouragement. The silence grew longer. Never during their entire relationship had Villot dropped his formality; always there was the mask, always there was the coldness. Luciani had tried directly and also via Felici and Benelli to inject some warmth into his dealings with Villot, but the cold professional aloofness that was his hallmark remained. Eventually it was Luciani who broke the silence, 'Well, Eminence?'

'You are the Pope. You are free to decide.'

'Yes, yes, but what do you think?'

Villot shrugged. 'These decisions will please some and distress others. There are cardinals within the Roman Curia who worked hard to get you elected who will feel betrayed. They will consider these changes, these appointments contrary to the late Holy Father's wishes.'

Luciani smiled. 'Was the late Holy Father planning to make appointments in perpetuity? As for the cardinals who claim to have worked hard to make me Pope – understand this – I have said it many times, but clearly it needs saying yet again. I did not seek to become Pope. I did not want to be Pope. You cannot name one single cardinal

to whom I proposed anything. Not one whom I persuaded in any form
to vote for me. It was not my wish. It was not my doing. There are men
here within Vatican City who have forgotten their purpose. They have
reduced this to just another market place. That is why I am making
these changes.'

'It will be said that you betrayed Paul.'

'It will also be said that I have betrayed John. Betrayed Pius. Each
will find his own guiding light according to his needs. My concern is
that I do not betray Our Lord Jesus Christ.'

The discussion continued for nearly two hours. At 7.30 p.m. Villot
departed. He went back to his own offices near by and, sitting at a desk,
studied the list of changes. Then, reaching into a drawer, he pulled out
another list – perhaps it was just coincidence. Every one of the clerical
personnel whom Luciani was moving was on the list of alleged Masons.
The list which the disenchanted P2 member Pecorelli had published.
Marcinkus. Villot. Poletti. Baggio. De Bonis. While each of the clerical
replacements so far nominated by Luciani was notably absent from the
list of Masons. Benelli. Felici. Abbo. Antonetti.

Cardinal Villot put the list to one side and studied another note on his
desk. It was the final confirmation that the proposed meeting between
the USA Committee on population control and Albino Luciani would
take place on October 24th. A Government group which was seeking to
change the Roman Catholic Church's position on the contraceptive pill
would in a few weeks meet a Pope who desired to make just such a
change. Villot rose from his desk leaving the various papers carelessly in
view. The lion had indeed revealed his claws.

Immediately after his meeting with Villot had finished at 7.30 p.m.,
Albino Luciani asked Father Diego Lorenzi to contact Cardinal
Colombo in Milan. A few moments later Lorenzi advised him that
Colombo was not available until about 8.45 p.m. While Lorenzi
returned to his desk, the Pope was joined by Father Magee. Together
they recited the final part of the daily Breviary in English. At ten
minutes to eight Luciani sat down to dinner with Magee and Lorenzi.
Totally unruffled by the long session with Villot he chatted amiably
while Sisters Vincenza and Assunta served a dinner of clear soup,
veal, fresh beans and salad. Luciani sipped a little from a glass of
water while Lorenzi and Magee drank red wine.

At one end of the table, Father Lorenzi was struck by the thought that
Luciani's Papacy must have already passed the shortest on record. He
was about to voice the thought when the Pope began to fuss with his new
watch. It was a present from Paul's secretary Monsignor Macchi after

39 *(Above)* An ebullient and zestful Luciani with Cardinal Sin of the Philippines. This last photograph of Luciani was taken a few hours before the Pope died. 40 *(Below left)* Father Magee. 41 *(Below right)* Sister Vincenza.

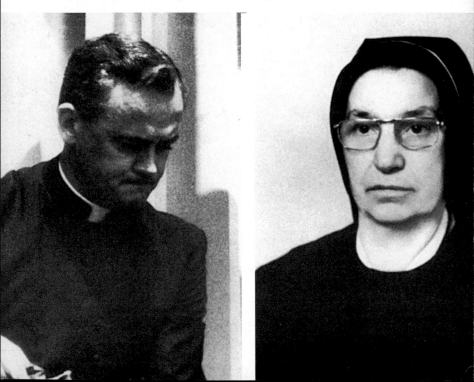

42 Ernesto and Arnaldo Signoracci, Papal embalmers.
43 Luciani, Pope John Paul I, lying-in-state.

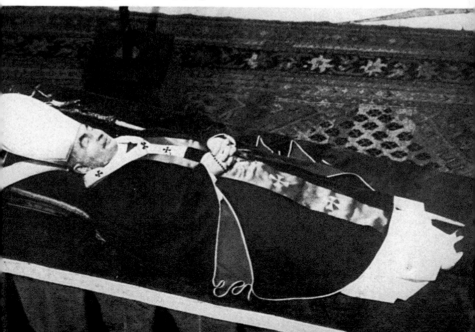

44 Prime Minister Andreotti *(kneeling, third from left)* prays by the body.
45 The new Pope with Cardinal Benelli, who was deprived by a mere handful of votes from succeeding Luciani.

46 On July 10th, 1976, the murder of Italian magistrate Vittorio Occorsio
halted the investigation into the links between a neo-Fascist movement
and the Masonic Order, P2.

47 *(Left)* and 48 *(Below)*
Emilio Alessandrini, a Milan magistrate, was murdered on January 29th, 1979, soon after he opened an investigation into Calvi's Banco Ambrosiano.
49 *(Opposite above left)* Mino Pecorelli was a disenchanted P2 member who began to talk. He, too, was murdered.
50 *(Opposite above right)* The deputy General Manager of the Bank of Italy, Mario Sarcinelli, leaves jail after being falsely imprisoned on trumped up charges arranged by Gelli.
51 and 52 *(Opposite below)* Giorgio Ambrosoli was murdered hours after he gave vital evidence against Sindona.

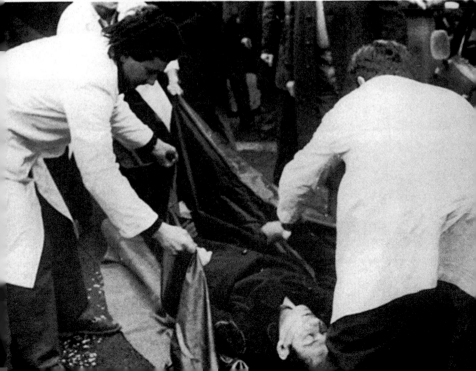

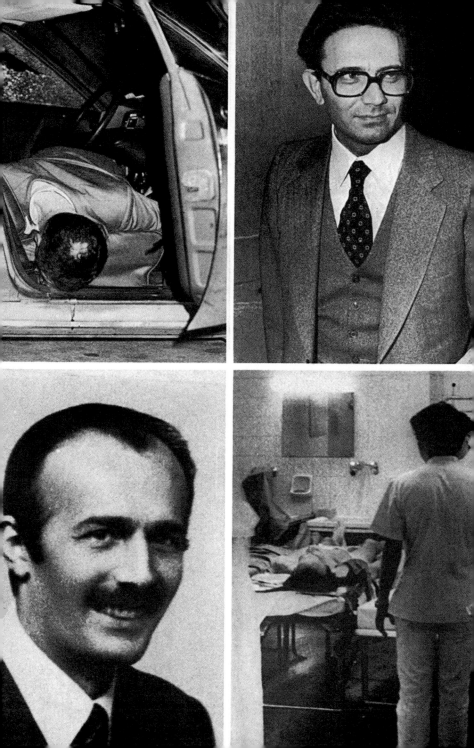

53 Two days before he was murdered Giorgio Ambrosoli had conferred
with Palermo police chief, Boris Giuliano. Within two weeks of
Ambrosoli's death, Giuliano was also murdered and laid to rest.

Felici had advised the Pope that some of the Curia considered his previous watch inadequate. A bad image apparently. In such a manner did the Curia seek to reduce the Pope to a second-hand-car salesman who took care that his trousers were always neatly pressed. The last time Luciani had seen his brother Edoardo he had offered him the old watch with the words, 'Apparently the Pope is not allowed to wear an old battered watch that needs to be constantly wound. Will you be offended if I give it to you?'

Eventually Luciani passed the new watch to Magee to reset when the television news began. It was one minute to eight.

Shortly after a pleasant, uneventful supper, the Pope went back to his study to consider the notes he had used during his discussions with Villot. At 8.45 p.m. Lorenzi connected him with Cardinal Colombo in Milan. The Cardinal declined to be interviewed but other sources indicate that they discussed the changes Luciani intended to make. Clearly there was no dissension. Cardinal Colombo has gone as far as recalling, 'He spoke to me for a long time in a completely normal tone from which no physical illness could be inferred. He was full of serenity and hope. His final greeting was "pray".'

Lorenzi noted that the phone call finished at about 9.15 p.m. Luciani then glanced over the speech he planned to make to the Company of Jesuits on Saturday the 30th. Earlier he had telephoned the Superior General of the Jesuits, Father Pedro Arrupe, and warned him that he would have one or two things to say about discipline. He underlined a part of the speech that was not without pertinence to the changes he had just made.

You may well know and justly concern yourselves with the great economic and social problems which trouble humanity today and are so closely connected with the Christian life. But in finding a solution to these problems may you always distinguish the tasks of religious priests from those of the laymen. Priests must animate and inspire the laity to fulfil their duties, but they must not take their place, neglecting their own specific task of evangelization.

Putting the speech to one side on his desk he picked up the notes on the dramatic changes he had earlier discussed with Villot. He walked to the door of his study and opening it saw Father Magee and Father Lorenzi. Bidding them both goodnight he said, 'Buona notte. A domani. Se Dio vuole.' (Good night. Until tomorrow. If God wishes.')

It was a few minutes before 9.30 p.m. Albino Luciani closed his study door. He had spoken his last words. His dead body would be discovered the following morning. The precise circumstances surrounding the discovery make it abundantly clear that the Vatican perpetrated a cover up. It began with a lie, then continued with a tissue of lies. It lied about little things. It lied about big things. All of the lies had but one purpose: to suppress the fact that Albino Luciani, Pope John Paul I, was murdered at some time between 9.30 p.m. on September 28th and 4.30 a.m. on September 29th, 1978.

Albino Luciani was the first Pope to die alone for over one hundred years, but then it has been a great deal longer since a Pope was murdered.

Cody. Marcinkus. Villot. Calvi. Gelli. Sindona. At least one of these men had decided on a course of action that was implemented during the late evening of the 28th or the early morning of the 29th. That course of action was derived from the conclusion that the Italian Solution must be applied. The Pope must die.

We Are Left Frightened

뀅

How and why did darkness fall upon the Catholic Church on September 28th, 1978?

The 'why' has already been established. There was a plethora of motives. The 'how' also has an alarming number of possibilities. If Albino Luciani was murdered because of any of the reasons already recorded then a number of factors had to apply.

1   The murder would have to be achieved by stealth. For that status quo of corruption which existed before Luciani's election to continue, then the act of murder had to be masked. There could be no dramatic shooting of the Pope in the middle of St Peter's Square; no public attack that would inevitably give rise to a full, searching enquiry as to why this quiet, holy man had been eliminated. The sudden death would have to be achieved in such a manner that public questions and anxiety would be reduced to a minimum.

2   The most efficient way to kill the Pope was by poison – a poison that when administered would leave no tell-tale external signs. Research indicates that there are over two hundred such drugs which would fulfil the task. The drug digitalis is but one of this number. It has no taste. No smell. It can be added to food, drink or existing proprietary drugs without the unsuspecting victim becoming alerted that he has taken a fatal dose.

3   Whoever planned to murder the Pope in such a manner would have to have an intimate knowledge of Vatican procedures. They would have to know that no matter what indications remained after the act, there would be no autopsy. Given that they could be confident of that one fact then any one of two hundred drugs could be used. A drug such

as digitalis would kill in such a way that upon an external examination of the body the Vatican doctors would conclude that death had been caused by a heart attack. The conspirators would be fully aware that there was nothing within the Apostolic laws directing that an autopsy should be carried out. Further, the conspirators would know that even if suspicions were aroused at the highest levels within the Vatican it would be virtually certain that Vatican officials and examining doctors would content themselves with an elementary examination of the body. If a drug such as digitalis was indeed administered to an unsuspecting Luciani in the late evening then there was the virtual certainty that the Pope would retire to his room for the night. He would go to bed and then to his final sleep. Death would occur between two to six hours after consumption of the fatal dose. The Pope kept beside his bed, on the small table with his battered alarm clock, a bottle of Effortil, a liquid medicine that he had been taking for some years to alleviate low blood pressure. A fatal dose of digitalis, half a teaspoonful, would be undetectable if added to the medicine.

The only other medicines the Pope was taking were vitamin pills three times a day with his meals and a course of injections for the adrenal cortex, drugs to stimulate the gland that secretes adrenalin. Again these were taken to assist the low blood pressure. Courses of these injections were given twice yearly, in the spring and in the autumn. The proprietary drugs varied. One of them frequently used was Cortiplex. These injections were administered by Sister Vincenza. Luciani was taking a course of them during his Papacy, hence the need for Vincenza in the Papal Apartments. The drugs used for the injections, like the Effortil by the bedside, could have been tampered with easily. No special precautions were made about the storage of these drugs. Access to them would not have presented any problem to a person with murder in mind. Indeed, as will be demonstrated, access to any part of the Papal Apartments presented no problem to anyone determined to end the life of Albino Luciani.

At 4.30 a.m. on the morning of Friday September 29th, Sister Vincenza carried a flask of coffee to the study as usual. A few moments later she knocked on the Pope's bedroom door and called out, 'Good morning, Holy Father'. For once there was no reply. Vincenza waited for a moment then padded away quietly. At 4.45 a.m. she returned. The tray of coffee in the study was untouched. She had worked for Luciani since 1959 in Vittorio Veneto. Not once in nineteen years had he overslept. Anxiously she moved to the bedroom door and listened. There was no sound. She knocked on the door, timidly at first, then with greater force. Still there was silence. There was a light shining from under the door of the bedroom. She knocked again on the bedroom door. Still there was no answer. Opening the door she saw Albino Luciani sitting up in bed. He was wearing his glasses and gripped in his hands were some sheets of paper. His head was turned to the right and the lips were parted showing his teeth. It was not the smiling face that had so impressed the millions but an expression of agony. She felt his pulse. Recently she recounted that moment to me:

'It was a miracle that I survived. I have a bad heart. I pushed the bell to summon the secretaries, then I went out to find the other Sisters and to awaken Don Diego.'

The Sisters resided on the far side of the Papal Apartments. Father Magee slept upstairs in the attic area. Father Lorenzi was sleeping on a temporary basis near to the Pope's bedroom while his own room in the attic area previously occupied by Paul's secretary, Monsignor Macchi, was being re-decorated. He was shaken out of his sleep by Sister Vincenza.

A number of early rising Romans had already noted with quiet satisfaction the light shining from the Pope's bedroom. It was good to know you were not the only one up at such an early hour. The light had remained unnoticed throughout the night by Vatican security gnards.

A half-dazed Diego Lorenzi gazed at the lifeless body of Albino Luciani. Next to respond was Father Magee. For the second time within two months he looked upon a dead Pope, but in markedly different circumstances. When Paul VI had died on August 6th, many were gathered around the death bed in Castel Gandolfo, the Papal summer residence just outside Rome. Medical bulletins gave a highly detailed account of the last twenty-four hours of Paul's life and an equally detailed account of the sequence of physical ailments that led to his death at 9.40 p.m.

Now after a mere 33 days as Pope, Albino Luciani had died alone. Cause of death? Time of death?

After one of the shortest Conclaves in history, one of the shortest reigns. No Pope had died so quickly after his election for nearly 400 years. To find a briefer Papacy it is necessary to go back to 1605, to the days of the Medici Leo XI who served for 17 days. How had Albino Luciani died?

Father Magee's first action was to telephone Secretary of State Villot, residing two floors below. Less than twelve hours earlier Albino Luciani had told Villot of his impending replacement by

Benelli. Now, far from being a former Secretary of State, the Pope's death not only ensured he would remain in office until a successor was elected, he also assumed the role of Camerlengo, virtually acting head of the Church. By 5.00 a.m. Villot was in the Pope's bedroom and had confirmed for himself that Albino Luciani was dead.

If Luciani died naturally, the subsequent actions and instructions given by Villot are completely inexplicable. His behaviour only becomes understandable when related to one specific conclusion. Either Cardinal Jean Villot was part of a conspiracy to murder the Pope, or he saw clear evidence in the Papal bedroom indicating the Pope had been murdered, and promptly determined that to protect the Church the evidence must be destroyed.

Beside the Pope's bed on a small table was the medicine that Luciani had been taking for low blood pressure. Villot pocketed the medicine and removed the notes on the Papal transfers and appointments from the dead Pope's hands. They followed the medicine into Villot's pocket. From his study desk his last Will was removed. Also to vanish from the bedroom were the Pope's glasses and slippers. None of these items has ever been seen again. Villot then created for the shocked members of the Pope's household a totally fictitious account of the circumstances leading to the finding of Luciani's body. He imposed a vow of silence concerning Sister Vincenza's discovery and instructed the household that news of the death was to be suppressed until he indicated otherwise. Then sitting in the Pope's study he began to make a series of telephone calls.

Based on the eye-witness accounts of people I have interviewed, the medicine, the glasses, the slippers and the Pope's last Will were all in the bedroom and the Papal study before Villot entered the rooms. After his initial visit and examination all the items had vanished.

News of the death was given to Cardinal Confalonieri, the 86-year-old Dean of the Sacred College. Then to Cardinal Casaroli, head of Vatican diplomacy. Villot instructed the nuns on the switchboard to locate his deputy and the number three in the Church hierarchy, Archbishop Giuseppe Caprio, who was on holiday in Montecatini. Only then did he telephone Doctor Renato Buzzonetti, deputy head of the Vatican's health service. Next he rang the guard room of the Swiss Guard. Speaking to Sergeant Hans Roggan, Villot told him to come immediately to the Papal Apartments.

Father Diego Lorenzi, the only man to have accompanied Luciani from Venice, wandered shocked and bewildered through the Apartments. He had lost a man who over the past two years had been a second father. In tears he attempted to understand, to find some meaning. When Villot eventually decided that the world could know, millions would share Lorenzi's grief and bewilderment.

Despite Villot's stricture that the news must not leak out, Diego Lorenzi telephoned Luciani's doctor, Antonio Da Ros. He had been Luciani's physician for over twenty years. Lorenzi vividly remembers the doctor's reaction. 'He was shocked. Stunned. Unable to believe it. He asked me the cause but I didn't know. Doctor Da Ros was equally mystified. He said he would drive to Venice immediately and catch a plane to Rome.'

Lorenzi's next phone call was to Albino's niece Pia, who was probably closer to her uncle than any other member of the family. Diego Lorenzi would appear to have been the only member of the Church to appreciate that even Popes have relatives. Lorenzi naturally felt that the family warranted a personal phone call rather than hearing the news on the radio.

'We found him this morning. You need a great faith now.' Many were going to be in need of a great faith. Many were going to have to suspend belief to swallow what Villot and his colleagues would say within the next few days.

The news was starting to spread through the Vatican village. In the courtyard near the Vatican Bank Sergeant Roggan met Bishop Paul Marcinkus. It was 6.45 a.m. What the President of the Vatican Bank, who lives in the Villa Stritch on Via della Nocetta in Rome and is not a renowned early riser, was doing in the Vatican so early remains a mystery. The Villa Stritch is a 20-minute drive from the Vatican. Roggan blurted out the news. 'The Pope is dead.' Marcinkus just stared at the Sergeant of the Swiss Guard. Roggan moved closer to the head of the Vatican Bank. 'Papa Luciani. Is Dead. They found him in his bed.'

Marcinkus continued to stare at Roggan without any reaction. Eventually the Swiss Guard moved on, leaving Paul Marcinkus staring after him.

Some days later during the Pope's funeral, Marcinkus proffered an explanation for his curious behaviour. 'Sorry, I thought you had gone mad.'

Dr Buzzonetti made a brief examination of the body. He advised Villot that the cause of death was acute myocardial infarction, a heart attack. The doctor put the time of death at about 11.00 p.m. on the previous evening.

To determine the time of death as 11.00 p.m. and the cause as myocardial infarction after such a brief external examination is a medical impossibility.

Villot had already decided before Buzzonetti's examination, which took place at approximately 6 a.m., that the body of Albino Luciani should be immediately embalmed. Even before his phone call to Cardinal Confalonieri at 5.15 a.m. Villot had put into motion the initial course of action to ensure a rapid embalmment. The Signoracci brothers Ernesto and Renato had embalmed the last two Popes. Now, a dawn telephone call and a Vatican car that arrived at 5.00 a.m. were the opening acts in what was to prove a long day for the Signoracci brothers. For them to have been contacted so early clearly establishes that the Vatican had spoken to the Institute of Medicine, who employ the brothers, and given instructions between 4.45 a.m. and 5.00 a.m.

At 7.00 a.m., more than two hours after the death had been discovered by Sister Vincenza, the world at large remained ignorant of the fact that Pope John Paul I was no more. The Vatican village, meanwhile, was totally ignoring Villot's edict. Cardinal Benelli in Florence heard the news by telephone at 6.30 a.m. Grief-stricken and openly crying, he immediately retired to his room and began to pray. All the hopes dreams, aspirations were shattered. The plans Luciani had made, the changes, the new direction, all had come to nothing. When a Pope dies, all decisions yet to be publicly announced, die with him. *Unless his successor decides to carry them through.*

By 7.20 a.m. the bells in the parish church in Albino Luciani's birthplace, Canale D'Agordo, were tolling. Vatican Radio remained silent on the death. Finally at 7.27 a.m., some two-and-three-quarter hours after the death had been discovered by Sister Vincenza, Cardinal Villot felt sufficiently in control of events:

> This morning, September 29th, 1978, about 5.30, the private Secretary of the Pope, contrary to custom not having found the Holy Father in the chapel of his private apartment, looked for him in his room and found him dead in bed with the light on, like one who was intent on reading. The physician, Dr Renato Buzzonetti, who hastened at once, verified the death, which took place presumably towards eleven o'clocck yesterday evening, as 'Sudden death that could be related to acute myocardial infarction.'

Later bulletins stated that the secretary in question was Father Magee who, according to the Vatican, usually said Mass with the Pope at 5.30

a.m., and that the Pope had been reading *The Imitation of Christ,* the fifteenth-century work usually attributed to Thomas à Kempis.

Along with the medicine, the Papal notes, the Will, the glasses and the slippers, Sister Vincenza and her discovery of the body at 4.45 a.m. had vanished. Even with two-and-three-quarter hours in which to concoct a story, Villot and those who advised him made a botch of it. While every newspaper and radio and television station in the free world was carrying stories based on the Vatican bulletins, Villot was having difficulties keeping his ship watertight.

The idea of placing a book that Luciani revered into his dead hands might have seemed inspired thinking to Villot. The problem was that there was not a copy in the Pope's bedroom. Further there was not a copy in the entire Papal Apartment. Luciani's copy was still in Venice and when a few days earlier he had wished to quote accurately from the book, Lorenzi was sent to borrow a copy from his Vatican confessor. Don Diego had returned the copy before the Pope's death. His complaints about an obvious fabrication could not be stilled. The Vatican continued to maintain that particular lie until October 2nd – for four days. Within those first four days the false information given out by the Vatican had become in the minds of the people, the reality, the truth.

Many were deceived by the dis-information that came out of the Vatican. There was the tale of Father John Magee going to the Pope's bedroom shortly before 10.00 p.m. on the 28th, for example. This story, emanating directly from the Roman Curia, recounted that Magee had told the Pope of the murder of a student in Rome. 'Are those young people shooting at each other again? Really, it is terrible.' These were widely reported around the world as being the Pope's last words. They provided the bonus of giving a possible explanation for the unexpected death of Luciani. He died of shock hearing such appalling news. The conversation between Magee and Luciani did not occur. It was a Vatican fabrication.

Another Vatican fabrication was perpetrated with the impression that Luciani was in the habit of saying Mass with Magee at 5.30 a.m. Mass in the Papal Apartments was not until 7.00 a.m. As previously noted Albino Luciani spent the time between 5.30 and 7.00 a.m. in meditation and prayer, usually alone, sometimes joined at about 6.30 a.m. by Magee and Lorenzi. The image of a disturbed, distraught Magee becoming alarmed by Luciani's non-appearance at 5.30 is Vatican fantasy.

The shock at such a tragic, unexpected death went around the world. The massive bronze doors to the Basilica were closed, the Vatican flag was flown at half mast – these were external indications – but news of

Albino Luciani's death was so stunning that the disbelief expressed by his personal doctor was echoed by millions. He had delighted the world. How could God's duly elected candidate pass so quickly from them?

Cardinal Willebrands of Holland, who had entertained great hopes for Luciani's Papacy said, 'It's a disaster. I cannot put into words how happy we were on that August day when we had chosen John Paul. We had such high hopes. It was such a beautiful feeling, a feeling that something fresh was going to happen to our Church.'

Cardinal Baggio, one of the men whom Luciani had determined to move out of Rome was less fulsome. 'The Lord uses us but does not need us.' He said this early in the morning after he had seen the dead body. He continued, 'He was like a parish priest for the Church.' Asked what would happen now he responded calmly, 'Now we will make another one.'

Baggio, however, was one of the exceptions. Most people displayed deep shock and love. When Cardinal Benelli finally emerged from his room at 9.00 a.m. he was immediately surrounded by reporters. With tears still running down his face he said: 'The Church has lost the right man for the right moment. We are very distressed. We are left frightened. Man cannot explain such a thing. It is a moment which limits and conditions us.'

Back in the Vatican Villot's plans for an immediate embalming had run into trouble. Cardinals Felici in Padua and Benelli in Florence, who knew very precisely the nature of the changes Luciani had been about to make were particularly disturbed and indicated so in telephone conversations with Villot. Already there were murmurs in Italy that an autopsy should be performed. It was a view that in the circumstances Benelli and Felici were inclined at least to consider. If the body were embalmed then a subsequent autopsy would be useless if the cause of death was poison.

Officially the Vatican created the impression that the body of Pope John Paul I was embalmed before being put on public display in the Sala Clementina at noon on Friday. In fact the mourners that day gazed upon an unembalmed Luciani in his natural state. Father Diego Lorenzi:

> The body was taken from the private apartment to the Clementina Hall in the Papal Apartment. At that time no embalming had been done. Papa Luciani was dressed by Father Magee, Monsignor Noè and myself. I stayed with the body as did Magee until 11.00

a.m. The Signoracci came at that time and the body was taken to the Sala Clementina.

The contrast to Pope Paul's death was startling. Then there had been little public emotion; now there was a flood. On the first day a quarter of a million people filed past the body. The public speculation that this death was not natural grew by the minute. Men and women were heard passing the body and shouting at the inert form. 'Who has done this to you? Who has murdered you?'

Meanwhile the debate about an autopsy was growing among the minority of Cardinals who were gathering in Rome. If Albino Luciani had been an ordinary citizen of Rome there would have been no debate. There would have been an immediate autopsy. Italian law states that no embalming can be undertaken until at least 24 hours after death without dispensation from a magistrate. If an Italian citizen had died in similar circumstances to those of Luciani there would have been an immediate autopsy. The moral would appear to be that Italian citizens who wish to ensure that after their death the correct legal steps are taken, should not become Head of State of the Roman Catholic Church.

For men with nothing to hide, the actions of Villot and other members of the Roman Curia continued to be incomprehensible. When men conspire to cover up it is inexorably because there is something to cover.

It was from a Cardinal residing in Rome that I learned of the most extraordinary reason given for the cover up:

He [Villot] told me that what had occurred was a tragic accident. That the Pope had unwittingly taken an overdose of his medicine. The Camerlengo pointed out that if an autopsy was performed it would obviously show this fatal overdose. No one would believe that His Holiness had taken it accidentally. Some would allege suicide, others murder. It was agreed that there would be no autopsy.

I have interviewed on two occasions Professor Giovanni Rama, the specialist who was responsible for prescribing the Effortil, Cortiplex and other drugs to alleviate Albino Luciani's low blood pressure. Luciani was a patient of Doctor Rama's from 1975. His observations on a possible self-administered, accidental overdose are illuminating.

An accidental overdose is not credible. He was a very con-
scientious patient. He was very sensitive to drugs. He needed
very little. In fact he was on the minimum dose of Effortil.
Normally it is 60 drops a day but 20 or 30 drops per day were
enough for him. We were always very prudent in prescribing
medicines.

Further discussion with my informant established that Villot had
arrived at his deduction of accidental self-administered overdose in
those few moments in the Pope's bedroom before he pocketed the
medicine bottle. Villot was clearly a highly gifted man. The Pope dies
alone, having retired to his bedroom a well man who has just made a
number of crucial decisions, including one that directly affects Villot's
future. Without any forensic tests, without any internal or external
evidence whatsoever the elderly Secretary of State deduces that the
rational Albino Luciani has accidentally killed himself. Perhaps in the
rarefied atmosphere of the Vatican village such a story has credibility.
In the real world outside actual evidence would be essential.

Some of the key evidence that would have established the truth
had already been destroyed by Villot – the medicine and the notes
Luciani had made that detailed the vital changes. A measure of
Villot's panic can be gauged from the disappearance of Albino
Luciani's Will. It contained nothing of significance with regard to
his death yet it was destroyed along with the other vital pieces of
evidence. Why the Pope's glasses and slippers also vanished remains
a mystery.

Rumours swept through the Vatican village. It was said that the
alarm light on a panel in the Papal Apartments had glowed
throughout the night and that no one had responded to the call for
help. It was said that signs of vomiting had been found in the
bedroom, staining various items, and that was why the slippers and
glasses were now missing. Vomiting is frequently one of the earliest
symptoms of a digitalis overdose. Groups of bishops and priests
huddled in various offices and recalled the curious incident of the
sudden tragic death of the Russian Orthodox Archbishop of
Leningrad, Nikodim. He had been received in a special audience by
Albino Luciani on September 5th. Suddenly, without warning, the
49-year-old Russian prelate had slumped forward in his chair.
Moments later he was dead. Now the word went around the Vatican
that Nikodim had drunk a cup of coffee intended for Albino Luciani.

Nikodim was of frail health and had previously suffered a number of heart attacks. In the frightened City State these facts were swept aside. His death was now seen in retrospect as a sign, a warning of the awful events that had now occurred in the Papal Apartments.

During the course of the day everything else within the Papal Apartments belonging to Albino Luciani was removed, including his letters, notes, books, and the small handful of personal mementoes such as the photograph of his parents with an infant Pia. Villot's colleagues from the Secretariat of State removed all the confidential papers. Rapidly all material evidence that Albino Luciani had ever lived and worked there was boxed and carried away. By 6.00 p.m. the entire 19 rooms of the Papal Apartments were totally bereft of anything remotely associated with the Papacy of Luciani. It was as if he had never been there, never existed. At 6.00 p.m. the Papal Apartments were sealed by Cardinal Villot. They were to remain unopened until a successor had been elected.

Unobtrusively the nuns and the two secretaries left. Magee kept as a memento the cassette tapes used by Luciani to improve his English. Lorenzi took with him a jumble of images and memories. Carefully avoiding the waiting reporters, the group took up residence in a house run by the Sisters of Maria Bambina.

John Magee was destined to be a secretary to a Pope for a third time, a unique and remarkable achievement. Diego Lorenzi, the intense young Italian, was totally devastated by the death of a man he loved. He would return to northern Italy to work at a small school. Vincenza would be sent even further north to an obscure convent. The Vatican machine would ensure that neither was easy to locate with this virtual banishment.

After the doors of the Clementina Hall closed to the public at 6.00 p.m. on Friday September 29th, surely the most relieved man in the Vatican was Villot. Finally the work of the body technicians could begin. Once the body had been embalmed it would be a difficult task during any subsequent autopsy to discover and establish poison within the body. If the Pope had indeed died because of acute myocardial infarction the embalming fluids would not destroy the naturally damaged blood vessels.

In what was presumably an ironic coincidence the Rome Association of Pharmacy Owners chose this of all days to issue a press release that a number of medicines essential for the treatment of certain cases of poisoning and heart ailments were not available. Of greater pertinence perhaps was the statement that the Italian reporters had finally managed to extract from Cardinal Villot: 'When I saw His Holiness yesterday evening, he was in perfectly good health, totally lucid and he had given me full instructions for the next day.'

Behind closed doors in the Clementina Hall the lengthy process of embalming continued for three hours. The care and preservation of the body was the responsibility of Professor Cesare Gerin, but the actual embalming work was performed by Professor Marracino and Ernesto and Renato Signoracci. When the two Signoracci brothers had examined the body before it had been moved to the Clementina, they had concluded from the lack of rigor mortis and the temperature of the body that death had taken place not at 11.00 p.m. on the 28th but between 4.00 a.m. and 5.00 a.m. on the 29th. They were given independent confirmation of their conclusion by Monsignor Noè, who advised the brothers that the Pope had died shortly before 5.00 a.m. I have interviewed both brothers at length on three separate orcasions. They are adamant that death occurred between 4.00 a.m. and 5.00 a.m. and that the Pope's body was discovered within one hour of his death. If they are accurate then either the Pope was still alive when Sister Vincenza entered his bedroom or he was barely dead. Only a full autopsy would have resolved these conflicting opinions.

At the Vatican's insistence, no blood was drained from the body, neither were any organs removed. Injections of formalin and other preserving chemicals were made into the body through the femoral arterial and vein passages. The entire process took over three hours. The reason the process took so long was because, contrary to normal practice when the blood is drained or cleared with a solution of salt water that is circulated around the body, the Vatican was adamant that no blood should be drawn off. A small quantity of blood would of course have been more than sufficient for a forensic scientist to establish the presence of any poisonous substances.

The cosmetic treatment given to the body eliminated the expression of anguish upon the face. The hands that had gripped the now missing sheets of paper were clasped around a rosary. Cardinal Villot finally retired to bed shortly before midnight.

Pope Paul VI, in keeping with Italian law, had not been embalmed until twenty-four hours after his death. Although there had been allegations of medical incompetence after Paul had died, there had not been a single suggestion of foul play. Now with not only the general public but radio and television stations and the press urging an autopsy, the body of Albino Luciani had been embalmed some twelve hours after it had been discovered.

By Saturday September 30th, one particular question was being asked with increasing urgency. 'Why no autopsy?' The news media began to seek an explanation for such a sudden unheralded death. The Curia had been very quick to remind enquiring reporters of an off-the-cuff remark Albino Luciani had made during his last General Audience on Wednesday, September 27th. Turning to a group of sick and handicapped people in the Nervi Hall, Luciani had said, 'Remember your Pope has been in hospital eight times and had four operations'.

The Vatican Press Office began to respond to requests for details of Luciani's health by repeating the late Pope's phrase. They used it so excessively it began to take on the quality of a telephone answering machine, with a comparable lack of satisfaction to callers.

The various media recalled that – Luciani had not appeared to be in ill health during his brief Papacy. On the contrary, they observed, he appeared to be the picture of health, full of life and zest. Others, who had known Luciani for considerably longer, began to be contacted for their views.

When Monsignor Senigaglia, Luciani's secretary in Venice for over six years, revealed that the late Pope had undergone a full medical check up shortly before leaving Venice for the Conclave and the medical examination had 'been favourable in all respects' the demands for an autopsy grew louder.

When a variety of Italian medical experts began to state categorically the need for an autopsy to ascertain the precise cause of death the panic within the Vatican reached new heights. It was clear that while doctors were prepared to put forward a variety of reasons that could have been contributory factors (the sudden stress of becoming Pope was a particular favourite), none was prepared to accept without an autopsy the Vatican's assertion that Albino Luciani died of myocardial infarction.

The Vatican countered by stating that it was against Vatican rules for an autopsy to be performed. This was yet another lie passed out to the world's Press. Further questioning by Italian journalists established that the Vatican was referring to the Apostolic Constitution announced by Pope Paul VI in 1975. This was the document which laid down the procedures for electing his successor, with its search for bugs in the Conclave area and its instructions on the size of voting cards. Careful reading of the document establishes that Paul had failed to cover the possibility of any controversy over the cause of his death. An autopsy was neither banned nor approved. It was simply not referred to.

The subject of Paul's death then became a matter of public debate. It is abundantly clear that Paul's life could have been prolonged. The medical treatment he had been given during his last days, had in the opinion of many of the world's experts, left a great deal to be desired. From his Cape Town Hospital, Dr Christian Barnard, when informed that Pope Paul had not been placed in an intensive care unit, said: 'If this was to happen in South Africa, the doctors responsible would have been denounced to their Medical Association for negligence.'

One of the principal doctors in control of Pope Paul's treatment had been Dr Renato Buzzonetti, the deputy head of the Vatican medical services. Now the same doctor, who in Dr Barnard's view had acted negligently in August, had performed a medical impossibility in determining the cause of Albino Luciani's lonely death. Without an autopsy his conclusion was totally without meaning.

It was against this background that Cardinal Confalonieri presided over the first meeting of the Congregation of Cardinals, the group which watches over and controls Church affairs in the interim after a Pope's death. This group comprises every cardinal – if they happen to be in Rome. When this initial meeting took place, at 11.00 a.m. on Saturday September 30th, the vast majority of cardinals were still scattered around the world. Of the 127 cardinals only 29 were present, and the majority of these were, naturally, Italian. This minority made a number of decisions. They decided that Albino Luciani's funeral would take place on the following Wednesday, October 4th. In the meantime the massive public desire personally to visit the Pope's body was causing havoc to Vatican officials. They had anticipated a similar degree of interest to that shown when Paul died – yet another example of how badly the Curia failed to understand Luciani's impact. The decision was taken to move the body that evening to St Peter's Basilica. The two most significant decisions taken that morning, however, were that the next Conclave should take place at the earliest possible date, October 14th, and that there would be no autopsy.

The doubts and concern of men like Benelli, Felici and Caprio about Luciani's death were overruled. Acutely aware that the controversy would grow until the public were given something to distract and deflect them, Villot and his colleagues totally reversed the way they had reasoned in August. Then the Conclave had been delayed until nearly the longest permissible time. Now it was to be the shortest. It was a shrewd ploy. Curial cardinals, in particular, reasoned that after the funeral the media would become preoccupied with Luciani's possible successor. If they could hold out until the funeral took place in a few days' time, they would be safe. Further, any of the majority of the cardinals yet to arrive, who felt like insisting on an autopsy, would be confronted with decisions already taken. To reverse such decisions in the limited time before the funeral would be a virtual impossibility. 'And ye shall know the truth, and the truth shall make you free', Jesus tells us, an injunction that 29 cardinals chose to ignore on behalf of the Roman Catholic Church on the morning of September 30th, 1978.

After the meeting had adjourned, Cardinal Confalonieri gave his considered opinion as to why the Pope had suddenly died.

He couldn't stand the solitude; all Popes live in a kind of institutional solitude, but perhaps Luciani suffered from it more. He, who had always lived among the people, found himself living with two secretaries whom he did not know and two nuns who did not even raise their eyes in the presence of the Pope. He did not even have the time to make any friends.

Father Diego Lorenzi had worked closely and intimately with Luciani for over two years. Sister Vincenza had worked with Luciani for nearly twenty years. Far from casting her eyes upon the ground at his approach she was a source of great comfort to Luciani. Indeed the man was cut off; but would a bevy of intimates have been able to prevent a solitary, mysterious death?

There can be no doubt that the Curial hostility and arrogance displayed during his last thirty-three days had not made for the happiest of experiences, but Albino Luciani had fought clerical hostility and arrogance for nearly a decade in Venice.

At 6.00 p.m. on Saturday September 30th the embalmed body was moved, uncovered, to the Basilica of St Peter. Much of the world watched on television as the procession, including 24 of the cardinals and 100 bishops and archbishops passed through the First Loggia, the Ducal Hall, the Hall and Stairway of the Kings and through the Bronze Door and out into St Peter's Square. At that point the singing of the Magnificat was unexpectedly drowned by one of those gestures that is so peculiarly Italian. The massive crowds broke into loud sustained applause, the Latin counterpart of Anglo-Saxon silence.

Throughout the world informed and uninformed opinion attempted to assess the life and death of Albino Luciani. Much of what was written tells a great deal more about the writers than about the man. The belief that minds could be quickly diverted from the death to the succession, expressed in the morning by the Curia, rapidly began to prove accurate. In England *The Times* neatly mirrored the transitory nature of life with an editorial entitled, 'The Year of The Three Popes'.

Some observers talked perceptively of a great promise unfulfilled, others of a pontificate that had promised to be fun. With regard to an explanation for the sudden death, the Roman Curia dis-information service achieved a remarkable coup. Writer after writer talked about a long record of illness. That someone as experienced as Patrick O'Donovan of the *Observer* could be deceived into writing the following indicates just how successful the lies were: 'It is only now generally known that Cardinal Luciani had a long record of all but mortal illness.'

Exactly what these mortal illnesses were was not stated. Fighting a deadline it is clear that O'Donovan and the other writers had no time for personal research but relied on Vatican contacts. Some talked of Luciani's heavy smoking, of the fact that he had only one lung, of his several bouts of tuberculosis. Since his death others have been told by Vatican sources of his four heart attacks, of the fact that he suffered from phlebitis, a painful circulatory disease. Others mention the fact that he suffered from emphysema, a chronic illness of the lungs usually caused by cigarette smoking. There is not a word of truth in any of it.

The overkill of Vatican lies is self-defeating. Would 111 cardinals gather in Rome in August 1978 and elect a man suffering from all of the above? And then permit him to die alone? Along with the lies about Luciani's medical history the Vatican disinformation service was busy in other areas. The Curia were pushing the non-attributable, off the record view that Luciani was no good as a Pope anyway. Why mourn what was worthless? I discussed this smear campaign with Cardinal Benelli who remarked:

> It seemed to me that their [the Roman Curia] aim was twofold. To minimize Luciani's abilities would reduce the sense of loss and consequently reduce the demands for an autopsy. Secondly the Curia were preparing for the next Conclave. They wanted a Curial Pope.

When Luciani had lunched with his niece Pia one of the subjects discussed had been Press distortion. Now in death Luciani became a victim of just this. The negative comments were mainly inspired by insignificant priests or monsignors who were normally busy writing irrelevant Vatican memos. They found it highly flattering to be asked for their opinion of the late Pope. The fact that none of them was near the corridors of power or had ever been within the Papal Apartment was masked by the all-embracing description, 'a highly placed Vatican source said today'. What they said was part of the great injustice done to the memory of the dead Pope. It enabled writers, who before the August Conclave had been dismissive of Luciani, to put behind them the uncomfortable fact that Luciani's election had been a major demonstration of how ill-informed they were. Their thinking appears to have been: well, yes, we discounted him, but you see he should have been discounted. Thus:

> The audiences attracted the immediate sympathy of the public but had disappointed and sometimes worried church officials. The Pope expressed a philosophy of existence that on occasion resembled the *Readers Digest*: common sense, a little simple at that, which broke the grand theological flights of oratory of Paul VI. Clearly he did not have the culture and the intellectual training of his predecessor.
>
> Vatican correspondent Robert Sole
for Le Monde

> We followed first with eagerness, then with a growing sense of the ridiculous, his generous efforts to discover who he was. He smiled, his father was a socialist, he rejected the tiara for a simple stole, he spoke informally at audiences.
>
> Commonweal

Newsweek considered that Luciani's rejection of the philosophy 'Ubi Lenin, ibi Jerusalem' was a betrayal of the Latin American cardinals who had played such a valuable part in his election. The periodical considered that in making this observation Luciani had rejected the theology of liberation. Because of Curia censorship they missed the fact that he had added an important qualification: 'There is some coincidence but we cannot make a perfect equation', and in doing so missed the point.

Peter Nichols, the very experienced *Times* correspondent, but writing on this occasion in the *Spectator*, compared Luciani with a popular Italian comedian of yesteryear who had but to stand there in sight of the populace to be given an ovation. He failed to explain why Paul VI had not received ovations on each appearance.

Others criticized the fact that he had re-confirmed all the Curia heads in office. They neglected to point out that this had also been done by the last three Popes before Luciani and that he retained the power and authority to move any of them at any time.

Much of the world's news media had, in the days following the Pope's death, carried stories about the Vatican ritual that surrounds this moment. The newspapers were full of accounts of how Cardinal Villot had approached the inert body and proclaimed three times, 'Albino, are you dead?', each question being followed by the symbolic striking on the Pope's forehead with a small silver hammer. The Press also gave dramatic descriptions of how Villot had then taken the Fisherman's Papal ring from Luciani's hand and subsequently smashed it to pieces.

With the death of Albino Luciani there was, in fact, no head tapping, no calling of names. These ceremonies had been abolished in Paul's lifetime. With regard to the Papal ring, Luciani's reign was so brief that the Vatican had not even created the ring. The only ring on Luciani's hand throughout his entire Papacy was the one given to all bishops who had attended the Second Vatican Council.

Why this highly inaccurate reportage is worth considering, when one is aware not only of how much Luciani did achieve in such a brief span, but also the very high regard in which such men as Casaroli, Benelli, Lorscheider, Garrone, Felici and many others held Luciani, is the fact that this was an orchestrated campaign. Not one single critical obituary or article carried any of the facts recorded in the previous chapter. One of the many expressions they are fond of quoting within Vatican City states, 'Nothing is leaked from the Vatican without a very specific purpose'.

On October 1st, the pressure for an autopsy on Luciani increased. Italy's most respected newspaper *Corriere della Sera* carried a front page article with the title, 'Why say no to an autopsy?' It was by Carlo Bo, a highly talented writer with considerable knowledge of the Vatican. That the article appeared at all is significant. In Italy, thanks to the Lateran Treaty and subsequent agreements between the Italian State and the Vatican, the Press is seriously muzzled when writing on the Catholic Church. The libel laws are very stringent. Critical comment, let alone an outright attack, can rapidly result in the newspaper concerned being brought to court.

Carlo Bo cleverly avoided any such risk. In a style rather reminiscent of Mark Antony's speech to the Roman populace, Bo talked of the suspicions and allegations that had surfaced after the sudden death.

He told his readers that he felt confident that the palaces and cellars of the Vatican had been free from such criminal actions for centuries. Because of this very reason he said he simply could not understand why the Vatican had decided not to perform any scientific checks, 'in humble words why there was no autopsy'. He continued:

> . . . The Church has nothing to fear, therefore nothing to lose. On the contrary it would have much to gain.
> . . . . Now to know what the Pope died of is a legitimate historical fact, it is part of our visible history and does not in any way affect the spiritual mystery of his death. The body that we leave behind when we die can be understood with our poor instruments, it is a leftover: the soul is already, or rather it always has been, dependent on other laws which are not human and so remain inscrutable. Let us not make out of a mystery a secret to guard for earthly reasons and let us recognize the smallness of our secrets. Let us not declare sacred what is not.

While the fifteen doctors who belonged to the Vatican's health services refused to comment on the desirability of performing autopsies on dead Popes, Edoardo Luciani, newly returned from Australia, failed to help the Vatican's position when he was asked about his brother's health:

> The day after the enthronement ceremony, I asked his personal doctor how he had found him, bearing in mind all the pressures he was now subjected to. The doctor reassured me, telling me that my brother was in excellent health and that his heart was in good condition.

Asked if his brother had ever had any heart trouble, Edoardo replied, 'As far as I know absolutely none'. It did not fit very well with the Vatican-orchestrated fantasy.

By Monday October 2nd the controversy surrounding the Pope's death had become world-wide. In France at Avignon, Cardinal Silvio Oddi found himself the object of many questions. As an Italian cardinal surely he could tell his French questioners the true facts? Oddi advised them that the College of Cardinals 'will not examine the possibility of an enquiry at all and will not accept any supervision from anyone and it will not even discuss the subject'. Oddi concluded: 'We know in fact, in all certainty, that the death of John Paul the First was due to the fact that his heart stopped beating from perfectly natural causes.' Clearly Cardinal Oddi had achieved a major medical break-through for the entire world – the ability to diagnose without an autopsy what is only diagnosable with an autopsy.

Meanwhile the protests of Father Lorenzi and other members of the Papal Apartments about one particular lie had finally borne fruit. The Vatican announced:

> After the necessary enquiries, we are now in a position to state that the Pope, when he was found dead on the morning of September 29th, was holding in his hands certain sheets of paper containing his personal writings such as homilies, speeches, reflections and various notes.

When the Vatican had previously announced that Luciani had been holding *The Imitation of Christ*, Father Andrew Greeley records in his book, *The Making of The Popes*, 'some reporters openly laughed'.

These papers, detailing the crucial changes that Albino Luciani was about to make, have undergone some extraordinary metamorphoses over the years: a report on the Church in Argentina; notes for his next Angelus speech; sermons made in Belluno/Vittorio Veneto/Venice; a parish magazine; the speech he was about to deliver to the Jesuits (in fact this was found on his study desk); a report written by Pope Paul. When a Head of State dies in apparently normal circumstances his last actions are of more than academic interest. When a Head of State dies in the circumstances surrounding Albino Luciani's death, the need to know becomes a vital matter of public interest. The fact that Luciani was holding his personal notes on the various crucial changes he was proposing to make has been confirmed to me from five different sources. Two are direct Vatican sources; the other three are external non-Vatican residents. With the Vatican officially retracting *The Imitation of Christ* version the Curial machine was beginning to show signs of strain.

The strain grew even greater when the world's Press began to comment on a number of disturbing aspects. For a Pope to have no one monitoring his welfare from mid-evening until the following day struck many observers as wrong. The fact that Dr Renato Buzzonetti worked mainly at a Rome hospital and consequently was not able to guarantee absolute availability seemed outrageous. If the observers had known the full scenario of Vatican inefficiency the outrage would have been even greater. The full facts illustrate not only the potential for a premature natural death but the scenario for murder.

In Spain, as in other countries, the controversy broke into public debate. Professor Rafael Gambra of the University of Madrid was one of a number who complained of the Vatican 'doing things in the Italian manner or in the Florentine manner as in the Renaissance'. Urging that an autopsy should be performed, Gambra voiced fears that a Pope who was manifestly going to bring a much needed discipline back into the Church might have been murdered.

In Mexico City the Bishop of Cuernavaca, Sergio Arceo, publicly demanded an autopsy declaring, 'To Cardinal Miranda and me it seems that it would be useful'. The Bishop ordered a detailed statement to be read out in all churches in his diocese. The Vatican machine moved fast. The detailed statement, like much else in this affair vanished from the face of the earth and by the time the Vatican had finished with Cardinal Miranda he was able to declare upon his subsequent arrival in Rome that he had no doubts whatsoever with regard to the death of the Pope.

On October 3rd, as people continued to file past the Pope's body at the rate of 12,000 per hour, the controversy roared on. The Will of Albino Luciani had vanished but by its extraordinary behaviour the Vatican was ensuring a bitter legacy. A Pope with an ability to speak openly, directly and simply was surrounded in death by deviousness and deceit. It was clear that the loss felt by ordinary people was immense. From the Vatican there was scant acknowledgment of that widespread feeling – rather a bitter rearguard action to protect not the memory of Albino Luciani but those to whom the evidence of complicity in his murder clearly pointed.

Non-Curial priests were now debating in newspapers the merits and demerits of an autopsy. Pundits and Vatican observers were castigating the Vatican for its obduracy. What had become abundantly clear, as Vittorio Zucconi observed in *Corriere della Sera*, was that, 'Behind the doubt about the Pope's death lies a vast dissatisfaction with "official versions"'.

The organization of traditionalist Catholics known as Civiltà Cristiana indicated just how deeply dissatisfied they were. Secretary Franco Antico revealed that he had sent an official appeal for a full judicial enquiry into the death of Pope John Paul I to the Vatican City State's chief justice.

The decision to make the appeal and the reasons for it made headlines around the world. Antico cited a number of the inconsistencies which had emerged to date from the Vatican. What his group wanted was not merely an autopsy but a full judicial enquiry. Antico said: 'If President Carter had died under such circumstances, you can be sure the American people would have demanded an explanation.'

Antico told the Press that his organization had initially examined the possibility of a formal allegation that the Pope had been killed by a person or persons unknown. Displaying a wonderful example of the complexity of the Italian mind, he said that they had refrained from such a step because 'we are not seeking a scandal'. Civiltà Cristiana had also sent their request to Cardinal Confalonieri, Dean of the Sacred College. Some of the issues they raised were the gap between the discovery of the body and public announcement of death, a Pope apparently working in bed without anyone checking on his welfare and the fact that no death certificate had been issued. No Vatican doctor had, via an official death certificate, taken public responsibility with regard to the diagnosis of the cause of Albino Luciani's death.

The rebel Archbishop Marcel Lefebvre's supporters who had already announced that Luciani had died because God did not want him to be Pope now announced through Lefebvre's right-hand man, Abbot Ducaud-Bourget, a different theory: 'It's difficult to believe that the death was natural considering all the creatures of the devil who inhabit the Vatican.'

Having previously been obliged to retract the statement that Papal autopsies were specifically banned, the Vatican was confronted on Tuesday October 3rd with the efforts of some tenacious probing by the Italian Press. Autopsies had been performed on other Popes. For example, Pius VIII had died on November 30th, 1830. The diary of Prince Don Agostini Chigi recorded that the following evening an autopsy was performed on the body. The result of the autopsy is officially unknown because officially the Vatican has never admitted that it took place. In fact apart from some weakness in the lungs all the organs were found to be healthy. It was suspected that the Pope had been poisoned.

On the evening of October 3rd at 7.00 p.m. a curious event occurred. The gates of St Peter's were closed to the public for the day. The church was deserted except for the four Swiss Guards posted at the corners of the catafalque, the traditional 24-hour protection accorded to the body of a dead Pope. At 7.45 p.m. a group of about 150 pilgrims from Canale d'Agordo, Albino Luciani's birthplace, accompanied by the Bishop of Belluno, were quietly let into the church through a side entrance. The group had only just arrived in Rome and had been granted special permission by the Vatican to pay their last respects to a man many of them knew personally, after the official closure for the day. Clearly someone in Vatican City with plans of his own in regard to the body of the Pope was not advised. Within a few minutes of their arrival the pilgrims found themselves being bundled out unceremoniously into St Peter's Square.

Vatican officials had appeared together with a group of doctors. Everyone else was ordered to leave. The four Swiss Guards were also dispensed with. Large crimson screens were placed all around the body preventing any onlooker who chanced to be still within St Peter's from observing precisely what the doctors were doing. This sudden unannounced medical examination continued until 9.30 p.m. When it was concluded, a number of the pilgrims from Canale d'Agordo who had remained outside asked if they could not finally pay their last respects to the corpse. The request was refused.

Why with less than 24 hours to the funeral did this examination take place? Many working in the news media were clearly in no doubt. An autopsy had been performed. Did the Vatican finally make a move to allay public anxiety? If it did, then the subsequent Vatican statements concerning this medical examination lead inexorably to the conclusion that the examination confirmed all those fears and anxieties that the Pope had been murdered.

There was no announcement after the examination and, despite being deluged with questions by the news media, the Vatican Press Office continued to maintain a total silence on what had occurred in St Peter's until after the Pope was buried. Only then did it give its version. Previously, off the record, it had advised the Italian news agency ANSA that the medical examination was a normal check on the state of preservation of the body and that it was carried out by Professor Gerin and Arnaldo and Ernesto Signoracci among others. ANSA was also told that several more injections of the embalming fluid were made.

When the Vatican Press Office finally spoke officially, it reduced the ninety-minute examination to twenty minutes. It also stated that everything was found to be in order and that subsequently the pilgrims from Canale d'Agordo were allowed back in. Apart from the errors or deliberate lies inherently contained within the Press statement there are a number of other disquieting facts. Professor Cesare Gerin, contrary to the Vatican informants questioned by ANSA, was not present. Furthermore when I interviewed the Signoracci brothers, they were adamant that they too were not present during this bizarre event. It was clearly a conservation check without the conservationists.

If, as many believe, an autopsy was indeed performed, even a partial autopsy – for in ninety minutes it could not have been the full standard post mortem – then the results, if negative, would have been announced loudly and clearly. What better way to silence the tongues? *Corriere della Sera* stated that 'at the last minute a famous doctor from the Catholic University joined the special team'. Subsequently the 'famous doctor' has vanished in the morning mists rising from the Tiber.

Catholic psychologist Rosario Mocciaro, commenting on the behaviour of the men entrusted with controlling the Roman Catholic Church during this period of the empty throne, described it thus: 'A sort of mafia-like "omertá" (silence) disguised as Christian charity and protocol'.

The dialogue of love that Albino Luciani had inspired between himself and the people continued until the bitter end. Ignoring the continuous rain nearly 100,000 people were in St Peter's Square for the open air Requiem Mass on October 4th. Nearly one million people had filed past the body during the previous four days. The first of the three readings, taken from the Apocalypse of St John, ended with the words, 'I am Alpha and Omega, the beginning and the end. I will give water from the well of life free to anybody who is thirsty.'

The body of Albino Luciani, hermetically sealed in three coffins, cypress, lead and ebony, went to its final resting place inside a marble sarcophagus in the crypt of St Peter's. Even as his mortal remains went into the cold Roman dusk to take their place between John XXIII and Paul VI the discussion continued as to whether before his death Albino Luciani had been given something other than water from the well of life.

A great many people remained disturbed about the sudden death, among them Albino Luciani's own doctor, Guiseppe Da Ros.

With the Pope buried within three coffins, it was clearly going to be virtually impossible to persuade the Vatican to change its mind. The formal request by Civiltà Cristiana to the Vatican Tribunal rested with a single judge, Giuseppe Spinelli. Even if the man had earnestly desired that there should be an autopsy and a full investigation it is difficult to see how he would have overcome the power of the Vatican City and the men who ran it – men who claim as an historical 'fact' that they and their predecessors have nearly two thousand years of practice at controlling the Roman Catholic Church.

It was all very well for the Jesuits to compare Luciani's death to a flower in a field that closes at night, or for the Franciscans to talk of death being like a thief in the night. Non-aesthetes continued to seek a more practical explanation. Sceptics could be found on both sides of the Tiber. Among those who were most disturbed within the Vatican was the group who knew the truth about the discovery of the Pope's body by Sister Vincenza. Concern mounted as the official lies increased. Eventually, with the Pope buried, several of them talked. Initially they spoke to the news agency ANSA and recently to me. Indeed it was several members of this group who convinced me that I should investigate the death of Albino Luciani.

On October 5th, shortly after lunch-time, they began to give ANSA the factual details of Sister Vincenza's discovery. Their information even correctly identified that the notes Luciani was holding in death, concerned 'certain nominations in the Roman Curia and in the Italian episcopate'. The group also revealed that the Pope had discussed the problem of Baggio's refusal to accept the Patriarchship of Venice. When the story exploded on the public the Vatican response was very reminiscent of Monsignor Henry Riedmatten's when confronted with questions about the Luciani document on birth control. That document, it will be recalled, was dismissed by Riedmatten as 'a fantasy'. Now confronted by literally hundreds of reporters demanding a Vatican comment on the latest leaks, the director of the Vatican Press Office, Father Panciroli, issued a one-line laconic denial. 'These are reports devoid of all foundations.'

Among those unimpressed by this denial were a number of the cardinals still arriving in Rome for the next Conclave. At the meeting of the congregation of cardinals which took place on October 9th their unease surfaced. Cardinal Villot in particular found himself under attack. As Camerlengo he had taken the decisions and authorized the statements which clearly indicated that the death of Luciani had been followed by a cover-up. Many of the non-Italian Princes of the Church demanded to know exactly what was being covered up. They wanted to know why the cause of death had not been precisely ascertained and why it had merely been presumed. They wanted to know why there was not greater clarification about the time of death. Why a doctor had not taken official responsibility in putting his name to a death certificate that could be made public.

They were unsuccessful in their efforts to obtain these facts. The next Conclave was fast approaching, thanks to the decision made by a minority the day after the discovery of the Pope's body. The minds of the cardinals began to concentrate on the lobbying and the intrigues surrounding the problem of who should succeed Albino Luciani: an indication that the men of the Roman Curia, with an inherited experience of nearly two thousand years, have indeed learned a great deal from their predecessors.

On October 12th, less than forty-eight hours before the next Conclave, the Vatican made its final public statement concerning the furore over the death of Albino Luciani. It was issued by Vatican press secretary Father Romeo Panciroli:

> At the end of the 'Novemdiales', when we enter a new phase of the Sede Vacante, the director of the Press Office of the Holy See expresses words of firm disapproval for those who in recent days have indulged in the spreading of strange rumours, unchecked, often false and which sometimes have reached the level of grave insinuations, all the more grave for the repercussions they may have had in those countries where people are not accustomed to excessively casual forms of expression. In these moments of mourning and sorrow for the Church one expected greater control and greater respect.

He repeated that 'what happened has been faithfully reported in the communiqué of Friday morning, September 29th, which maintains its full validity and which reflected the death certificate signed by Professor Mario Fontana and Dr Renato Buzzonetti so faithfully as to render its publication unnecessary'.

He also noted with satisfaction, 'the rectitude of many professionals who in such a difficult moment for the Church, showed loyal participation in the events and informed public opinion with considered and objective reports'.

Wishing to avoid 'grave insinuations' I will make instead a categoric statement. I am completely convinced that Pope John Paul I, Albino Luciani, was murdered.

To this date no death certificate has ever been made public and despite repeated requests the Vatican refused to make one available to me. Undoubtedly it would state that the cause of death was myocardial infarction. The continued refusal to make the death certificate available means that no doctor is prepared to accept publicly the legal responsibility for diagnosing Albino Luciani's death. The fact that the diagnosis was based on an *external* examination which is unacceptable medically may have something to do with that Vatican refusal.

The fact that a full autopsy or post mortem was not performed despite international unease and concern is powerful evidence that the

Pope was murdered. If Luciani's death was natural then why not have an autopsy and allay that concern?

It is clear that, officially at least, the Vatican does not know when Luciani died or what killed him. 'Presumably towards eleven o'clock' and 'sudden death that could be related to' are statements that clearly demonstrate a high degree of ignorance, of presumptions and assumptions. The body of a beggar found in the gutters of Rome would be accorded a greater degree of professional care and attention. The scandal is all the greater when one is aware that these examining doctors had never medically cared for the living Albino Luciani. When I spoke to Dr Renato Buzzonetti in Rome I asked what medicines the Pope had been taking in the weeks before his death. He replied, 'I don't know what medicines he was taking. I was not his doctor. The first time I saw him on a doctor/patient relationship he was dead.'

Dr Seamus Banim is a heart specialist with over twenty years' professional experience. He is the Senior Consultant at St Bartholomew's Hospital, London and the Nuffield Hospital. During my interview with him he said:

> For a doctor, any doctor, to diagnose myocardial infarction as the cause of death is wrong. I would not be satisfied. If he had known the patient before, had treated him for a period of time, had cared for him during a previous heart attack, had observed the living man after what was to prove to be a fatal heart attack, then the diagnosis might just be permissible. But if he had not known the patient before he is not entitled to make that diagnosis. He is taking a very grave risk and he certainly would not be entitled to take such a risk and make such a diagnosis in this country. Such a diagnosis can only be given after an autopsy.

We have, therefore, an unacceptable conclusion concerning the cause of death and an equally unacceptable conclusion about the time of death.

The Vatican told the world that it happened, 'Presumably towards eleven o'clock on the evening of September 28th'. Dr Derek Barrowcliff, a former Home Office pathologist with over fifty years' experience, advised me:

> Unless there were a graded series of temperature readings in the rectum it is a very very brave man who will say that death occurred at such and such a time. A very brave man indeed.

Rigor mortis tends to be detectable after five or six hours depending on a number of factors including the heat of the room. A hot room brings it on quicker – a cold room slower. It may take 12 hours to develop, then remain firmly fixed for 12 hours, then start to weaken during a further 12 hours. This is very very approximate. If *rigor mortis* is present, it is reasonable to assume that death occurred some six hours or more before. Certainly a liver temperature reading [which was not taken] would have helped. If one is examining a body very very carefully in a medico-legal sense, then one does detect slight degrees of rigor. It comes on very gently. Hence if the body were stiff at 6 a.m. it would be reasonable to say death occurred at 11.00 p.m. the previous evening. But it could equally have been 9 p.m. the previous evening.

So, two facts have been indisputably established:
1   We do not know what caused the death of Albino Luciani.
2   We do not know with any degree of certainty what time he died. When Pope Paul VI died in August 1978 he was surrounded by doctors, secretaries and priests. Consider the detail contained in the official bulletin that was published and signed by doctors Mario Fontana and Renato Buzzonetti.

During the course of the past week, the Holy Father Paul VI suffered a serious accentuation of the painful symptoms referable to the arthritic illness with which he has been affected for many years. On the afternoon of Saturday 5th of August he suffered from fever due to the sudden resurgence of an acute cystitis. Having taken the opinion of Professor Fabio Prosperi, chief urologist of the United Hospitals of Rome, the appropriate curative measures were begun. During the night of 5–6 August and all through Sunday 6th of August the Holy Father was suffering from high fever. About 18.15 of Sunday 6th of August sudden, serious and progressive heightenmg of arterial pressure was observed. Now there followed rapidly the typical symptoms of insufficiency of the left ventricle with the clinical picture of acute pulmonary oedema.

Despite all the precise attentions which were at once applied, His Holiness Paul VI died at 21.40 hours.

At the time of death, the doctors in attendance indicated the following general clinical picture: cardiopathic arteriosclerotic polyarthritis, chronic pyelonephritis and acute cystitis. Immediate cause of death: hypertensive crisis, insufficiency of the left ventricle, acute pulmonary oedema. Less than two months later, Paul's successor dies 'like a flower in a field that closes at night' with not a single member of the medical profession in sight.

In contrast to the plethora of lies that poured from Vatican City about the medical history of Luciani it is worth stating the facts.

In his infancy he had shown signs of a tubercular illness, the symptoms being enlarged neck glands. At the age of eleven his tonsils were removed; at the age of fifteen his adenoids. Both these operations were performed in the general hospital in Padua. In 1945 and again in 1947 he was admitted to a sanatorium with suspected tuberculosis. Tests on both occasions produced negative results and the pulmonary illnesses were diagnosed as bronchitis. He made a complete recovery and every subsequent chest X-ray was negative. In 1964 he was operated on in April for gallstones and a blocked colon and in August for haemorrhoids. Professor Amedeo Alexandre, who performed both operations at the Pordenone hospital, checked his medical records of the period before advising me that Albino Luciani was suffering from no other ailments and that all of his pre- and post-operative medical tests confirmed that Luciani was in perfect health. These tests included X-rays and a number of ECGs, a test specifically designed to record heart abnormalities. The Professor stated that his patient's recovery from both of these minor operations was total and complete. 'I re-examined him in the summer after the second operation. Then too he was in excellent health.'

An illustration of how healthy Albino Luciani was can be found in the daily routine his then colleague Monsignor Taffarel described to me. It is virtually identical to his routine in Venice and subsequently in the Vatican. He awoke at 4.30 to 4.45 a.m. and retired for the night some sixteen hours later between 9 p.m. and 10 p.m. Monsignor Taffarel advised me that Luciani, apart from his many other functions, made pastoral visits to every one of his 180 parishes and was two-thirds of the way through a second round of pastoral visits when he was promoted to go to Venice. He suffered a blood clot in the central vein of the retina of the left eye in December 1975. No operation was required and his specialist Professor Rama advised me:

The treatment was only general and was based on haemokinetic medicine, anti-coagulants and mild medicines to dilate the blood vessels and, above all, a few days rest in hospital. The result was almost immediate, with a complete recovery of vision and general recovery. He was never what one would call a 'physical colossus' but he was fundamentally healthy and the tests carried out on several occasions never revealed heart troubles.

Professor Rama noted that Luciani had low blood pressure which under normal conditions oscillated around 120/80. Low blood pressure was considered by the twenty-three members of the medical profession whom I consulted, to be 'The best possible diagnosis for life expectancy.'

During his time in Venice Luciani occasionally had swelling in the ankles. His doctors thought this attributable to the low blood pressure and the need for more exercise. In July 1978 he spent ten days at the Stella Maris Institute on the Lido to counteract a possible re-occurrence of gallstones. He was put on a bland diet and took extensive walks in the morning and the evening to alleviate the slight swelling in the ankles. A medical check-up after this stay concluded that he was in excellent health. The check-up included an ECG.

The above is the sum total of Albino Luciani's medical history during his entire life. It is based on interviews with the doctors who cared for him, relations, friends and colleagues. It should be closely compared with the farrago of lies concerning his health that poured out of Vatican City. The overriding question that surely springs immediately to mind is, why all the lies? The more one probes into Luciani's life the greater grows the belief that this man was murdered. For nearly six years the Vatican lies concerning the late Pope have run unchecked and unchallenged. The Roman Curia would have the world believe that Albino Luciani was a simple, near idiot; a gravely ill man whose election was an aberration and whose natural death was a merciful release for the Church. In such a manner they hoped to mask murder. The past 400 years have not been: we are back with the Borgias.

While the news media of the world carried details of the Vatican fantasy about Luciani's health, there were many who, if they had been asked, would have provided a different picture:

I knew him from 1936 onwards. Apart from the two periods of confinement for suspected tuberculosis he was perfectly healthy. He made a complete recovery after the second confinement. Certainly up to 1958 when he became Bishop of Vittorio Veneto there were no major illnesses. (Monsignor Da Rif, to author.)

His health while in Vittorio Veneto was excellent. He had the two operations in 1964 for gallstones and haemorrhoids and made a complete recovery. His work-load remained exactly the same. I have heard about the low blood pressure and the swollen legs. Neither occurred while he was here [Vittorio Veneto] and subsequently after he had gone to Venice I saw him many times. He was always in excellent health. Between 1958 and 1970 apart from those two operations his health was perfect. (Monsignor Taffarel, to author.)

In the eight years he was in Venice I only once saw Cardinal Luciani in bed because he was unwell, that was for simple influenza. For the rest, the Patriarch of Venice was very healthy and he did not suffer from any illness. (Monsignor Giuseppe Bosa, Apostolic Administrator of Venice.)

He had absolutely no cardiopathic characteristics, besides, his low blood pressure should, at least in theory, have made him safe from acute cardio-vascular attacks. The only time I needed to give him treatment was for the influenza attack. (Dr Carlo Frizzerio, Venice physician.)

Albino Luciani did not have a bad heart. Someone with a bad heart does not, as the Patriarch did every year with me from 1972 to 1977, climb mountains. We would go to Pietralba, near Bolzano, and we would climb the Corno Bianco, from 1,500 metres to 2,400 metres, at a good speed . . . There was never a sign of cardiac insufficiency. On the contrary, at my insistence in 1974 an electrocardiogram was carried out, which recorded nothing irregular. Immediately before leaving for the Conclave in August 1978 and after his visit to the Stella Maris Clinic he had a full medical check-up. The results were favourable in all respects. As for the theory of stress or exhaustion, it's a nonsense. His working day in the Vatican was no longer than here in Venice and in the Vatican he had many more assistants, a great deal more help and goodness knows how many more advisers. Mountain men do not die of heart attacks. (Monsignor Mario Senigaglia, Secretary to Albino Luciani 1970–6, to author.)

Doctor Da Ros said to me: 'Do you have a secret medicine? Albino Luciani is in perfect health and he is so much more relaxed. What magic drugs do you have?' (Father Diego Lorenzi, Secretary to Albino Luciani 1976 to his death, to author.)

All of the above plus over a further twenty people, who knew Albino Luciani from childhood onwards, confirmed that he had never smoked, he drank alcohol rarely and ate sparingly. This life style plus his low blood pressure could not be improved upon if one wished to avoid coronary disease.

Apart from the members of the medical profession already referred to who had been concerned with specific ailments, there was his regular physician Dr Giuseppe Da Ros. His relationship with Albino Luciani reveals that the Pope's health was constantly and regularly monitored for over the last twenty years of his life.

Dr Da Ros was also a friend and in Vittorio Veneto visited Luciani every week. In Venice he came once a fortnight at 6.30 a.m. and stayed for a minimum of ninety minutes. They would breakfast together but the visits were professional as well as social.

The visits continued after Luciani's election to the Papacy. Da Ros gave Luciani three full medical examinations during his 33-day Papacy. The last was on Saturday, September 23rd, immediately before Luciani left the Vatican for his first public engagement in Rome, meeting Mayor Argan and officially accepting the Church of St John Lateran – a public ordeal that would surely have highlighted any physical ailment from which Luciani might have been suffering. Dr Da Ros found his patient in such good health that he advised Luciani that, instead of seeing him in two weeks as planned, he would not come for three weeks. When Father Lorenzi asked the doctor about the Pope's health on that Saturday, Dr Da Ros declared, 'Non sta bene, ma benone' – 'He's not well but very well'.

Da Ros consulted Dr Buzzonetti of the Vatican the same day and they discussed Luciani's medical history. Obviously the Pope would eventually need a regular general practitioner based in Rome, but the doctors agreed that there was no immediate urgency. Da Ros would continue for the time being to travel down from Vittorio Veneto on a regular basis. That the doctor who had cared for him for over twenty years and the Vatican medical staff were content with an arrangement whereby the Pope's physician resided nearly 600 kilometres from his patient is perhaps the most illuminating evidence possible. That such an arrangement was satisfactory to all leads to only two conclusions. Either that Dr Da Ros and the Vatican medical staff were guilty of the most appalling negligence and that none of them is fit to practise medicine, or Albino Luciani was a perfectly healthy man without any illness whatsoever at the time of his death. In view of the care and attention Dr Da Ros provided, not to mention the very real affection he felt for his patient, clearly the latter conclusion must be drawn. Da Ros, you will recall, was 'shocked, stunned and mystified' when told of the death.

Dr Da Ros stated that he found the Pope in such good health that in future he would come every third Saturday rather than every second because the Pope was so well. On the last evening he was perfectly fit. During his Papacy this business of leg swelling did not occur. He took daily exercise either in the Vatican Gardens or in the big hall. (Father John Magee, Secretary to Pope John Paul I from late August 1978 until his death, to the author.)

Largely because of his personal friendship with Dr Da Ros, few men could claim to have received greater medical attention than Luciani – weekly, then fortnightly visits for over twenty years. Medical attention of a remarkable degree was followed by a sudden unexpected death, followed by a false diagnosis and the failure to publish a death certificate.

How then do we explain the inexplicable? A popular theory at the time of the Pope's death was that it was caused by stress. It is not a theory given any credence by the many doctors I have interviewed. Many were scathing about what they termed 'the stress business', an industry where fortunes are made by playing on popular fears. Too much sexual intercourse causes stress. Too little sexual intercourse causes stress. Playing space invader machines causes stress. Watching sports events causes stress. Too much exercise causes stress. Too little exercise causes stress.

I see an awful lot of people with stress symptoms but they don't have coronary disease. They are a pain in the neck. They are all working long hours, overworked, six, seven days a week, totally involved in their work, they lose perspective. My impression is that, after a while, they build up this tremendous negative balance, if they don't relax. They see a neurologist about headaches, a specialist about stomach disorders such as ulcers, they come to me with chest pains. It is never heart disease they are actually suffering from. Here in St Bartholomew's we have a very busy coronary unit. It's not the whizz kids from the City we have as patients, it's the porters and the messengers. If the myth of stress had any validity we would not see the change in mortality that we are seeing. What we are seeing are the upper classes reducing their coronary attacks and the lower classes increasing theirs. Your risk factors if you are social class five are much higher than if you are social class one or two. The vast amount of people with stress symptoms are not turning up coronary problems, they are turning up funny chest pains, they are turning up funny breathlessness, they are turning up feeling funny. It's never the heart. They merely need a great deal of reassurance. You dare not tell them what the real heart symptoms are or otherwise they will be back with them. (Dr Seamus Banim, to author.)

Research indicates that stress can sometimes lead to heart disease and indeed to a fatal heart attack, but the heart disease caused by stress does not occur overnight. Symptoms manifest themselves for months or even years. No such symptoms were ever noted by any of the doctors who cared for Albino Luciani throughout his entire life.

The Vatican lied when it stated that an autopsy on the Pope was forbidden under Vatican rules.

The Vatican lied when it stated an autopsy on a Pope had never been performed.

The trickle of lies became a flood.

The Pope's Will. The Pope's health. The time of his embalming. The exact nature of the medical examinations on the body before the funeral. It lied on each and every one of these aspects.

Consider the Will of Albino Luciani. No Will has ever been produced or made public. Luciani's family have been told that no Will exists. And yet:

It certainly exists. I don't know the length or even less what it says. I remember that the Pope spoke about it at table about a fortnight before he died. Edoardo, his brother, spoke with great enthusiasm about Paul VI's Will. 'My Will is of another tone and less weighty,' he said. Then indicating a small gap between his index finger and thumb, Papa Luciani said 'Mine is like this'. (Father Diego Lorenzi, to author.)

When Cardinal of Venice he drew up a three-line Will that left everything to his seminary in Venice and appointed his auxiliary bishop as executor. When the auxiliary bishop died, Luciani crossed out the bishop's name and put in mine and showed me the Will. (Father Mario Senigaglia, to author.)

When he died his Will was never found although I am sure he made one. Some money that he had in account in Venice was sent to my family because he had in theory died intestate. We sent it back to the Venice diocese knowing that was his intention. Part went to his successor and part to nominated charities. I know there was a Will. When he went from Belluno to Vittorio Veneto he destroyed his Will and made a new one, similarly when he went to Venice he destroyed that Will and made a new one. Equally when he became Pope, Father Carlo, one of his secretaries in Venice, was asked to bring that Will down. Don Carlo took it to the Vatican. Either there should be a Will dating from the thirty-three days or the Venice Will. He was always very meticulous about this. I do not know why they were unable to find it. (Pia Luciani, to author.)

As has already been established, worldly goods held no interest for Luciani but a Papal Will invariably includes more than instructions on material assets. There is always a spiritual message – comments and reflections on the state of the Church. Was the Will of Albino Luciani destroyed because it accurately reflected the Pope's feelings and views on what he had discovered in those 33 days? Luciani, an accomplished writer, one of the most literary Popes in modern times, failed to leave a final written observation? Were there no last reflections from the revolutionary Pope?

It may be considered shocking that so much false information emanates directly from the Vatican, a place considered by millions to be the spiritual home of Christianity. Is it any less shocking that men who have dedicated their lives to Jesus Christ should destroy so much vital evidence? Is it any less shocking that the Secretary of State, Cardinal Villot, should impose a vow of silence on members of the Papal Household? Is it any less shocking that Villot, acting in his capacity as virtual caretaker Pope, should take medicine, reading glasses, slippers from the Papal bedroom? That he should remove and destroy the papers clutched in the dead Pope's hands – papers which detailed the important changes Albino Luciani was about to make and which he had discussed with Cardinal Villot a short time before the Pope's totally unexpected death? Was Villot a party in a conspiracy to murder the Pope? Certainly his subsequent actions were those of a man determined to cover up the truth of that death. Doubtless he took the Will as he sat at Luciani's desk in his study and made his series of early morning phone calls. Having removed the papers from Luciani's hands Cardinal Villot was clearly determined that no trace of those changes that had so concerned him on the last evening of the Pope's life should remain. God alone knows what else was stolen from the Papal Apartments. We know beyond all doubt that the items already mentioned vanished.

> Father Magee and the Sisters and I searched everywhere in the apartment for these things. We could not find them. We searched during the morning of the 29th of September. (Father Diego Lorenzi, to author.)

We know beyond any doubt that these items were in the apartment before Villot was summoned. Indeed the glasses were upon Albino Luciani's face. When Villot left the items had vanished.

The Vatican lied when it stated that the initial discovery of the dead body was made by Father Magee at 'about 5.30 a.m. on the morning of September 29th'. Sister Vincenza recounted directly to me the moment when she discovered the dead Pope. Previously she had used virtually the same words to Monsignor Mario Senigaglia, to Luciani's niece Pia and his sister Nina. 'It was a miracle that I survived. I have a bad heart. I pushed the bell to summon the secretaries, then I went out to find the other Sisters and to awaken Don Diego.' She also told me that as she stood for a moment looking transfixed at the body of the dead Pope, the alarm clock began to ring. Instinctively she reached out and turned it off.

There is a curious external fact that confirms the veracity of Sister Vincenza's statements. Conan Doyle had his fictional creation Sherlock Holmes observe on one occasion that there was an odd and significant fact about a dog. It did not bark. In the Papal Apartments there was beside the Pope's bed an alarm clock that did not ring. I have questioned both Papal secretaries and other members of the Papal Apartments very closely about this. All of them are adamant. On the morning that Albino Luciani was found dead the alarm clock he had set every day for many years did not ring. It was set for 4.45 a.m. His body was not officially found until after 5.30 a.m. Diego Lorenzi, who slept so closely to the Pope's bedroom that he could hear the Pope moving about, heard no alarm.

When Pope Paul VI died in August 1978 a full twenty-four hours elapsed before his body was embalmed, in accordance with Italian law. When Albino Luciani died in September 1978 Italian law was thrown out of the window, and Vatican, let's make it up as we go along, law applied.

The body of Albino Luciani was embalmed within 14 hours of his death. Why the haste? Evidence suggests that Villot desired an even quicker embalming; evidence that indicates the embalmers were summoned before the body was 'officially' found. If Magee found the body at 'shortly after 5.30 a.m.' why were the Vatican morticians, the Signoracci, summoned 45 minutes earlier? Prudence carried to unusual lengths.

On September 29th, the Italian news agency ANSA, a highly reputable organization on a par with the Press Association or Reuters, carried on their wire service one of the many news items they ran that day on the Pope's death. In part it reads:

> The two Signoracci brothers, Ernesto and Arnaldo (the others are Cesare and Renato) were awoken this morning at dawn and at five were collected from their homes by a Vatican car which took them to the mortuary of the little state where they began the operation.

I have traced and interviewed the journalist responsible for that news item, Mario de Francesco. He confirmed the accuracy of his story which was based on an interview with the Signoracci, conducted the same day. I have interviewed the Signoracci brothers on a number of occasions. With regard to the time that they were first contacted they are now, some five years later, uncertain. They confirmed that it was early on the morning of September 29th. If Francesco's story is accurate then a Mafia-like situation is established. Morticians ordered before a body is found.

Embalmers were summoned before the cause of death had been even guessed at. Why would the Vatican wish to destroy the most valuable evidence before the official cause of death had been determined?

Was there a secret autopsy on the eve of the Pope's funeral? The evidence clearly established a long and detailed examination. What was the purpose? A routine embalming check would have taken only minutes. What were the examining doctors doing behind screens, in a locked church for nearly one and a half hours?

It must be recorded that Albino Luciani's personal doctor flew from

Venice to Rome on September 29th and agreed with the Vatican doctors that the cause of death was myocardial infarction. It must equally be recorded that as he observed a body that had been dead for 15 hours and contented himself with an external examination, his medical opinion was worthless on this occasion.

If there was one man in Italy who was in a position to confirm that Albino Luciani did in fact die of a myocardial infarction that man was Professor Giovanni Rama, the eye specialist who had been treating Luciani since 1975 for a blood clot that had occurred to the left eye. He holds the view that this vascular complaint may have led ultimately to Luciani's death but he freely admitted to me that as a medical opinion it was worthless without an autopsy. If Cardinal Villot and his senior Vatican colleagues really did believe that Albino Luciani had died naturally of a myocardial infarction, Professor Rama, with over three years' experience of treating Luciani, was *the* man to call to the Vatican. He advised me that he had no contact whatsoever from the Vatican after Albino Luciani's death and remarked: 'I was very surprised that they did not ask me to come and examine the Pope's body.'

Easily the most significant observation from a member of the medical profession was the comment attributed to Professor Mario Fontana. Apparently he gave his opinion privately shortly after the Pope's death but it did not become public knowledge until after his own death in 1980.

'If I had to certify, under the same circumstances, the death of an ordinary, unimportant citizen, I would quite simply have refused to allow him to be buried.'

Professor Mario Fontana was the head of the Vatican Medical Service.

How and why did darkness fall upon the Roman Catholic Church on September 28th, 1978?

To establish that a murder has taken place it is not essential to establish a motive. But it helps, as any experienced police officer will confirm. Without a motive you are in trouble. With regard to the death of Albino Luciani there are a frightening number of motives. I have clearly identified a number of them within this book. I have also identified the men with those motives.

The fact that three of those men, Villot, Cody and Marcinkus, are priests does not rule them out as suspects. Men of the cloth should in theory be above suspicion. They should be. Sadly many have demonstrated since the birth of Christianity the ability to commit appalling crimes.

Villot, Cody, Marcinkus, Calvi, Sindona, Gelli: each had a powerful motive. Might Cardinal Villot have murdered to protect his position as Secretary of State, to protect other men who were about to be moved, and most of all to avoid the furore that undoubtedly would have ensued when Albino Luciani took a different stance publicly on the issue of birth control?

Might Cardinal Cody, aided by some of his many friends within the Vatican, attempting to cling corruptly to office in Chicago, have silenced a Pope who was about to remove him?

Might Bishop Marcinkus, sitting at the head of a demonstrably corrupt bank, have acted to ensure he remained President of the IOR?

It is possible that one of these three men is guilty. Certainly Villot's actions after the Pope's death were criminal: destruction of evidence; a false story; the imposition of silence. It is conduct that leaves much to be desired.

Why was Bishop Paul Marcinkus wandering in the Vatican at such an early hour? A normal police investigation would demand many answers from these three men, but over five years later such vital interrogations are impossible. Villot and Cody are dead and Marcinkus is hiding inside the Vatican from the Italian police.

The most pertinent evidence in defence of these three men is not their own inevitable protestations of innocence. It is the very fact that they were men of the cloth; men of the Roman Catholic Church. Two thousand years has taught such men to take the long view. The history of the Vatican is the history of countless Popes eager to make reforms and yet hemmed in and neutralized by the system. If the Church in general and Vatican City in particular so wishes it can and does dramatically influence and affect Papal decisions. It has already been recorded how a minority of men imposed their will upon Paul VI on the issue of birth control. It has also been recorded how Baggio flatly refused to replace Luciani in Venice.

As for the changes Luciani was about to make, many within the Vatican would have welcomed them, but even those most deeply opposed were more likely to react in a manner less dramatic than murder. This does not rule out Villot, Cody and Marcinkus. Rather it places them at the bottom of the list of suspects and moves Calvi, Sindona and Gelli to the top. Did any of these men have the capacity for the deed? The short answer is yes.

Whoever murdered Albino Luciani was clearly gambling that the next Conclave and the next Pope would not reactivate Luciani's instructions. All six men stood to gain if the 'right' man was elected. Would any kill merely to buy a month's grace? If the 'right' man was elected, that month would extend into the future. Two of these men, Villot and Cody, were in the perfect position to influence the next Conclave. Marcinkus was not without influence. Neither were Calvi, Sindona and Gelli.

It was at the villa of Umberto Ortolani that the final plans were made by a group of cardinals that resulted in the election of Pope Paul VI. Gelli, as the ruler of P2, had access to each and every part of Vatican City, just as he also had access to the inner sanctum of Italian Government, the banks and the judiciary.

On a practical basis how could the murder of Albino Luciani have been achieved? Surely Vatican security could not be penetrated? The truth is that Vatican security at the time of Luciani's death could be penetrated with consummate ease – with the same ease that a man called Michael Fagin calmly entered Buckingham Palace in the middle of the night and, after wandering about, sat in Her Majesty's bedroom and asked the Queen of England for a cigarette.

Vatican security in 1978 could be penetrated as easily as the security surrounding President Reagan was penetrated when John Hinckley wounded the President and members of his staff. Or as easily as it was on Wednesday May 13th, 1982, when Mehmet Ali Agca fired three bullets into Pope John Paul II.

John XXIII had abolished the practice of the Swiss Guard maintaining an all-night vigil outside his apartment. Nevertheless Albino Luciani really did deserve better protection than he was accorded. Vatican City, a little larger than St James's Park in London, with six entrances, presented no serious problem to anyone intent on penetration.

The Conclave that had elected Luciani was in theory one of the most stringently guarded places on earth. The reader may recall the extraordinary lengths that Pope Paul VI had gone to to ensure that no one could get in or out during the sessions that chose the new Pope. After his election, Luciani kept the Conclave in session on Saturday, August 26th. Yet one simple unassuming priest, Father Diego Lorenzi, has graphically recounted to me how, anxious to join Luciani, he had wandered unchallenged into the very heart of the Conclave. Only when he was within sight of the 110 cardinals and his newly elected Pope did someone ask him who he was and what he was doing. By then he could have blown the entire building to the next world, if he had so chosen.

At the time of the August Conclave, many writers commented on the total lack of security. To quote just two:

> There was too, on this occasion, the unceasing if unspoken threat of terrorism. In my view, security around the Vatican has not been impressive over the past week, and the rambling place which opens on to the streets in many places, poses perhaps insuperable problems. All the more reason for getting the Conclave over quickly.
>
> Paul Johnson, *Sunday Telegraph*
> August 27th, 1978

> As far as I can see, the security cops are mostly interested in talking to pretty girls in sidewalk cafés. I hope the Red Brigades don't have anything in mind for the evening (the day of Paul VI's funeral). They could arrive and knock out many of the world's leaders in one fell swoop.
>
> Father Andrew Greeley, *The Making of the Popes*

Then less than two months later at the funeral of Albino Luciani, 'The security precautions are enormous'. (Father Andrew Greeley, *The Making of The Popes*).

It was curious that after the death the security which had been non-existent during Albino Luciani's lifetime should suddenly appear. 'There were no security guards in the area of the Papal Apartments when I was there with Albino Luciani,' Father Diego Lorenzi advised me.

I interviewed Sergeant Hans Roggan of the Swiss Guard. He was the officer in charge on the night Luciani died. He recounted how earlier in the evening he had been out in Rome for a meal with his mother. They saw the light on in the Papal bedroom when they returned at 10.30 p.m. Roggan's mother retired for the night and he went on duty. He told me:

> For some reason that was a terrible night for me. That night I was the officer in charge of the Palace. *I simply could not get to sleep.* Eventually I got up and went to the office and worked on a couple of ledgers. Normally I sleep well.

This is the officer in charge of Palace security on the night of Luciani's sudden death, tossing and turning in his bed as he tries to *sleep*. To add that no one saw fit to query and check the fact that the Pope's bedroom light continued to shine throughout the night seems almost superfluous. Much criticism was made at the time of the assassination of President Kennedy about the appalling security, or lack of it, in Dallas. By comparison with what passed for security around Luciani, the President was extremely well protected.

Further research has established that at the time of Luciani's Papacy, there was a Swiss Guard at the top of the stairs on the Third Loggia. His function was merely ceremonial, as few people ever entered the Papal Apartments by this route. Access to the Apartments was usually by the lift – for which many had the key. The lift entrance was not guarded. Any man dressed as a priest could enter and leave the Papal Apartments unchallenged.

Further instances of the chaotic security within the Vatican City abound. Recently, since the death of Albino Luciani, a staircase near the Papal Apartments has been re-discovered. It was not hidden, not masked by later building work. Quite simply no one knew of its existence. Or did they? Did someone perhaps know of it in September 1978?

Swiss Guards officially asleep on duty. Swiss Guards who guard an entrance no one uses. A staircase that no one knew about. Even an amateur assassin would not have experienced any great difficulty and whoever killed Albino Luciani was no amateur. To assist any would-be murderer *L'Osservatore della Domenica* published a detailed plan, complete with photograph, of the Papal Apartments. Date of publication, September 3rd, 1978.

If Mehmet Ali Agca had carried out even elementary homework, Pope John Paul II would now be dead; murdered as his predecessor was. The more I probed the more apparent it became that anyone bent upon murdering Albino Luciani had a relatively simple task. To obtain access to the Papal Apartments in September 1978 and to tamper with either the medicines or food or drink of the Pope with any of two hundred lethal drugs would have been a simple task.

The virtual certainty that there would not be an official autopsy merely makes the deed that much easier. There was not even a doctor on 24-hour duty. The Vatican health service did not have at that time the standard equipment of an ordinary modern hospital. There was no emergency medical structure. And in the centre of this shambles was an honest man, who by the various courses of action he had embarked upon, had given at least six men very powerful motives for murder.

Despite the appalling attack on Luciani's successor, little has changed with regard to security within the Vatican. During my research I walked in the gardens of the Augustinian residence where Luciani had walked before the August Conclave. It was a Sunday in September 1982. Across St Peter's Square His Holiness came out on to the balcony to deliver the mid-day Angelus. From where I stood he was in a direct firing line of less than 2,000 yards, the top half of his body entirely unprotected. If Agca or one of his kind had been standing there, the Pope would have been dead and the assassin back in the heart of Rome within minutes. I had walked into the gardens unchallenged.

A few days after this I walked unchallenged through the Vatican's Saint Anna Gate. Carrying a case large enough to contain bombs, I went unchecked to the Vatican Bank. The following week in the company of two researchers, all three of us carrying cases and bags, we walked unsearched through the very heart of the Vatican on our way to see Cardinal Ciappi. These events took place only seventeen months after Pope John Paul II had been nearly murdered in St Peter's Square.

Is it possible that in a country with one of the lowest death rates for coronary heart disease in Europe, a perfectly fit man, whose one unusual physical characteristic, that of low blood pressure, which mitigates against a death from heart disease, did in fact die of a myocardial infarction? Is it possible that the non-smoking, moderately eating, abstemious Luciani, who was doing everything that heart specialists would have had him do, was merely unfortunate? Unfortunate that despite taking every conceivable health precaution, he died? Unfortunate that despite constant medical check-ups including numerous ECGs, not a single trace in 65 years indicated any heart weakness? Unfortunate that his death was so sudden, so immediate that he did not even have time to press the alarm bell a few inches from his hand? In the words of Professors Rulli and Masini, who were two of the experts I consulted in Rome: 'It is very very unlikely that death is so quick that the individual does not take any action. Very very rare.'

Indeed the evidence is all against Luciani's death being a natural one. The evidence very strongly suggests murder. For myself I have no doubt. I am totally convinced that Albino Luciani was murdered and that at least one of the six suspects I have already identified holds the key.

At 65 years of age, Albino Luciani was considered by the Conclave that elected him to be exactly the right age for the Papacy. Paul VI had been 66 when elected and had ruled for fifteen years. John XXIII had been 77 when elected as a stop-gap Pope, yet he ruled for five years. The Conclave had felt that Luciani would rule for a minimum of ten years. Conclaves are expensive affairs. The death of Paul VI and the election of his successor cost 5 million dollars. The Church is not disposed towards frequent Conclaves or short Papacies. As a result of Luciani' s sudden and unexpected death there were two Conclaves in less than two months.

It is not of course my contention that the plot to murder Albino Luciani was conceived on September 28th, 1978. The final act was obviously carried out on that day but the decision had been taken earlier. How much earlier is a moot point.

It could have been within days of Luciani's election when the new Pope initiated his investigations into Vatican Incorporated. It could have been within the first two weeks of September when the fact that Luciani was investigating Freemasonry within the Vatican became known to some members of the Vatican village. It could have been mid September when the attitudes of the new Pope on birth control and his plans to implement a liberal position on the issue were causing deep concern within the Vatican. It could have been the third week of September when the fact that Marcinkus and others at the Vatican Bank were about to be removed became a certainty. It may have been a few days before his death that the plan was put into motion, days during which Albino Luciani arrived at other far-reaching and crucial decisions. Whenever the plan originated, for the suspects already identified its final act came not a moment too soon. If they had allowed even a few more days to elapse they would have been too late.

Doubtless it will be observed by some that much of the evidence already adduced is of a circumstantial nature. When one is dealing with murder the evidence is very frequently entirely circumstantial. Men and women who plan murder are not given to announcing their intentions on the front page of *The Times* or *Le Monde* or the *Washington Post*. It is relatively rare for independent observers to be present and in a position to offer incontrovertible evidence. Circumstantial evidence on its own has been deemed sufficient to send many a man and woman to the gallows, the electric chair, the firing squad and the gas chamber. One fact is of overriding importance when considering the murder of Albino Luciani. If it was to succeed in its aim, then the murder had to be committed by stealth in such a manner that there was a reasonable chance of the death appearing to be a natural one. For nearly six years the perpetrators of the murder of

Albino Luciani have succeeded in what must rank as one of the crimes of the century.

To identify correctly who was responsible for the murder of Albino Luciani one should consider what occurred at the second Conclave and what has happened subsequently. An examination of certain events should establish which of the six men was at the heart of the conspiracy to murder God's candidate.

By Benefit of Murder –
Business as Usual

❦

When voting in the Conclave to select a successor to Albino Luciani began on Sunday, October 15th, 1978, the Holy Ghost was noticeably absent. A long, bitter struggle, principally between the supporters of Siri and Benelli, was the predominant theme of the first day's voting. Whoever had been responsible for the murder of Luciani very nearly found themselves faced with the task of ensuring that a second Pope should suddenly die. During the course of eight ballots over two days, Cardinal Giovanni Benelli came within a handful of votes of winning. If Benelli had been elected there is no doubt whatsoever that many of the courses of action Luciani had determined upon would have been carried out. Cody would have been removed. Villot would have been replaced. Marcinkus, de Strobel and Mennini would have been thrown out of the Vatican Bank.

But Benelli fell nine votes short and the eventual winner, a compromise candidate, Cardinal Karol Wojtyla, bears little resemblance to Albino Luciani. Wojtyla has given countless demonstrations that all he has in common with his predecessor is the Papal name John Paul.

Despite the efforts of Benelli, Felici and others, the Papacy of John Paul II has been a case of business as usual. The business has benefited immeasurably not only from the murder of Albino Luciani, but also from the murders that have followed that strange, lonely death in the Vatican in September 1978.

Upon his election the current Pope learned of the changes that Luciani had proposed making. He was advised of the various consultations that his predecessor had had on a variety of problems. The fiscal information collected by Benelli, Felici, members of APSA and others on behalf of Luciani was made available to Wojtyla. He was shown the evidence that had led Luciani to conclude that Cardinal Cody of Chicago should be replaced. He was shown the evidence that indicated that Freemasonry had infiltrated the Vatican. He was advised of Luciani's dialogue with the US State Department and the planned meeting with the Congressional Committee on Population and Birth Control. Villot also made the new Pope fully conversant with Albino Luciani's attitude on birth control. In short Pope John Paul II was in the unique position to bring all Luciani's plans to fruition. Not one of Luciani's proposed changes became a reality. Whoever had murdered the Pope had not murdered in vain.

Villot was again appointed Secretary of State. Cody remained in control of Chicago. Marcinkus, aided by Mennini, de Strobel and Monsignor de Bonis continued to control the Vatican Bank and continued to ensure that the criminal activities with Banco Ambrosiano flourished. Calvi and his P2 masters Gelli and Ortolani were free to continue their massive thefts and frauds under the protection of the Vatican Bank. Sindona was able, at least in the short term, to maintain his freedom in New York. Baggio did not go to Venice. The corrupt Poletti remained Cardinal Vicar of Rome.

Many millions of words have been written since the election of Karol Wojtyla in attempts to analyze and understand what manner of man he is. He is the kind of man who could allow men like Villot, Cody, Marcinkus, Mennini, de Strobel, de Bonis and Poletti to remain in office. There can be no defence on the grounds of ignorance. Marcinkus is directly answerable to the Pope and for the Pope to be unaware of the degree of guilt that clings to Marcinkus defies belief. With regard to Cody, His Holiness was made aware of the full facts in October 1978 by Cardinals Benelli and Baggio. Wojtyla did nothing. We have a Pope who publicly berates Nicaraguan priests for their involvement in politics and simultaneously gives his blessing for large quantities of dollars to be made available, secretly and illegally, to Solidarity in Poland. It is the Papacy of double standards: one set for the Pope and another for the rest of mankind. The Papacy of John Paul II has been a triumph for the wheeler dealers, for the corrupt, for the international thieves like Calvi, Gelli and Sindona, while His Holiness has maintained a very highly-publicized image not unlike some perpetual rock and roll tour. The men behind the tarmac-kissing star are ensuring that it is business as usual and takings at the box office

over the past five years have boomed. It is to be regretted that the
severely moralizing speeches of His Holiness cannot presumably be
heard backstage.

As I have recorded earlier, after the election of Luciani Bishop Paul
Marcinkus cautioned his colleagues in the Vatican Bank and Roberto
Calvi in Buenos Aires: 'Remember that this Pope has different ideas
from the previous one and that many things will be changing here.'

With the election of Wojtyla it was straight back to the values of
Paul VI, with interest. With regard to the infiltration of the Vatican by
Freemasons, for example, the Vatican, though not the current Pope,
has not only taken on board a variety of Masons from a variety of
Lodges but it has also acquired its own in-house version. Its name is
Opus Dei – God's Work.

On July 25th, Albino Luciani had written on Opus Dei in *Il
Gazzettino,* the Venetian newspaper. His remarks were confined to a
short history of the movement and some of the organization's aspirations towards lay spirituality. With regard to the more controversial
aspects of Opus Dei either Luciani was ignorant of them, which is
unlikely, or was yet again displaying his own quiet discretion.

With the election of Karol Wojtyla quiet discretion has become a
rare commodity. His espousal of Opus Dei is well documented. In
view of the fact that this Catholic sect shares many views and values
with the corrupt P2 and that Opus Dei is now a force to be reckoned
with inside Vatican City, a few basic details should be recorded.

Opus Dei is a Roman Catholic organization of international
dimensions. Though its actual membership is relatively small
(estimates vary between 60,000 and 80,000), its influence is vast. It is
a secret society, something which is strictly forbidden by the Church.
Opus Dei denies that it is a secret organization but refuses to make its
membership list available. It was founded by a Spanish priest,
Monsignor Josemaria Escriva, in 1928. It is to the extreme right wing
of the Catholic Church, a political fact that has ensured that the organization has attracted enemies as well as members. Its members are
composed of a small percentage of priests, about 5 per cent, and lay
persons of either sex. Though people from many walks of life can be
found among its members, it seeks to attract those from the upper
reaches of the professional classes, including students and graduates
who are aspiring to executive status. Dr John Roche, an Oxford
University lecturer and former member of Opus Dei, describes it as
'sinister, secretive and Orwellian'. It may be that its members' preoccupation with self-mortification is the cause for much of the news

media hostility that has been directed towards the sect. Certainly the idea of flogging yourself on your bare back and wearing strips of metal with inward-pointing prongs around the thigh for the greater glory of God might prove difficult for the majority of people in the latter part of the twentieth century to accept. No one, however, should doubt the total sincerity of the Opus Dei membership. They are equally devoted to a task of wider significance: the takeover of the Roman Catholic Church. That should be a cause of the greatest concern not only to Roman Catholics but to everybody. Undoubtedly there are aspects to admire within this secret society. Albino Luciani eloquently praised some of the basic spiritual concepts. He was discreetly silent on the issues of self-mortification and the far more potent Fascist political philosophy. Under Pope John Paul II Opus Dei has flourished. If the present Pope is not a member of Opus Dei, he is to its adherents everything they could wish a Pope to be. One of his first acts after his election was to go to the tomb of the founder of Opus Dei and pray. Subsequently he has granted the sect the status of a personal prelature, a significant step on the journey to Cardinal Cody land, where one becomes answerable only to Rome and God.

This organization has, according to its own claims, members working in over 600 newspapers, reviews and scientific publications, scattered around the world. It has members in over fifty radio and television stations. In the 1960s three of its members were in the Spanish dictator Franco's Cabinet, creating Spain's 'economic miracle'. The head of the huge Rumasa conglomerate in Spain, José Mateos, is a member of Opus Dei; he is also currently on the run after building a network of corruption similar to that of the Calvi empire, as recently revealed.* Opus Dei is massively wealthy. Until recently, when it changed hands, anyone walking into an Augustus Barnett wine store in England was putting money into Opus Dei.

José Mateos, known as Spain's richest man, funnelled millions into Opus Dei. A considerable amount of this money came from illegal deals with Calvi, perpetrated in both Spain and Argentina. P2 paymaster and Opus Dei paymaster: could this be what the Church means when it talks of God moving in mysterious ways?

Since the death of Albino Luciani and his succession by Karol Wojtyla, the Italian Solution that was applied to the problem of an honest Pope has been frequently applied to the problems that have confronted Marcinkus, Sindona, Calvi and Gelli. The litany of murder

*In late April 1984 Mateos was arrested in West Germany. The Spanish authorities have begun extradition proceedings.

and mayhem perpetrated to mask plundering on an unimaginable scale makes grim reading. It also serves as powerful evidence after the deed to confirm that Albino Luciani was murdered.

Roberto Calvi, Licio Gelli and Umberto Ortolani did not return to Italy while Luciani reigned as Pope. Calvi eventually returned in late October after the election of Karol Wojtyla. Gelli and Ortolani continued to monitor events from Uruguay. Was the fact that the three men stayed in a variety of South American cities just mere coincidence? Did their business discussions really need to continue from August to October? Was it really necessary for either Gelli or Ortolani to insist on staying close to Calvi throughout September 1978? Did it really take all that time to meet important officials to discuss opening new branches of Banco Ambrosiano?

The breathing space gained for the P2 paymaster by Luciani's death looked like being of a temporary nature after Calvi's meeting with Bank of Italy Inspector Giulio Padalino on October 30th in Milan. Again Calvi, with his eyes focused firmly upon his shoes, declined to give straight answers to a variety of questions. On November 17th, the Bank of Italy inspection of Banco Ambrosiano was completed.

Despite the fraudulent letter from Marcinkus and his Vatican Bank colleagues concerning the ownership of Suprafin, despite the lies and evasions of Roberto Calvi, despite the help of his protector Licio Gelli, the central bank inspectors concluded in a very lengthy report that a great deal was rotten in the state of Calvi's empire.

From South America and using his own special code name, Gelli telephoned Calvi at his private residence. For Calvi, wallowing ever deeper in a mire of Mafia/Vatican/P2 dealings, the news was bad.

Within days of Inspector Giulio Padalino handing in his report to the Head of Vigilance of the Bank of Italy, Mario Sarcinelli, a copy of the full report was in Gelli's hands in Buenos Aires. Not from Sarcinelli or Padalino but by courtesy of the P2 network. Gelli advised Calvi that the report was about to be sent from the Bank of Italy to the Milan magistrates and specifically to the man Gelli had predicted in September, Judge Emilio Alessandrini.

Again Calvi was teetering on the edge of exposure and total ruin. Emilio Alessandrini could not be bought. Highly talented and courageous, he represented for Calvi, Marcinkus, Gelli and also Sindona a very serious threat. If he pursued this investigation with his customary vigour then Calvi was certainly finished, Marcinkus would be exposed, Gelli would have lost the crock of gold that the continuing thefts from Ambrosiano represented and Sindona would be confronted with the most powerful argument yet for his immediate extradition from the United States.

By early January 1979 the financial circles of Milan were yet again preoccupied with rumours about The Knight, Roberto Calvi. Judge Emilio Alessandrini, having carefully studied a summary of the 500-page report compiled by the Bank of Italy, ordered Lt-Colonel Cresta, the commander of the Milan tax police, to send his men into the 'priests' bank'. The brief was to check point by point the many criminal irregularities that were detailed in the report. No one outside official circles had access to the report, no one, that is, apart from Calvi and Gelli.

On January 21st *L'Espresso* commented on the rumours that were flying around the city, including the alarming news that Calvi and his entire board of directors were about to be arrested and that Calvi's passport was about to be withdrawn. Something had to be done quickly before the general public created a run on Banco Ambrosiano.

On the morning of January 29th Alessandrini kissed his wife goodbye, then drove his young son to school. Having dropped the boy he began to drive to his office. A few seconds before 8.30 a.m. he stopped at the traffic lights on via Muratori. He was still gazing at the red light when five men approached his car and began firing bullets into his body.

Later in the day a group of left-wing terrorists called Prima Linea claimed responsibility for the murder. The group also left a leaflet about the murder in a telephone booth in Milan Central Station. Neither the phone call nor the leaflet gave any clear reason for the murder.

Why would an extreme left-wing group cold-bloodedly murder a judge who was nationally known for his investigations into right-wing terrorism? Emilio Alessandrini was one of the leading investigators into the Piazza Fontana bombing, which was acknowledged to be a right-wing atrocity. Why would Prima Linea murder a man who was clearly attempting, through legal and proper channels, what they, in theory, would most applaud – to bring right-wing criminal elements to task for their acts?

Groups such as Prima Linea and the Red Brigades do not merely kill and maim to political and ideological order. They are guns for hire. The links, for example, between the Red Brigades and the Naples Camorra (local Mafia) are well documented.

At the time of writing, five men who have already confessed to the murder of Alessandrini are standing trial. Their evidence concerning the actual murder is full of detail, but when it comes to the motive their evidence raises more questions than it answers.

Marco Donat Cattin, the second man who opened fire on the trapped, unarmed and helpless judge, observed: 'We waited for the newspapers to come out with reports of the attack and we found in the magistrate's obituaries the motives to justify the attack.'

Three days after the murder on the afternoon of February 1st, Roberto Calvi was enjoying a drink at a Milan cocktail party. The conversation inevitably turned to the recent outrage. Calvi promptly attempted to elicit sympathy, not for Signora Alessandrini and her fatherless children, but for himself: 'It really is such a shame. Only the day before this happened Alessandrini had told me that he was taking no further action and that he was going to have the case filed.'

The murder of Luciani had given Marcinkus, Calvi, Sindona and their P2 friends a momentary breathing space. Now the murder of Emilio Alessandrini bought them further time. The investigation initiated by Judge Alessandrini continued, but at a snail's pace.

In the Bank of Italy, Mario Sarcinelli was acutely aware of the lack of momentum. Sarcinelli and the Governor of the Bank, Paolo Baffi, were determined that the long, complex investigation which had been carried out during the previous year would not be a wasted exercise.

In February 1979 Mario Sarcinelli summoned Calvi to the Bank of Italy. Calvi was questioned closely about Suprafin, about the Ambrosiano relationship with the IOR, about the Nassau branch and about who precisely owned Banco Ambrosiano. With Alessandrini dead Calvi was a new man, or rather his old self. The eyes were again ice cold. Licio Gelli's protection had inspired an even greater degree of arrogance than normal. He flatly refused to answer Sarcinelli's questions, but the encounter left Calvi in no doubt that the Bank of Italy investigation had not been inhibited by the latest murder.

Again he discussed his problems with Gelli, who reassured him the matter would be dealt with. Before that problem was resolved there was, however, another matter causing the Masons of P2 considerable concern. This was the problem posed by the lawyer journalist Mino Pecorelli. Among Pecorelli's many activities was that of editor of an unusual weekly emanating from the agency referred to earlier, OP.

OP has been variously described as 'muck-raking' and 'scandal-istic'. It was both. It was also accurate. Throughout the 1970s it acquired and subsequently printed an astonishing number of exposés and allegations on Italian corruption. It became required reading for anyone who was interested in knowing exactly who was robbing whom. Despite the stringent laws on libel in Italy it led a charmed life. Pecorelli clearly had access to the most highly sensitive information. Italian journalists frequently went into print with OP-inspired articles. Privately they tried to ascertain who was behind this news agency which was clearly above the law, but OP remained a mysterious organism. Pecorelli's sister Rosita alleged during a television interview that the news agency OP was financed by Prime Minister Andreotti.

In the early 1970s the name of Michele Sindona was frequently linked with OP. Pecorelli obviously had sources working within the Italian Secret Service, but his major contacts were inside an organization more powerful and indeed more secret than such official Government agencies. Mino Pecorelli was a member of P2 and it was from this illegal Masonic Lodge that he derived much of the information that set the Italian news media buzzing. At one Lodge meeting Licio Gelli invited members to contribute documents and information which would be passed on to OP. The prime function of OP during this period was therefore to further Gelli's ambitions and the aims of P2. In mid-1978, however, Pecorelli decided upon a little private enterprise. He obtained information about one of the biggest thefts in Italian financial history. The mastermind behind the theft was Licio Gelli. In the early 1970s the scheme was responsible for robbing Italy of 2.5 billion dollars in oil tax revenue. In Italy, the same petroleum product is used to heat property as to drive diesel trucks. The oil for heating is dyed to distinguish it from that used for vehicles and is taxed at a rate fifty times lower than the diesel fuel. It was a situation ready-made for a criminal like Gelli. Under his guidance oil magnate Bruno Musselli, a P2 member, doctored the dyes. Head of the Finance Police, General Raffaele Giudice, a P2 member, falsified the paperwork to ensure that all the fuel was taxed at the lower rate. The fuel was then sold to petrol outlets which paid the conspirators at the higher rate.

The profits were then transferred, thanks to P2 member Michele Sindona, through the Vatican Bank to a series of secret accounts at Sindona's Swiss bank, Finabank. Licio Gelli became a familiar sight walking through the Saint Anna gate with large suitcases containing billions of stolen lire.

General Giudice was appointed head of the Finance Police by Prime Minister Giulio Andreotti, a close friend of Licio Gelli. This particular appointment had been made after Cardinal Poletti, Cardinal Vicar of Rome, had written to the Prime Minister strongly recommending Giudice for the post. Poletti, it will be recalled, was one of the men

Albino Luciani had planned to remove from Rome. The Vatican link with this scandal was unknown to Pecorelli, but he had learned enough about this gigantic theft from the State to begin the publication of small titbits of information. A deputation that included Christian Democrat Senator Claudio Vitalone, Judge Carlo Testi and General Donato lo Prete of the Finance Police bought his silence. The articles on the scandal ceased.

Realizing that more money could be obtained by such dubious techniques, Pecorelli began to write about the Masons. His issue of early September 1978, containing the names of over one hundred Vatican Masons, had been a warning shot across Gelli's bows. The fact that a copy arrived on the desk of Albino Luciani who, having carefully checked it, began to act upon the information, was the supreme irony for Licio Gelli, who was already acutely aware of the threat Luciani posed to his paymaster Roberto Calvi.

With Luciani dead, Gelli attempted to deal with Pecorelli. He bribed him. Inevitably Pecorelli demanded more money for his silence. Gelli refused to pay. Pecorelli published the first of what he promised would be a series of articles. It revealed that Gelli, the pillar of extreme right-wing Fascism, had spied for the Communists during the war and had continued to work for them afterwards. Pecorelli, having now embraced the mantle of a fearless investigative journalist, promised his readers he would reveal everything about P2. For good measure he revealed that Licio Gelli, former Nazi, ex-Fascist and late Communist, also had very strong links with the CIA. By revealing so much of the truth, Pecorelli's colleagues in P2 concluded that he had betrayed them.

On March 20th Gelli telephoned Pecorelli at his Rome office. He suggested a peace talk over dinner the following day. 'If that is convenient.' It was. During the course of the conversation Pecorelli mentioned that he would be working late at the office that evening but dinner on the following day would be possible. It was a dinner that Pecorelli never ate.

Mino Pecorelli left his office in via Orazio at 9.15 p.m. and headed towards his car parked a short distance away. The two bullets that killed him as he sat in his car were fired from within his mouth, a classic Sicilian Mafia gesture of *sasso in bocca,* a rock in the mouth of a dead man to demonstrate he will talk no more.

Unable to have dinner with his old friend, Licio Gelli passed the time by opening up his secret files of P2 members and writing 'deceased' alongside the entry for Mino Pecorelli.

No one has ever 'claimed' responsibility for Pecorelli's murder but in 1983 Antonio Viezzer, at one time a high-ranking officer in SID, Italy's Secret Service, was arrested and charged on suspicion of involvement in the killing of Pecorelli. Antonio Viezzer was a member of P2.

A few days before Pecorelli was silenced for ever, one of the men he had named on the list of Vatican Masons, Cardinal Jean Villot, preceded him to the grave. He died still holding the vast array of official titles that had been his during Luciani's brief reign. For a man who, if not a party to the criminal conspiracy to murder Albino Luciani, most certainly gave that conspiracy vital aid, Villot's own death, with its various stages described in a series of well-documented medical reports, serves as a curious contrast to that of Luciani, who 'died like a flower in the night'.

While the Vatican buried its late Secretary of State, the battle for a little temporal purification continued across the Tiber. The Head of Vigilance of the Bank of Italy, Mario Sarcinelli, and his Governor Paolo Baffi were by now demanding swift action on the Calvi investigation. They insisted that there was more than sufficient evidence to justify immediate arrest. Clearly Gelli and Calvi agreed with them.

On March 25th, 1979 the arrests were made – but not of Roberto Calvi and his colleagues. The men arrested were Sarcinelli and Baffi. Rome magistrate Judge Mario Alibrandi, a man of known right-wing sympathies, granted Baffi bail because of his age, 67 years. Sarcinelli was less fortunate and was thrown into prison. The charges against the two men, of failing to disclose knowledge of a crime, were clearly specious and after two weeks Sarcinelli was granted bail. The charges, however, would hang over both him and Baffi until January 1980 when it was admitted that they were totally false and without a shred of justification. In the interim the magistrate refused to lift his order which barred Sarcinelli from returning to his position as Head of Vigilance at the Bank for a year. With this action P2 had effectively drawn the teeth of the Bank of Italy. Paolo Baffi, the shocked and distressed Governor of the Bank, resigned in September 1979. The demonstration of the power Calvi and his criminal associates had convinced Baffi that he and his men were fighting a force that was far greater than any wielded by the Bank of Italy. Between the scandal of Sarcinelli's wrongful imprisonment and Baffi's resignation, Baffi and his staff were given an ultimate demonstration of just how powerful were the forces ranged against them. The demonstration occurred in Milan. It was organized and paid for by Michele Sindona.

While Calvi and his friends were coping in their own particular way with their problems in Italy, their fellow P2 member, Michele Sindona, was getting his fair share in New York. Sindona had finally beaten the attempts to have him extradited to Italy, but the manner of his victory brought him little comfort.

On March 9th, 1979 the Justice Department indicted Sindona and charged him with 99 counts of fraud, perjury and misappropriation of bank funds. The charges stemmed directly from the collapse of the Franklin National Bank. Sindona, having posted a 3 million dollar bond, was granted bail upon the condition that he presented himself daily to the US Marshal's office.

In the first week of July 1979 a Federal Court Judge ruled that Sindona could not be extradited to Italy to face bank fraud charges because he was soon to face similar charges in the United States. The extradition treaty between Italy and the United States had a double jeopardy clause. Assistant District Attorney John Kenney commented that the US Government intended to send Sindona back to Italy after the case against him in the United States had been completed.

Kenney, still alive despite the 100,000 dollar contract that had been put out by Sindona's colleagues, owed his continuing survival to one fact alone. In Italy, to kill a judge or prosecuting counsel is often an effective ploy in persuading the authorities to slow down a prosecution. The Alessandrini murder is an excellent example. In the United States, such a murder would have precisely the opposite effect. A 100,000 dollar fee was very tempting but the professionals knew that Kenney's murder would result not only in a ruthless pursuit of the killer but also a vigorous acceleration of the prosecution against Sindona.

With Sindona confronting the reality of a New York trial with the tenacious Kenney prosecuting, he decided to use the Italian Solution on another man who was causing him an even greater degree of discomfort: Giorgio Ambrosoli.

On September 29th, 1974, the attorney Giorgio Ambrosoli was appointed the liquidator of Sindona's Banca Privata Italiana. As previously recorded, Banca Privata had been created by Sindona in July 1974 when he merged two of his banks, Banca Unione and Banca Privata Finanziaria – one large bent bank to replace two medium-sized bent banks. By 1979 no man knew more about Sindona's crooked dealings than Giorgio Ambrosoli. Appointed liquidator by the Treasury Ministry and the Governor of the Bank of Italy, Ambrosoli had begun the nightmare task of unravelling the affairs of a modern Machiavelli. As early as March 21st, 1975 the cautious and careful Ambrosoli, in a secret report to Italy's Solicitor General, showed he was convinced of the criminality of Sindona's activities. The evidence he had studied at that date satisfied him that far from the bankruptcy being caused merely by bad business practices, Sindona and the management running his banks in early 1974 'wanted the February operations to create the circumstances for bankruptcy'. It had been a coldly planned looting.

Giorgio Ambrosoli was a most courageous man. At about the same time that he was advising the Solicitor General of his preliminary findings, he confided some of his inner feelings to his wife. 'Whatever happens, I'll certainly pay a high price for taking this job. But I knew that before taking it on and I'm not complaining. It has been a unique chance for me to do something for the country . . . Obviously I'm making enemies for myself.'

Slowly and methodically Ambrosoli began to make sense of what Sindona had deliberately made senseless. The parking of shares, the buy-backs, the dazzling transfers through the myriad of companies. While Sindona was talking to USA university students of his dreams of cosmic capitalism, the quiet, circumspect Milanese lawyer was establishing beyond all doubt that Sindona was corrupt to his highly manicured fingertips.

In 1977 Ambrosoli was approached by Rome lawyer Rodolfo Guzzi with a complicated offer to buy Banca Privata out of bankruptcy. Ambrosoli discovered that Guzzi was working on behalf of Michele Sindona. He declined the offer despite the fact that at least two Christian Democrat Ministers supported it.

The power Sindona still wielded can be gauged from this Ministerial support. Ambrosoli was given a further illustration of that power when the Governor of the Bank of Italy told him of the pressure being exerted by Franco Evangelisti, Prime Minister Andreotti's right-hand man, who was urging the Bank of Italy to arrive at a typically Italian solution. He wanted Governor Baffi to authorize the central bank to cover Sindona's debts. Baffi bravely refused. The Ambrosoli investigation went on.

Ambrosoli continued to come across references in the mountain of papers he was diligently working his way through to 'the 500'; other references made it clear that these 500 people were the super exporters on the black market. The men and women who, with the aid of Sindona and the Vatican Bank, had poured currency out of Italy illegally. The actual list of names might continue to elude Ambrosoli but very little else did. He ascertained that a large number of public organizations, respectable institutions like the insurance giant INPDAI, placed their funds at Sindona's banks for a lower rate of interest than was generally current – 8 per cent rather than 13 per cent. They received, however, a secret interest rate that went directly and privately into the pockets of the directors of INPDAI and the other august companies.

Ambrosoli identified many of the devices that Sindona had used to export money illegally, including buying dollars at higher than the market rate with the balance paid to a foreign account in London, Switzerland or the USA.

Ambrosoli began to compile his own list of guilty names. It never reached 500 – Michele Sindona saw to that – but it reached 77 names and included those trusted men of the Vatican, Massimo Spada and Luigi Mennini. The liquidator collated irrefutable evidence of Vatican Bank complicity in many of Sindona's crimes. Throughout the entire period of his work on behalf of the Bank of Italy this man, working virtually single-handed, was subjected to the range of Sindona behaviour. Sindona brought actions alleging embezzlement against Ambrosoli. Then the actions would be dropped to be replaced by a different approach from Sindona's son-in-law, Pier Sandro Magnoni, inviting Ambrosoli to become President of Sindona's new bank, 'once you have settled this tiring business of the bankruptcies'.

Sindona's P2 infiltration of those whom Ambrosoli considered he could trust was so total that Magnoni was able to quote verbatim a passage from a secret report compiled by Ambrosoli that had been officially seen by only a handful of bank officials.

By March 1979 Ambrosoli was able to put a figure on the size of Il Crack Sindona as far as Banca Privata was concerned. The loss was 257 billion lire. Also by March 1979 Ambrosoli had been subjected to a series of threatening phone calls. The callers always had Italian/American accents.

The threats and the insults grew in intensity from late 1978. The callers varied their tactics from tempting Ambrosoli with offers of vast amounts of money to outright threats. It was made quite clear on whose behalf the calls were being made. 'Why don't you go and see Sindona in the States? As a friend,' said one caller with a heavy American accent. Ambrosoli declined the invitation and began taping the phone calls. He told his friends and colleagues of the calls. Eventually he played one of the tape recordings to one of Sindona's lawyers. A few days later the next call came. 'You dirty bastard. Think you've been clever taping the calls, eh?' The Sindona lawyer was later to admit that after hearing the tape he had immediately called Sindona in New York.

On April 10th, 1979 Sindona confronted another man he considered an enemy, Enrico Cuccia, managing director of Mediobanca, a publicly-owned investment bank. Sindona's assessment was accurate. Cuccia had thwarted the Sindona takeover of Bastogi in 1972. He had arrived at the conclusion long before many others that Sindona was a megalomaniac crook. During their April 1979 meeting Cuccia was given ample evidence to justify the conclusion he had arrived at nearly eight years earlier. What had promptod Cuccia's visit to New York was a series of phone calls that *he* had been receiving from men with American/Italian accents. These calls, like those to Ambrosoli, were of a threatening nature. While Ambrosoli chose to stay with his work in Milan, Cuccia elected to confront Sindona.

Sindona made a number of demands. One was that Cuccia should have the Italian arrest warrant withdrawn – the fact that in his absence he had been sentenced to three-and-a-half years' imprisonment in 1976 Sindona brushed aside as a trivial point. Sindona further demanded that Cuccia should find 257 billion lire and bail out Banca Privata. For good measure he also demanded that Cuccia should find even more money to provide for the Sindona family. Apart from making the gracious gesture of allowing Signor Cuccia to continue to live, it is unclear what Sindona was offering in return.

During the course of this extraordinary conversation Sindona, perhaps by way of demonstrating Cuccia's very real danger, introduced the subject of Giorgio Ambrosoli. 'That damned liquidator of my Bank is harming me and therefore I want to have him killed. I will make him disappear in such a way that he leaves no trace.' This is the reality of Mafia mentality. Al Pacino and well-cut suits, lovable children and doting fathers is the fantasy world of Mafia. The reality is men like Michele Sindona.

These threats were uttered less than one month after Sindona had been indicted on 99 counts. The same mentality which concluded that the extradition proceedings would vanish if Assistant District Attorney John Kenney were murdered was at work again. If Ambrosoli could be silenced, the criminal charges would presumably dribble away like the morning mist. A mind which functions with such perverted reasoning could plan to kill a Pope without hesitating.

Enrico Cuccia left the meeting unimpressed. In October 1979 a bomb exploded under the front door of Cuccia's flat in Milan. Luckily no one was injured. Giorgio Ambrosoli was less fortunate.

It was apparent to all parties concerned with the forthcoming trial of Sindona that the evidence of Giorgio Ambrosoli was of paramount importance. On June 9th, 1979, the Judge who had been appointed to try the Sindona case, Thomas Griesa, arranged for Ambrosoli to swear a deposition in Milan.

By that date the man who was given a 100,000 dollar contract to kill Giorgio Ambrosoli had been in the Hotel Splendido, Milan for 24 hours. He was booked in as Robert McGovern. He was also known as 'Billy the Exterminator'. His real name is William Arico. At the first class hotel, less than 50 metres from Milan Central Station, Arico dined with the five men who were to assist him with the murder. His two main accomplices were Charles Arico, his son, and Rocky Messina. Their weapons included an M11 machine gun, specially fitted with a silencer, and five P28 revolvers. Arico hired a Fiat car and began to stalk Ambrosoli.

The request to take a detailed and lengthy statement from Ambrosoli had initially been made by Sindona's lawyers. They had hoped to demonstrate the absurdity of the charges with which their client stood accused in New York. Their awakening which began on the morning of July 9th was rude in the extreme. Four years of work, over 100,000 sheets of carefully, meticulously prepared notes plus the mind of an exceptionally gifted lawyer began quietly to reveal the appalling truth in front of a cluster of American lawyers, two special marshals representing New York Judge Griesa and the Italian Judge Giovanni Galati.

When the court adjourned after the first day's hearing, Sindona's lawyers could easily be identified as they left. They were the men with worried faces.

With Arico trailing him, the oblivious Ambrosoli went on to another meeting. This was with the deputy superintendent of the Palermo police force and head of that city's CID, Boris Giuliano. The subject was the same as the one on which Ambrosoli had been testifying all day – Michele Sindona. Giuseppe Di Cristina, a Mafia enforcer employed by the families Gambino, Inzerillo and Spatola, had been murdered in Palermo in May 1978. On his body Giuliano had discovered cheques and other documents which indicated that Sindona had been recycling the proceeds from heroin sales through the Vatican Bank to his Amincor Bank in Switzerland. Having compared notes on their separate investigations the two men agreed to have a fuller meeting once Ambrosoli had finished his testimony to the US lawyers.

Later that day, Ambrosoli was still not finished with Sindona. He had a long telephone conversation with Lt-Colonel Antonio Varisco, Head of the Security Service in Rome. The subject was the matter Varisco was currently investigating, P2.

On July 10th, as his deposition continued, Ambrosoli dropped one of a large number of bombshells. Detailing how Banca Cattolica del Veneto had changed hands and how Pacchetti had been unloaded by Sindona to Calvi, Ambrosoli stated that Sindona had paid a 'brokerage fee of 6.5 million dollars to a Milanese banker and an American bishop.'

On July 11th Ambrosoli completed his deposition. It was agreed that he would return the following day and sign the record of his testimony and that the week after he would be available for questioning and clarification of his evidence by the US prosecutors and Sindona's lawyers.

Shortly before midnight on the 11th, Ambrosoli arrived outside his apartment. From the window his wife waved. They were about to have a belated dinner. As Ambrosoli moved towards his door Arico and two of his aides appeared from the shadows. The question came out of the darkness.

'Giorgio Ambrosoli?'

'Si.'

Arico aimed at point blank range and at least four bullets from a P38 entered the lawyer's chest. He died instantly.

By 6 a.m. Arico was in Switzerland. One hundred thousand dollars was transferred from a Sindona account at Calvi's Banca del Gottardo into an account Arico had under the name of Robert McGovern at the Crédit Suisse in Geneva. The account number is 415851-22-1.

On July 13th, 1979, less than forty-eight hours after the murder of Giorgio Ambrosoli, Lt-Colonel Antonio Varisco was being driven in a white BMW along the Lungotevere Arnaldo da Brescia in Rome. It was 8.30 a.m. A white Fiat 128 pulled alongside. A sawn-off shotgun appeared through its window. Four shots were fired and the Lt-Colonel and his chauffeur were dead. One hour later the Red Brigades 'claimed' responsibility.

On July 21st, 1979, Boris Giuliano went into the Lux Bar in Via Francesco Paolo Di Biasi in Palermo for a morning coffee. The time was 8.05 a.m. Having drunk his coffee he moved towards the cash desk to pay. A man approached and fired six shots into Giuliano. The cafe was crowded at the time. Subsequent police questioning established that no one had seen anything. No one had heard anything. Boris Giuliano's position was taken by Giuseppe Impallomeni, a member of P2.

Not even the members of the Red Brigades 'claimed', falsely or otherwise, the responsibility for the murders of Giorgio Ambrosoli and Boris Giuliano. When news of the murder of Ambrosoli was flashed to New York, Michele Sindona, the man who had paid to have the liquidator taken care of by an exterminator, responded in typical fashion. 'No one must link me with this act of cowardice and I will take decisive legal action against anyone who does.'

Two years earlier during an interview with *Il Fiorino* Sindona had made a far more significant statement. Talking of the 'plot that exists against me', he had listed the leaders who in Sindona's mind included Giorgio Ambrosoli. Sindona observed: 'There are many who should be afraid . . . I repeat, there are very many.'

Giorgio Ambrosoli did not die in vain. His many years of work plus the unsigned deposition were to prove powerful aids for the prosecution during the forthcoming trial of Michele Sindona.

The Milanese banker and the American bishop referred to in Ambrosoli's sworn deposition were quickly identified as Calvi and Bishop Paul Marcinkus. Marcinkus was to deny flatly receiving such a commission. Ambrosoli was most certainly not the kind of man to make such an accusation without overwhelming proof. With regard to the veracity of statements made by Bishop Marcinkus, it will be recalled that shortly after the Sindona crash he denied ever having met Sindona.

Who were the main beneficiaries of this series of appalling and inhuman crimes? The list begins to have a familiar ring: Marcinkus, Calvi, Sindona, Gelli and Ortolani.

In Milan the terror after the series of murders was most discernible in the Palace of Justice. Men who had worked alongside Ambrosoli suddenly found difficulty in remembering that they had assisted him during his investigation of Sindona's affairs. Judge Luca Mucci, who had taken over the criminal investigation after Alessandrini's murder, moved into the continuing investigation so slowly that spectators might have thought he had been turned to stone. An initial evaluation of the Bank of Italy's investigation into Banco Ambrosiano astonishingly concluded that Calvi's explanations were perfectly acceptable. This at least was the view of the Finance Police.

Padalino, the Bank of Italy official who had actually headed the 1978 probe, found himself frequently summoned to Milan where he was confronted by doubting magistrates. As the summer of 1979 wore on, Padalino was threatened and harassed by elements of the Milan judiciary. He was warned that his report on Ambrosiano amounted to a libel. Gelli's P2 and Sindona's Mafia were reducing the concepts of justice to a depravity.

An example of just how powerful the Calvi/Gelli axis was can be gauged from events that occurred in Nicaragua at about the time of Emilio Alessandrini's murder in January 1979. Calvi had opened a branch of his empire in Managua in September 1977. The bank was called Ambrosiano Group Banco Comercial. Its official function was 'conducting international commercial transactions'. Its actual function was to move from the Nassau branch, with director Bishop Paul Marcinkus's approval, a large amount of the evidence that would reveal the fraudulent and criminal devices used in the share pushing/acquisition of the Milan parent bank. Nicaragua removed the evidence even farther from the eyes of the Bank of Italy. As always there was a price to be paid. Gelli had smoothed the way with introductions to Nicaragua's dictator Anastasio Somoza. After several million dollars had been dropped into the dictator's pocket, he announced that it would be an excellent idea for Calvi to open a branch in his country. One of the side benefits for Calvi was the acquisition of a Nicaraguan diplomatic passport, something he retained to the end of his life.

Calvi and Gelli appraised the political situation in Nicaragua with its growing possibility of Sandinistan rebel rule in the not too distant future. These men, who had carried both Fascist and Partisan membership papers during the Second World War, had not changed a lifetime's habit of being double-faced or, in banking terms, prudent. Calvi gave equally large amounts of money to the rebels – some went to buy grain, some went to buy arms.

Early in 1979 the left-wing takeover of Nicaragua became a reality. Like many left-wing takeovers before, this one promptly nationalized all foreign banks – with one exception: the Ambrosiano Group Banco Comercial continued to trade under Roberto Calvi. Even left-wing idealists, it would seem, have a price.

In New York with a large array of his Italian enemies silenced either permanently or temporarily, Michele Sindona decided towards the end of July 1979 that he would after all return to Italy. Illegally. The fact that he was on a 3 million dollar bail in New York and had to report daily to the Marshal's office, and that he had already been sentenced to three-and-a-half years' imprisonment in Italy and was wanted on further charges, might appear good reason not to return. Sindona's solution was simplicity itself. With the aid of his Mafia associates in New York and Sicily he arranged his own 'kidnap'.

The reasons Sindona had for a secret return to his native land included his need to marshal maximum support for his forthcoming New York trial. Sindona took the view that a great many people owed him favours. He now wished to collect. To persuade his Italian friends and colleagues to repay him Sindona was prepared to play the one ace he still held. He would name the 500.

The list of 500 major Italian exporters of black currency had proved elusive to Italian authorities during the past ten years. A number of investigators apart from Giorgio Ambrosoli were continually stumbling over references to the list of 500, which allegedly includes the names of many of the most powerful men in Italy. It has become the Holy Grail of Italian finance but the list is not merely legendary. It exists. Sindona and Gelli certainly have copies of it, and Calvi had one too. Sindona believed that the threat to make the mysterious names public would be sufficient to effect his complete rehabilitation in Italian society. The prison sentence would be quashed, all other outstanding charges against him would be dropped, he would re-acquire his Italian banks and the New York Court would be confronted by a man who would claim that he was the victim of wicked conspiracies, probably Communist inspired. An array of very respectable people would testify that Michele Sindona was not only a very much wronged man, but also the world's most brilliant banker, a man who personified good, clean, healthy capitalism. All of this would be achieved by the use of a technique of which Sindona had frequently boasted to Carlo Bordoni he was a master – blackmail.

Later Sindona would claim there was another reason for his trip. He will insist to anyone who cares to listen to him today, that it was to overthrow the Italian Government in Sicily and declare the island an independent State. According to Sindona, he would then offer Sicily to the USA as the fifty-first State of the Union in exchange for all criminal charges he faced in the USA being dropped. Sindona asserts that the plan would have succeeded except for the fact that, after the Mafia had arranged a phoney kidnap, they proceeded to carry out a real one. Fantasies and delusions such as this are laughable until one remembers that good honest men like Giorgio Ambrosoli did not die laughing.

The madness of Michele Sindona is perhaps nowhere more clearly revealed than in the fine detail of this plan. Sindona asserts that the Gambino family was fully prepared to give up its heroin factories in

Sicily, a murderous industry that was bringing in profits to the Gambino, Inzerillo and Spatola families estimated by the Italian authorities at 600 million dollars minimum a year. In exchange for this public-spirited action, the Gambino family would be given control of the trade in oranges and Rosario Spatola would be allowed to build a casino in Palermo.

Sindona duly vanished from the streets of New York during the afternoon of August 2nd, 1979. He was clearly going to be extremely busy if Sicily was to be annexed and a deal with the President of the United States was to be effected before the trial, which was scheduled to begin on September 10th. Carrying a false passport in the name of Joseph Bonamico (Italian for good friend) and accompanied by Anthony Caruso, Sindona, wearing glasses, a white wig and false moustache and beard, boarded TWA flight 740 to Vienna at Kennedy Airport. The farce, complete with ransom demands to a variety of people from 'kidnappers' calling themselves the 'Proletarian Committee for the Eversion [sic] of an Improved Justice' continued until October 16th when an 'emotionally exhausted and physically weak' Sindona with a healing bullet wound in the thigh, telephoned one of his New York lawyers from a phone booth on the corner of 42nd Street and Tenth Avenue in Manhattan.

By any standards his trip had been less than an overwhelming success. Sicily had not become part of the Union. Many of Sindona's former friends remained just that, former friends. The list of 500, despite all threats, had not been revealed and Sindona would in the near future face additional charges of perjury, bail-jumping and arranging a false kidnap. The main gain for Sindona appears to have been 30 billion lire. This sum was paid by Roberto Calvi after the kindly Licio Gelli had interceded yet again on Sindona's behalf. It was paid to Sindona's 'kidnappers' from a Calvi-owned bank, the Banca del Gottardo, in Switzerland. In theory the sum was paid to Mafioso Rosano Spatola, for the 'release' of Sindona – an Italian version of the three-card trick.

The main conspirators, apart from Sindona himself, were Anthony Caruso, Joseph Macaluso, Johnny Gambino, Rosano Spatola, Vincenzo Spatola and Joseph Miceli Crimi. The Italian authorities established that Rosario Spatola, who could normally be found wandering about the lines of cement mixers at the large construction company he owned in Palermo, had been in New York at precisely the time that Sindona had vanished. Asked the reason for his visit he replied, 'Family business'.

Sindona's trial on the massive array of charges arising from the collapse of the Franklin Bank finally began in early February 1980. Immediately before it started the Vatican gave clear indication that the Roman Catholic Church at least was going to stand by its former financial adviser.

Cardinal Giuseppe Caprio, Cardinal Sergio Guerri and Bishop Paul Marcinkus had agreed to a defence counsel request that they help Sindona's case by swearing depositions on video-tape. Intrigued by what these devout men might say about Sindona, the prosecution had raised no objection to this unusual gambit. It is normal for witnesses to have their statements tested on oath, in courtroom, in front of judge and jury. For the men from the Vatican, trial judge Thomas Griesa waived this consideration and instructed Sindona's lawyers to fly to Rome on Friday February 1st. The understanding was that the deposition would be taken the following day and the lawyers would report back to the Judge on the Monday. Their report, contained within the trial transcripts of United States of America *v.* Michele Sindona, makes extraordinary reading.

At the last minute, or more exactly four hours before the depositions were to be sworn, Secretary of State Cardinal Casaroli intervened. There would be no depositions. 'They would create a disruptive precedent. There has been so much unfortunate publicity about these depositions. We are very unhappy about the fact that the American Government does not give diplomatic recognition to the Vatican.'

The sophisticated New York lawyers were still in a state of disbelief when they reported to Judge Griesa. At 11.00 a.m. on the Saturday morning, Cardinal Guerri's secretary, Monsignor Blanchard, had telephoned the American Embassy to confirm that the cardinals and Marcinkus would be there at 4 p.m. A few minutes later he had called back to say Casaroli had withdrawn them from the arena. He was asked about his earlier call. The Monsignor promptly denied making any earlier call. He compounded that lie with another when he told the Embassy the 'American judge knows all about this'.

The bemused Embassy official, unaccustomed to such a graphic display of Vatican dishonesty, set about contacting Cardinal Guerri direct. When she eventually located His Eminence, he confessed that he did not know if he was coming to swear a deposition or not. In the event he did not. Guerri, Caprio and Marcinkus all assured the American lawyers that their depositions would have been full of praise for Michele Sindona – that was not their difficulty. The problem had arisen when Cardinal Casaroli saw the appalling implications. If the jury found Sindona guilty, then three high prelates of the Roman Catholic Church would in effect be branded as liars. Further, to allow the three to testify, even through voluntary depositions, would open a Vatican gate through which would come pouring every Italian magistrate demanding the same co-operation. That would lead to a breach of the Lateran Treaty which granted a cardinal complete immunity from arrest in Italy. The next step would be a very unwelcome light shining on Vatican Incorporated.

Casaroli had shrewdly saved the Vatican at the eleventh hour. What the American lawyers did not know was that in doing so he had actually overridden a decision taken by the Pope. John Paul II had happily agreed to the request that Marcinkus and the others should tell the world how highly they regarded Michele Sindona.

On March 27th, 1980, Michele Sindona was found guilty on 65 counts, including fraud, conspiracy, perjury, false bank statements, and misappropriation of bank funds. He was imprisoned in the Metropolitan Correctional Center, Manhattan, to await sentence.

On May 13th, two days before he was due to be sentenced, Sindona attempted to commit suicide. He slashed his wrists superficially, but more significantly consumed a quantity of digitalis. Acting on Grand Master Gelli's advice, Sindona had carried with him everywhere for many years, a lethal dose of digitalis. Gelli had advised not only Sindona, but other top P2 members always to carry the drug. It was P2's insurance against members being forced to reveal details of the organization.

How such a quantity of the drug had been brought into the prison remains a mystery. Sindona has apparently claimed to have it sewn into the lining of a suit for years. To smuggle digitalis into his prison would have been a far more difficult feat than to get it into the Papal Apartments in September 1978.

Initially it appeared that Sindona would die, particularly as the doctors were at a loss to know what drug he had taken, but the dose was inadequate. Having eventually established that it was digitalis, they were able to administer an antidote. Sindona made a full recovery and on June 13th, 1980 was sentenced to 25 years' imprisonment and fined over 200,000 dollars. Carlo Bordoni, who had been the main prosecution witness against Sindona, received a seven-year prison sentence and a 20,000 dollar fine. Sindona was subsequently found guilty of arranging his own false kidnap and sentenced to a further two-and-a-half years. Also found guilty of conspiring with him and assisting him in bail-jumping were

Anthony Caruso and Joseph Macaluso. Both were sentenced to five years' imprisonment.

While these events were unfolding in New York, Sindona's P2 comrades Calvi and Gelli were continuing business as usual on the other side of the Atlantic. By 1979, Roberto Calvi was seeking protection in all directions: a private army of eight bodyguards; twenty-four-hour guards for Calvi, his family, his Milan, Rome and Drezzo homes; armour-plated Alfa Romeos with bullet-proof tyres. These manifestations of the master thief's personal fears were costing the shareholders of Ambrosiano over one million dollars a year. No one in Italy, including the President or the Prime Minister, was as well protected. He sought protection from political parties of every shade or colour – the Christian Democrats, the Socialists, the Communists, all were illegally bank-rolled by Calvi. He had the protection of Gelli's P2 and his Mafia associates, but both of these were two-edged swords which could be used against him.

The illegally purchased shares in Banco Ambrosiano were concealed in Panamanian companies beyond the jurisdiction of the Bank of Italy, but always the fear for Calvi was the possibility that officialdom would discover this aspect of his many criminal activities. First the Nassau branch had been used to bury the illegal transactions. When the Bank of Italy came within an ace of proving what they suspected, Calvi moved the axis of the fraud to Nicaragua. Then in 1979 he moved much of the central activity that governed the fraud even further away, to Peru. On October 11th, 1979 Banco Ambrosiano Andino opened its doors in Lima. Shortly afterwards the majority of the loans that had been extended to the shell Panamanian and Liechtenstein companies were transferred to Peru. These small shell companies, many with a nominal capital of a mere 10,000 dollars, continued to proliferate. Eventually there would be seventeen. The majority were owned by a Luxembourg company aptly named Manic SA which in turn was owned by the Vatican Bank.

If the international banks queueing up over the years to lend Calvi millions upon millions of dollars had carried out even elementary homework, Calvi would have been exposed years before he suffered his ultimate fate. It is true that the Bank of Italy 1978 report on Banco Ambrosiano was highly confidential and not freely available. That was still the position when I obtained it in 1981. If one author can obtain such a report, so presumably can the Midland, Lloyds, National Westminster or any of the other 250 banks scattered throughout the world who were taken in by Calvi, who had stolen *our* money. These bankers have a much-vaunted reputation for shrewdness and astuteness, yet they believed the doctored accounts Calvi showed them. The statements he made assuring them that the vast loans were to finance Italian exports were accepted. Did no one check? Did no one subsequently monitor? That over 450 million dollars should be loaned by the international banks, not to another bank, but to a mere holding company called Banco Ambrosiano Holdings, based in Luxembourg – a company manifestly unsupported by any central bank – is a savage condemnation of the lending practices of the interbank market. The men who sit on the boards of these lending banks should be made to answer to their shareholders and to all who have accounts with them. It is not pleasant to reflect that some of us in Great Britain undoubtedly financed the purchase of Exocet missiles for Argentina, missiles that were used to kill so many men during the Falklands war. Yet there is no doubt that this evil chain did occur. Calvi diverted millions of dollars to Licio Gelli, who in turn used some of that money to purchase Exocets for Argentina. Investing in the future is fine, but investing to ensure that your own kith and kin have no future is another matter. Doubtless the men who negotiated these huge loans to Calvi would claim that at the time it looked like very good business.

Just how obscene this particular transaction was can only be appreciated when one is aware that this money was diverted to Gelli and Ortolani through a Panamanian company owned by the Vatican.

The company in question, Bellatrix, was controlled by Marcinkus at the Vatican Bank but created by a trinity of P2 members, Gelli, Ortolani and Bruno Tassan Din, managing director and financial strategist to the giant Rizzoli publishing group. These Masons milked the Ambrosiano cow of 184 million dollars. The capital of Bellatrix? Ten thousand dollars. The vast non-returnable loan was secured on paper against a large helping of Rizzoli shares. Rizzoli was jointly owned by P2 and the Vatican. The value placed on the Rizzoli shares far exceeded their real worth.

Astolfine, yet another of the Panamanian companies owned by the Vatican was able, on a capital of 10,000 dollars, to run up debts of 486 million dollars. Its security? A large helping of grossly over-valued Banco Ambrosiano shares.

With business practices of this order capitalism need have no fear that it will be ultimately destroyed by Marxism. All Marxists have to do is to sit back and wait for capitalism to self-destruct automatically.

It is understandable that ENI, one of the biggest conglomerates in the world, should suddenly start lending Calvi money; that this huge state-owned oil company should suddenly start functioning as a bank and lend to instead of borrow from Banco Ambrosiano Holdings in Luxembourg – the Chairman of ENI, Giorgio Mazzanti, and the head of its financial department, Leonardo di Donna, are both members of P2. To date no P2 members have been discovered in the higher reaches of the many international banks which continuously poured millions of dollars down Calvi's throat between 1978 and 1980.

When the man in the street in London, Paris, New York, Copenhagen, Tokyo, Ottawa, Sydney and Wellington curses the high rate of his bank charges he should tilt his hat at the ghost of Roberto Calvi and at the ever elusive Licio Gelli and Umberto Ortolani. He should also spare a thought for Vatican City. When we pay our high bank charges we are helping to pick up their tab.

Incontrovertible evidence that the Vatican owns these mysterious Panamanian companies reaches back to 1971, to the time when Calvi and Sindona put Bishop Paul Marcinkus on the board of Calvi's section in Nassau.

In Milan, during 1979, the magistrate Luca Mucci spasmodically questioned Calvi. Calvi would study his shoes or the floor intently, mutter about his need to preserve banking secrecy, discuss Inter Milan's chances of winning their next football match and leave an outmanoeuvred judge.

By the end of 1979 the financial exposure of the Vatican-owned front companies that Calvi controlled was in excess of 500 million dollars. Fortunately the intercosmic banking fantasies of Sindona had not yet become a reality. There were still financial situations Calvi could not control. The dollar began to rise against the lira. Ambrosiano's assets, such as they were, consisted very largely of lira-denominated shares. The game became frenetic. Just to keep up with the fraud required demented juggling, particularly when the running costs included 30 billion lire for buying the Venice newspaper *Il Gazzettino* to keep the Christian Democrats happy, and 'lending' the Rome daily *Paese Sera* 20 billion lire to keep the Communists content. Everyone had their hands out and it always seemed that the man with the biggest hands was Licio Gelli.

In January 1980 Banco Ambrosiano de America del Sud opened its doors in Buenos Aires. There was practically no banking activity but it was this arm of the Calvi empire which helped finance Argentinian purchases of Exocet missiles. It also provided funds for arms purchases by other South American regimes.

In July 1980 Judge Luca Mucci felt sufficiently impressed by the investigation that the Guardia di Finanza, the financial police, had carried out in the wake of the Bank of Italy 1978 enquiry, to order Calvi to surrender his passport and to warn the banker that he would be facing criminal charges. It was a small step forward in the name of justice.

It took a smart step backwards when a few months later Calvi obtained his passport back again through the good offices of Gelli. The Grand Master was less inclined to intercede when Massimo Spada, late of the Vatican Bank and currently Chairman of Banca Cattolica del Veneto, was arrested and charged with involvement of a criminal nature in Il Crack Sindona. Next to feel the handcuffs, at least momentarily, was Luigi Mennini, still active in the Vatican Bank, on similar charges.

As the net began to draw tighter around Calvi, despite the valiant efforts of Gelli to corrupt all and sundry, the Milanese banker's hopes of continuing to plunder relied very largely on Marcinkus. The game was becoming much rougher and without the constant co-operation of the Vatican Bank, concealment of Calvi's crimes would cease. It had always been so but in the past the pressure on the Vatican had been minimal; now with the arrest of Mennini the pressure intensified. Calvi began to fear that, despite the massive amounts of money he had channelled into the hands of Bishop Paul Marcinkus, the time might be fast approaching when the man across the Tiber might withdraw his active support and leave Calvi alone and highly vulnerable.

Early in 1981 Treasury Minister Beniamino Andreatta, who had been promoted to the post the previous October, concluded that the Vatican should withdraw its support immediately. He had studied the 1978 Bank of Italy report at length and felt compelled to make an attempt to protect the Church. He went to the Vatican and spoke at length to Foreign Minister Cardinal Casaroli. He outlined the entire situation. He urged the Vatican to break all links with Banco Ambrosiano before it was too late. The advice was ignored. Marcinkus would claim later that he had no knowledge of this meeting. In any event, if the devout Catholic Andreatta had been aware of the full facts, he would have known that it was an impossibility for the Vatican to sever the links. It actually owned Banco Ambrosiano. Through the array of Panamanian and Liechtenstein companies, it had acquired control of over 16 per cent of Banco Ambrosiano. With the rest of the shares in the bank so widely scattered among small shareholders, that gave the Vatican a controlling interest.

At noon on March 2nd 1981 the Vatican Press Office released a document that puzzled many. Issued without explanation, it reminded all Catholics of the Canon Laws covering Freemasons and stressed the fact that the present code 'forbids Catholics under pain of excommunication from joining Masonic or similar associations'. No one could understand the timing. Roman Catholics had been subjected to automatic excommunication if they became Freemasons since 1738. Why remind them in early March 1981? The answer was not long in coming and indicates that the intelligence-gathering network of the Church is at least as efficient as Licio Gelli's. The Vatican statement did not explain how all the good Catholics who featured on the membership list of P2 could have their names expunged from the records before the Italian authorities discovered them. For P2 member Calvi, this apparently insurmountable problem was to have disastrous consequences.

When public exposure finally came, it was ironically through Calvi's association with his protector Licio Gelli. Italian magistrates in 1981 were still attempting to clarify the facts concerning Sindona's self-arranged kidnap. On March 17th police raided Gelli's palatial villa in Arezzo and his office at the Gio-Le textile factory. They sought links of Gelli's involvement in Sindona's surprise trip to his homeland. What they found was a Pandora's box of scandal. In Gelli's safe they discovered a list of the 962 members of P2. They also found dossiers and secret Government reports.

The list of P2 members was a veritable Who's Who of Italy. The armed forces were heavily represented with over fifty generals and admirals. The Government of the day was there with two Cabinet Ministers, as were industrialists, journalists (including the Editor of *Corriere Della Sera* and several of his senior staff), 36 parliamentarians, pop stars, pundits, and police officers. It was a State within a State. Many have said that Gelli was planning to take over Italy. They are wrong. He *had* taken over Italy. Of the Grand Master himself there was no sign. The arrangements for the police raid had been top secret, which translated meant: only tell trusted police officers and Licio Gelli. He had fled to South America.

The ensuing scandal brought down the Italian Government and gave considerable momentum to the Milan magistrate's investigation of Calvi. Judge Mucci was replaced by Gerardo d'Ambrosio. It had been over two years since the murder of Judge Emilio Alessandrini; two years of procrastination. Now with a new investigating judge, helped by the compromising documents found in Gelli's safe, within two months Calvi was arrested and placed in a prison cell in Lodi.

Now was the time for all good friends to come to the aid of the man who had so often helped other parties. In the weeks following Calvi's arrest, Bettino Craxi, the leader of the Socialist party, and Flaminio Piccoli, the president of the Christian Democrats, got to their feet in Parliament and made pleasant remarks about Calvi and his Bank. The Vatican stayed silent. Demonstrably its entire attention was focused on a far graver situation. Seven days before Calvi's arrest, Pope John Paul II had his near fatal meeting in St Peter's Square with Mehmet Ali Agca.

While much of the world prayed that the Pope would survive, Roberto Calvi in his prison cell was totally preoccupied with what seemed to him an infinitely more important problem: his own survival. Through his family he began to press Marcinkus to admit publicly that over the years he had been standing side by side with Calvi in the kitchen as they cooked the books.

After many futile telephone calls, Calvi's son Carlo finally got through to Marcinkus. He pleaded with the Bishop that the gravity of his father's position would be greatly reduced if the Vatican Bank admitted its involvement. The deals had been channelled through Calvi's Banca del Gottardo in Lugano which could not reveal the truth because of the very stringent Swiss banking regulations, but the Vatican Bank was its own master. It could volunteer information. Marcinkus, however, had no intention of publicly accepting responsibility. He told Calvi's son: 'If we do, it's not only the IOR and the Vatican's image which will suffer. You'll lose as well, for our problems are your problems too.'

Indeed they were. The two banks were completely interlocked. They had been for years. Bishop Marcinkus was in a bind. To tell the truth would bring down on the Vatican the wrath of Italy. The alternative was to leave Calvi unsupported in the hope that the Vatican's deep and continuing involvement would remain secret and that after Calvi's trial it would be a case of business as usual. Bishop Marcinkus took the latter course. Undoubtedly this decision was based on the fact that, of all the crimes perpetrated by Calvi, the charges he now faced involved only two of his illegal transactions, when Calvi had sold himself shares in Toro and Credito Varesino that he already happened to own, at vastly inflated prices. This had involved illegally exported currency out of Italy and that was the offence the Milan magistrates were hoping would enable them to convict Calvi. Marcinkus reasoned that if everyone kept calm the game could continue. Calvi, sitting in Lodi prison, was unimpressed by the messages from his sanguine partner in the Vatican. International bankers shook their heads in disbelief as Calvi continued to run Banco Ambrosiano from inside prison.

On July 7th, the Italian Government charged Michele Sindona with ordering the murder of Giorgio Ambrosoli. Calvi's reaction to the news was particularly interesting. He tried to commit suicide the following evening. He swallowed a quantity of barbiturates and slashed his wrists. He later explained his reasons: 'Because of a kind of lucid desperation. Because there was not a trace of justice in all that was being done against me. And I am not talking about the trial.' If, of course, he had really wanted to end his life, he had merely to obtain the quantity of digitalis recommended by Gelli by having it smuggled into prison. His trial judges were unimpressed.

On July 20th he was sentenced to four years imprisonment and a fine of 16 billion lire. His lawyers immediately lodged an appeal and he was freed on bail. Within a week of his release, the board of Banco Ambrosiano unanimously reconfirmed him as chairman of the bank and gave him a standing ovation. The international bankers again shook their heads in disbelief. As Marcinkus had predicted, it was indeed business as usual. P2 was a continuing power. The Bank of Italy allowed Calvi to return. The Italian Government made no move to end the extraordinary spectacle of a man convicted of banking offences running one of the country's biggest banks.

One banker did raise objections. Ambrosiano's general manager Roberto Rosone pleaded with the Bank of Italy to approve the removal of Calvi and replace him with the previous chairman, Ruggiero Mozzana. The Bank of Italy, with its eyes still firmly fixed on the power of P2 and the political muscle that Calvi had bought over the years, declined to intervene.

The second threat to Calvi's banking empire came from Peru and Nicaragua. To counter it, Calvi enlisted the help of Marcinkus. The Bishop had declined to give Calvi any support, public or private, during his trial but he was now about to give him every assistance to ensure that the criminal fraud perpetrated by both men should remain secret.

During the time of Calvi's trial the Vatican announced that Pope John Paul II had appointed a commission of fifteen cardinals to study the finances of the Roman Catholic Church. The function of the commission was to recommend improvements that would increase Vatican revenue.

Bishop Paul Marcinkus was not included as a member of the

commission but he obviously felt that as head of the Vatican Bank he could nevertheless make a powerful contribution to the vexed question of Vatican finances. He held a number of secret meetings with the convicted Calvi which resulted in the Vatican Bank officially admitting an increase in its outstanding debts of nearly one billion dollars. This was the sum that was owed to the Calvi banks in Peru and Nicaragua, as a result of their having loaned on Calvi's instructions hundreds of millions of dollars to Bellatrix, Astolfine, etc. Peru and Nicaragua, in spite of being Calvi subsidiaries, were finally displaying a little independence. The securities backing these enormous loans were negligible.

Peru and Nicaragua wanted greater cover. Who picked up the bill in the event of a default? Who exactly owned these mysterious Panamanian companies? Who had borrowed so much with so little? The gentlemen from Peru were particularly anxious, having loaned some 900 million dollars.

At this stage, in August 1981, Calvi and Marcinkus perpetrated their biggest fraud. The documents would become known as 'letters of comfort'. They offer no comfort to any Roman Catholic; no reassurance to any who believe in the moral integrity of the Vatican. The letters were written on the headed paper of the Instituto per le Opere di Religione, Vatican City and were dated September 1st, 1981. They were addressed to Banco Ambrosiano Andino in Lima, Peru and Ambrosiano Group Banco Comercial in Nicaragua. On the instructions of Bishop Paul Marcinkus, they were signed by Luigi Mennini and Pellegrino De Strobel. They read:

Gentlemen:

This is to confirm that we directly or indirectly control the following entries:

Manic SA Luxembourg
Astolfine SA Panama
Nordeurop Establishment, Liechtenstein
UTC United Trading Corporation, Panama
Erin SA Panama
Bellatrix SA Panama
Belrosa SA Panama
Starfield SA Panama

We also confirm our awareness of their indebtedness towards yourself as of June 10, 1981 as per attached statement of accounts.

The attached accounts showed that the 'indebtedness' to the Lima branch alone was 907 million dollars.

The directors in Nicaragua and Peru relaxed. They had now clear admission that the massive debts were the responsibility of the Vatican Bank. The Holy Roman Catholic Church was the guarantor. No banker could wish for a better security. There was just one small problem. The directors in Peru and Nicaragua knew only half of the story. There was another letter. This one was from Roberto Calvi to the Vatican Bank, dated August 27th, 1981. It was safely in Marcinkus's hands before he acknowledged that the Vatican Bank was liable for the debts of one billion dollars. Calvi's letter made a formal request for the letters of comfort in which the Vatican would admit that it owned the Luxembourg, Liechtenstein and Panamanian companies. This admission, Calvi assured the Vatican, 'would entail no liabilities for the IOR.' His letter concluded with a paragraph confirming that whatever happened the Vatican Bank would 'suffer no future damage or loss'. Hence the Vatican Bank was secretly absolved from debts to which it was about to admit.

For Calvi's secret letter to Marcinkus to have any legal validity, its existence and precise contents would have had to be revealed to the directors in Peru and Nicaragua. Further, the arrangement between Calvi and Marcinkus would have had to be agreed upon by the majority of the directors in Milan. Moreover, to have been a legal agreement, it would have been essential for the contents of both letters to have been public knowledge to all the shareholders of Banco Ambrosiano, including the many small shareholders in the Milan area.

The two letters and the agreement between Calvi and Marcinkus constitute a clear case of criminal fraud by both men. That all of this should have transpired on the third anniversary of the election of Albino Luciani to the Papacy adds to the obscenity. Luciani, a man committed and dedicated to the elimination of corruption within the Vatican, had been succeeded by Pope John Paul II, a man who whole-heartedly approved of Bishop Paul Marcinkus.

This appalling effrontery grew when on September 28th, 1981, the third anniversary of Luciani's death, Marcinkus was promoted by the Pope. It was announced that he had been appointed Pro-President of the Pontifical Commission for the State of Vatican City. This virtually made him Governor of Vatican City. He still retained his position as

head of the Vatican Bank and the new post gave him automatic eleva-
tion to Archbishop.

Through his Lithuanian origins, his continual espousal, in fiscal
terms, of Poland's needs and his close proximity to the Pope because
of his role as personal bodyguard and overseer of all security on
foreign trips, Marcinkus had discovered in the person of Karol
Wojtyla the most powerful protector a Vatican employee could have.
Sindona, Calvi and others like them are, according to the Vatican,
wicked men who have deceived naive, trusting priests. Either
Marcinkus has misled, lied to and suppressed the truth from Pope John
Paul II since October 1978, or the present Pope also stands indicted.

While Karol Wojtyla displays remarkable charisma and tells the
world that a man who looks at his wife with desire could well be
committing adultery of the heart, Marcinkus has continued to seduce
many of the world's bankers. While the Pope from Krakow demonstrates his preoccupation with maintaining the Roman Catholic status
quo by his declarations that divorced Roman Catholics who had re-
married could only be given Holy Communion if they totally abstained
from sexual relationships with their married partners, the Pope's
bankers have shown themselves to be less fastidious about whom they
sleep with. While Pope John Paul II has justified the Roman Catholic
Church's continuing treatment of women as second class citizens with
assertions such as 'Mary, the mother of God, was not among the
Apostles at the Last Supper', the men from Vatican Incorporated have
continued to display a more liberated attitude: they will steal and
embezzle from either sex.

In the years since the election of Wojtyla, Licio Gelli, the
unbeliever, has continued to demonstrate his own power and charisma.
None would call him God's representative but many would continue
to jump when the Puppet Master tugged the string.

From the sanctuary of his home in the Uruguayan capital of
Montevideo, Licio Gelli remained in contact with Calvi. Still pulling
that particular string, still extorting huge amounts of money from the
banker, he would frequently telephone when Calvi was at his villa in
Drezzo. His wife Clara and his daughter Anna have confirmed that the
number was known only to Gelli and Umberto Ortolani – a P2 hotline.
Gelli would never give his name when the Calvi family would ask who
was calling. It was always the special codename: 'Luciani'.

Why would the Grand Master of P2 ascribe to himself Albino
Luciani's name – a name Gelli had used since 1978 when contacting
Calvi? Was it a constant reminder of a certain event? A constant

threat that this master blackmailer might reveal details of that event unless the money kept pouring into Gelli's bank accounts? Undoubtedly the money did continue to flow to Gelli. Right until the end, Calvi was still paying Gelli off. With the Grand Master disgraced and in hiding in South America, wanted by the Italian authorities on a variety of charges, his protection of Calvi was limited. Why then the millions of dollars that each mention of the name 'Luciani' sent pouring into Gelli's pocket? Calvi personally estimated that Gelli and Ortolani eventually were worth over 500 million dollars each.

Months before the P2 scandal broke, when the Grand Master was still in Italy, Calvi was clearly attempting to break all links with Gelli. Why did Calvi avoid the phone calls? Tell his family to say he was ill or was not there? From the accounts of the Calvi family Gelli, the insatiable collector of secrets and information, had a frightening hold over Roberto Calvi. What was the ultimate secret that Gelli knew which sent Calvi into fits of perspiring terror at the mere mention of Gelli's name?

Gelli's hold on Calvi continued until the end of the banker's life. When he whistled Calvi danced. Late in 1981 Carlo De Benedetti, chief executive of Olivetti, became deputy chairman of Banco Ambrosiano at Calvi's request. It gave his Bank's tattered public image a healthy injection of respectability. In Uruguay Gelli and Ortolani heard the news with alarm. An honest deputy chairman was not consistent with their plans to continue the plunder of Banco Ambrosiano. 'Luciani' picked up his telephone and dialled the private number at the Drezzo villa. Having persuaded De Benedetti to join his bank, Calvi then made life impossible for the man from Olivetti. 'You must take the greatest care,' he said to Benedetti. 'The P2 is preparing a dossier on you. I advise you to take care, because I know.' Little more than a month later De Benedetti had left.

A long letter of complaint, complete with highly detailed appendices, from a group of Milanese shareholders in Banco Ambrosiano was sent to John Paul II. The letter, dated January 12th, 1982, was a slashing attack on the Bank. It set out the links between Marcinkus, Calvi, Gelli and Ortolani. The shareholders were particularly distressed that the previously staid Catholic Ambrosiano and the Vatican Bank had bred such an unholy alliance. As the troubled Catholics of Milan observed:

> The IOR is not only a shareholder in the Banco Ambrosiano. It is an associate and partner of Roberto Calvi. It is revealed by a

growing number of court cases that Calvi stands today astride one of the main crossroads of the most degenerate Freemasonry (P2) and of Mafia circles, as a result of inheriting Sindona's mantle. This has been done once again with the involvement of people generously nurtured and cared for by the Vatican, such as Ortolani, who moves between the Vatican and powerful groups in the international underworld.

Being a partner of Calvi means being a partner of Gelli and Ortolani, given that both guide and influence him strongly. The Vatican is therefore, whether it likes it or not, through its association with Calvi also an active partner of Gelli and Ortolani.

The letter contained an appeal to Pope John Paul II for help and guidance. Though the Pope speaks many languages, including Italian, the Milanese thoughtfully had the letter translated into Polish and also took steps to ensure that neither the Curia in general nor Villot's replacement Casaroli should prevent the letter reaching the Pope. In any event the letter was ignored. The Milanese shareholders were not even graced with a formal acknowledgment.

Calvi was aware that the letter had been sent and was equally aware that it had the approval of his general manager and deputy chairman Roberto Rosone. He discussed with his close friend and fellow P2 member, Flavio Carboni, the threat that Rosone's attempts to clean up the bank were posing.

The range of Carboni's friends and contacts was wide. It included such men as the two rulers of Rome's underworld, Danilo Abbruciati and Ernesto Diotavelli.

On the morning of April 27th, 1982, Rosone left his apartment at a few minutes before 8.00 a.m. Fortunately for Rosone, he happened to live directly above a branch of Ambrosiano which, like all Italian banks, is protected on a 24-hour basis by armed guards. As Rosone emerged into the street a man approached and began firing. Wounded in the legs, Rosone collapsed to the ground. The armed bank guards retaliated. Moments later the assailant was also laid out on the pavement. Dead. His name was Danilo Abbruciati.

The day after the attempted murder of Rosone, April 28th, Flavio Carboni paid the surviving leader of the Rome underworld 530,000 dollars. The job had been botched but Calvi was a man who honoured his debts with other people's money.

Calvi, who undoubtedly had ordered the assassination of his own deputy chairman, was quickly at the bedside of his wounded colleague, complete with the statutory bunch of flowers. 'Madonna! What a world of madmen. They want to frighten us, Roberto, so that they can get their hands on a Group worth 20,000 billion lire.'

In May 1982 the screws began to tighten on Calvi. Consob, the Milan Stock Market Regulatory Agency, finally forced him to list his shares publicly on the Milan Stock Exchange. Such a listing would necessitate an independent audit of the Bank's books.

Roberto Calvi's wife Clara has stated under oath that earlier that year in a private audience with Pope John Paul II, Calvi had discussed the problem of the billion dollar debt the Vatican had incurred very largely through the efforts of Calvi, Gelli, Ortolani and Marcinkus. The Pope allegedly made Calvi a promise. 'If you can extricate the Vatican from this debt you can have full control of rebuilding our finances.'

If this offer was indeed made then His Holiness was obviously seeking more of the same. It was to be business as usual for ever and ever with no Amen.

The Pope and Calvi were only two of many beginning to show real concern about the fortune in dollars that had poured into the Vatican-owned off-shore companies. On May 31st, 1982, the Bank of Italy wrote to Calvi and his board of directors in Milan. They demanded that the board give a full account of foreign lending by the Banco Ambrosiano Group. The board of directors, in a pitifully late show of resistance to Calvi, voted 11 to 3 to comply with the central bank's demand.

Licio Gelli, who had secretly returned from Argentina to Europe on May 10th, was another making demands on Calvi. Gelli was in the market for more Exocet missiles to help his adopted country in their Falklands war with Great Britain. With the bulk of Argentina's foreign assets frozen and an official arms embargo operating, Gelli was obliged to turn to the black market arms dealers, who displayed some scepticism about Gelli's ability to pay what he was offering for the deadly missiles. He was offering four million dollars per missile, with a minimum order of twenty. At six times the official price there was considerable interest in the order, subject to Gelli raising the necessary money. He was well known to the arms dealers as a man who in the past had purchased radar equipment, planes, guns, tanks and the original Exocets on behalf of Argentina. Now he was in need of at least 80 million dollars and the need was urgent. The war in the Falklands hung in the balance.

Thus, Calvi, already juggling the needs of Pope John Paul II, his

Mafia clientele, his irate shareholders, the Consob watchdogs on the Milan Stock Exchange, a recalcitrant board of directors and an incompetent assassin who had succeeded in getting himself killed, yet again found Gelli with his hand out.

Calvi saw only two avenues of survival. Either the Vatican had to help him fill the ever-growing hole that was appearing in the Bank's assets or Gelli, the Puppet Master, must yet again demonstrate that he still controlled the Italian power structure and save his P2 paymaster from ruin.

Calvi discussed the options with Flavio Carboni, who continued secretly to run tape on their conversations.

It is clear from Calvi's remarks that he considered the Vatican Bank should fill the huge hole in Banco Ambrosiano if for no other reason than that they were the main beneficiaries of the missing millions and further that they were legally obligated. Calvi observed: 'The Vatican should honour its commitments by selling part of the wealth controlled by the IOR. It is an enormous patrimony. I estimate it to be 10 billion dollars. To help the Ambrosiano the IOR could start to sell in chunks of a billion at a time.'

If any layman in the world should have known the worth of the Vatican that man should have been Roberto Calvi. He was privy to virtually all of its financial secrets. For over a decade he had been *the* man to whom the Vatican had turned in financial matters. I have previously noted that at the time Albino Luciani became Pope in 1978 the wealth controlled by both sections of APSA and the Vatican Bank was conservatively in the region of three billion dollars. Now in early 1982 the highly conservative Roberto Calvi placed the patrimony of the IOR alone at 10 billion dollars.

It is clear that as 1982 progressed the man who is mistakenly known to the world as 'God's Banker' had a multitude of problems, the majority of them self-created. 'God's Thief' would be a more appropriate title for this man who stole millions on behalf of the Vatican and P2. Since the late 1960s there has been only one man who deserves the sobriquet of 'God's Banker' and that is Archbishop Paul Marcinkus.

In spite of the formidable range of problems confronting him at the time, problems that were only partly known to me, Roberto Calvi was initially calm when I interviewed him by telephone during the evening of June 9th, 1982. The interview had been arranged by an intermediary whom Calvi trusted. It covered a wide range of subjects. Through my interpreter, I began to question Calvi closely about the Banca Cattolica del Veneto transaction. He had been told that I was writing a book about the Vatican and when I mentioned the bank in Venice he asked what the central subject of the book was. I told him, 'It's a book on the life of Pope John Paul I, Papa Luciani.'

Calvi's manner suddenly underwent a complete change. The calmness and control vanished, to be replaced with a torrent of loud remarks. His voice became excited and very emotional. My interpreter began to translate the stream of words for me.

'Who has sent you against me? Who has told you to do this thing? Always I pay. Always I pay. How do you know Gelli? What do you want? How much do you want?'

I protested that I had never met Licio Geili. Calvi had barely stopped to listen to me before he began again.

'Whoever you are, you will not write this book. I can tell you nothing. Do not call me again. Ever.'

Eight days later the body of Roberto Calvi was found hanging under Blackfriars Bridge in the City of London.

Within days a hole was discovered in Banco Ambrosiano Milan. A 1.3 billion dollar hole.

The central purpose of my investigation has been the death of another man, Albino Luciani. Villot, Calvi, Marcinkus, Sindona, Gelli, Cody: one of these men was at the very heart of the conspiracy that resulted in the murder of Luciani. Before you, the reader, consider your verdict, let us take one final look at these men.

Cardinal Jean Villot, whom Albino Luciani had decided to remove from office, retained his position as Secretary of State upon the election of Karol Wojtyla. He also retained his many other posts including the control of the vital financial section, the Administration of the Patrimony of the Holy See, APSA. It was APSA that took the role of bride in the Sindona/Vatican marriage. Archbishop Marcinkus has frequently been castigated for bringing Sindona inside Vatican City. He bears no responsibility for that act. The decision was taken by Pope Paul, Monsignor Macchi, Umberto Ortolani and the gentlemen of the APSA, including, naturally, its head, Cardinal Villot. If Luciani had lived, then Villot's removal from the Secretariat of State would also have meant his automatic removal from the APSA. It is this organization with its immense portfolio of investments, not Marcinkus's Vatican Bank, that is recognized as a central bank by the World Bank, the International Monetary Fund and the Bank of International Settlement in Basle. It is a section that has much to hide, dating back to its deep involvement with Sindona.

At the time of Luciani's election, Villot had only a short while to live. He was a sick, tired man who by September 1978 knew he was seriously ill. He died less than six months after Luciani on March 9th, 1979. His death, according to the Vatican, was due to 'bilateral bronchial pneumonia attacks with complications, circulatory collapse, renal and hepatic insufficiency'. It was known that he had wanted to retire but it was also known he wished to determine his successor, and the man he had in mind was not Benelli. If Benelli discovered the scandal of the APSA section he would undoubtedly alert the new Pope. This, combined with the other changes that Villot knew Luciani was about to make, created a powerful motive. If he was at the heart of any conspiracy to murder Luciani the motive would have been the future direction of the Church. On the testimony of three Vatican witnesses, Villot considered the changes that were about to be implemented 'a betrayal of Paul's will. A triumph for the restoration'. He feared that they would take the Church back to pre-Vatican Council II. That his fear was invalid is not relevant. Villot felt it and felt it profoundly. He was also bitterly opposed to Luciani's plan to modify the Roman Catholic Church's position on birth control, which would have permitted Catholics throughout the world to use the contraceptive pill. With Paul VI, the creator of *Humanae Vitae*, barely dead, Villot was watching at close range the destruction of an edict he had many times publicly supported. Did Villot conclude that the greater good of the Church would be served with Luciani's death?

His behaviour after the Pope's death was either that of a man who was responsible for or deeply involved in that death, or of a man suffering a severe moral crisis. He destroyed evidence. He lied. He imposed a vow of silence on members of the Papal household. He rushed through an embalming before a majority of the cardinals were in Rome, let alone consulted. If Villot is blameless with regard to Luciani's death, then he most certainly materially assisted whoever was responsible. His actions and statements ensured that someone got away with murder. He himself clearly had a motive; it is also clear he had opportunity. In addition, by dint of his position as Camerlengo, he had virtually total control over immediate subsequent events or, as in the refusal to perform an official autopsy, non-events.

It may well be that the various illegal actions perpetrated by Villot after the discovery of Albino Luciani's body were motivated by what Villot considered the paramount factor, the greater good of the Catholic Church, if he saw clear evidence of murder, clear proof that Albino Luciani did not die a natural death. Many would contend that his subsequent actions were to protect the Church. Even given that rationale, I would still contend that morally he would appear to have been in need of help.

Cardinal John Cody, another of the men Luciani had been determined to remove from office, retained his position as Cardinal of Chicago upon the election of Albino Luciani's successor Karol Wojtyla. In his book, *The Making of The Popes*, Father Andrew Greeley observes:

> Cardinal Cody parlayed his past financial contributions to Poland (and some new contributions, according to Chicago sources), the size of the Polish population in Chicago, and his alleged friendship with the Pope, into a successful counter offensive against his enemies. John Paul II, according to what the Cardinal told visitors in early December [1978], offered him a job in Rome, which he declined. The Pope, the Cardinal intimated, indicated the matter was closed.

My own research confirms this. Further, the financial contributions Cody subsequently made to the Vatican and which were secretly funnelled into Poland, were part of a much larger operation that Marcinkus and Calvi undertook on behalf of Pope John Paul II.

Cardinal Cody continued to be a lavish donor of gifts. In October 1979 Pope John Paul II visited the USA. When he arrived at O'Hare airport in Chicago he was met by Cardinal Cody who thrust a small wooden box into the Pope's hands as 'a personal gift'. Inside the box were 50,000 dollars. No one would deny the Cardinal the right to give the Pope a gift but, apart from the crassness of the gesture, the question this act raises is, where did the money come from? Was it from diocesan funds? Was it from funds exclusively controlled by Cody? From exactly what source had 50,000 dollars so mysteriously appeared?

Within a year of this incident, the United States Government had mounted an official but secret investigation into Cody. US attorneys began to probe allegations that Cardinal Cody had illegally diverted up to one million dollars of Church funds to his life-long friend Helen Wilson. They also began to investigate a variety of other allegations including that he had commingled personal and Church funds, that he had paid Helen Wilson a secret salary over many years, that he had improperly awarded her pension benefits, that he had bought for her a 90,000 dollar home in Florida. That all of this had been done allegedly with Church funds which are tax exempt, made it a Government issue.

In view of the highly sensitive political implications of such an investigation, the fact that the Government initiated the enquiry is indicative of the very strong prima facie case that existed. The investigation began in September 1980.

In January 1981 the Federal Grand Jury served a number of subpoenas on Cody, demanding to see his financial records. If Cody was as pure as the driven snow, his subsequent behaviour is unaccountable. Only the Cardinal, his lawyers and one or two very close confidants knew of the investigation and subpoenas. Cody kept the developments from the people of Chicago, from the Apostolic Delegate in Washington and from the Vatican. He also refused to comply with the Government requests to hand over the diocesan financial records. For an ordinary citizen to decline to co-operate would have meant prison but Cody, who is on record as declaring, 'I don't run the country but I do run Chicago', demonstrated that the boast was not an empty one.

In September 1981, when the *Chicago Sun Times* broke the story, Cody had still not complied with the subpoenas. The *Sun Times* had been conducting its own investigation of the Cardinal for nearly two years. It proceeded to give its readers chapter and verse on a large array of allegedly appalling crimes committed by Cody.

The Cardinal refused to produce a shred of evidence that would have rebutted the wide variety of charges and attempted instead to rally behind him the 2,440,000 Catholics of the city with the assertion: 'This is not an attack on me. It is an attack on the entire Church.'

Many responded to this totally fallacious statement. Many did not. The massive damage to the image and reputation of the Roman Catholic Church which Albino Luciani had rightly foreseen was now a reality. The city was divided. Initially it is clear that the majority supported Cody but, as the months dragged by, one fundamental fact began to sink in. Cody had still not complied with the Government subpoenas. His own close supporters began to demand that he obey the Government. His initial response through his lawyers had been, 'I am only answerable to God and Rome.' It was a concept that he took to the grave. In April 1982, with the Government still waiting for answers, Cardinal Cody died. Notwithstanding that he had a long history of illness, Cody's body, unlike Albino Luciani's, was subject to an autopsy. His death had been caused by 'severe coronary artery disease'.

He had left a final message to be read out after his death. It contained no proof of his innocence with regard to the very serious charges that he had faced. It contained instead that arrogance which had been such a feature of his entire life. 'I forgive my enemies but God will not.'

With the tyrannical despot Cody dead, there had been immediate speculation about his successor. A name frequently mentioned was that of Archbishop Paul Marcinkus, citizen of Cicero, Chicago, who was currently drowning in scandal in Italy. The US Church hierarchy demurred and advised the Vatican that to give Chicago to Marcinkus, 'would be more of the same'. In the event the position went to Archbishop Joseph Bernardin of Cincinatti who promised an immediate Church investigation into L'Affaire Cody.

The Government announced that it was closing its own enquiry and the Federal Grand Jury investigation was terminated without any charges being brought. In view of the fact that the man who had been accused was dead, there was little alternative.

In December 1982, Bernardin issued a two-page pastoral letter to Chicago's Catholics. The letter was not supported with any documentary evidence. Bernardin concluded that a probe of Cody's finances showed no wrong-doing, that he may have unfairly awarded a pension to Helen Wilson, that he 'did not always follow preferred accounting procedures'. More significantly, accountants whom Bernardin had employed, refused to certify the 'accuracy of the estimated receipt and expenditure figures' though they found the figures 'within an acceptable range of reasonableness for the purposes of the inquiry'. The reason the accountants refused to certify the records was because, as Bernardin admitted, some of the financial records of the archdiocese could not be located and, 'if they were subsequently to become available, then the conclusions might require reevaluation'. Nearly two years later, those financial records are still missing.

The despotic, arrogant Cody clearly had a motive, and a powerful one, to involve himself in a conspiracy to murder Albino Luciani. A question mark may remain with regard to his financial corruption. There can be no doubt that Cody suffered from acute paranoia. If he was a paranoid psychotic it is entirely consistent that he would have sought to solve his problems, real or imagined, in a violent manner. Clearly if any Pope was going to remove Cody from Chicago it would be over his dead body – either Cody's or the Pope's. Through his many early years in Rome and then during his numerous visits, Cody had succeeded in ingratiating himself with two future Popes, Pacelli and Montini, and he had built up a large network of friends and informants.

That this man could put two fingers in the air to Pope Paul VI is an indication of his power. The many cash gifts, not only to Poland but to favoured members of the Roman Curia, also consolidated a peculiar brand of loyalty. Cody had his own Mafia or P2 planted deep within Vatican City – men with constant access to the Papal Apartments.

Archbishop Paul Marcinkus, the third of the men Albino Luciani had been determined to remove from office, retained his position as head of the Vatican Bank upon the election of Karol Wojtyla. Indeed, as previously recorded, he has been promoted to Archbishop and given even greater power. For a man who observed upon his initial appointment to the Vatican Bank, 'my only previous financial experience is handling the Sunday collection', Marcinkus has come a long way. He has far greater claim to the title of 'God's Banker' than either of his two former close friends and business associates, Roberto Calvi and Michele Sindona. He can also justly claim to have brought the Roman Catholic Church into greater disrepute than any other priest in modern times.

It is abundantly clear that in the mid-1970s Calvi and Marcinkus devised a scheme that spawned a multitude of crimes. It is equally clear that the Panamanian and other off-shore companies the Vatican owned, and still own, were run for the mutual benefit of Banco Ambrosiano and the Vatican Bank.

The Vatican has claimed since Calvi's death that the first it knew of the off-shore companies and its ownership of them was in August 1981. This is yet another Vatican lie. Documentary evidence established that, as early as 1978, Bishop Marcinkus was actively ensuring that the fact that these companies were owned by the Vatican was suppressed. As for the Vatican's lack of knowledge of the companies it owned, one example will suffice. UTC, United Trading Corporation of Panama, is one of the companies referred to in the letters of comfort, a company that the Vatican now claims it knew nothing about until shortly before the notorious letters were written by Marcinkus. Documentation dated November 21st, 1974, duly signed by Vatican Bank officials, requests that Calvi's Banca del Gottardo arrange on behalf of the Vatican Bank the formation of a company called United Trading Corporation.

For Calvi the illegal scheme had many virtues. And what did the Vatican Bank gain? It gained money. Vast amounts of it. Calvi bought his own shares, from himself; at greatly inflated prices, but on paper these shares were legally owned, *and still are legally owned*, by the Panamanian companies who, in turn, are owned by the Vatican. Calvi duly turned over the annual dividend on the huge block of shares to their rightful owners, the Vatican Bank. The sum involved varied over the years but averages out annually at 2 million dollars.

That was but the tip of the iceberg. More substantial gains can be traced. For example, in 1980 the Vatican Bank sold 2 million shares in a Rome-based international construction company called Vianini. The shares were sold to a small Panamanian company called Laramie. It was the first stage of a deal in which it was planned that the Vatican would sell to Laramie 6 million shares in Vianini. The price of the shares was grossly inflated. The first 2 million cost Laramie 20 million dollars. Laramie is yet another of the companies owned by the Vatican. It might be considered a futile exercise to sell yourself your own shares at an inflated figure. It becomes less futile if you are using someone else's money, as Calvi had demonstrated over the years. The 20 million dollars to pay for the shares came from Roberto Calvi. And the Vatican Bank kept the shares it already owned and the 20 million dollars as well. Further, it did not and never has owned 6 million shares in Vianini. Its maximum stake in the company has never been more than 3 million shares. It was with schemes like this that Calvi paid off Marcinkus.

In March 1982, Archbishop Marcinkus granted a rare interview. It was given to the Italian weekly *Panorama*. His comments about Roberto Calvi are particularly illuminating, coming as they did just eight months after Calvi had been fined 13.7 million dollars and sentenced to four years' imprisonment, and only seven months after the Vatican and Marcinkus discovered (if we believe the Vatican version) that Calvi had stolen over a billion dollars and left the Vatican to pay the bill.

> Calvi merits our trust. This I have no reason to doubt. We have no intention of ceding the Banco Ambrosiano shares in our possession: and furthermore, we have other investments in this group, for example in the Banca Cattolica, which are going very well.

It is on a par with that other eulogy given by Marcinkus to the USA Government attorneys and the men from the FBI, who were investigating the alleged involvement of Marcinkus in a billion dollar counterfeit bond swindle in April 1973. On that occasion, it may be remembered, Marcinkus was extolling the virtues of a man he now claims to have hardly ever met, a man who, for his part, insists, 'We met many many times over the course of the years in which we did business together. Marcinkus was my partner in two banks.' That man is Michele Sindona who, apart from his many other crimes, is responsible for the biggest single banking disaster in United States history, a man whom Marcinkus considered to be 'well ahead of his time as far as banking matters are concerned'.

It may be argued on behalf of Marcinkus that his observation was made a year before Il Crack Sindona. In 1980, six years after the Sindona crash, Marcinkus was ready to testify on behalf of Sindona and was only stopped by the intervention of Cardinal Casaroli, who felt obliged to overrule Pope John Paul II.

Today, there is only one reason why Marcinkus has not been further elevated to cardinal. Despite the massive world-wide disgrace that his activities have brought upon the Vatican and Roman Catholicism, Karol Wojtyla was still going ahead with plans to give the man from Cicero a red hat. Again, only the insistence of Casaroli saved the day. It would seem the Pope takes a more tolerant view of sins perpetrated behind a bank counter than he does of sins perpetrated in bed.

With regard to the murder of Albino Luciani, Marcinkus had the motive and the opportunity. One of the many functions he performed for Paul VI was that of the role of personal Papal bodyguard and security adviser. As such his knowledge of the security arrangements, such as they were, was unsurpassed. Exactly why the President of the IOR was wandering around the Vatican City shortly after 6.30 a.m. on the morning on which Albino Luciani was discovered dead had yet to be established. Research indicates that Marcinkus could not normally be found near the bank premises at such an early hour. Unlike Villot he did not live inside the Vatican walls but at the Villa Stritch in Rome. Marcinkus brought many facets to his work in the Vatican Bank; not least were elements of his early childhood in Al Capone's Cicero. 'How are your gangster friends in Chicago, Paul?' was a running joke in the early 1970s. It was heard less after Sindona's trial. It is not heard at all after the Calvi débâcle.

If not actively involved in the conspiracy to murder Albino Luciani it is possible that Marcinkus acted as a catalyst, wittingly or unwittingly. Many years ago an English king cried out, 'Will no one rid me of this meddlesome priest?' and soon after, the Roman Catholic Church had a martyr in the person of Thomas à Becket. There is no doubt that Marcinkus conveyed in full his fears on the new Papacy to Roberto Calvi. There is equally no doubt that Albino Luciani was about to remove Marcinkus from the Vatican Bank and cut off all links with Banco Ambrosiano. Did the fears that Marcinkus expressed not only to Calvi but to others about this new Pope provoke the course of events that, on the morning of September 29th, left Bishop Marcinkus open-mouthed and stunned when a Swiss Guard told him the Pope was dead?

Michele Sindona is often incorrectly referred to as 'God's Banker'. A more accurate label would be 'God's Speculator'. At the time of Albino Luciani's murder, Sindona was fighting an extradition order served by the Italian Government. He was also wanted for questioning in regard to a wide variety of financial crimes in a number of other countries. By September 1978 the likelihood of the United States authorities initiating criminal proceedings against him, with regard to the Franklin Bank collapse, was becoming more of a certainty daily. These proceedings would save him from extradition but would place him in immediate jeopardy in the United States. The one remaining ace he could hope to play was dependent on Vatican co-operation. Sindona reasoned that if Bishop Marcinkus, Cardinal Guerri and Cardinal Caprio gave evidence on his behalf; a jury would be very heavily influenced by statements from three such august people. With Albino Luciani as Pope, the possibility of any Vatican testimony, let alone favourable testimony, did not exist.

Sindona, as a member of both the Mafia and P2, had not only the motive and opportunity for murder but, as has been amply demonstrated, he also had the capacity. He was a man deranged enough to believe that if an Assistant District Attorney were murdered his troubles in the United States would be at an end – a man deranged enough to believe that if he ordered the murder of Giorgio Ambrosoli his Italian problems would vanish. Such a man clearly had the capacity to remove an honest, reforming Pope.

Sindona remains a man very much in demand. There is the three-and-a-half-year prison sentence already passed on him in Italy. There is the continuing American investigation into the helicopter attempt in January 1981 to rescue him from his United States prison. There is the July 1981 Italian Government indictment charging him with having ordered the murder of Giorgio Ambrosoli. Also named in that arrest warrant are his son Nino Sindona and his son-in-law Pier Sandro Magnoni. There is the January 1982 indictment from Palermo, Sicily in which he and 65 members of the Gambino, Inzerillo and Spatola Mafia families were charged with operating a 600 million dollar per year heroin trade between Sicily and the United States. There are the further Sicilian indictments which charge Sindona with illegal possession of arms, fraud, using a false passport and violating currency regulations. Then there are the further indictments issued by the Italian government in July 1982 charging Sindona and others, including the Vatican's Massimo Spada and Luigi Mennini, with a long list of criminal offences connected with the fraudulent bankruptcy of Banca Privata Italiana. It is only fitting that the prosecution's case with regard to these last alleged offences be based, very largely, on the valiant work of the murdered Giorgio Ambrosoli. No words of mine could describe so exactly what manner of man Sindona is and what manner of family he has spawned, as those uttered by his son Nino Sindona. He was talking on tape with the writer Luigi di Fonzo. (The tape is now with the New York prosecutor's office.) The long interview took place during the evening of March 18th and the early hours of March 19th, 1983.

> My father admitted to me that it was Arico . . . who committed the murder.* They were threatening Ambrosoli and it was effective for a while. Billy Arico was sent to Milan by Venetucci [a heroin smuggler and alleged member of the Gambino family] at my father's request, and was supposed to shoot at Ambrosoli, but not kill him. Arico committed the murder . . . Ambrosoli's family do not deserve any pity. I have no compassion for the fucking guy and this is not enough for a son of a bitch like him. I'm sorry he died without suffering. Let's make sure on this point. I'm never going to condemn my father because Ambrosoli doesn't deserve to be on this earth . . . My father has gone through enough. Now it's time our enemies go through something. Griesa, Kenney, it's their turn to suffer. Not my father again, not us. We have done nothing . . . To obtain justice there could be no crime that I would be afraid of committing. People like Kenney, Griesa, they could die of the worst pain, and for me it would be only a case for a big champagne celebration. I believe in justifiable homicide.

Thomas Griesa was the trial judge in the United States *v*. Sindona. John Kenney was the chief prosecutor. Luigi di Fonzo asked Nino Sindona how he could justify murder.

---

*On Sunday February 19th William Arico fell to his death while trying to escape from the Metropolitan Correctional Center in lower Manhattan. Arico and Michele Sindona were due to face an extradition hearing two days later. The Italian authorities wanted to place both men on trial for the murder of Giorgio Ambrosoli.

I could justify it in about a second and a half. Like I could justify political murder in a second and a half. Let's assume I want to kill Judge Griesa. For me it's self defence . . . because he committed the enormous crime of putting my father in jail for life. And there is no chance of a re-trial as long as Judge Griesa is alive. So by killing him we will obtain a chance for a re-trial. So self defence.

Clearly for people like Michele Sindona and his son to murder a Pope who stood in their way would be 'self defence'.

Roberto Calvi. It was once said by Lenin: 'Give a capitalist enough rope and he will hang himself.' Clearly the first coroner's jury that considered the death of Calvi agreed with Lenin. It returned a verdict of suicide. The fact that the hearing was compressed into a day, that witnesses were missing, that witnesses committed sustained perjury, and very little of the highly relevant background evidence was presented did not appear to disturb the Coroner. In Italy the verdict was greeted with incredulity. In 1983 a second Coroner's jury got nearer the truth when it returned an open verdict on the man who had been found hanging appropriately next to a sewer outlet.

I am in no doubt that Calvi was 'suicided' by his P2 friends – yet another example of the very high risks that are attendant if one pursues a career in Italian banking. Hours before Calvi died, his secretary in Milan, Graziella Corrocher, was 'suicided' from a fourth floor window at the Banco Ambrosiano headquarters in Milan. Her 'death note', which showered curses on Roberto Calvi, was discovered by Roberto Rosone, still walking with the aid of sticks after the attempt on his life. A few months later on October 2nd, 1982, Giuseppe Dellacha, an executive at the bank, was also 'suicided' from a window in the Milan headquarters. Calvi's widow, Clara, is on record as laying the blame for her husband's death at the bronze doors of the Vatican: 'The Vatican had my husband killed to hide the bankruptcy of the Vatican Bank.'

If it did, and it is not a view I share, then it would perhaps be poetic justice. The case against Roberto Calvi with regard to his direct involvement in the death of Albino Luciani is strong. Very strong.

Calvi was engaged in the progressive, continuing theft of over one billion dollars, a theft that would have been completely exposed if Luciani had lived. That exposure would have occurred in 1978. With Luciani dead, Calvi was free to continue his colossal and frightening array of crimes. Over 400 million dollars of the money that has apparently vanished in a Panamanian triangle was borrowed by Calvi from the world's banks *after* the death of Albino Luciani.

Calvi advised everyone to read *The Godfather* because, as he used to say, 'Then you will understand the ways of the world.' It was certainly the way of the world he inhabited.

Until the end of his life he was laundering money for the Mafia, the role he had inherited from Michele Sindona. He was also recycling money for P2. These functions were carried out with the assistance of the Vatican Bank, with money moving from Banco Ambrosiano into a Vatican account in Italy, then on to Banco Gottardo or UBS in Switzerland. He laundered money from kidnappings, drugs sales, arms deals, bank raids, hold-ups, thefts of jewellery and works of art. His criminal contacts ranged from what is known as High Mafia to ordinary, run-of-the-mill murderers, through to right-wing terrorist organizations.

The 1.3 billion dollar hole in Banco Ambrosiano was not only created by the fraudulent purchase of shares in Calvi's own bank. Many millions went to sustain Gelli and Ortolani. Fifty-five million dollars, for example, were diverted by Calvi from Peru to a numbered account at UBS Zürich. The owner of that account is Licio Gelli. Another 30 million dollars were diverted into Swiss accounts owned by Calvi's close friend Flavio Carboni.

In early 1982 Calvi transferred direct from the mother bank in Milan 470 million dollars to Peru. He then gave his secretary an air ticket to Monte Carlo and a pile of Telex messages. The messages duly sent from Monte Carlo moved the money into a variety of Swiss numbered accounts.

The Italian political parties of Christian Democrats, Communists and Socialists were not the only political factions to have a bite at the golden apple. Millions were given at Gelli's direct instructions to the military regimes which then controlled Argentina, and still control Uruguay and Paraguay. Money stolen by Calvi was used by the Argentine military junta to purchase Exocet missiles from the French; Calvi's bank in Peru assisted in that deal. Millions went secretly and illegally to aid Solidarity in Poland. This particular transaction was a mix of money that Calvi had stolen and Vatican bank funds collected from the Catholic faithful. Calvi often talked about these transactions to trusted friends. They included Carboni who, like all good Masons, was secretly running a tape recorder:

> Marcinkus must watch out for Casaroli, who is head of the group that opposes him. If Casaroli should meet one of those financiers in New York who are working for Marcinkus, sending money to

Solidarity, the Vatican would collapse. Or even if Casaroli should find just one of those pieces of paper that I know of – Goodbye Marcinkus. Goodbye Wojtyla. Goodbye Solidarity. The last operation would be enough, the one for 20 million dollars. I've also told Andreotti but it's not clear which side he is on. If things in Italy go a certain way, the Vatican will have to hire a building in Washington behind the Pentagon. A far cry from St Peter's.

The total amount that was secretly and illegally funnelled on behalf of the Vatican to Solidarity was in excess of one hundred million dollars. Many who hold the strongest sympathies with Solidarity might well applaud such action. To interfere in such a manner, however, with the affairs of another country creates a dangerous precedent. Why not a hundred million funnelled secretly to the IRA to kill and maim on the British mainland? A billion dollars to the Sandinistans to blow up a few skyscrapers in New York, Chicago and San Francisco? Playing God, even for a Pope, can be a dangerous occupation. For Karol Wojtyla publicly to upbraid Nicaraguan priests for participating in politics while he interferes in such a profound manner with the affairs of Poland is breathtaking hypocrisy.

We have no temporal goods to exchange, no economic interests to discuss. Our possibilities for intervention are specific and limited and of a special character. They do not interfere with the purely temporal, technical and political affairs, which are matters for your governments.

Thus spoke Albino Luciani to the Diplomatic Corps accredited to the Vatican. It is clear that the man who has succeeded him takes precisely the opposite point of view.

With regard to the murder of Albino Luciani, Roberto Calvi had the motive, the opportunity and undoubtedly, like Michele Sindona, the capacity.

Before Luciani's murder, Calvi associates in P2 had demonstrated their capacity to kill with a variety of appalling bomb outrages. Their ability to kill a specific subject was demonstrated with the murder of Vittorio Occorsio. After the death of the Pope, murder and mayhem began to match the tempo of the gigantic thefts in which Calvi was indulging. The fact that Emilio Alessandrini, Mino Pecorelli, Giorgio Ambrosoli, Antonio Varisco and Boris Giuliano are all dead, is the most telling evidence of the kind of company that

54 The Milan headquarters of Roberto Calvi.
55 Bologna railway station, 1980, when 85 people were killed and 182 injured in a bomb explosion masterminded by P2.

56 By 1980 Roberto Rosone *(left)*; deputy chairman of Banco Ambrosiano, was becoming a threat to Calvi's activities. On April 27th, 1980 Rosone was shot and seriously wounded.

57 The body of Rosone's assailant, Danilo Abbruciati, after he was shot dead by Banco Ambrosiano guards.

58 Flavio Carboni *(centre right)*, friend of Roberto Calvi.
59 Roberto Calvi 'suicided' in London on June 17/18th, 1982.

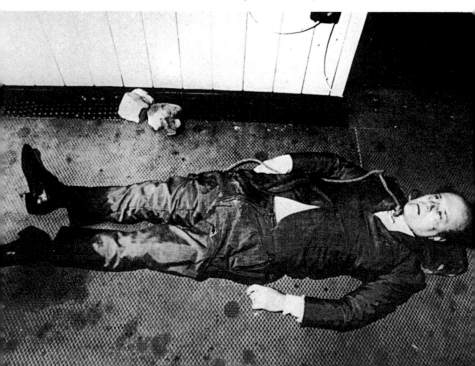

60 A few hours before Calvi's death his secretary, Graziella Corrocher, was also 'suicided' from the fourth floor of the Banco Ambrosiano headquarters. An ambulance leaves with her body.

61 With all the other suspects dead, in prison, or fugitives from justice, Marcinkus *(centre foreground)* remains inside the Vatican.

62 'God's Banker' in his bank.
63 Umberto Ortolani.

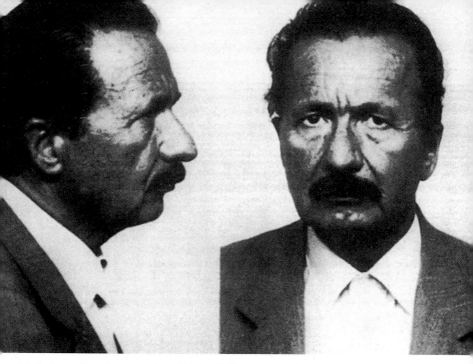

64 Swiss police photographs of Licio Gelli.
65 Michele Sindona is serving 25 years in prison in the U.S.A.

Roberto Calvi kept. The fact that the Governor of the Bank of Italy and one of his most trusted colleagues could be falsely charged, that Sarcinelli was forced to endure two weeks of imprisonment, that for years men who knew the truth were frightened to act, is a demonstration of the terrifying power at the command of Calvi: power that came from many sources including Licio Gelli, Grand Master of P2.

Licio Gelli was the Puppet Master with a few thousand strings from which to select. Strings appear to have led everywhere: to the heart of the Vatican, to the White House, to Presidential palaces in a wide range of countries. It was Gelli who gave his singular advice to senior P2 members that they should always carry a fatal dose of digitalis. A lethal dose will cause, to use a lay term, a heart attack. Any subsequent examination by a doctor that is merely external, will confirm that death has been caused by a myocardial infarction. The drug is odourless and is impossible to trace unless an autopsy is performed.

Why did Licio Gelli use such a strange codename, 'Luciani', whenever he called his P2 paymaster on the special hotline? Was mere mention of the name enough to send the millions upon millions flowing from Calvi into Gelli's various bank accounts?

According to the members of Calvi's family, he attributed all his problems to 'the priests'. He made it clear which priests he had in mind – those in the Vatican. In September 1978 one priest in particular represented to Roberto Calvi the greatest threat with which he had ever been confronted. Calvi was with Gelli and Ortolani in South America in August 1978, planning new schemes. Can anyone really believe that Gelli and Ortolani would have merely shrugged their shoulders when Calvi told them that Albino Luciani was about to take a course of action that would mean the party was over?

The murder of a magistrate or a judge or a policeman could be effected openly. The death would remain a mystery or be blamed on one of the many terrorist organizations then rampaging throughout Italy. But the murder of a Pope to cover up what was ultimately a billion dollar theft would have to be achieved by stealth. It would have to arouse as little concern as possible. For the murder to achieve its aim, the death would have to appear natural.

The cost, no matter how high, in bribes, contracts, fees or commissions, was irrelevant. If the object of the Pope's death was to protect and sustain Roberto Calvi while he continued to steal millions, then there was a virtual well of truth to draw upon. The problem of deputy chairman Roberto Rosone, which Calvi discussed at great length with fellow Mason Carboni, was intended to be resolved with the contract murder of Rosone. He lived, but Carboni still paid 530,000 dollars, the day after the attack, to the surviving gangster Ernesto Diotavelli. Half a million for a deputy chairman. How much for a Pope? When you have an entire bank at your disposal?

After the death of Roberto Calvi, the most pertinent obituary came from Mario Sarcinelli, one of the many who had personally experienced the powers upon which Calvi could call. 'He began as a servant, then became a master, only to become the servant of other masters later on.' Calvi's ultimate master was the man I believe to be at the very heart of the conspiracy to murder Albino Luciani. Licio Gelli.

This book has already recorded many instances of the power and influence that Gelli has exerted. At the time of Albino Luciani's death in September 1978, Licio Gelli, to all practical purposes, ran Italy. His access to any person or any place within the Vatican City State was unrivalled. The fact that he was in South America at the time of Luciani's death is no alibi in the conventional legal sense. Sindona was enjoying an early evening dry Martini in New York at the precise moment that Giorgio Ambrosoli was murdered by William Arico in Milan. That arrangement will not save Sindona if the Italian authorities ever manage to have him extradited from the USA.

The Puppet Master, who uses the secret code-name 'Luciani', continues to give impressive demonstrations that he is a man of extraordinary influence. In 1979 Gelli and Ortolani began working to bring about a political reconciliation between Christian Democrat leader and former Prime Minister Giulio Andreotti and the Socialist leader Bettino Craxi. The exposure of nearly one thousand P2 members in 1981 slowed down these delicate negotiations. They have now flowered. At the time of writing the Prime Minister of Italy is Bettino Craxi, the Foreign Minister, Giulio Andreotti. Both men have much for which to thank Licio Gelli.

On April 8th, 1980, Gelli wrote from Italy to Phillip Guarino, a senior member of the Republican Party National Committee, which at the time was concentrating all its efforts on getting Ronald Reagan elected President. Gelli wrote: 'If you think it might be useful for something favourable to your Presidential candidate to be published in Italy, send me some material and I'll get it published in one of the papers here.'

Without any knowledge of the power that Gelli wielded it might seem a curious offer. How could a man who officially owned no newspapers guarantee a favourable mention and sympathetic coverage for Reagan? The answer was a consortium of P2 members plus the Vatican-controlled Rizzoli, the massive publishing group, with interests stretching as far as Buenos Aires. Among the many magazines and newspapers was *Corriere Della Sera*, Italy's most prestigious newspaper. Other P2 members were planted throughout the television, radio and newspaper media of the country. The favourable comments about Ronald Reagan, carefully placed by Licio Gelli, duly appeared in Italy.

In January 1981, Licio Gelli was an honoured guest at the Presidential inauguration. Guarino later ruefully observed, 'He had a better seat than I did.'

In May 1981, after the discovery of the list of nearly one thousand members of P2 that included several current Cabinet Ministers had led to the collapse of the Italian Government, Gelli continued his exercise of power from a variety of South American bases. An indication that Gelli was far from being a spent force can be seen in the movement of 95 million dollars by Calvi from Banco Ambrosiano to the Panamanian company of Bellatrix, one of the P2-controlled shell companies. This transfer, via a number of exotic routes including Rothschild in Zürich, Rothschild in Guernsey and the Banque Nationale de Paris in Panama, sprayed money in the most unlikely directions, including some 20 million dollars into Ansbacher & Co, a small merchant bank in Dublin.

One year later, in May 1982, with the Falklands war at its height, Licio Gelli, a man in hiding, on the run, wanted on countless charges, calmly came to Europe to help his Argentinian friends. The original Exocet missiles which Gelli had purchased for the junta had proved themselves to be a devastating weapon. As previously recorded, Gelli came to buy more. He stayed with Ortolani at a villa at Cap Ferrat and began secret negotiations not only with a variety of arms dealers but also with Aerospatiale, the makers of the missile. British Intelligence became aware of these negotiations and alerted their counterparts in the Italian Secret Service who promptly began to descend on the Cap Ferrat villa. They were prevented from getting to Gelli by the DST, the French Secret Service, who blatantly prevented all attempts to arrest Gelli. That is an example of the power of Licio Gelli.

While negotiating with a variety of potential Exocet suppliers, Gelli was also in daily contact with Calvi. The two Freemasons still had so much in common. By the second week of June 1982 Calvi, like Gelli, was also a man on the run. With his Ambrosiano empire on the verge of collapse he had illegally left Italy, first travelling to Austria and subsequently to London. He and Gelli once again had a deep mutual need for each other. Calvi needed protection from the Italian authorities, Gelli needed many millions for the Exocet purchase. My research indicates that the French were planning to find a way round the arms sales embargo then operating against Argentina. The missiles would find their way to Argentina via Peru. French technicians were standing by to be flown out to modify the Exocets for the Argentinian Air Force.

For Gelli and Calvi their priorities clashed fatally. The war would not wait while the Puppet Master pulled his Italian strings. Calvi, at Gelli's suggestion, travelled to London and to his death. He was 'suicided' on June 17th, 1982, the same day that General Galtieri was replaced as President of Argentina by General Bignone. Argentina had lost the war. Calvi's P2 colleagues considered that by failing to divert money promptly for the Exocets he had contributed to that defeat.

In August 1982, the Argentinian junta secretly decided to recommence hostilities against the British forces guarding the Falklands. They considered that a quantity of Exocets could bring them victory and the islands.

This time Gelli dealt with a former officer of the Italian Secret Service, Colonel Massimo Pugliese, a member of P2. Again British Intelligence learned of the proposed deal. They ensured it aborted.

During the same month, August 1982, Gelli was encountering a problem with one of his secret bank accounts in Switzerland. It was not performing to order. Every time that Gelli, in South America, attempted to transfer money, the UBS in Geneva declined to comply with the instructions. Gelli was advised that he would have to appear at the bank personally.

Using a false Argentinian passport, he flew to Madrid and then to Geneva on September 13th, 1982. He presented his false documentation and was advised there would be a short delay. Minutes later he was arrested. He had walked into a carefully prepared trap. The account had been frozen at the request of the Italian Government who had been advised by the Swiss of the real identity of the account holder.

The account had been created for Gelli by Roberto Calvi. Into it the Milanese banker had poured over 100 million dollars. At the time of his arrest Gelli was attempting to have the 55 million dollars remaining in the account transferred to Uruguay.

Extradition proceedings began immediately, with Gelli singing the same song that had previously been chanted by Sindona and Calvi. 'I am a victim of political persecution. It is a plot of the left.' While Swiss magistrates considered the issues, Licio Gelli was held in one of Switzerland's maximum security prisons, Champ Dollon. Extradition proceedings involving any member of P2, as this book has already established, tend to be protracted. Gelli was still in Champ Dollon in the summer of 1983.

With Italy about to face another General Election in June, the parliamentary commission which had been investigating P2 was suspended. The Christian Democrat party fielded at least five P2 members at the election. Signorina Tina Anselmi, who had been chairman of the commission, was asked her views on P2 after two years' intensive study of the secret society. She said:

> P2 is by no means dead. It still has power. It is working in the institutions. It is moving in society. It has money, means and instruments still at its disposal. It still has fully operative power centres in South America. It is also still able to condition, at least in part, Italian political life.

The evidence overwhelmingly confirms the validity of Signorina Anselmi's statements. When news of Gelli's arrest became known in Argentina, Admiral Emilio Massera, a member of the ruling junta, remarked, 'Signoi Gelli has rendered invaluable service to Argentina. This country has much to thank him for and will forever be in his debt.'

Admiral Massera, like General Carlos Suarez Mason, the First Army commander, like the organizer of the Argentine Death Squads, José Lope Rega, is a member of the Argentine section of P2. In Uruguay P2 membership includes the former Commander in Chief of the Armed Forces, General Gregorio Alvarez.

If anyone in Italy or elsewhere considered that Tina Anselmi was merely attempting to score political points before an election they must have received a jolt on August 10th, 1983. Champ Dollon had one prisoner fewer than the day before. Licio Gelli had escaped. The Swiss authorities, attempting to cover their deep embarrassment, are now in the process of laying the entire blame at the feet of one corrupt guard, Umberto Cerdana, who officially took a derisory bribe of just over £6,000 from Gelli.* If any reader of this book believes that Gelli escaped from Switzerland with the help of only one prison guard, they also probably believe that Albino Luciani died a natural death. A guard takes the equivalent of four months' salary for an act that could now give him a prison sentence of seven-and-a-half years?

Nine days after Gelli's escape the Swiss authorities approved the extradition request from Italy. The trouble was that there was no Gelli to extradite. Driven first to France by his son in a hired BMW, the pair were transported by an unwitting helicopter pilot to Monte Carlo. The excuse given to the pilot for diverting from Nice and landing at Monte Carlo was that Gelli was in urgent need of dental treatment. Via a yacht belonging to Francesco Pazienza, a man who claims to have been a good friend of the late Roberto Calvi, Gelli continued his search for a good dentist in Uruguay, where at the time of writing he sits still pulling strings from a ranch a few miles north of Montevideo. He is wanted in many countries, accused of many crimes, but the mass of information that he has so diligently acquired over the years ensures that he continues to be protected.

The Italian election in June 1983 resulted in Signor Bettino Craxi, one of the many beneficiaries of Calvi's largesse, becoming Prime Minister. Told of Gelli's escape he said: 'The flight of Gelli confirms that the Grand Master has a network of powerful friends.'

If, and it is indeed a very large if, Licio Gelli is ever handed over alive to the Italian Government, he faces a variety of criminal charges. They include the following: extortion, blackmail, drug smuggling, arms smuggling, conspiracy to overthrow the legal Government, political espionage, military espionage, illegal possession of State secrets, involvement with a series of bomb outrages including the Bologna Station attack in which 84 people died.

The chain that link by link leads from a murdered Pope to Bishop Paul Marcinkus to Roberto Calvi to Umberto Ortolani and Licio Gelli is strong. For circumstantial evidence to succeed it must be strong, must sustain the closest scrutiny before a jury can bring in a verdict of 'guilty'. No jury confronted with the evidence contained in this book could return a verdict of 'death by natural causes'. No judge, no coroner in the world, would accept such a verdict on this evidence. That is beyond all argument. No evidence exists to indicate that

---

*Early in 1984 Cerdana was sentenced to eighteen months in prison. The sentence was suspended. The court received a letter from Gelli in which the Puppet Master recommended leniency. He also apologized for escaping and stated that he was a Victim of political persecution.

Albino Luciani's death was the result of an accident. We are left with murder. Not, in my view, by person or persons unknown, but by persons all too well known, with, at the heart of the conspiracy, Licio Gelli. Gelli was a man who happened to number among his P2 members the brother of Cardinal Sebastiano Baggio, Francesco. His meetings with the powerful and famous included audiences with Pope Paul VI. Gelli was a man whose close friends included Cardinal Paolo Bertoli. Gelli's closest P2 adviser, Umberto Ortolani, knew his way around Vatican City better than many cardinals. Ortolani, with his drawer full of Vatican honours and awards, was so close to the nerve centre of Vatican power that his was the villa, and he the host, at the pre-Conclave secret meeting that finalized strategy and brought about the election of Paul VI. It was Ortolani who conceived the idea of the multi-million dollar sale of the Vatican interests in Società Generale Immobiliare, Ceramiche Pozzi and Condotte d'Acqua. Ortolani was the P2 marriage broker, joining as partners the Mafioso and fellow P2 member Michele Sindona and Pope Paul VI. He collected vast commissions from one and Papal honours from the other. Gelli was also that collector of curious knowledge and information, including photographs of Pope John Paul II completely nude next to his swimming pool. When Gelli showed these snapshots to senior Socialist Party politician Vanni Nistico he remarked, 'Look at the problems the secret services have. If it's possible to take these pictures of the Pope, imagine how easy it is to shoot him.' Indeed. Or poison his predecessor.

> And Jesus went into the temple of God, and cast out all them that sold and bought in the temple, and overthrew the tables of the moneychangers, and the seats of them that sold doves,
>   And said unto them, It is written. My house shall be called the house of prayer; but ye have made it a den of thieves.
>   Matthew 21:12/13

Albino Luciani had a dream. He dreamt of a Roman Catholic Church which would truly respond to the needs of its people on vital issues such as birth control. He dreamt of a Church which would dispense with the wealth, power and prestige that it had acquired through Vatican Incorporated; of a Church which would get out of the market place and reject the moneylenders where the message of Christ had become tainted; of a Church that would once again rely upon what has always been its greatest asset, its source of true power, its greatest claim to a unique prestige: the Gospel.

By the evening of September 28th, 1978, Albino Luciani had taken the first steps towards the realization of his extraordinary dream. At 9.30 p.m. he closed his bedroom door and the dream ended.

In Italy now, there is talk of making Albino Luciani a Saint. Already petitions of many thousands of signatures have been collected. Ultimately if this man who was 'a poor man, accustomed to small things and silence' is beatified, it would be more than fitting. On September 28th, 1978 he was martyred for his beliefs. Confronted with a man like Albino Luciani, with the problems his continuing presence would pose, the Italian Solution was applied. The decision that the Pope must die was taken and God's Candidate was murdered.

Epilogue

❦

If the good that Albino Luciani represented was interred with his bones the evil perpetrated by Roberto Calvi has most certainly lived after him.

Within hours of his body being identified in London alarm bells were ringing in many places throughout Italy. On Monday, June 22nd, the first day the banks were opened after The Knight had been found hanging not far from where the White Friars had offered sanctuary to embezzlers, swindlers and thieves in the Middle Ages, the Banco Ambrosiano, Milan began to experience a heavy run of withdrawals. What is not public knowledge, until now, is that the Vatican Bank suffered the same fate. Many millions of dollars were withdrawn by those members of the Italian Establishment who, privy to the facts, were aware that a 1.3 billion dollar hole in the Ambrosiano group would soon be public knowledge and that the hole was not unconnected with Calvi's long-standing business and personal relationship with Paul Marcinkus and the IOR.

By September 1982, Marcinkus, the man who had never left the Pope's side during his visit to Britain in May and June, had become a virtual prisoner within the Vatican. He was replaced as organizer and advance guard of international Papal trips – to have ventured out of Vatican City would have been to invite immediate arrest by the Italian authorities.

Marcinkus continued to function as head of the Vatican Bank and declared that the Vatican did not and would not accept any responsibility for the 1.3 billion dollars which had gone missing.

The Roman Curia refused to accept judicial papers that the Italian

Government attempted to serve on Marcinkus and others at the Vatican Bank. Protocol must be observed at all times, the Curia insisted, even when the theft of over a billion dollars is involved. The papers would have to be handed to the Italian Ambassador to the Vatican.

Vatican City did establish a commission of enquiry after a great deal of prodding from the Italian Government. Simultaneously, the Vatican Bank's own lawyers busied themselves with an enquiry and at the same time the Italian Government created a commission of enquiry. By now there were jobs for nearly everyone. The lawyers working for Marcinkus came up with their conclusions first.

1 The Institute for the Works of Religion has not received either from the Ambrosiano Group or from Roberto Calvi any monies, and, therefore, does not have to refund anything.
2 The foreign Companies indebted to the Ambrosiano Group have never been run by the IOR which has no knowledge of the operations carried out by the same.
3 It is established that all the payments made by the Ambrosiano Group to the aforementioned Companies were made prior to the so-called 'letters of comfort'.
4 These latter, by their date of issue, have not exercised any influence on the same payments.
5 In any future checking of the facts, all the above will be proved to be true.

I have already established that these Vatican 'facts' are very far from the truth.

The commission of enquiry set up by the Vatican has yet to report. Their conclusions were due at the end of March 1983, then the end of April 1983, then August 1983, then October, then November.

The commission comprises 'four wise men'. Two of them, by their presence on a commission of enquiry that Cardinal Casaroli has predictably called 'objective', completely invalidate any findings they may eventually reach. One is Philippe de Weck, the former Chairman of UBS Zürich. Le Weck still maintains very close links with the UBS bank. This is the bank which holds on behalf of Licio Gelli, 55 million dollars of the stolen money. It is the bank which holds on behalf of the late Roberto Calvi and Flavio Carboni over 30 million dollars of the stolen money. It is the bank which holds on behalf of Carboni's Austrian mistress, Manuela Kleinszig, 2 million dollars of the stolen money.

Philippe de Weck is also the man at the centre of what the French call 'the sniffer planes affair'. This involved a wonderful invention, the brainchild of an Italian technician, Aldo Bonassoli, and Count Alain de Villegas, an elderly Belgian. The invention came in two parts, one housed in a plane which beamed back to the second part on earth cross sections of the geological strata many thousands of feet below the earth's sufface which were then seen as technical data on a computer screen.

The potential was limitless. Along with instant mineral and oil prospecting at a fraction of the traditional cost, there were also military implications: any eye that could locate oil thousands of feet below the earth's surface could also pinpoint a submerged nuclear submarine. Encouraged by President Giscard d'Estaing the French oil giant Elf poured about 120 million dollars into the Count's Panamanian company Fisalma. Villegas was the sole shareholder and the company was administered by Philippe de Weck. By the time the French realized that Le Sting had been played on them, 60 million dollars had vanished. De Weck told the French that the money had gone on research and 'charitable works'. One of the men acting for UBS Zürich, who had been keeping an eye on this interesting pioneering work in the art of international theft, was Ernst Keller, who at the same time was also a shareholder of Ultrafin AG, a Calvi-owned company linked to Ambrosiano Holding, Luxembourg. Ultrafin was the conduit by which the Count's Panamanian company received its initial payments.

Another member of the commission is Herman Abs who was head of the Deutsche Bank from 1940 to 1945. The Deutsche Bank was the Nazis' bank throughout the Second World War. Abs was in effect Hitler's paymaster. During this period Abs was also on the board of I.G. Farben, the chemical and industrial conglomerate that gave such whole-hearted assistance to Hitler's war efforts. Abs participated at board meetings of I.G. Farben when members discussed the use of slave labour at a Farben rubber plant located in the Auschwitz concentration camp.

No matter how many ex-bank chairmen or Nazi paymasters the Vatican employs, the truth will not go away. At least one billion dollars of the monies owed to the various banks is the Vatican's responsibility. It is perhaps the sweetest irony of all that no matter how much or how little it benefited from the phantom companies littered in Panama and elsewhere, it owned the companies when the debts were incurred. In truth it has benefited vastly, but if the banks who are owed money are really determined to get it back, then there is only one logical course of action: sue the Vatican. More specifically sue the Vatican Bank and Pope John Paul II, for 85 per cent of the profits from the bank go directly to the Pope.

At the time of his death Calvi was, according to subsequent sworn statements made by members of his family, negotiating with Opus Dei, who had agreed to buy the 16 per cent of Banco Ambrosiano that the Vatican owned. If this deal had been completed the 1.3 billion dollar hole would have been filled, Calvi's empire would have remained intact and Archbishop Paul Marcinkus would have been removed from office. Many, including Marcinkus, objected to that eleventh-hour deliverance from such a quarter.

Now, with Calvi dead, the Vatican has been wrangling with the Italian Government and a consortium representing international banking for nearly two years. Eventually in February 1984 news that agreement had finally been reached began to filter out of the Geneva conference rooms. By mid-May 1984 the details were clear. The international banks will get back approximately two-thirds of the 600 million dollars they had loaned Calvi's Luxembourg holding company. *Of that some 250 million dollars will be paid by the Vatican Bank*. The Vatican is due to hand over this sum on June 30th, 1984. This payment is being made by the Vatican 'on the basis of non-culpability' but 'in recognition of a moral involvement'. The reader may care to re-study the Vatican denials of any involvement, recorded on page 306, in the light of this impending payment.

The faithful should ignore all appeals that will undoubtedly be made in Roman Catholic churches throughout the world. All the Vatican Bank is doing is repaying a part of the vast amount of money it acquired through the activities of Calvi and Marcinkus. The Vatican Bank has still walked away from the entire affair with millions upon millions of dollars that represent a substantial amount of the still missing monies.

At the time of writing, Archbishop Paul Marcinkus still clings to office. He has been written off many times, yet he still survives. He still hides in the Vatican, fearful of emerging in case of being immediately arrested by the Italian authorities. He has recently appealed to the Italian courts asking for immunity from prosecution. It is to be hoped that before the Italian judiciary consider Marcinkus's plea they have obtained access to the still secret reports of the negotiations between Italy and Vatican City State. Possibly the most extraordinary information the official reports contain is the revelation that the secret criminal agreement between Marcinkus and Calvi that occurred in August 1981 was not, as the Vatican would have the world believe, a singular aberration by a kindly Archbishop towards a devout Catholic banker. The evidence now available clearly shows that other illegal and criminal agreements between Marcinkus and Calvi existed. They reach back as far as November 1976. The criminal conspiracy, therefore, began during the reign of Pope Paul VI. These facts serve powerfully to underline what would have occurred if Albino Luciani had lived. Also still hiding within the Vatican are the Archbishop's colleague and partner in so many crimes, Luigi Mennini. Also hiding in the Vatican is Pelligrino De Strobel. In such a manner does Pope John Paul II preside over his Vatican Bank in May 1984.

While all three remain fugitives from Italian justice, the authorities have sequestered all Italian property belonging to Mennini and de Strobel. All three are wanted by a wide range of Italian authorities in a variety of cities. Yet another colleague who would also have been promptly removed by Luciani if he had lived, Monsignor Donato De Bonis, the secretary of the IOR, is hiding within the Vatican walls from Turin magistrates, who are investigating a billion-dollar tax evasion scandal. De Bonis, who has had his passport withdrawn by the magistrates, continues, like his three colleagues, to work in the Vatican Bank. In such a manner does Pope John Paul II, to whom these men are answerable, preside over his Vatican Bank in May 1984.

Cardinal Ugo Poletti, the Cardinal Vicar of Rome, whom Luciani wished to remove, is another for whom there is ample evidence to illustrate the wisdom of Luciani's decision. Poletti was responsible for recommending to the then Prime Minister Giulio Andreotti that General Raffaele Giudice should be placed in command of the Finance Police. Subsequently P2 member Giudice organized the billion-dollar tax evasion scandal, diverting massive amounts of money to Licio Gelli. In 1983 Cardinal Poletti indignantly denied using any influence to get Giudice his job. The Turin magistrates then showed the Cardinal Vicar of Rome a copy of his letter to Andreotti. Poletti remains Cardinal Vicar of Rome. In such a manner does Pope John Paul II preside over the Roman Catholic Church in May 1984.

The new Concordat recently signed between the Vatican and the Italian Government makes a fitting epitaph for the current Pope's reign. Italy, for nearly two thousand years regarded by Catholics as the home of their faith, no longer has Roman Catholicism as 'the religion of the State'. The Church's privileged position in Italy is ending.

Another change must be bringing a warm smile to the face of Licio

Gelli. The new Canon Law that took effect on November 27th, 1983, has dropped the ruling that Freemasons are subjected to automatic excommunication. The survivors on the list of Vatican Masons that Albino Luciani considered are now safe. The purge that he had planned will not be reactivated by his successor.

As previously recorded, none of Luciani's proposed changes has been implemented. Vatican Incorporated is still functioning. In all markets.

Postcript to this Edition

❧

Since initial publication in 1984, the Holy See has failed to address either the evidence contained or the issues raised within this book. Events in the world beyond the Vatican City State have, however, served as a powerful vindication of both the evidence and many of the conclusions.

Michele Sindona
Among the crimes of which I accused Sindona were the fraudulent bankruptcy of his Italian empire and the contract murder of Giorgio Ambrosoli. Three months after initial publication of this book in the United States, and although he was still serving a 25-year term of imprisonment, the US Justice Department felt compelled to return Sindona to Italy to stand trial accused of precisely those same crimes. Sindona's first reaction upon hearing the news of his extraction is particularly significant. 'If I finally get there, if no one does me in first – *and I've already heard talk of giving me a poisoned cup of coffee* – I'll turn my trial into a circus. I'll tell everything.'

After he had arrived in Italy, Sindona was visited in prison by other members of P2. Subsequently he had a change of mind about telling all. He requested that his trial on the various fraud charges should proceed without his being present in the courtroom. A request that was surprisingly granted. In 1985, a Milan court found Sindona guilty of fraudulent bankruptcy and sentenced him to a term of 15 years' imprisonment. On March 18, 1986, another Milan court found Michele Sindona guilty of ordering the murder of Giorgio Ambrosoli and he was sentenced to life imprisonment. Before he could commence either of these sentences he was due to be returned to the United States to serve the remainder of the initial 25-year prison sentence.

Confronted with the realization that he would undoubtedly die in prison, the 66-year-old man made a decision. He would break his Mafia oath of *Omertá*. He would tell all. Not least, he intended to barter information concerning the circumstances surrounding the death of Albino Luciani. On Thursday, March 20, after drinking his breakfast coffee, he screamed, 'They have poisoned me!' Two days later, on Saturday, March 22, he was dead. The murder of Sindona was a classic example of the power of P2. Because of fears that an attempt might be made on his life, Sindona was being held in a maximum-security prison. He was subjected to constant 24-hour TV surveillance. There were never less than three guards with him and his food and drink came into the prison in sealed containers.

Paul Marcinkus

Archbishop Marcinkus was accused of direct criminal involvement with regard to the crash of Banco Ambrosiano and the disappearance of $1.3 billion. Like the murder of Albino Luciani, this is yet another crime that the Vatican insists never occurred. Since the initial publication of this book, the Vatican has repaid $250 million to the creditors of Calvi's ruined financial empire. This money was repaid on a 'no fault' basis thus enabling the Vatican to continue to deny any liability.

Within this book Luigi Mennini the managing director of the Vatican Bank was yet another accused of perpetrating criminal fraud. In July 1984, one month after the first publication, Mennini was sentenced by a Milan court to seven years' imprisonment after being convicted of fraud and other charges related to *Il Crack Sindona*. It continued to prove far more difficult to bring the President of the Vatican Bank to the bar of justice, but then Archbishop Marcinkus had very powerful protectors ranging from Pope John Paul II to senior members of the then United States Government.

In June 1984, Pope John Paul II lectured the Swiss on banking ethics: 'The world of finance, too, is a world of human beings, our world, subject to the consciences of all of us.' The one conscience exempted from this doctrine would appear to have been the late Pope's. When he uttered these words his Vatican City State was continuing to offer safe refuge to a number of alleged criminals including Archbishop Paul Marcinkus, Pellegrino de Strobel and Luigi Mennini, all senior executives of the Pope's bank.

The activities of Marcinkus continued to put that Vatican conscience under strain. When the Holy Father roundly condemned apartheid, the response of the Vatican bank was to secretly lend $172 million to various agencies of the pro-apartheid South African Government. During late December 1985, terrorist attacks at Rome and Vienna airports resulted in twenty deaths. The Pope, taking as his text the Commandment 'thou shalt not kill', condemned absolutely those who bore the responsibility for these deaths. President Reagan stated that his administration had 'irrefutable proof' indicating that Libya was responsible. On December 29, two days after the attacks, the United States Ambassador to the Vatican, William Wilson, paid a secret visit to Libya and met Muammar Qadafi. Acting on behalf of Marcinkus and the Vatican Bank, Wilson negotiated the terms of a multi-million dollar loan to enable Libya to acquire an Italian oil refinery.

For more than five years Ambassador Wilson proved a source of strength for Marcinkus. Wilson's efforts included bringing pressure to bear on the United States Justice Department to halt investigations into the Marcinkus/Sindona relationship. He also seriously compromised US Attorney General William French Smith by arranging for Smith to meet Marcinkus in Rome, this at the very time when the Justice Department was investigating Marcinkus. In May 1986, Wilson resigned his post. Marcinkus observed, 'I am sorry to see a man I've gotten to know and appreciate leave'. Pope John Paul II was also heard warmly praising the late Ambassador.

On February 25, 1987, Milan magistrates issued warrants for the arrest of Archbishop Marcinkus and his Vatican Bank colleagues Mennini and de Strobel. The warrants alleged that all three were accessories to fraudulent bankruptcy. All three continued to hide inside the Vatican, protected by Pope John Paul II.

Acting on the instructions of Pope John Paul II, the Secretariat of State, while negotiating a wide-ranging concordat with Italy in 1984, succeeded in obtaining immunity from arrest and trial for Archbishop Paul Marcinkus. This was achieved by invoking a particular clause of the original Lateran Treaty between the Holy See and the Italian State. This clause allowed for Cardinals to enter or leave Italy without let or hindrance. The original purpose of this clause was to ensure that Cardinals of the Church would be free at all times to assemble for a Conclave to elect a new Pope. No matter that Marcinkus was not a Cardinal. No matter that there was no Conclave pending. Marcinkus – despite constant pleas by Cardinal Casaroli and other Cardinals to the

Pope that the Archbishop should be immediately replaced – remained in charge of the Vatican Bank for a further six years.

When, finally, in 1989 the Pope reluctantly approved the appointment of a group of laymen to run the bank Marcinkus blithely carried on as if nothing had changed. It was only when the lay group insisted that Marcinkus must vacate the premises before they were prepared to take over that both he and the Pope accepted the inevitable. He finally left in March 1990, secretly departing for the United States and ultimately Phoenix, Arizona, where according to the Vatican he engaged 'in unspecified work on behalf of the Diocese'. Namely saying the occasional Mass and attempting to improve his golf handicap.

Licio Gelli

In July 1984, it was established by an Italian parliamentary commission that the list of P2 members referred to within this book was authentic. Italian Budget Minister and *P2 member Pietro Longo* was forced to resign from the Italian Government. For the Puppet Master himself it appeared that the day of reckoning was near. But Gelli is a master of illusion.

From his luxurious hideaway on the outskirts of Sao Paulo, Brazil, Gelli offered to repay $8.5 million to the creditors of Banco Ambrosiano. Like the Vatican, Gelli denied any liability in billion-dollar theft. My accusation of criminal links between Italian freemasonry and the Mafia was officially confirmed in March 1986 by investigating magistrates in Palermo. In the same week the interior Minister Oscar Scalfaro told Parliament: 'Until Licio Gelli is arrested he will continue to be a threat to Italian democracy'.

And not only Italian democracy. Evidence continued to repeatedly confirm how close Gelli's links remained with various members of the late Argentinean junta. On instructions of P2 member Admiral Emilio Massera, five false passports were created for Gelli during his brief stay in a Swiss prison. Gelli subsequently utilized several of these passports after escaping. In May 1986, a bomb was discovered at the Cordoba headquarters of the Argentinean Third Army Corps, just prior to a visit from President Raul Alfonsin. The assassination attempt was planned by P2 members in the Army. During the last week of January 1987, P2 member General Suarez-Mason was arrested in San Francisco. Extradition proceedings began to return him to Argentina where he was wanted on several counts of torture and torture resulting in death.

Within the book I accuse Gelli's P2 of the bombing of Bologna railway station. This atrocity, in which 85 people were murdered and 182 injured occurred in 1980. Since this book was first published, P2 member General Pietro Musumeci the former head of the internal section of SISMI, the Italian military intelligence, has been arrested and subsequently charged with perpetrating a cover-up. Fellow P2 members Francesco Pazienza and Giuseppe Belmonte and the Puppet Master himself, Licio Gelli, were also charged. After a series of trials and appeals all four were finally found guilty and sentenced to terms of imprisonment.

On April 16, 1992, in a Milan court, 33 men were found guilty of criminal fraudulent conspiracy relating to the collapse of Banco Ambrosiano. Among those to be sentenced was Umberto Ortolani, to 19 years' imprisonment, and Licio Gelli to 18 years and six months' imprisonment. Needless to say, none of the 33 men actually commenced serving their prison sentences; they were all granted bail pending appeals.

Having enjoyed a further six years of freedom Licio Gelli's sentence was reduced on appeal in April 1998 to 12 years but again Gelli was disinclined to sample prison food. He negotiated with the authorities and it was agreed that instead of languishing in prison he would serve his sentence in his villa under constant police surveillance. He also surrendered his passport. For most people to hand over such a document means that they are unable to leave the country. Gelli merely took another passport out of his safe. The authorities acting under great secrecy began to prepare another attempt to apply Italian justice to Licio Gelli. Yet again his friends, including the doyen of Italian politics, Giulio Andreotti, came to his assistance. Advised that further charges against him were imminent, the Puppet Master yet again vanished. He was subsequently arrested at a residence on the French Riviera. Three days later the police searched his villa in Tuscany and discovered one hundred and fifty gold bars hidden in the flowerpots on the patio: minimum value at the time was £1.5 million. The following May after serving just a few months of his sentence he was released from prison on 'health grounds'.

On July 19, 2005, Gelli was finally indicted for yet another crime that I had first accused him of in 1984. The murder of Roberto Calvi. As of January 2007 the trial of Gelli, Flavio Carboni and the other three defendants meanders on its way with no sign of reaching a conclusion.

P2. The immortal lodge

In February 1993, nine years after I had originally accused Bettino Craxi, the leader of the Italian Socialist Party, of receiving from Roberto Calvi and Michele Sindona some of the plundered funds of Banco Ambrosiano, Craxi, who in the interim had been for a substantial period of time Prime Minister of Italy, was forced to resign from party leadership when Italian magistrates finally decided to act upon my accusations.

Italy continued to stagger from political crisis to political crisis. Again and again the source of this turmoil can be traced to P2 elements. In early 1994 a 'new' personality entered the political ranks. The multi-media mogul Silvio Berlusconi ran for election on an anti-corruption platform. He was swept to power in March 1994 and became Prime Minister. Silvio Berlusconi is a member of P2. In December 1994 Berlusconi was forced to resign his office after charges of corruption were brought against him. *P2 members are resilient people*; in 2001 Berlusconi was again elected Prime Minister, a post he held until his election defeat in April 2006. Berlusconi grudgingly departed from office.

Some three months earlier Archbishop Paul Marcinkus had departed from all earthly office. He died in Phoenix, Arizona, in February 2006. He had resisted to the end all attempts by the Italian Courts to have him returned to Rome to testify in the trial of the five accused of the murder of Roberto Calvi. The death of Marcinkus left unresolved the accuracy of an extra-ordinary allegation made during the lifetime of the Archbishop by a member of the Mafia that Marcinkus had been present at a meeting when the decision was taken to 'suicide' Calvi in a Masonic manner.

Over the decades the real identity of the ultimate head of P2 was a question that exercised many. A repeated whisper invariably settled on one particular man, Giuilo Andreotti. But surely the figurehead of Italian politics for over fifty years, seven times Prime Minister and Life Senator could not possibly also be the real Puppet Master? The sceptics suffered a severe jolt when in 2002 Andreotti was found guilty of complicity in the murder of the investigative journalist Mino Pecorelli. The Italian magistrates also had abundant evidence that linked Andreotti to a world of illicit financing. The magistrates established that people 'close to Andreotti' had met with Pecorelli shortly before his murder in an attempt to persuade him not to publish further 'embarrassing material'. The former Prime Minister was sentenced to twenty-four years' imprisonment. Because of his age, he was 83 years old at the time, it was decided that he would not serve the sentence. After a series of appeals Andreotti was cleared of having connections with the Mafia and in October 2003 he was cleared of complicity in the murder of Pecorelli the man who had ensured that a list of senior members of the Roman Catholic hierarchy who were allegedly also members of the Masonic lodge P2 had been sent to Albino Luciani.

Pope John Paul I

Described by the Vatican as 'a fantasy' this book continued to be vindicated by further realities. One of my allegations that had particularly infuriated the Vatican was the assertion that the body of the murdered Pope John Paul I had been discovered by Sister Vincenza. It was an assertion that many within the Church condemned as a wicked lie. Among their number was Father John Magee, who continued to claim that it had been he who had found the Pope's body. In 1985, I was flying back to London from Dublin, and chanced to find that I was sitting next to Father Magee's brother. He assured me that he had questioned his brother closely on this aspect and that Father Magee had insisted that I was wrong and his version was correct.

In September 1988, Father John Magee finally admitted that he had lied, not only to his brother, but along with his fellow Papal secretary Father Diego Lorenzi and numerous other Vatican officials, to the world since 1978. He confirmed that it had indeed been Sister Vincenza and not he that had found the body of the dead Pope. Magee had therefore, by such admittance, finally confirmed the first crucial stage of the Vatican cover-up.

This aspect had in fact been confirmed, albeit grudgingly and very obliquely by the Vatican, four years earlier in June 1984. Within weeks of the initial publication of this book apart from denouncing it as 'infamous rubbish' a memorandum created by the Commission for Social Communications, the media and public relations arm of the Vatican, was distributed to Episcopal Conference. It attempted in typical Vaticanese to address several of the many issues raised within this book. One of these concerned the identity of who had found the body of Pope John Paul I.

The memorandum while aspiring to minimize the issue admits that it was Sister Vincenza.

> While it makes no difference whether the Pope was found by a sister, or as the Vatican communiqué said, by the private secretary of the Pontiff, in fact, the secretary instantly ran to the

bedside of Pope John Paul I when he was summoned by the sister who suspected that something might be wrong. The secretary touched the Pope to awaken him and discovered that he was dead. The secretary then called Cardinal Villot.

If, as the Vatican memorandum asserts, 'it makes no real difference' then why where the Papal secretaries obliged to take a vow of silence on this and other issues? Why did both secretaries continue to lie for years? Lie both before the Vatican Memorandum and for years afterwards. If those responsible for the Vatican Memorandum had questioned the author Camilo Bassotto, a close personal friend of Pope John Paul I for many years, they would have received confirmation that the account within this book describing how Sister Vincenza discovered the body of the Pope is entirely accurate. Prior to her death in 1983 Bassotto had twice interviewed the nun. The account she gave Bassotto of her grim discovery is the same as that previously given to me. The various reforms detailed within this book that Pope John Paul I had been planning to implement was another aspect which that Vatican Memorandum addressed. 'Pope John Paul I did not have in mind to make revolutionary changes in the Vatican hierarchy, as can be seen from the following facts'.

The 'facts' including his re-appointment of Cardinal Villot, his confirmation of the various Cardinal heads of departments and Secretaries of the Curia are not in dispute and are recorded within this book. The Memorandum's comments about the late Pope's prudence, his habit of reflecting, meditating and allowing his thinking to mature before taking decisions could well have been taken directly from my text, as could the comments on his ability after that process had been completed of acting 'firmly and decisively'. The evidence within this book that details fact after fact that led to the various reforms that were about to be implemented at the time of Albino Luciani's death is not addressed or considered. Also ignored is the fact that the late Pope's decisions had not been based merely upon a one-month investigation but on knowledge acquired over a six-year period.

The only aspect of this section of the Memorandum, which is in conflict with this book concerns the heated discussion that Luciani had with Cardinal Baggio regarding the Pope's desire to send Baggio to Venice as his successor. In June 1984 six years after the confrontation Baggio denied being asked and declared that if he had been he 'would have gone there – flying'.

I only became aware of this Vatican Memorandum while preparing this postscript. Not only are both Luciani and Baggio dead but so are my primary sources. It is the only proposed change that is specifically challenged. It is reasonable therefore to assume that those responsible for the Vatican Memorandum were unable to find anyone or any evidence that refuted the many other changes that Albino Luciani planned to make that are recorded within this book.

The Memorandum then turns to the question of the papers found in the dead Pope's hands 'The pages found in the hands of Pope John Paul I after his death could not, therefore, have been lists of the prelates to be transferred'. It would have immeasurably assisted the Vatican's position if they had then identified the precise content of these pages. This they fail to do. They quote Father Magee 'indicating' that it was the 'Pope's custom to review points of sermons and meditations for Wednesday audience discourses and Angelus talks on Sundays'. Demonstrably Magee had no knowledge of what the Pope was reading on that fatal evening or what happened subsequently to those documents.

The most glaring deficiency in this exercise conducted by the Vatican was their failure to talk to others still alive in June 1984 who knew the truth concerning the 'revolutionary changes' that Pope John Paul I was about to implement. The failure to talk to these crucial witnesses or if they were spoken to, the failure to report what they said is highly significant.

Father Germano Pattaro brought from Venice by Pope John Paul I as an adviser has stated that among the documents that the Pope was studying were his notes covering the range of changes he had discussed with Cardinal Villot a few hours before retiring for the night. The previously mentioned Camilo Bassotto, is also on record as having discussed with Luciani the various changes he was proposing to make. Then there were others. Men such as Archbishop Giuseppe Caprio who had taken a leading role in the investigation ordered by the late Pope, or Monsignor Giovanni Angelo Abbo, the man chosen by the Pope to replace Marcinkus, or Cardinal Ugo Poletti, the man that the Pope planned to place in charge of the Florence archdiocese.

Archbishop (later Cardinal) Caprio was at the time of Luciani's death the deputy head of the Secretariat of State and as such if asked he would have been able to make available to the Vatican spin doctors responsible for the Memorandum a copy of the crucial dossier that the late Pope was studying shortly before his death. If there was ever within this entire affair a smoking gun it is the Vagnozzi dossier.

As of September 1978 Cardinal Egidio Vagnozzi knew more about the inner workings of Vatican finances than anyone else in or out of the Vatican. From 1967 he had been in control of the Prefecture of the Economic Affairs of the Holy See. His role was comparable to that of the Chancellor of the Exchequer in the United Kingdom or the Auditor General in the United States. Vagnozzi had intimate knowledge of the Sindona and Calvi relationships with the Vatican and their various dealings with the Holy See. As recorded earlier within this book in 1968/69 Vagnozzi was still struggling to prise out many of the Vatican's financial secrets that lay buried but long before Pope John Paul I was elected he had the answers.

When Albino Luciani sought an urgent investigation the information that Vagnozzi had acquired over a decade ensured that a highly detailed dossier was soon in the Pope's hands. Immediately after the discovery of the Pope's body the Vagnozzi report along with the papers covering the various changes were removed by Cardinal Villot, whose deputy Caprio was most certainly aware of the contents of that report. An indication of just how explosive the contents were can be gauged by the fact that Roberto Calvi subsequently became aware of the Vagnozzi report and its contents and after being offered a copy by a Vatican contact for three million dollars haggled the price down to one point two million dollars then kept the copy close to himself for the rest of his life.

Finally the first two paragraphs of the Vatican Memorandum of June 1984 deserve to be quoted in full. They have assisted immeasurably in the growth of a myth that is still vibrant twenty-eight years later. While the death of Pope John Paul I came as a great surprise only a month after his election to the papacy, the Cardinals who gathered in daily meetings in preparation for the (next) Conclave saw no reason to question the report of Dr Renato Buzzonetti, Director of Vatican Health Services, that the death of Pope John Paul I was attributable to natural causes.

In addition, there was the fact that the Pope's health had been rather frail. Some time previously, he had complained of swollen ankles. His close relatives did not have any doubts regarding the naturalness of his death, but cited no less than three cases of similar deaths of relatives.

Dr Buzzonetti had never been Albino Luciani's doctor. His sole medical experience of the late Pope had been to establish cause of death. His conclusion that the Pope died from myocardial infarction – a heart attack – has been dismissed not only by members of the medical profession in Italy, the US, Australia, New Zealand and the United Kingdom but also by other Vatican doctors including the man who had co-signed Luciani's death certificate, the Head of the Vatican Medical Service Professor Mario Fontana who subsequently observed 'If I had to certify under the same circumstances, the death of an ordinary, unimportant citizen. I would quite simply have refused to allow him to be buried'.

Albino Luciani's condition was far from frail as a study of his factual medical history would have confirmed. Buzzonetti was offered that medical history by Dr Da Ros, the Pope's physician for more than twenty years. Astonishingly the Vatican medical staff refused to consider that history, a course of action that would have resulted in a very severe medical censure in a great many countries. Quite a number of Cardinals did indeed question Buzzonetti's 'report' including Cardinals Benelli, Felici, Willebrands, Pironio Lorscheider, and there were others. Confronted with the implications of this book in 1984 'close relatives' of the dead Pope recalled three relatives who had 'similar deaths' events that lay forgotten in 1978 and again between 1980-1984 when I was engaged in active research. For example the Pope's brother Edoardo's response in 1978 when asked if Albino had ever had heart trouble was 'As far as I know absolutely none'.

Once the allegations contained within this book became public knowledge the memories of a number of the people that either I or my researchers had interviewed underwent remarkable transformations. This phenomenon occurred on both sides of the Tiber. Albino Luciani in fact was in excellent health at the time of his sudden death and his ankles were not swollen. The reader may wish to re-read the factual medical history of Pope John Paul I contained in Chapter Six. A detailed medical history that the Vatican has ignored for nearly three decades.

In late 1988 my literary agent was contacted by a journalist named John Cornwell. He told her that he was preparing a major two-part article on my book and that he was the European Editor of the Sunday *Observer* who would be publishing the articles. He wished to interview me. We met in early January 1988 and he at once confessed that he had lied about the reason for the interview. Contrary to what he had pitched repeatedly to my agent and then to me he was not working on a two-part article for the *Observer* either about me or *In God's Name*. He was, he admitted, working with the 'Vatican's full permission and unlimited co-operation' on a full-length book on the death of Albino Luciani.

I considered throwing him out there and then, what stopped me was his remark about the Vatican assistance he was getting. I reasoned that with that kind of backing it should be possible to finally establish the ultimate truth concerning the murder of Albino Luciani. With hindsight that was very naive of me. A reading of his book *A Thief in the Night* made it clear to me that this was not an author approaching an investigation with an open mind but the work of a man striving to create on behalf of the Vatican a pre-determined version of truth. His conclusions appear to have been arrived at by largely ignoring the body of factual evidence contained within my book.

The book makes a remarkable contribution to the Vatican-created myths concerning the health of Albino Luciani. Remarkable because the author notwithstanding the promises that had been made to him concerning cooperation was denied access to the medical records of the murdered Pope, failed to persuade the Pope's personal doctor of more than twenty years to talk to him and failed to interview the Pope's specialist Professor Rama. There were numerous other omissions but this is not the time or the place to dwell upon them. One should be positive and record just a little of what John Cornwell gleaned from those he did manage to talk to: 'A few days before coming down to the Conclave after Paul VI's death, Luciani visited a parish priest in this friend of mine's home town, and he had to rest a while because his feet were swelling up, which is a sign of certain sorts of heart problems . . . Another thing I've heard is that there had been problems with his health before he became Bishop. There was a doubt. You're going to need to document that somehow.' *An anonymous Monsignor referring an anonymous friend who is referring to an anonymous priest.*

'We also know that he had extremely swollen ankles. I could show you photographs of his ankles, very swollen . . .' Dr Navarro Valls, Vatican Press spokesman. In the event, however, we are never told if Navarro Valls did show Cornwell the photographs and there is no record of the author requesting that he should.

Father Farusi was yet another who contributed to the picture of a mortally ill Albino Luciani. Father Farusi was the head of Radiogiornale at the Vatican Radio at the time of Luciani's brief papacy. He told Cornwell that once he realized that Luciani was a 'front-runner' for the papacy and that Cardinals were 'asking about the health of the Patriach of Venice' he made it his business to acquire from 'contacts in the policc' a 'thorough dossier on this man Luciani's health. When the information came back I was shocked, because I learned that he was in very poor health . . . they should never have elected him.' Farusi did not volunteer a copy of the medical dossier.

We are not told why, if Albino Luciani was so clearly at death's door, he was elected Pope or if the Cardinals who were apparently enquiring about Luciani's health received copies of the medical dossier.

During October 1988, former Papal Secretary Father Diego Lorenzi while taking part in a television debate had produced a large white rabbit. He had revealed for the first time that on the last evening of his life shortly before 8.00 p.m. the Pope had come to the door of his study complaining of 'dreadful pain' in his chest. Lorenzi had then recounted how he had urged the Pope to call a doctor but the Pope 'absolutely forbade me to do this'. It was, Lorenzi declared, months later before he connected these chest pains with Luciani's death. This extraordinary tale was recounted to Cornwell with additional details including how both he and the other papal secretary Father John Magee had subsequently gone to the Pope's bedroom and said to Luciani: 'Now look, if anything should happen tonight, if you have need of any us, just push the button and we will hear the bell and we'll rush through to help you'.

Fellow Papal secretary Father John Magee was yet another whose memory post-publication of *In God's Name* and more than six years later had 'improved' greatly. Interviewed on my behalf by researcher Phillip Willan he had observed 'On the last evening he was perfectly fit. During his Papacy this business of leg swelling did not occur. He took daily exercise in the Vatican gardens or the big hall.' To John Cornwell, Father Magee said '. . . They were terribly swollen . . .'

Father Magee's version of the sudden attack of alleged violent chest pain suffered by the Pope differed markedly from Lorenzi's. Magee was adamant that his fellow secretary was not even in the Papal Apartments at the time, and that the incident occurred not in the evening at 8.00 p.m. but in the afternoon about 5.30 p.m. That Luciani called out 'I have a pain! Send Sister Vincenza to me. She knows what to do.' Magee wanted to call a doctor but the Pope was adamant that he should not. Magee then advised Sister Vincenza who took 'some medicine' to the Pope. Later when Father Lorenzi had eventually appeared Magee told him what had occurred and according to Magee when they asked Luciani how he was he responded 'Sto bene! Sto bene! Eccomi' ('I am well! I am well! Here I am.') Pummelling his chest he declared 'Andiamo (Let's go). Those tablets of Sister Vincenza are miraculous. Let's go to supper.'

One of Albino Luciani's nieces, Lena Petri, herself a doctor discussed her uncle's medical history with Cornwell. She talked of a conversation that she had with her uncle in 1975 after he sustained a blood clot in his left eye. The conversation had occurred shortly after the condition had been treated successfully by Professor Rama. 'He [Albino Luciani] said in so many words that if it recurred he could be seriously ill. He also said he would be a slave to medicines anticoagulants and so forth – for the rest of his life'.

It had not recurred. The gloomy scenario painted by Luciani did not become a reality but Lina Petri speculated about the possibility that during his short papacy the Pope through stress may have 'neglected to take his anti-coagulants, which may have proved fatal.' There is in fact no evidence that after Professor Rama's successful treatment in 1975 Luciani was ever again obliged to take anti-coagulants. But Cornwell seized on what was no more than supposition which through a series of further speculations hardened to fact in his mind.

Thus in his conclusions we read: 'The description of his swollen legs was all over the Vatican . . . During the weeks that I spent in the Vatican talking with scores of officials I gathered John Paul I's difficulties both in health and in coping, had been common knowledge throughout the four weeks of his reign . . . It was common knowledge that he was seriously ill . . . By the second week of his Papacy his legs were swelling up to elephantine proportions . . . It would not be difficult to construct a plausible hypothesis that accounts for John Paul's death. Did he as his niece believes, neglect to take life-saving medicines? What is the dividing line between "giving up", suicide by deliberate neglect, and "resignation", or "abandonment" in a religious sense where a person believes that it is God's will that he should die and eagerly embraces that prospect . . . It was common knowledge that John Paul I was overwhelmed by his task . . .'

Someone reading the Cornwell book might well think that here was an author who was taken up and down the Vatican garden path. The Pope's doctor was less charitable. Doctor Da Ros considers Cornwell's conclusions inconceivable: 'Luciani was very careful and always took his medication. In addition, Sister Vincenza was not only a nun but a qualified nurse and she was in control of the medication.'

Based upon my research Albino Luciani on the last day of his life was not a man planning to ensure his premature death. The last photograph taken of Luciani just a few hours before he died shows a man ebullient and zestful. He was fit and well. He was planning for the future and not only with the various changes he had discussed with Villot that are detailed within this book. He also discussed with his Secretary of State a series of Papal letters he was planning 'The Unity of the Church.' 'The Bishops Collegiality with the Pope.' A third letter on the role of women in, 'Civil society and in Ecclesial Life.' and a fourth on 'The Poor and Poverty in the World.' The Curia were to be reformed. The Conclave would be revolutionized with access being granted to the Bishops and to the 'Presidents of the Episcopal Conferences of all the world.' This was a man at the height of his powers, brimming over with ideas. He was not as Cornwell has portrayed him, an incompetent lost in endless Vatican corridors as he forlornly sought death.

In September 2003 Doctor Antonio Da Ros the man who had been Albino Luciani's doctor for the last twenty years of the late Pope's life finally broke the silence he had maintained since the death of his former patient. He gave two interviews. His interview with Andrea Tornelli was published on the 27 September 2003 in *Il Giornale*. The following extracts come from that source.

Doctor, it has been said that during the month of his pontificate Pope Luciani had been abandoned by the doctors neither treated or visited.

It is not true. I visited him on Sunday 3 September, the day of the Mass for the beginning of the pontificate after the audience granted to the pilgrims of Vittorio Veneto. There are photos that demonstrate that I was there. I saw him. I measured his blood pressure, subjected it to the usual control. On the 13th September I again went to the Vatican and I visited for the third time on Saturday 23rd September and on that occasion I was invited to lunch with the Pope, after meeting with his secretary Father John Magee and with Dr Renato Buzzonetti.

What was the reason for meeting with Buzzonetti?

It was established that I was to be the doctor in charge of John Paul I.

Can you document this?

Look I have the note here that I made during the meeting, about which I spoke to the Pope at lunch. In any case my presence and those three visits must be recorded in the registries of the Vatican, because there was a car of the Holy See that came to take me to the airport of Fiumicino.

Why did you visit the Pope three times? Were you worried about his health?

Not at all. It was not bad. These control visits were a habit. Since the times in 1959 in Vittorio Veneto I checked him once a week.

Da Ros then revealed that on the evening of September 28, 1978 the last evening of the Pope's life he had phoned the Pope at approximately 9.00 p.m. It was a 'routine call, nobody had contacted me.'

With whom exactly did you speak?

I spoke with John Paul I and also with Sister Vincenza Taffarel, the nun who was also a nurse who attended to Luciani.

What did you say to the Pope on the telephone? Were you worried about his health? Was there some omen of what was to happen a few hours later?

No absolutely not. All was calm, normal.

And Sister Vincenza. What did you say to her?

She explained to me that the Pope had spent his day as usual and that all was normal. We arranged the visit that I would have made to the Pope on the following Wednesday.

Some years after the death of the Luciani, his secretary Diego Lorenzi, revealed during a television transmission that in the late afternoon of September 28th, John Paul I had had a strong pain in his chest. The sign of a heart attack or, in any case the symptom of a serious illness. Is it true that on that evening nobody spoke to you about this?

I was astounded, not to say bewildered, when I heard Diego making these affirmations. That evening nobody told me of these symptoms, neither the Pope, much less Sister Vincenza, who, I repeat was a nurse, and she would certainly have informed me if Luciani had been ill. John Paul I had a day of intense work as always, as in Venice. Also Cardinal Giovanni Colombo, the Archbishop of Milan, who spoke with me that evening, said that the Pope was calm, not worried about anything. I have never understood why it was not stated immediately.

It has been said that Pope Luciani during those 33 days had swollen ankles, that he had serious circulatory problems?

I visited him three times. There was a slight swelling up, which had also to do with the fact that life in the Vatican was much more sedentary than in Venice. I had advised him to move around a little and, from the time that he begun to walk in the hanging garden, the situation had improved. I do not exclude the fact that he had to become accustomed to the papal red slippers, without a heel.

Before the death of Paul VI on 6th of August 1978, Cardinal Luciani had spent one week at the Alberoni Institute, at the Lido of Venice. Had he gone for treatment?

No. He had gone to spend seven days on holiday. To be able to read, to walk and rest.

According to you, therefore, nothing made it possible to foresee the premature death of John Paul I?

I think it can be said that he enjoyed good health.

Early on the morning that the body of Luciani was discovered, his niece Pia upon hearing the news came to pay her respects to her uncle still lying in his bed. The papers he had been clutching had already been removed. Among those Pia spoke to was Sister Vincenza, who told her that 'Papa Luciani had been feeling really well the evening before'.

The doctor's observations concerning Luciani's general level of good health are shared by many who knew him. Some of their number are quoted within this book another who spoke out some four years earlier that the doctor was Cardinal Aloisio Lorscheider of Brazil who had enjoyed a close friendship with Albino Luciani over a number of years. 'I was dumbstruck. I found it hard to accept the sad news. I would never have expected it. No clue, no negative sign had come to me about the health of Pope John Paul I. Suggestions that the Pope had been in poor health are nonsense.'

Commenting on the Vatican's refusal to allow a post-mortem examination. Cardinal Lorscheider said he had to 'record with sorrow' that the official version of John Paul I's death was open to question. 'It pains me to say so, the suspicion remains in our heart. It is like a bitter shadow, a question not fully answered.'

As long as the lies, the cover-up and the disinformation exercise are officially permitted to continue that bitter shadow will remain. By the end of 2006, the first phase of the beatification process of Albino Luciani had been completed. In the fullness of time Pope John Paul I will indeed be beatified then ultimately canonized. He will be acclaimed for his manifest goodness and holiness. He should also be acknowledged as a modern martyr, a man who died in the worthy cause of renovation and purification of the Roman Catholic Church.

David A. Yallop
January 2007

Index

❦

Note: in sub-entries Pope John Paul I is referred to as J.P.I. and Pope John Paul as J.P.II.